ZYGMUNT KRASIŃSKI

DRAMATIC WORKS

DRAMATIC WORKS

by Zygmunt Krasiński

Translated from the Polish and introduced by
Charles S. Kraszewski

This book was published with the support
of the Hanna and Zdzislaw Broncel Charitable Trust

Publishers
Maxim Hodak & Max Mendor

© 2018, Charles S. Kraszewski

© 2018, Glagoslav Publications

www.glagoslav.com

ISBN: 978-1-912894-07-9

A catalogue record for this book is available from the British Library.

This book is in copyright. No part of this publication may be reproduced, stored in a retrieval system or transmitted in any form or by any means without the prior permission in writing of the publisher, nor be otherwise circulated in any form of binding or cover other than that in which it is published without a similar condition, including this condition, being imposed on the subsequent purchaser.

ZYGMUNT KRASIŃSKI

DRAMATIC WORKS

Translated from the Polish
and introduced by Charles S. Kraszewski

GLAGOSLAV PUBLICATIONS

Contents

INTRODUCTION. DO YOU NOT KNOW?
ZYGMUNT KRASIŃSKI, THE REACTIONARY
AND INQUISITIVE ROMANTIC 7

THE UNDIVINE COMEDY 47

IRYDION 153

AUTHOR'S NOTES TO IRYDION 348

1846 379

FIRST PART OF THE UNDIVINE COMEDY
(AN UNFINISHED POEM) 408

BIBLIOGRAPHY 554

ABOUT THE AUTHOR 555

ABOUT THE TRANSLATOR 556

Zygmunt Krasiński

1812 – 1859

Do You Not Know?

ZYGMUNT KRASIŃSKI, THE REACTIONARY AND INQUISITIVE ROMANTIC

As far as I know, Zygmunt Krasiński is the only bard of Romantic Poland ever to be punched in the nose.

This happened whilst he was a student at Warsaw, which at the time lay in the Russian partition of Poland. A student demonstration was taking place, in support of Polish independence, and Krasiński, whose father Wincenty was a Tsarist general, took the brave — or foolhardy — course of being the only person to break the striking students' picket line. The story is given a literary treatment in the author's *Unfinished Poem*, which Krasiński intended as an introductory work to his masterpiece, the *Undivine Comedy*:

> I see those staircases, spiralling like snakes, and that turning, that stony entrance, where you first appeared to me! I was a bold boy, was I not? Although immature and of slender strengths? I had come from home — I strode through them all with pride seated upon my brow, conscious of their hatred — but then again, why? Unconscious! — They tightened round me in a ring, an ever tighter ring, jeering "Little lord! Little lordling!" — as if it were a shameful thing to be able to point out where any given one of my forefathers had sacrificed his throat for the sake of the fatherland, and in which crypt of which church he rests. God! It was then that Hell was first born in this breast — the breast of a child!

It is Czesław Miłosz who hands down the anecdote about the young Krasiński.[1] Although the future poet may have been animated by a praiseworthy desire to defend his father's honour — for unlike

---

[1] Czesław Miłosz, *The History of Polish Literature* (Berkeley and London: University of California Press, 1983), p. 243. It was a slap, rather than a punch.

Wincenty, Zygmunt was no supporter of the Tsarist occupation of his country — the upshot of it is the same: Krasiński's devotion to Polish independence, which we have no reason to doubt, seems to have had its limits. For, scion of an ancient magnate clan — one of twelve or so families who constituted the blue-blooded "one percent" so to speak — it is worth considering whether or not he was also acting in defence of his caste.

Such seems to be hinted at in the above-cited passage, as the Youth (Henryk) still bristles at the memory of his classmates' jeering: "as if it were a shameful thing to be able to point out where any given one of my forefathers sacrificed his throat for the sake of the fatherland!" During an age when nationality was ever more associated with the common people, the "folk," in his plays, Krasiński associates Polish nationhood with Polish history, and the historical families who made it. In a heated exchange between Aligier and Pankracy towards the end of the *Unfinished Poem*, the former responds to the latter's revolutionary apotheosis of the people with:

> Pankracy! Pankracy! Where do you come from? And who was it poured the Polish language into your spirit? Who, Polish customs? Who set within you the desire for freedom? The strength of action? Were you born in the future? Of course not! So, what exactly are you, although you lack fathers that you can name, if you are not a son of the Polish Commonwealth? Tell me — what might you be able to say on the earth, with what might you form your lies, with what would you commit your treason, with what misappropriate the past, if not with all the gifts she has given you? You ungrateful thing! Who would give ear to your voice on behalf of the people, who among your own land, or among strangers, if not for the sword of Bolesław Chrobry, the immaculate person of Jadwiga, the wise love of Zygmunt, the fortitude of Batory, the Roman virtue of the Zamoyskis, the heroic death of the Żółkiewskis, the heroic life of Czarniecki, the toils of Sobieski and his great European Deed? Without them there is nothing. And you choose to stand upon nothing? Why do you rise up against History and Immortal

---

Of course, that makes little difference: it was a personal affront that might have had serious consequences in that age of duels.

Deeds? Against that, which you yourself cannot do without, cannot make one step, or pronounce one single word? It is the very breath of your lungs! Lead further, man, if the Lord's blessing rests upon you; lead your own nation further! But lead your nation not out of its national identity, as the cruel tyrant would, those who have torn the motherland apart! Be not her fourth hangman, given by Hell in addition to the other three! Pankracy! Pankracy!

Now, for most Poles of the period stretching between the complete loss of independence in 1795, and its restoration following World War I in 1918, the universal tragedy was the carving up of the once powerful country between Russia, Prussia and Austria. For Krasiński, the jettisoning of the history of the noble republic for an internationalist's dream of levelling all to universal democracy, would be just as tragic a partition. It would divide the classes, and in so doing, destroy the poet's idea of what the Polish "nation" is: a paternalistic, hierarchically organised society, with the nobility playing its God-given, natural role as leaders, with the broad swaths of the faithful and loyal peasantry gratefully accepting their tutelage — and with the rising mercantile bourgeoisie grudgingly allowed their own place in the top-heavy mosaic, as long as they behave themselves, avoid greed, and prove themselves adept at wielding both rapier and rosary.

Perhaps this is why the vision of guillotines is so frequently found in the closet-dramas of this reactionary Romantic. Zygmunt Krasiński is deathly afraid of the democratic Pankracys of the world slicing the noble head of his society from the obedient, healthy body of the peasantry. Should that happen, he feels, it would lead to the death of both. It is for this reason that Aligier (the spirit of none other than Dante Alighieri, who leads young Count Henryk on his journey in the *Unfinished Poem*) chides Pankracy (who is said to represent, in part, the more republican-leaning Adam Mickiewicz),[2] with the words: "Pankracy! Pankracy! Choragos of the Polish chorus, yourself not a Pole at all! You who are constantly repeating 'the People, the People,' whilst 'the Nation' is never found on your lips!" For the "people" may indeed signify those merely united in language and custom, but the "nation" can only be the entirety of the historical complex that is

---

2   Cf. Alina Witkowska, *Literatura romantyzmu* (Warsaw: PIW, 1986), p. 205.

Poland, led by those magnates, kings, and nobles. For Krasiński, it's all, or nothing.

THE NATION, AND NATIONALITY

Questions of nationality, ethnic loyalty, and social castes play an important, and sometimes troubling, role in the plays of Zygmunt Krasiński. One often speaks of his conservatism. This may be fair, especially when he is compared, politically, to Mickiewicz, Słowacki, or the younger, fourth bard, Cyprian Kamil Norwid. But he is not the conservative that his father was — although devotion to that father, despite their political differences, is what shaped the poet's outlook on caste. Wincenty, once an officer in Napoléon's Grande Armée waging war against the Russian Empire, went over to the dark side after the Congress of Vienna, accepting a post in the Tsarist forces, and, as a result, implicitly accepting the partitions as a fait accompli. He became (to his son's chagrin) a stalwart defender of the Muscovite system. As if poor Zygmunt needed any more reminders of this equivocal situation, the scathing depiction of the Tsarist ball in the third part of Mickiewicz's *Forefathers' Eve* is set in the Warsaw salon of his father Wincenty.[3]

Like his father, Krasiński was fiercely attached to the idea of patriarchy. References to fathers abound in his works, whether that be the Count's (or Aligier's) pious defence of ancestry, or the immediate duty it imposes upon fathers and sons in present moments of crisis — as during the showdown-like summit of Pankracy and the Count in the *Undivine Comedy*:

> PANKRACY
> Time mocks us both. If you're tired of your own life, save at least that of your son...
>
> HUSBAND
> His pure soul is already reserved for heaven — and on earth, his father's fate awaits him.
> *He lets his head droop in his hands, then rises.*

---

[3] Miłosz, p. 243.

Yet whereas it can be argued that Count Henryk — known in the play as "the Husband" — dies defending the feudal system that he has inherited from ages past, his earlier incarnation as "the Youth" in the *Unfinished Poem*[4] sets national patriotism on the same level as loyalty to family, or caste. In a ritualistic initiation scene, when he is brought before the massed "choruses of the nations" and the quasi-sacerdotal figure of the "President," to offer himself as one more soldier in the moral struggle to speed on the coming Age of the Spirit, nationality is depicted as a primary characteristic of the human person, following hard after his individual identity:

> UNSEEN CHORUS
> Let him pronounce before us the merited name, the sacred name with which he was christened when born as a man.
>
> YOUTH
> Henryk.
>
> UNSEEN CHORUS
> Let him now confess the name common to the spirits, for whose sake the Lord determined that he should live and die, when He ordained his birth among them on the earth.
>
> YOUTH
> Poland.

For Krasiński, then, it is clear that, whatever it also may mean for the creation of the human soul, the foresight of God predetermines his or her role on earth as sealed to a particular nation, among which he or she must live and act, and to which he or she must dedicate herself — or else:

> POLISH CHORUS
> Thou, our brother thrice over, thou spirit among spirits, thou man among mankind, thou Son of Poland among Her sons,

---

[4] A prequel of sorts to the *Undivine Comedy*, which gives us the backstory of Count Henryk's youth. Krasiński worked at it during the 1840s and 1850s. It was only published after his death.

we greet thee! And now as a spirit merely in the guise of a man, know that thou art only a man under the appearance of a Pole; shouldst thou take upon thee another guise, thou shalt fall lower than cattle!

Such rather strongly conceived theories are problematic, to say the least. People "take upon themselves the guise" of another nationality quite frequently, and for divers reasons. Perhaps marriage leads them to a different country, where they settle for good. Perhaps it is life-threatening political or religious oppression in their native land that spurs their emigration. In neither case can such a person be classified as a traitor "fallen lower than cattle," nor, we trust, would Krasiński consider them as such. The latter case prompts an even bigger question: do we not owe a greater debt of loyalty to right action, to justice, to the Good which concerns every man and woman, than we do to the nation to which we are haphazardly attached by the accident of birth?

Of course, such questions do not occur in the context provided by Krasiński. It seems obvious that the Unseen Chorus is warning against frivolous action, or, which is part of the main nexus of conflict in these plays, international movements inimical to nationality.

In considering questions of nationalism and ethnicity in plays like the *Undivine Comedy* and the *Unfinished Poem*, we must remember that Krasiński was a person caught in pincers: between love and respect for a father upholding political views abhorrent to him and most of his generation, and the desire to prove himself in service to his nation enchained. In choosing exile over the danger of being associated with Russian servitude because of his father, who once (to his son's great embarrassment) officially presented him at the court of the Tsar in Sankt Petersburg, perhaps the desire to identify himself ethnically as a Pole was all the more exacerbated. Given his background, how might Krasiński, living in political exile in Paris, *not* put the following lines into Count Henryk's mouth, in that dramatic face-to-face meeting with Pankracy on the eve of the decisive battle:

HUSBAND
No use. You'll never understand me. Because every single one of your fathers has mixed his dust with the common mob, like a dead

thing, not like a man of strength and spirit. *He raises hand toward portraits.* Look at these figures — the very spirit of Fatherland, of home, family, a thought inimical to yourself, written in the furrows of their brows, and whatever was in them now lives in me. But you, fellow, tell me — Where is it your land lies? In the evening you stake your tent on the ruins of someone else's home; at sunrise you strike camp and wander elsewhere. You've not found your own hearth yet, nor will you ever, as long as one hundred repeat with me "Praise to our fathers!"

Here we are led to one of the more troubling aspects found in Krasiński's masterpiece. Such words in Husband-Henryk's mouth, with keywords like "where is it your land lies?" and "In the evening you stake your tent on the ruins of someone else's house; at sunrise you strike camp and wander elsewhere," to say nothing of "you've not found your own hearth yet," cannot but conjure in our minds images of anti-Jewish sentiment. Consider the scene of the conniving Jewish converts on the eve of the decisive battle:

CONVERT
My villainous brothers, my vengeful brothers, my dear brothers, let us suck at the pages of the Talmud as at a milky breast, a life-giving breast flowing with strength and honey for us, and for them — bitterness and poison!

CHORUS OF CONVERTS
Jehovah is our Lord, and no one else! He has scattered us everywhere, winding us around the world of the venerators of the Cross, our masters proud, stupid, illiterate, like the folds of an immense reptile. Let us spit thrice to seal their doom — thricely may they be accurst!

CONVERT
Let us rejoice, my brethren. That Cross, our enemy, undermined, rotten, now teeters over a puddle of blood, and once it falls, it will never rise again. Now only the bluebloods defend it.

CHORUS
The labour of ages is consummated, our labour sad, painful, dogged. Death to the bluebloods! Let us spit thrice to seal their doom — thricely may they be accursed!

CONVERT
On freedom without order, on slaughter without end, on conflict and malevolence, on their stupidity and pride we shall establish the power of Israel. We've only this handful to deal with — only this handful of bluebloods to topple into the abyss; then we shall sprinkle over their corpses the dusty ruins of the Cross.

CHORUS
The Cross, our holy sign; the water of baptism has joined us to the nations; those who held us despised ones in contempt, the despised, have been duped into believing in our love!
The freedom of the people is our law — The good of the people our goal — The sons of Christians have believed the ruse of the sons of Caiaphas!
Centuries ago our fathers put our enemy to torture — We shall torture Him again today and He will rise no more from the dead!

CONVERT
A few moments more, a few more drops of viper's venom, and the world is ours, ours, O my brethren!

CHORUS
Jehovah is our Lord, and no one else. Let us spit thrice to seal their doom — thricely may they be accurst!

This is hard to read. Krasiński's converts are conniving hypocrites, who have accepted initiation into the Christian religion of the majority among whom they live, only so as to undermine their adopted society all the more easily under the cloak of assimilation. If one of the great values of the *Undivine Comedy* is the manner in which it foresees the Marxist and totalitarian upheavals of the twentieth century,[5] one of its

---

5   "The *Undivine Comedy* is a rarity in world literature by virtue of its

great vices is this canard of the Jewish Convert "sleeper cell," to use the modern terminology of our terrorist nightmares.

It is surprising how, on the one hand, the same man can be so prescient about the dangers that can be unleashed by the ideology of class warfare, and yet so viciously insouciant as to peddle the baseless stuff that pogroms are made on. Nor is it a mere aberration. In the later *Unfinished Poem*, the "merchant-kings of the world" that haggle over the price of the blood of the labouring class are presented as members of the "wandering generations of the East," one of whom purchases the goblet of gore at the price of a diamond unpinned "from the purple band on his brow," and this is one of the nails of the True Cross, "which crystallised on the night in which your God expired. On the next morning, my great-great-grandfather pried it from the wood."

De mortuis nil nisi bonum. One would like to place such passages in a context that would, if not exculpate the author, at least explain why he chose to express himself thus. The *Undivine Comedy* is no more a political broadside than the *Divine Comedy* is a work of theology. These are words placed in the mouth of fictional characters, and in the context of an artistic argument for national identification, national loyalty. And yet, it is hard to even attempt a contextualisation of these sentiments without appearing to be an apologist for racism, which we completely, utterly, reject. Zygmunt Krasiński, as a thinker sensitive to universals and eternal truths, ought to have known better. Certainly, by contrast, Adam Mickiewicz, who treated Jewish topics with much more sympathy in his writing, and underscored complete civil rights for the Jews as one of the "Declared Principles" of the revolutionary legions he formed when he set about practical action, is seen in a much better light.

There is no excuse for any sort of racism, and we will not be apologists for it. Out of fairness to Krasiński, however, we must point out that it is the "stateless" condition of the Jewish diaspora that rankles him. For in his oddly Hegelian understanding of the manner in which the history of the world is tending through the ages from

---

dialectical conception of *The* Revolution (not just any revolution). It is difficult to believe that the *Comedy* was written when Karl Marx was scarcely a stripling, more than eighty years before 1917 in Russia." Thus Czesław Miłosz in "Krasiński's Rereat," in Wacław Lednicki, ed., *Zygmunt Krasiński: Romantic Universalist* (New York: PIASA, 1964), p. 219.

infancy to maturity, it is through nationalism that the "fulfilment" of man's history is to be effected. This is how he puts it in the catechetical portion of the *Unfinished Poem*:

> PRESIDENT
> Speak on! Now, Christ was God, in one man?
>
> YOUTH
> Yes.
>
> PRESIDENT
> And who will be Christ in all people?
>
> YOUTH
> Humanity, I reckon!
>
> PRESIDENT
> But when? It was not yesterday. And not today? So, when?
>
> YOUTH
> At the final, greatest moment of Humanity's fulfilment!
>
> PRESIDENT
> And who shall bring about this fulfilment? Where are the members of that body in which one spirit resides? What sort of rites are celebrated in this Church universal, varied, and established by God? Where are the hues of that rainbow, from which the shining whiteness shall arise?
>
> YOUTH
> But I am not mistaken, Father, am I? It is of nationalities that you wish to speak?
>
> PRESIDENT
> Thou hast said it thyself.

And again we must remind ourselves that Krasiński can have had no idea what sorrow and suffering nineteenth century nationalism's dividing up of human beings according to ethnicity and language would lead to in the post World War I era. Whether or not the *Undivine Comedy* is a work that continues to speak to our world, nowhere else in the literature of Polish Romanticism are we confronted with writing that is so divided from us, by the yawning gulf of attitude and presupposition. Krasiński's words have a much different sound today, after Auschwitz.

The "national choruses," which greet the Youth in that strange underground chamber, are many and varied. We hear the Irish Chorus, the Italian, German and French Choruses, greet the initiate along with the Polish and Slavic Choruses; presumably, there is room for a Jewish Chorus, an Arab and a Chinese Chorus as well. For Krasiński, the main thing is to know who you are, and to be true to that ethnic identity. This, more than anything, seems to be at the bottom of his characterisation of the Converts, as, curiously enough, it is, in his basing of the character of Pankracy on Mickiewicz.[6] Again, one wonders whether or not Krasiński's insistence on ethnicity did not arise from concerns about his own identity. However, nationality itself is a stereotypical construct; in Krasiński's philosophy of historical determinism, it is the stereotype, not necessarily the truth, that shall set you free.

THE NEW AGE AND THE SOCIAL QUESTION

Despite the foregoing, it cannot be said of Zygmunt Krasiński that he is an unquestioning partisan of the caste from which he springs, and which he so values. He is no jingo who would declare "my people, right or wrong," as is evidenced from the — at times agonising — debate in the *Undivine Comedy* between Count Henryk and the revolutionary leveller Pankracy. Although he will not be swayed by the blandishments of that Moses of the new age, who, for some reason,[7] wishes to save

---

[6] In a letter to Delfina Potocka dated 6 August 1847, Krasiński refers to Mickiewicz as "that little Jew" who "adds Jewish inflexibility to Lithuanian stubbornness." Cited by Artur Sandauer, *Pisma Zebrane* (Warsaw: Czytelnik, 1985), Vol. 4, p. 357.

[7] According to Miłosz, "only the amalgamation of Pancras [sic] and Count Henry would produce a complete Man. And Pancras is wise enough to know this; hence his weakness for Henry, as a suppressed part of his own person." To this he

him and his son from amongst the thousands of nobles marked for tomorrow's slaughter, Henryk must give ear to the counter-argument made by Pankracy in response to his panegyric on the portraits of his ancestors, quoted above. What is more, Krasiński is sober enough to acknowledge the gripes of his class enemies by creating a speech of real emotional, logical, and… historical power:

> PANKRACY
> Oh, sure — praise to thy fathers and grandfathers on earth as in … Yes, there's quite a lot to look at around here.
>   That one there, the Subprefect, liked to shoot at women among the trees, and burned Jews alive. — That one, with the seal in his hand and the signature, the "Chancellor," falsified records, burned whole archives, bribed judges, hurried on his petty inheritances with poison — To him you owe your villages, your income, your power. That one, the darkish one with the fiery eye, slept with his friends' wives — that one with the Golden Fleece, in the Italian armour, fought — not for Fatherland, but for foreign pay. And that pale lady with the black locks muddied her pedigree with her squire — while that one reads a lover's letter and smiles because the sun is setting… That one over there, with the doggie on her farthingale, was whore to kings. — There's your genealogies for you, endless, stainless! — I like that chap in the green caftan. He drank and hunted with his brother aristocrats, and set out the peasants to chase deer with the dogs. The idiocy and adversity of the whole country — there's your reason, there's your power. — But the day of judgement is near at hand and on that day, I promise you, I won't forget a single one of you, a single one of your fathers, a single scrap of your glory!

This is one of the most persuasive speeches enunciated by a revolutionary democrat, whether in this *Undivine Comedy*, or in the more reflective *Unfinished Poem*. Most often, it seems that the enemy party — the revolutionaries — are more motivated by a blind hatred of the old system, the nobility, Christianity, and authority in general, as well as a cynical lust to snatch power for themselves, than any true

---

wisely adds, "But such a union can exist only in dreams." Cf. "Krasiński's Retreat," p. 219.

humanistic or just impulse toward the righting of wrongs. They are a blind, elementally destructive force. As he writes in a letter to Princess Izabella Sanguszko, "communism arouses seething passions in every human soul [...] it is no joke to the hungry and the freezing."[8] In his treatment of the revolutionary masses, Krasiński can be just as dismissively stereotypical as he is of the Jewish Converts. And yet, the difference here is that, even though he paints them with a broad brush, he also recognises their complaints:

FIRST LACKEY
I did in my old master a'ready.

SECOND LACKEY
I'm still lookin' for my sweet baron. To your health!

VALET
Citizens, hunched over shoetree in sweat and misery, polishin' boots, clippin' hair — we've come to recognise our rights all the same. Health to the entire club!

CHORUS OF LACKEYS
To the health of our president, who leads us on the path of honour!

VALET
Thank you, citizens.

CHORUS OF LACKEYS
From the foyers, from our prisons, all together, with one strong push, we've broken free. Vivat! Don't we know the idiocy and whoring that goes on in the bluebloods' salons? Vivat! Vivat!

---

8   Krasiński, letter to Isabella Sanguszko dated Heidelberg, 1 May 1851. Collected in Halina Gacowa, ed. "Nowe listy Zygmunta Krasińskiego do Izabelli z Lubomirskich Sanguszko z lat 1841–1851," in Jarosław Maciejewski, ed. *Archiwum Literackie: Miscellanea z okresu romantyzmu* (Wrocław: Ossolineum, 1972), vol. XV (2), p. 254. In referring to the appeal of revolutionary theory to the "hungry and freezing," Krasiński again shows some understanding of the topic; in a note, the editor adds that, at the time, "Krasiński had a foreboding of coming political upheavals in Europe."

Remembering both the slaughter of the French aristocracy during the terror of Robespierre and the more recent "Galician massacre," during which the Polish peasants, under the leadership of Jakub Szela (and instigated by the Austrian authorities) rose up and cut down the oppressive nobles who had been their masters (memories of which haunt the unfinished play *1846*), these vignettes of revolutionary cénacles lend first-hand weight to Pankracy's assertions, above. Rather than merely fashioning painted devils with which to frighten his noble readers, in passages like this, Krasiński dons prophetic robes to warn his "brethren" of the coming catastrophe, if they don't shape up:

CRAFTSMAN
Curses… Curses!

HUSBAND
What are you doing there under the tree, poor fellow? Why do you cast your eyes about so wildly, so moodily?

CRAFTSMAN
Curses to the merchants and factory directors! I wasted the best years of my life — When other fellows were out chasing girls, winning fame on the battlefield or sailing the open seas, I was slaving away in a cramped little space in a silk manufactory.

HUSBAND
Down the cup that you hold in your hand!

CRAFTSMAN
I haven't got the strength… can't even raise it to my mouth. I was hardly able to crawl here on hands and knees, and now I won't see any dawn of freedom rising for me… Curses to the merchants who sell silk, and to the bluebloods who wear it. Curses — Curses!
He dies.

The words of the Chorus of Lackeys and the Craftsman contain a stinging criticism of the social system that had been in place up until then, from the lips of one of those who derived great advantage from it. The poet calls out his noble peers for their idiocy and whoring. Perhaps they have little control over the former (depending on what exactly is covered by the broad term), but there is no excuse for the latter; Krasiński decries his own class here as hypocrites, strongly implying that, if it should come to such a levelling revolution against them, it is they who are at least partially to blame.

Not far from where I am sitting, the Polish Democratic Society (Towarzystwo Demokratyczne Polskie) had its headquarters, after having been forced to leave Paris for London. Headed by Wojciech Darasz, the Society was one of the many movements and organisations among Poles in exile who were struggling for Polish independence from the partitioning empires of Russia, Prussia, and Austria. What distinguished them from the rest were their social postulates. In their view, the nobility of Poland bore much of the blame for the failure of the 1830 uprising. Not only did they fail to mobilise the peasants under their influence to join the colours of the insurrectionist forces, but they were all too conservative in their political thinking, which means: they chose their own comfort and material stability over the independence of their nation. Zygmunt Krasiński, as the scion of one of the greatest magnate clans in Poland, was especially sensitive to such views, which, judging from his major plays, he entertained with some sympathy. It is not just the Lackeys and Craftsmen of the world who cry aloud for justice, acknowledging that Europe has had a less than stellar record of living out Christ's commandments of equality and brotherhood. Count Henryk himself is moved deeply by his antagonist's pleas and reasonings:

> HUSBAND
> Progress, the happiness of the human race... I myself once believed... Ha! here — take my head, if only... it come true... One hundred years ago, two hundred... a mutual agreement could still have... But now, I know... Now we need mutual slaughter, 'cos now it's only about a switch of places.

What does Henryk mean when he suggests that "one hundred years ago, two hundred... a mutual agreement could still have" been arrived at — a compromise which, presumably, would have cast oil upon the churning waters of social inequality, and forestalled the angry uprising of the masses? Is he referring to the stubbornness of the French king

Louis and the earlier British king Charles who might have saved their own heads, and those of so many others, by a more pliant acquiescence to the petitions of their aggrieved subjects? What matters is that Henryk himself is attracted to such "progress" and "human happiness;" he once had liberal tendencies, the like of which can still move his heart. But although Pankracy is correct in assessing that now "I've placed my finger right beneath his heart, and touched the nerve of poetry," Henryk cannot be finally moved: "Vain dreams — who will realise them? Adam died in the wilderness, and we won't get back into Eden." And is not Henryk at least a little bit right? Despite the vitriolic attitude of Pankracy towards traditional religion (one of the props of the social order he is attacking), something he shares with Robespierre earlier, and Marx later, all he is proposing is another sort of messianism, another sort of utopian parousia, which is just as unlikely to come about in our lifetimes, as is that foretold in the New Testament:

> PANKRACY
> From this generation, over which I brood with the strength of my will, the final tribe shall emerge — the greatest, bravest. The earth has yet to see such men: free people, lords of the earth from pole to pole. And the earth herself shall be one city flourishing, one happy home, one workshop of happiness, riches and industry.

And this is something for which Count Henryk has no patience. In one of the Dantean scenes from the *Undivine Comedy*, Henryk has the Convert (under duress) lead him among the revolutionary mobs, disguised, on the night before his meeting with Pankracy. (It is during this "underworld" journey that the hero of the play witnesses the conversation of the Chorus of the Lackeys, and holds his brief exchange of words with the Craftsman, both cited above). I'll have none of your idealistic claptrap, he tells Pankracy after shaking off that momentary lapse to sympathy, for, just as Peter Townshend and Roger Daltrey were to assert decades later, all this is just another case of "meet the new boss, same as the old boss:"

> HUSBAND
> [...]I too know you, and your world. Amidst the shades of night I watched the dancing of the mob, upon whose necks you

climb upward, and saw all the old crimes of the world dressed up in new clothes, swaying to the rhythm of a new dance, the end of which, however, hasn't changed in one thousand years: dissipation, gold, and blood. But you were nowhere there to be seen. You didn't deign descend among your children, 'cos in the depths of your soul you hold them in contempt! A few minutes more, and if your reason doesn't abandon you, you'll hold yourself in contempt as well. Don't torment me any further.

There's something to this assessment. We see with our own eyes how Pankracy, lord and master of the revolutionary mobs, assumes the distant air of the lords he seeks to overthrow, in relation to the people who acknowledge him their leader:

> PANKRACY. And have you put the shoemakers' subscription into our strongbox?
>
> LEONARD. With unfeigned enthusiasm they contributed — every one of them — they collected one hundred thousand.
>
> PANKRACY. I'll invite them to supper tomorrow.

Similarly, when Henryk and the Convert come across the revolutionary warlord Bianchetti during that foray through the nighttime camp, it's hard not to appreciate, at least, the sardonic reasoning behind Henryk's conclusions:

> HUSBAND
> And what is the general musing on, may one inquire?
>
> BIANCHETTI
> See that space between the sycamores, Citizens? Take a good look. Up through there you can see the castle. With my glass I can even make out the walls, fosses and the four bastions.
>
> HUSBAND
> Difficult to take.

BIANCHETTI
Thousands and thousands of kings! One might steal along the ravine, undermine a bit and…

[…]

CONVERT
[…] So, what've you thought up, Citizen General?

BIANCHETTI
In thought
You may be my brothers in freedom, but not in genius. Everyone will learn of my plans… after my victory.
Moves off.

HUSBAND
To convert
Kill him. That's my advice. Because that's the way all aristocracy gets its start.

When we come to speak of the manner in which poetry, idealism, and, in particular, Byronism and "great soulled" Romantic tropes are dealt with in Krasiński's work, we will come across Henryk's guardian angel advising him to turn away from the dream world, and concentrate instead on practical love. Whether or not he is correct in so thinking, this is what the revolutionary movement is lacking, as far as Krasiński is concerned. It is for this reason that he sees republicanism, in its guise as revolutionary, or popular, democracy, not as progress, but rather as a simple changing of the ruling guard, and revolution itself — despite his constant harping on the need for Action — as nothing more than gratuitous bloodshed. As he says in his own voice, in his opening prose statements to Part III of the *Undivine Comedy,* the programme of the revolutionaries can be reduced to the following slogan: "Away with the heart, with superstition; long live the word of comfort and slaughter!" Witness also the words of Henryk, in his nocturnal reconnaissance, when he comes across the Chorus of Butchers:

CHORUS OF BUTCHERS
Poll-hammer, cleaver — them's our weapons, the shambles is our life! It's all the same, capon or count, swine or seigneur, we put to the knife.

Children of strong-arm, children of blood, we look with impassive eye on weaker, on whiter. Well and good, whoever hires us: be it the bluebloods to slaughter their cattle, be it the people to slaughter their lords.

Poll-hammer, cleaver — them's our weapons, the shambles is our life. O, the shambles, the shambles, the shambles!

HUSBAND
These I like — at least they make no pretensions to honour or philosophy.

Other examples of this gloomy view of social revolution can be cited. The real issue with the topic, as dealt with in the *Undivine Comedy*, is that we are offered no solution to the problem. The impatient revolutionaries want power and blood; the aristocrats and the old guard, whether they are able to sympathise with the demands of the long-downtrodden classes or not, have nothing to offer except resistance, and an insistence upon a paternalistic view of society which would keep the status quo in place. "I have placed my trust in the Lord, who gave my forefathers the right of rule," Henryk declares, rather quaintly, if not infuriatingly, to our tastes; and a little later, in the same interview he says to Pankracy:

> Neither you, nor any one of yours would have lived were it not for the grace of my fathers which nourished you, the power of my fathers that defended you, and them. In time of famine they gave you grain; in time of plague they founded hospitals, and when you'd lifted yourselves up from the levels of the cattle you tend to that of children, they gave you schools and churches. And during time of war they left you at home, knowing that you're not made for the battlefield.

He will, of course, learn that this is not the case; the common people may lack the scutcheons and the shining armour, but their anger — and numbers — will carry the day in the end.

No compromise can be reached. One of the constant themes in the plays of Zygmunt Krasiński is this philosophical intractability. After bringing the two implacable enemies Pankracy and Henryk together (Why? Is Miłosz's psychological assessment correct? Or was Krasiński writing blind, exploring, curious himself as to how their interview would turn out?) he has them part from each other, neither changed by the meeting:

> HUSBAND
> [...] Your words dash themselves against their glory and shatter, just as, long ago, the arrows of the pagans did, against their breastplates. These words of yours can't even stir their ashes — they die away like the howling of a mad dog, racing about frothing until he croaks beside the road. And now it's time for you to take your carcass from my home. My guest, you leave a free man.
>
> PANKRACY
> Until we meet again, on the battlements of Holy Trinity. And when you run out of powder and shot...
>
> HUSBAND
> Then we'll meet at sword's-point.
>
> PANKRACY
> We are two eagles. But your aerie is shattered by the lightning bolt. *Takes up his cap of liberty.* Crossing this threshold, I cast a curse upon it befitting ancient trash. And you, you and your son, I devote to destruction.

It is the same at the conclusion of the *Unfinished Poem*. There, it is the President of that none-too-defined association of national spirits working to further the advent of God's Kingdom on Earth who chases the rebellious ones off with a curse, unable to compromise with evil. The young Henryk, an initiate to the society, is little more than a witness at this point. But, true to form, Pankracy (at the start of his career, though the play was written long after the *Undivine Comedy*) is unable to bend from his side, either:

PRESIDENT
Carry their coffins behind them — See them off to the very threshold of the mysteries. Open the wall of the underworld before them!

PANKRACY
My thanks to you, most reverend sir! We shall fight, you and I, for I — how well you spoke — I am the destroyer! But fear no treason — the surface of the earth will never hear of you, or your men!

PRESIDENT
Who has played Judas to the Idea, may yet turn Judas among men!

PANKRACY
No, no! You cannot think so of me!

PRESIDENT
The living hold no commerce with the dead. Enough already. Amen!

PANKRACY
The keys, the keys! Here is the threshold — How stuffy it is here! You ought not to strain your lungs so, singing in this atmosphere. Open it up, already!

UNSEEN CHORUS
Sing, sing them the funeral dirge to the end!

PRESIDENT
And now, let each say to them, "You are extinguished."

PANKRACY
Will this ritual ever end?

And finally, even in Krasiński's early-Christian costume drama *Irydion*, implacability seems to be an heroic attribute. Despite his sympathy for Alexander Severus, who, it seems, wishes to reform the Rome that Irydion hates so in a direction that ought to please the Greek, Irydion will not join forces with the young pretender against Heliogabalus, whom both oppose, who incarnates in his person everything that both hate about corrupt Rome:

ALEXANDER
Son of Amphilochus, insult me not with equivocal words. For you owe me a debt of gratitude, that I do not believe my own eyes, although clearly, they testify to your perversity. Ah! I don't understand myself, why I always wished to trust you!

IRYDION
I thank you, Severus! If the fates had made me a man, and if I had wished to gladden my heart with the blessed gift of a man's friendship, it is you that I would have desired. But now, these bosoms of ours, which might have met in a friendly embrace, will confront one another only on the field of battle.

ALEXANDER
It is not too late yet — Abandon the tyrant! Peer out of the mist with which you have been engulfed and pronounce but one word of friendship, and I will never doubt of your faith. Irydion, where is your sister?

IRYDION
There, where fate has pinned her.

It is not odd that, in the semi-pagan world of *Irydion*, a lot should be made of moira, that destiny written in the stars that even the gods cannot oppose. But fate has no predetermining role in the Christian conception of history. Even though Krasiński's concept of God's plan for the world seems almost to shade into Calvinism, he never does abandon the tenet of man's free and unfettered will. As Aligier warns Pankracy for the final time before the schism noted above:

I warn you — because at this moment your future failure stands reflected before me! There is still time! You have free will! If you won't listen to me, perhaps you shall be powerful; perhaps you shall stand before people for a moment, a moment and a half. But you will fall away from the sight of God, and no trace of you will be found in His heart!

But perhaps this is one of the keynotes of Krasiński's plays. Man has a free will; in each of these plays, theoretically, peace might be restored, or preserved, by one of the protagonists coming to his senses and bending. Irydion could have joined his men to those of Alexander Severus, and cleansed Rome of its contagion. Yet he has vowed Rome's destruction, and nothing — not even common sense — can turn him from his determination. Pankracy could have stepped away from his disastrous heresy in the concluding scenes of the *Unfinished Poem*, but the hatred he bears the aristocracy will not permit him to lower the horns of his pride. Like Lucifer, whom in many respects he resembles, he can only exclaim *Non serviam!*

It is only the Husband, Count Henryk, who is in a completely impossible position when he and Pankracy meet at the crisis point of the *Undivine Comedy*. Pankracy offers him no compromise, nothing but shameful personal immunity from the massacre that looms over the other aristocrats, for himself and his son, in exchange for betraying his people (who, as we learn in the end, are rather base fellows anyway). But when Henryk, tempted, cries out that once compromise might have been possible, but now blood must be shed, he is merely speaking the truth. No synthesis can arise from this clash of thesis (revolution) with antithesis (reaction, status quo), and it is for this reason that, after the final victory of Pankracy's revolutionary forces, they themselves are overcome by, of all things, the Second Coming of Christ. It is an ending that appealed to Mickiewicz. In his discussion of the play, he writes:

> The end of this drama is sublime. I know of nothing comparable. It is that truth was neither in the camp of the Count nor in that of Pancras; it was above them; it appeared in order to damn them. [...] The author has been accused from two sides: some have seen nothing else in his work but the expression of violent hatred for the ideas of progress: for he has exaggerated to caricature the language of modern reformers and heightened the character of their adversaries; others have blamed the

seeming irreligion in the spectacle of triumphant evil. But the truth is that this poem is merely the cry of despair of a man of genius who recognizes the greatness and difficulty of social questions and who, unfortunately, did not raise himself to a height from which he could glimpse the solution of them.[9]

As effective as this may be, dramatically speaking, there can be no greater expression of despair on behalf of the author, no stronger indicator of his pessimism for the future of a mankind determined to turn everything he holds dear upon its head. As he wrote to Sanguszko: "This is a horrid age, my dear Princess. It is ever more sinful and perverse; the very essence of sin and perversity. Punishment simply must come again, be it another flood, or new Gomorrahs!"[10]

PROMETHEUS DEAD: KRASIŃSKI'S ANTI-HEROES

Judging from his plays, Krasiński had a very sceptical attitude toward the creative prowess of man. In this, he is out of step with the modern age of individualism, which is ushered in by the Romantic movement of the nineteenth century, and in his insistence on sensitivity — indeed obedience — to the plan of God, he seems most akin to the poets and thinkers of the Baroque age. At that moment in the *Unfinished Poem* when Pankracy interrupts the ritual of Henryk's initiation, he turns to him with the following characteristic words:

> Listen, boy, you scion of fathers, you who know your fathers! I, who have none, I who walk the earth as if I had arisen directly from her womb, from the gravel and muck and the grass, as once the Titans, and as today the people of the peoples, I say unto you — there is to be an end to the Polish nobility, and that of all Slavdom!

---

9   Adam Mickiewicz, *Les Slaves*, pp. 91-92, cited by Wacław Lednicki in his article "The *Undivine Comedy*," collected in Lednicki, p. 78.
10 Krasiński, letter to Izabella Sanguszko, dated Warsaw, 24 July 1850. In Maciejewski, p. 251.

To a great degree, these claims are attractive. Pankracy identifies himself as the man with no antecedents, the man from nowhere, the Great Soul, a force of nature whose power rests not upon ancient lineage or societal approval, but personal talent, the justice of his cause, the might of his will. He continues in this prideful strain when rebuked for his presumption by the Unseen Chorus:

> UNSEEN CHORUS
> Hold, hold, you errant soul! Do you not recall how deep the stain of shame is upon him who breaks his faith? Abandoned he is, on this and on the other side of the tomb; perverse, wretched, vile is he!
>
> PANKRACY
> I'll take that on the other side of your tomb, but not here. On this side, I am the son of my own deeds! I generate my own fathers. O my deeds, to my succour!

But here the pride and bravado devolves into farce. So stubborn is Pankracy in his pride that, consciously or not, he begins to utter absurdities. He is the "son of his own deeds," which "fathers" he "generates" himself! Here we have a more puzzling conundrum than the familiar riddle of the chicken and the egg. But more than that, here we have the author's characterisation of the Great Soul as the Great Usurper — unfettered will as nothing heroic, but rather, as villainy. Pankracy repeats the prideful absurdity blurted out by Milton's Lucifer in Book V of *Paradise Lost*, when that anti-hero is reproached for his ingratitude towards the God Who created him:

> That we were formed then say'st thou? And the work
> Of secondary hands, by task transferred
> From Father to his son? Strange point and new!
>   [...] who saw
> When this creation was? Rememb'rest thou
> Thy making, while the maker gave thee being?
> We know no time when we were not as now;
> Know none before us, self-begot, self-raised
> By our own quickening power.
>   (V: 853-861)

Created? Me? Lucifer asks, with rebellious rhetoric. Rubbish! I created myself! It is as close to comedy as Milton comes in his epic, and, as there, so here: the hubris of the "great soulled" hero is not only absurd, it is damnably sinful. The only route to happiness for mankind is submission to God's wisdom, God's will, God's plan. Stubborn insistence on one's own will can only lead to tragedy. It draws a man — or mankind — to the lip of such an abyss that he has no way out of the impending catastrophe, and God Himself, in His mercy, must intervene.

That is what happens at the conclusion of the *Undivine Comedy*; the two implacable camps of Count Henryk and Pankracy lead mankind to such a situation of pat, that Christ Himself must wipe the chessboard clean with His second coming. It is also what happens in the individual life of humans with an unnatural sense of their own elevation above the common rout. Alongside the political and social crises described by Krasiński in the *Undivine Comedy*, we witness, earlier on, the personal crisis of the Husband, Count Henryk, brought about by his romantic, poetic nature.

It is one of the curious paradoxes of cultural history that the Slavic peoples are often characterised as idealistic, dreamy Romantics. How often is Lord Byron invoked as the patron saint of the Romantic strain in the literatures of Slavdom. Of course, his influence, like that of Shakespeare, is huge. But it is not unchallenged, and it is the Polish and Russian traditions, which provide us with three of the greatest unmaskings of the Byronic hero that we possess.

Among the Russians, it is Aleksandr Pushkin who, in his marvellous novel in verse *Evgenii Onegin*, uses his protagonist, that "Harold in Muscovite dress" to prove that Byronism, as entertaining as it may be on the printed page, can lead only to tragedy should one attempt to live according to its dictates in the real world. Among the Poles, Pushkin's friend Adam Mickiewicz lays bear the bankruptcy of the great soul when Konrad, the eloquent shaman-poet of *Forefathers' Eve*, learns that poetic powers promise more than they can deliver, and that common, real, small acts of charity such as we all can perform are of much greater practical value to the brothers and sisters we wish to help. In Krasiński's *Undivine Comedy*, the lesson is much the same.

The story of Count Henryk told therein, which will reach its crescendo with the apocalyptic end-times, begins as a domestic drama: his marriage, and the birth of his son Jerzy Stanisław (soon to be given the rather humorously romantic monicker of "Orcio.") The marital bliss is very short-lived, as, before long, the devils of Hell, in an effort to enlarge their infernal kingdom by the addition of Henryk's soul, tempt him away from goodness, from his sacramental union, and indeed from reality by animating the corpse of a dead whore in the guise of his vision of ideal, poetic female pulchritude. The scene where she appears to both Husband and Wife, to separate the former from the latter, is both terrifying, and comic, in respect of how duped the Husband is, while his poor Wife sees everything all too clearly:

> WIFE
> What's that?
> *She pulls the child close to her breast. The music stops.*
>
> *Enter the maiden.*
>
> MAIDEN
> O my darling, I bring thee blessing and delight — Come with me. Throw away the earthly chains that hold thee bound. I am from a fresh world, endless, nightless… and I am thine.
>
> WIFE
> Blessed Mother, save me! — This phantom is as pale as death itself — snuffed-out eyes and a voice like the creaking of a corpse-laden wagon!
>
> HUSBAND
> Thy forehead shineth; thy locks are blossom-laced, my darling.
>
> WIFE
> A shroud hangs from her shoulders in rags!
>
> HUSBAND
> Light pours about thee… Speak to me once more — then I can die.
>
> MAIDEN
> She who restraineth thee is an illusion — her life is fleeting — her love, like a leaf that perisheth among desiccated thousands. But I pass not away.

> WIFE
> Henryk, Henryk, screen me from her, don't give me over! I smell sulphur and decay!
>
> HUSBAND
> Woman of clay and mud, envy not, slander not — blaspheme not! God's intent was thus to fashion thee, but thou didst follow the serpent's crooning and didst become what thou art!
>
> WIFE
> No! I will not let you go!
>
> HUSBAND
> *To maiden*
> O darling! I shall abandon her and follow thee!
> *Exits.*

So joyously flummoxed is the aether-treading poet Henryk, that the diabolical maiden achieves what seems impossible: convincing him that *she* is real, and that his actual wife, a woman of flesh and blood, is an "illusion." He will not see clearly again until he is led to the lip of an actual abyss by the Maiden, flying before him, leading him on. It is only when the devils have him exactly where they want him, that they allow the self-imposed scales to fall from his eyes, so that they might mockingly torment him with his stupidity before the final push into the black pit:

> HUSBAND
> Where has she got to? — Of a sudden, the morning's perfumes have disappeared, the weather has clouded over — I'm standing on a summit, before an abyss, and how terribly the winds blow!
>
> MAIDEN'S VOICE
> *From afar*
> Come to me, love.
>
> HUSBAND
> But thou art far from me, and I cannot overstep the abyss.

VOICE
Near at hand
Where are thy wings?

HUSBAND
Devil, who mockest me, I do contemn thee.

SECOND VOICE
Here at the summit of the world, thy great soul, thy immortal soul, which was to race through the heavens — What? 'Tis perishing! And, poor thing, begs thy feet to go no further — Great Soul — Great Heart!

[…]

MAIDEN
From the other side of the abyss
Take my hand in thine and take wing!

HUSBAND
What's happening to you? — The flowers are tearing away from your brow, falling down — and as soon as they touch earth, they squirm away like reptiles — they crawl away like snakes!

MAIDEN
My darling!

HUSBAND
Good God, your dress is in rags!

MAIDEN
Why dost thou linger?

HUSBAND
Your hair is — all wet … Bones are poking from your chest!

Once more, a human being has wilfully got himself into a fix from which there is no way out. God must step in again to save the day; but — true to the traditional Christian understanding of God's respect for the unfettered free will of the human agent — it is only when Henryk calls out to Him, albeit grudgingly, for His aid, that He sends Henryk's Guardian Angel to his side to quite literally pluck him out of the mess into which he's rushed headlong: "At this very moment, holy water falls upon your child's brow. Return home and sin no more. Return home and love your child."

This is a truly beautiful passage, sublime in its powerful simplicity. Poetry is lovely, and we ought to celebrate our unique individuality, each of us. But we are not just made for ourselves and the Ideal; we are made for one another. It is for this reason, perhaps, that throughout the play Krasiński refers to Henryk as "Husband" rather than "Count" or "Poet" or even "Henryk." Any vocation he may have to poetry (or lordship), can only be secondary to that vocation of husband and father, which are sacred in a way that the writing of verses or dallying with philosophical questions of Form and Reflection, Ideal and Real, are not. It is a lesson taught us by Mickiewicz's Konrad, whose greatest act on behalf of others is giving his signet to be sold on behalf of the poor on earth, and the suffering souls in Purgatory; it is the lesson taught us by Tatyana who, even though she admits her continued attraction to, nay, love for, the roguish Evgenii, determines not to accept him when he throws himself at her feet, but rather remain faithful to the man she has married. It is to her husband that she has a real, sacramental, responsibility, and giving in to Evgenii's blandishments would be selfish, destructive, wrong. It is a lesson that is taught us not only by Christianity. It is as old as humanity itself. The Guardian Angel's words are a repetition of those spoken by Siduri to Gilgamesh in that ancient, first great monument of western literature. Catching sight of the ratty looking fellow out chasing dreams of immortality, she says: "Gilgamesh, you will never find what you are seeking. The gods have reserved eternal life for themselves. Return home, rejoice in the embraces of your wife, and love the child who places his hand in your own. For this too is the lot of man."

This, above all, is the lot of man.

There is no room for heroes in the world presented by Zygmunt Krasiński. Perhaps this is his chief virtue as a poet — he shows us an unvarnished world, where outlandish hopes are reduced to moderate expectations, where the real levelling has less to do with politics, and all to do with recalling the improbable superman to the squalor, and dignity, of human quotidianity. Henryk falls from the clouds, as do most of us, who attempt to displace the world with the petty levers that fit our hands. Besides the fanciful character of Irydion, whom (in yet another apocalyptic scene) is saved from the jaws of Hell after many centuries, and sent north to the "land of graves and crosses" (Poland) where he is to carry on his suffering on behalf of liberty until he achieves his apotheosis ("you and my Word shall never pass away," God promises him, with grandiosity), only Napoléon triumphs:

> Who can equal him, of those who have passed away? Everything that ever existed scattered and divided, is given to him to unite in marvellous manner! Both the flesh of ancient demi-gods, unfatigued, sleepless, beautiful, and the Christian soul, of plumbless depth, tender and yearning, and the spirit creative, the magnetic master of time and space!
>
> All the fates of humanity are gathered together in him: all trial and triumph, might and catastrophe, rejoicing and misfortune! Just as God created the world from nothing, so shall he appear among people, from nowhere, and arise! He shall be a hero like Alexander the Greek, an emperor like the Roman Caesar, and a martyr like a saint of the first springtimes of Christianity. He shall die, like Moses, alone, face to face with the Lord; he shall die prophesying the Lord's will to the future days of the tribe of man!

Now there's a paean for you. But — as we, and Krasiński himself, writing in the middle of the nineteenth century — know, this hero-emperor-martyr-prophet ultimately failed. Another artistic representation of the Corsican, painted at this same time by Turner and hanging today in Tate Britain, is closer to the truth: "War. The Exile and the Rock Limpet" depicts the French warlord alone on a wild, empty beach, gazing at a shellfish at his foot (how the mighty have fallen) while his British guard watches over him, from a respectful distance.

Napoléon — that darling of Romantics idealising the great souled individual who triumphs by might of will, snatching the crown from the hands of the Pope — and rightly so, for he rose to empire by his own efforts, and not through the grace of any potentate — that model of the superman to both the Onegins and Raskolnikovs of the world — even he failed. Even if we grant that, according to Dostoevsky's hero, there do exist here and there such supermen who are beyond good and evil, who make their own rules and shape their world according to their will — such figures are few and far between. How can any one of us dare to suggest that we belong to their number? As Raskolnikov bitterly realises after his horrid attempt at transgressing the petty laws of humanity, "Can anyone imagine Napoléon creeping under an old woman's bed" to fish out a handful of coppers?[11]

So what remains us? The frustration of the pianist Kęta from the play *1846*, scandalised by the behaviour of his compatriots who are too terrified to intervene, to help the needy, to stand up to brazen evil when they witness it?

> I'm ashamed, ashamed to speak of this, Madame! O, you simply can't believe what terror reigns in the city! In our veins there runs, not blood, but mistrust — fear has found a lodging in the marrow of our bones. Please note Madame, that not I alone, but other passers by too had halted on the street. — The while the horrid scene was playing out, it's true, one couldn't say a word, but later, there was nothing to prevent, nothing to oppose. And yet when that scoundrel drove away — can you comprehend it? — none of those present moved a muscle. Each of us stood there as motionless as a pole planted in the pavement. Meanwhile, in the middle of the road, all bloodied, the cabbie rolled about, moaning "Jesus, Jesus, Jesus!" Yet none of them, and there were many, dared to bring him aid [...] It seemed to me that I was ringed round by coffins, moving across the ground on their short ends —

---

11   It is also worth pointing out that both Napoléon and Irydion are not human beings like Henryk, Pankracy, or us. They are symbols, the former being described by Aligier as "one soul, which yet contains whole ages — An idea formed of millions of thoughts, trembling, incarnate," and the latter, by Alina Witkowska, as "a symbolic figure in the play, in which the poet concentrates both a condemnation of an act saturated with hatred, and the hope of redemption for an act truly Christian." Witkowska, p. 197. Even his curious apotheosis as he is sent by God into contemporary Poland is a confirmation of his essence as a vengeful spirit implacably devoted to liberty and justice, not a well-rounded, real man.

Since the play just cited is such a brief fragment, it is difficult to say how Krasiński might have developed his thought. Perhaps it was to be toward boldness, as *1846* contains mention of a poet, whose idealism sparks him to self-sacrifice, as well as a Count, who not only seeks to broaden his peasants' emancipation even further than they themselves wish it, but defends the idea of popular uprising, directly blaming his own caste for their role in turning the common people against them. Instead, we may turn our eyes again to the *Unfinished Poem*, which, despite its inchoate nature, most clearly describes Krasiński's understanding of the significance of time. As young Count Henryk is led to the doors of the underworld near the conclusion of the play, he is greeted with these words from the chorus who await him:

> CHORUS
> In the name of the Lord I receive you at these doors! The Lord Triune, Three, though One, and the history of the world is threefold, though one!
>
> YOUTH
> I've never heard such tones as these. The whole air is vibrating with this music. This hymn enters my very core, like the Sound-Redeemer of all the groans of the heart!
>
> CHORUS
> At last the promised day approaches! The Age to be known as that of the Comforter! the Hour, to be known as that of the Fulfiller! Christ was not taken from us forever — not for always was the Light of the World darkened! At last the Son will be adored through the Spirit, and the Spirit is from both Father and Son, uniting Both in Love!

This is, of course, the theory of the "three ages" first popularised by the curious figure of Joachim di Fiore (c. 1135–1202) and re-enunciated in Krasiński's own days by Hegel. The Age of the Holy Ghost, an age of harmony and brotherhood — the closest we shall ever see, perhaps, to the establishment of the Kingdom of God upon earth — can be hastened, not by social or political revolution, nor by the conservation of outdated feudal forms. It only can, and must, be brought about through the internal regeneration (or "revolution") of each man and woman, here and now:

> PRESIDENT
> To them all, to them all the Lord still says, "You cannot bear them," for only he adores Him, who makes visible and tangible His commandment in all its reality — only then shall the glory of such a world, being truly of God, bear testimony to itself. And so, my son? What now? The execution thereof will be the descent of the Spirit, the act itself, the Comforter! And where is that act? Dost thou see it?
>
> YOUTH
> No.
>
> PRESIDENT
> Look within thyself, for it is there!
>
> YOUTH
> How can that be, Father?
>
> PRESIDENT
> It is in thy breast, as it is in that of each human being!
>
> YOUTH
> How?
>
> PRESIDENT
> Eternal Grace can effect nothing at all for individual, or for nation, or for Humanity entire unless they lift their hands unto the heavens for it — for one half of creation is the will of the created! Although what was to pass away has passed away, and although the ages are drawing close to their fulfilment; although the wings of the promised Spirit already beat above this earthly vale, if we do not earn His coming, truly desire and indeed work earnestly toward it; if we do not become ourselves tabernacles to house Him, he shall not shine forth to us, and we shall not be comforted!

YOUTH
What then is your command?

PRESIDENT
It is no longer for us to command anything. We can only reveal the truth, and he who comprehends it, will command himself!

It can certainly be argued that this advice is dangerous. It can lead to atomisation and self-satisfaction, the safe belief that one is doing one's bit by merely looking within and working at self-perfection; in a word, the comfortable, drawing room apathy known as quiescence. But it needn't do; withdrawing from the arena of loud, earth-shattering acts (to which so few are called, and which often go awry) does not preclude engagement with one another on humbler, yet more meaningful levels. This, after all, is the lesson that even Mickiewicz's Konrad comes to learn. And Krasiński is not writing for the Konrads of the world, but rather for the "millions" that heroes such as he — and Henryk, and Pankracy — strive to elevate and make happy, while never quite ceasing to despise them. It is the message of Voltaire's Candide. If all of us really were to tend our own gardens, would we not have a better chance of making the world even so much better than if we took it in mind to trim all of Hyde Park with our weed whacker?

KRASIŃSKI THE POET OF PROSE

One of the better known of Krasiński's lyric poems begins with the lines "God hath denied me that angelic measure / Without which no man sees in me the poet" (*Bóg mi odmówił tej anielskiej miary / Bez której ludziom nie zda się poetą*). Czesław Miłosz states the matter as diplomatically as possible when he says, "Krasiński's poems are not regarded as important in the development of Polish poetry; opinion is in general agreement on this point."[12] While some of his poems still grace the pages of anthologies, it is a fact that his two most noteworthy works, the *Undivine Comedy* (*Nieboska komedia*, 1835) and *Irydion* (1836), both plays, are written in prose. In this he is unusual amongst

---

12 Miłosz, "Krasiński's Retreat," p. 214.

the Polish romantics, who excelled at verse. Indeed, all of his plays are prose, including the two fragments also collected in this translation, the so-called *Unfinished Poem* (*Niedokończony poemat*) and *The Year 1846* (*Rok 1846*), both of which he worked at later in life, and were published only after his death.

Besides their prose, the great characteristic that these plays share is volubility, coupled with an inquisitiveness, which at times suggests that the author was pursuing paths, the end of which he himself couldn't see at the time of composition. As far as their windiness is concerned, they do seem endless at times. This is particularly true of the *Unfinished Poem* with its extended mystical journeys, the patriotic/erotic motif of Princess Rahoga, which ends, abruptly and unexpectedly, in a dead end, and the sermonising and rituals that accompany the expulsion of Pankracy from the ranks of the pious choruses. From time to time, that anti-hero cries out "Get to the point already!" and "Will this never end?" — sentiments with which, perhaps, the weary reader has some sympathy…

Certainly, although both the *Undivine Comedy* and *Irydion* have been staged, it is clear that they were meant, first and foremost, as closet dramas, to be read, rather than seen. The author's novelistic approach justifies the extended introductions to each section of these works, spoken in his own voice, which would be rather unwieldy in a stage performance. It is this "living voice" of the author, present in the introductory paragraphs, which turn our eyes to the matter of inquisitiveness. In the extended introduction to *Irydion*, the poet's voice calls out:

> Begone! Away from me! — Not for you, my companions, these wild spaces… It is better for you to remain in the Roman Campania, at the foot of the Apennines. I shall go; I wish to look upon him once more before he dies, before he dies for all ages!

This is surely something new in the history of literature. Usually, when the author addresses his imagined readership, it is in the tones of an invitation, something along the lines of "Come with me and explore…" Here, we have just the opposite: the author is waving us *away* from the journey, telling us to "wait here a bit," while he goes off exploring by himself. In this, I think, we catch a glimpse of what Krasiński was about in writing the *Undivine Comedy*, *Irydion*, and that most elaborate of his incomplete plays, the *Unfinished Poem*. In the first place, these works are not primarily intended for us. They arise from the author's own inner need, from his wish to understand, to make sense out of, the past, present, and the future; to comprehend, as much as he is able, the sweep of history as "planned" by God, and his role therein.

And so, the plays are not calls to action. They are meditations on time and eternity — "compositions of place," to borrow a term from St Ignatius' *Spiritual Exercises*, the intent of which is to make plastic and immediate places, persons, and situations; a conscious effort to become vicariously present at them, and thus to open oneself to the enlightenment that only physical presence can provide.

It is for this reason that, as I state above, in reading through these plays, one often has the feeling that we are being led along a path by the author, which tends toward a goal of which he himself is unconscious. The enlightenment doesn't always come, or, at least, not in the manner in which it was expected.

This, I believe, is at the bottom of the apocalyptic conclusion of the *Undivine Comedy*. It is as if Krasiński were seeking an answer to the problems of social unrest that were beginning to plague industrialising Europe from the two polar opposite protagonists, Count Henryk and Pankracy, themselves. Each of them is given a platform to speak from, and, despite his obvious leanings toward the former, both of them are given free rein to make the best arguments they can. And yet, no satisfying answer is forthcoming, neither from the democrat, nor from the feudal conservative. Both of them fail; both of them fail *us*, and the only way this particular circle can be squared is with the intervention of Christ.

However, even here we are not completely satisfied. Although Christ certainly appears to Pankracy, overwhelming him with His light — Leonard seems not to see him. Is this really the end of the world? Or will the massacre of the nobles, who were being led to the guillotine just before Pankracy's vision, take place? Is this merely the end of Pankracy's world?[13] It's the end of the play, that's for sure. Satisfied or not, this is as much as Krasiński will tell us. Or maybe

---

13   Such is suggested by the poet himself in a letter to Henry Reeve, dated Rome, 19 December 1833: "He has seen the Cross, and his work has appeared false

it's as much as he *can* tell us — still unsure himself, perhaps, since later he will feel impelled to set his hand to the more philosophical "prequel" of the *Unifinished Poem*.

In this, the *Undivine Comedy* more than deserves its curious title. For, despite its surface similarities — Count Henryk being led amongst the unfamiliar groups of revolutionaries by his own reluctant Virgil, the Convert — where Dante learns, and transmits to us, solid knowledge at the end of his magnum opus, Krasiński only points the way, shows us, and allows us to draw our own conclusions, if we can. It could not have been otherwise. For Dante comes of the Age of Faith, when everything was explainable, if at first confusing. With the aid of theology and revelation, one might always emerge from the dark wood into the clean sunlight of certitude. Krasiński is a man of the troubled modern age. It is no coincidence that the skies described in these plays are so often covered in clouds.

Even in those places where he, or his characters, seem to state something with certainty, as, for example, in Dante's castigation of modern capitalism, in comparison to the "heroic" age of his Florentine burghers:

> And again the figure flamed, but this time with the blood of inspiration, saying: "Would you even understand me, were I to prophesy future times to you? When still on the far side of the grave my body marched toward the tomb in the open brightness of the sunlight, there were such labourers on the earth too, and the banners of their guilds fluttered from the arcades of high towers. They hawked amaranth and all sorts of precious stone about the city markets — but a sword was sheathed, a rosary looped, at their sides; their hands knew how to manage the tiller on the swelling sea, and to build impregnable ramparts on the land. They took silver, and washed off the stain of that silver in the blood of battle! What shall such as you begin today — you with fingers as soft as wax, you whose lips have never formed a prayer! You, without strength on earth, and without hope in heaven, and all athirst for gold?"

---

to him. He is vanquished at the moment of his victory; his edifice is smashed, and he dies repeating the last words of Julian the Apostate." Cited by Lednicki, p. 71.

or when, so ahead of his time, he comforts the oppressed women with a vision of coming gender equality:

> "Up until now, you all have been like to the lilies of God, who grow, knowing nothing of their splendrous colours and aromas. But the day will come when you shall each be transformed into thinking roses. The reins of inspiration will fall from the hands of men and be given into yours. And they, prostrate at your feet, will beg of you but one song of sweetness — one prophecy of hope, one image of beauty — for their fate of unbearable difficulties and demanding acts will be a hard fate indeed, and a low one. But you, gazing upwards to God, will not glance their way; your ears will not hear their sobbing. Then will their hearts break as yours have, through so many ages! […] Thus shall it be, until the hour of your second transformation strikes, and once more you shall extend your hand to them, and you shall save their perishing hearts with love. And for all time you shall be to them as sisters, their equals on earth as in heaven […] Call back your soul and fear not — for if anything is to perish, the star of male praise will sooner grow dim at the judgement of God than the tear of one misfortunate woman dry up in vain,"

no positive statement is actually made. Does Dante really imagine that the nascent capitalists and industrialists of the nineteenth century will resume the swashbuckling ways of their pious and sword-bearing predecessors in pre-Renaissance Italy? And if the future equality of the sexes is to come about, when, exactly, will that be, and how will it be effected?

Perhaps the value of such inquisitive, but nebulous, works as Krasiński's plays is just this. Maybe the posing of important questions is just as important as answering them. If we are offended by this nineteenth century playwright's attitude toward the Other, and repulsed by his nationalistic ideas, how do we, in the twenty-first century, approach the Other in our midst? Is our self-image, as Americans, Britons, Poles, or what have you, consciously or unconsciously, triumphalist, messianic, bigoted? If it would be anachronistic to judge Krasiński's attitudes by a post World War II yardstick, how do we measure up? To paraphrase Pope Francis, are we wall-builders, or bridge-builders? What is the sense of our labour? Where do labour issues stand in our day, and what are our obligations, to ourselves and others, when we cash the weekly paycheque? How are women and other marginalised groups faring today, in our enlightened century? As the President challenges Young Henryk, "Which age of these [now twenty-one] Christian centuries has advanced Christ?" What are we doing so that, finally, we might say that it is our own?

ACKNOWLEDGEMENTS

As always, I thank, from the bottom of my heart, Ksenia Papazova, and everyone at Glagoslav, for their patient and enthusiastic help in bringing this, and other, of my translations of the Polish classics to the attention of the English-reading public.

This particular translation has received generous funding from the Broncel Trust, London, which greatly aided its publication. I am deeply thankful for their support.

This introduction was completed five days after the book launch of my translation of Stanisław Wyspiański's *Acropolis: the Wawel Plays*, hosted at the Hearth Club in South Kensington, under the aegis of the Union of Polish Writers Abroad, of which I have the honour of being a member, and the Polish Cultural Institute in London. I would here like to express my debt of gratitude to Mrs. Regina Taylor of the former organisation, and Mr. Robert Szaniawski, of the latter, for their support in my endeavours.

Above all, I am grateful to (and for) my wife Aleksandra, for absolutely everything.

London, 6 March 2018

The Undivine Comedy

FOR MARIA

To the errors, accumulated by their forefathers, they added something unknown to their ancestors — hesitation and fear — and so it happened that they were wiped clean from the face of the earth and a great silence is all that remains after them.

— Author unknown

To be, or not to be, that is the question.

— Hamlet

PART I

Stars about thy head — beneath thy feet the waves of the sea — before thee on the waves a rainbow rushes, cleaving the mist — whatever thou beholdest is thine — coasts, cities and peoples are thy property — heaven is thine — 'tis as if nothing can thy glory equal.

*

Thou playest to the ears of others inconceivable delights — Twining hearts together and rending asunder, as if they were but wreaths, trifles in thy hands — thou wringest tears from eyes — to dry them with a smile, yet only to hurl the smile from thy lips again, for a moment — for a few moments — sometimes for ages — But what dost thou feel thyself? — What art thou creating? — Of what art thou thinking? — And through thee flows the stream of the beautiful, but thou art not the beautiful. — Woe to thee — Woe! — The child, which weepeth on the bosom of his mother — the flower of the field, which knoweth not its own fragrance, have far greater merit before the Lord than thou hast.

*

Whence thy genesis, cheap shadow, which givest to know of the light, yet knowest not the light thyself? Which seest not! Which shalt not see the light! — Who created thee in ire or in irony? — Who hath given thee thy scoundrel life, that thou art able to put on the Angel, a moment before thou art hurled to the mire to creep along like a toad and choke thyself on slime? — For thee and the woman the origin is one.

*

But now thou sufferest as well, although thy torture produces nothing; it is good for nothing — The groan of the basest wretch is told among the strains of heaven's harps. — Thy despairings and sighs sink downward, and Satan collects them, adding them gaily to the sum of his own lies and deceits — And some day the Lord will deny them, as they have denied the Lord.

*

Not for this do I cry thee down, o Poetry, mother of the Beautiful and the Salvific. — He alone unhappy among men, who, conceived on worlds destined to perish, must recall, or have a presentiment of, thee — For such alone dost thou lead astray, who have dedicated themselves unto thee, who have become the living voices of thy glory.

*

Blessed is he, in whom thou dost take up residence, as God did upon the earth: unseen, unheard, in each of His parts magnificent, great, the Lord, before Whom all of creation humbles itself and declares: "He is here" — Such a one will bear thee like a star upon his forehead, and not separate himself from thy love by an abyss of words — He will love people and appear as a Man among his brethren — Yet he who will not preserve thee, who betrayeth thee too early and casteth thee about amongst people for empty delight; on his head thou strewest a few blossoms and then dost turn away. And he will play with the withered petals throughout his life, weaving for himself a charnel wreath — For him and the woman the origin is one.

Of all buffooneries, the most serious is marriage.

— Figaro

GUARDIAN ANGEL
Peace to men of good will — blessed is he amongst creation, who hath a heart — he may yet be redeemed — Good and humble wife, appear unto him — and may a child be born unto your house.
Flies away.

*

CHORUS OF EVIL SPIRITS
To the air, take wing, phantoms, fly to him! — Thou first, take the lead, shadow of a whore dead but yesterday, freshened with mist and wrapped in blossoms — maiden, poet's lover, take the lead. And thou as well, take wing, o Fame, old eagle of hell's taxidermy, filched from the stake upon which the hunter hung thee last Fall — Fly forth and spread wide thy wings, grand, sun-blanched, over the poet's head. Come out of our cellars, rotten likeness of Eden, thou work of Beelzebub's brush — we shall patch up thy holes and smear varnish over thy surface — and then, magic canvas, curl a cloud about thyself and fly to the poet — spread thyself about him, girdle him with cliffs and waters, night and day in turn — Mother, Nature, surround the poet!

*

A village church. Above the church hovers the Guardian Angel.

GUARDIAN ANGEL
If thou wilt persevere in thy vows to the end, thou wilt bask in the presence of the Heavenly Father, for all time, as my own brother.
He disappears.

The inside of the church — witnesses — a large, consecrated wax candle on the altar. The priest is performing a wedding ceremony.

PRIEST
Remember this well.

The couple rise from their knees. The husband squeezes his wife's hand and relinquishes her to her relatives' care — everyone exits — the husband remains in the church alone.

GROOM
I have deigned to enter into the bonds of earthly wedlock, for I have found the one of whom I have always dreamt — May a curse fall on my head, should I ever cease to love her.

*

A large chamber full of people — a ball — music — candles — flowers. The bride waltzes — after a few turns she pulls up, happens upon her husband in the crowd, and rests her head upon his shoulder.

GROOM
How beautiful thou art in thy weariness — in a disorder of flowers, with pearls in thy hair — thou art flaming from shyness and fatigue — Eternally, O eternally wilt thou be my song.

BRIDE
I'll be faithful to you, as mother told me to, and as my own heart dictates. — But there's so many people here — It's so hot and loud.

GROOM
Go and dance once more, and I shall stand here and gaze upon thee, as I've more than once looked upon the gliding angels with my mind's eye.

BRIDE
If that's what you want, but I've hardly any strength left.

GROOM
I beg thee, my love.

Dancing, music.

*

A cloud, night. An evil spirit in the guise of a maiden, flying.

MAIDEN
Not that long ago I was running around on the streets at this hour — now, demons drive me before them and have me put on the holy virgin. *She flies above a garden.* Flowers, tear yourselves from the earth and bedeck my hair. *She flies above a cemetery.* Freshness and grace of deceased maidens, dispersed through the air and hovering above the grave mounds, sink into my cheeks. Here some fine black hair is going to waste — Shadow of her curls, come and adorn my brow — And beneath this headstone, two blue eyes snuffed out — to me, to me, O fire, which once smouldered in them! — Behind these gates a hundred candles burn for a princess buried just today — milk white gown of silk, tear away from those bones! — Here it flutters to me through the bars like a bird. — Now, onward, onward!

*

A bedroom — a nightlamp stands on a table and palely illuminates the husband sleeping beside his wife.

HUSBAND
In his sleep
From whence comest thou, O unseen, unheard for such a long time — As water flows, thus thy feet, two ripples of white — a peace of holiness shineth forth from thy brows, — Everything of which I have dreamed, everything which I have loved, has come together in thee. *He wakes.* Where am I!? — Ha, next to my wife. This is my wife. *Stares at his wife.* I thought that thou wert my dream. And now, after a long absence, she hath returned and she differs from thee — Thou art good and kind, but she… My God! — what's that? — For real!

MAIDEN
Thou hast betrayed me.
She disappears.

HUSBAND
Curséd be the moment, in which I took a wife unto myself, in which I abandoned the lover of my youthful years, thought of my thought, soul of my soul...

WIFE
Waking
What is it? — Is it morning? — Is the carriage ready? — We've got a lot of things to do today.

HUSBAND
'Tis night, deaf night. — Sleep. — Sleep deeply.

WIFE
Are you ill, my dear? I'll get up and fetch you some ether.

HUSBAND
Go back to sleep.

WIFE
Tell me what's wrong, dear — Your voice is strange, and it looks as if you had a fever.

HUSBAND
Starts up violently
I need fresh air. — Stay where thou art. — In God's name, don't come after me — I repeat, do not get out of bed.
He exits.

*

A moonlit garden — beyond the wooden fence, the church.

HUSBAND
Since the day of my wedding I have slept the sleep of the torpid, the sleep of gluttons, the sleep of a German merchant beside his German wife — The world around me fell asleep in my own image and likeness — I have been running to relatives, to doctors, to stores,

and now, that a child is born unto me, I have been thinking of... a wet nurse!

The church clock strikes two.

Come to me, my ancient dominions, alive, flocking together beneath the aegis of my thought — attentive to my inspirations — Once, the echo of a bell at night was your call to action. *He walks about, wringing his hands.* God, can it be that Thou Thyself hast sanctified the union of two bodies? Can it be that Thou Thyself hast declared that nothing may them sunder, e'en though their souls beat each other off, going each his own way, leaving the bodies together as if they were but two corpses lain in the same tomb? Again thou art beside me — O mine — O mine! — Take me with thee. — If thou art but an illusion, if it be that I have but imagined thee — If thou hast created thyself from me, and but showest thyself as nothing but a dream, O let me become a dream as well! I would become of mist and smoke if only to unite myself with thee!

MAIDEN
And wilt thou then follow after me when I come to you, on whatever day I choose to come?

HUSBAND
At each and every moment I am thine.

MAIDEN
Remember.

HUSBAND
And thou *be*! Don't dissolve like a dream — If thou art indeed that beauty above all beauty, thought above all thought, why is it that thou never lastest longer than the space of one wish, one thought?

A window in the house adjoining opens.

WOMAN'S VOICE
Come back in, my dear — you'll catch cold out there. And I'm afraid to be alone in this big, dark room.

HUSBAND
All right, in a moment. The spirit hath disappeared, yet promised me that she would return. And then — farewell garden, farewell home! And farewell to thee, who wert created for home and garden, though not for me!

VOICE
For pity's sake — it gets colder and colder towards the dawn.

HUSBAND
And my child… O God!
Exits.

*

A salon — two candles on the piano — a child in a corner crib — the husband sits sprawled on a chair with his face in his hands, the wife at the piano.

WIFE
I was to see Father Benjamin. He promised to come the day after tomorrow.

HUSBAND
Good. Thanks.

WIFE
And I sent to the confectioner's so they'd have some cakes ready — It seems you've invited quite a few guests to the christening — You know, chocolate cakes, with "JS" — the initials of Jerzy Stanisław.

HUSBAND
Good. Thanks.

WIFE
Thank God that this christening will soon take place — and that our little Orcio will become a Christian in the full sense of the word. Even though he was already baptised with water, I always felt that something was missing. *She goes over to the crib.* Sleep my child — Can you already be dreaming of something, that you've thrown off your blanket? — There now — Just like that — Lie down this way. You're uneasy today, my little one — sleep, my lovely boy, sleep.

HUSBAND
Aside
Sultry — humid — It's getting ready to storm — Soon a thunderbolt will take voice, and my heart — will it burst?

WIFE
Returns to the piano, plays and stops, begins to play again, stops again
Today, yesterday — Ah, my God! All week long, all month long, you haven't spoken as much as a word to me — and everyone tells me that I look awful.

HUSBAND
Aside
The hour is upon us. I shall put it off no longer. *Aloud.* Nay, it seemeth to me that thou lookest well.

WIFE
It's all the same to you, 'cos you don't even look at me anymore. You turn your back on me when I enter a room, and you cover up your eyes when I sit down beside you. — Yesterday I went to confession, but in recalling my sins, I couldn't call to mind anything that would have offended you so.

HUSBAND
Thou hast not offended me.

WIFE
My God — my God!

HUSBAND
I feel as though I should love thee.

WIFE
You've finished me off with that one: "should!" — Better to speak plainly: "I don't love you." Then at least I'd know everything — everything. *She starts up violently and lifts the child from the crib.* Just don't abandon him, and I'll sacrifice myself to your anger. Love the child — my child, Henryk.
She kneels.

HUSBAND
Rising
Take no notice of what I've just said — Bad moments often come upon me of a sudden — It's ennui.

WIFE
Just one word, one promise, I beg of you — promise that you will always love him.

HUSBAND
Both thee and him — believe me.

He kisses her forehead — she embraces him — then a peal of thunder is heard — music follows immediately — chord after chord becoming ever more wild.

WIFE
What's that?
She pulls the child close to her breast. The music stops.

Enter the maiden.

MAIDEN
O my darling, I bring thee blessing and delight — Come with me. Throw away the earthly chains that hold thee bound. I am from a fresh world, endless, nightless… and I am thine.

WIFE
Blessed Mother, save me! — This phantom is as pale as death itself — snuffed-out eyes and a voice like the creaking of a corpse-laden wagon!

HUSBAND
Thy forehead shineth; thy locks are blossom-laced, my darling.

WIFE
A shroud hangs from her shoulders in rags!

HUSBAND
Light pours about thee… Speak to me once more — then I can die.

MAIDEN
She who restraineth thee is an illusion — her life is fleeting — her love, like a leaf that perisheth among desiccated thousands. But I pass not away.

WIFE
Henryk, Henryk, screen me from her, don't give me over! I smell sulphur and decay!

HUSBAND
Woman of clay and mud, envy not, slander not — blaspheme not! God's intent was thus to fashion thee, but thou didst follow the serpent's crooning and didst become what thou art!

WIFE
No! I will not let you go!

HUSBAND
To maiden
O darling! I shall abandon her and follow thee!
Exits.

WIFE
Henryk! — Henryk!

She faints and falls with the child — a second peal of thunder.

*

The christening — guests — Father Benjamin — Godfather — Godmother — wet nurse — the wife sits on a sofa apart — servants in the background.

FIRST GUEST
Softly
Funny, where's the Count got to?

SECOND GUEST
Off dawdling somewhere, or dribbling doggerel.

FIRST GUEST
The Countess is awfully pale. She hasn't said a word to anyone. Looks as if she hadn't slept for weeks.

THIRD GUEST
Today's christening reminds me of a ball hosted by someone who's lost his shirt at cards and greets the guests with the politeness of despair.

FOURTH GUEST
And to think that I abandoned a perfectly delightful princess to come here. I thought there'd be a nice little breakfast, but instead of that we have, as the Good Book reads, "wailing and gnashing of teeth."

FR BENJAMIN
Jerzy Stanisław, dost thou accept the holy unction?

GODPARENTS
I accept.

ONE OF THE GUESTS
Look — she's got up and is walking as if she were asleep.

SECOND GUEST
She throws her arms out in front of her — walking over toward her son on drunken legs.

THIRD GUEST
Come on, let's give her an arm to lean on. She'll faint!

FR BENJAMIN
Jerzy Stanisław, dost thou reject Satan and all his pride?

GODPARENTS
I do.

ONE OF THE GUESTS
Shh! — Listen.

WIFE
Placing her palm on the child's forehead
Where is thy father, Orcio?

FR BENJAMIN
Please don't interrupt.

WIFE
I bless thee, Orcio, I bless thee, my child — Be thou a poet, so may thy father love, and not abandon thee.

GODMOTHER
Let us continue, Marysiu.

WIFE
Thou wilt wrest esteem from thy father and endear thyself to him — and then he will forgive thy mother.

FR BENJAMIN
Fear God, Countess!

WIFE
I curse thee, if thou wilt not prove a poet.
She faints — servants carry her out.

GUESTS
Something strange is going on in this house — let's get out of here!

Meanwhile, the ceremony has run its course. The godfather carries the wailing child back to his crib.

GODFATHER
Over the crib
Jerzy Stanisław, you've just become a Christian and a member of Christian society. Later you'll become a citizen, and with the help of your parents and the grace of God, a fine civil servant. — Remember that one must love the Fatherland above all things, and that to die for the Fatherland is a beautiful thing…

Exit all.

*

Beautiful surroundings — hillocks and forests — mountains in the distance.

HUSBAND
This is what I have desired; for this I have spent long years in prayer! At last I am near my goal — I have left the world of people behind me — let each little ant down there scurry about and play with his blade of grass, and when he drops it, let him foam in anger and perish from sorrow!

MAIDEN'S VOICE
Come — come.
She walks through and exits.

*

Mountains, a cliff above the sea — thick clouds — storm.

HUSBAND
Where has she got to? — Of a sudden, the morning's perfumes have disappeared, the weather has clouded over — I'm standing on a summit, before an abyss, and how terribly the winds blow!

MAIDEN'S VOICE
From afar
Come to me, love.

HUSBAND
But thou art far from me, and I cannot overstep the abyss.

VOICE
Near at hand
Where are thy wings?

HUSBAND
Devil, who mockest me, I do contemn thee.

SECOND VOICE
Here at the summit of the world, thy great soul, thy immortal soul, which was to race through the heavens — What? 'Tis perishing! And, poor thing, begs thy feet to go no further — Great Soul — Great Heart!

HUSBAND
Show thyself! Take some form, which I might grapple with and crush! And should I take fright of thee, may I never possess her!

MAIDEN
From the other side of the abyss
Take my hand in thine and take wing!

HUSBAND
What's happening to you? — The flowers are tearing away from your brow, falling down — and as soon as they touch earth, they squirm away like reptiles — they crawl away like snakes!

MAIDEN
My darling!

HUSBAND
Good God, your dress is in rags!

MAIDEN
Why dost thou linger?

HUSBAND
Your hair is — all wet … Bones are poking from your chest!

MAIDEN
Thy promise! Thou hast sworn.

HUSBAND
The lightning lights up your face — You have no eyes! Empty eye-sockets!

CHORUS OF EVIL SPIRITS
Get thee back to Hell, old whore. Thou hast deceived a great soul and a proud heart. The wonder of people and his own self. Great Heart, hie thee after thy darling.

HUSBAND
God, are you damning me for this, because I believed that your beauty exceeds the beauty of this earth by a heaven's measure? Am I doomed because I chased after it, tortured myself to possess it — all to become the sport of Hell?

EVIL SPIRIT
Listen, brothers — listen!

HUSBAND
My last hour has tolled. — The storm whips up in black spirals — the sea rushes up the cliffs and reaches out for me — What is this force that pushes me ever further, ever nearer the edge? A whole nation has seated itself upon my shoulders, pressing me toward the abyss!

EVIL SPIRIT
Rejoice, brothers — rejoice!

HUSBAND
Vain to struggle — the delight of the abyss is ripping me away — my soul is fainting — God — your enemy is winning!

GUARDIAN ANGEL
Above the sea
Peace, billows, quiet yourselves. At this very moment, holy water falls upon your child's brow. Return home and sin no more. Return home and love your child.

*

Salon with piano — the husband enters — a servant with a candle follows.

HUSBAND
Where's your lady?

SERVANT
My lady the Countess is ill.

HUSBAND
I was in her room. It's empty. —

SERVANT
My lord. My lady is not here.

HUSBAND
So where is she?

SERVANT
They took her away yesterday…

HUSBAND
Where?

SERVANT
To the asylum.
He hurries out of the room.

HUSBAND
Listen, Maria — maybe you're pretending? Hiding somewhere, to punish me? Say something, please — Maria — Marysiu…

No…No one answers. Jan! Katarzyna! The whole house is deaf and dumb.

Her, to whom I swore fidelity and happiness, I have myself thrust into the ranks of those already damned in this world. Everything I've touched, I've destroyed, and I shall destroy my own self in the end. — Is it for this that Hell has released me from its clutches, that I might live a little longer as its image and likeness on the earth?

On what sort of pillow does she rest her head this evening? — What sort of sounds surround her at night? — The howling and singing of the crazed. I see her: the brow, upon which quiet thought always reigned, invitingly, pleasantly, transparently — she holds in her hands, bowed low — and that good thought of hers she has sent abroad, into the unknown, perhaps after me, and lost, weeping…

VOICE FROM SOMEWHERE
What a leading man.

HUSBAND
Ha! My devil speaks up. *Runs toward the doors, pushes both open.* Saddle up Tatar! — My cape, and my pistols!

*

A lunatic asylum, in a mountainous region, surrounded by a garden.

DOCTOR'S WIFE
At the door, with a ring of keys
I suppose you are a relative of the Countess?

HUSBAND
I'm a friend of her husband's. He sent me.

DOCTOR'S WIFE
You must understand, sir — you shouldn't expect too much of her… My husband's away — left yesterday… He'd be the better one to talk to. They brought her here two days ago — she was in convulsions. — What a fever! *Wipes her brow.* We've got lots of patients here, but none of them as sick as her. Just imagine, sir: this institution costs us two hundred thousand. But have you seen what a view of the mountains we have? — But you're getting impatient, I see. So it's not true that the Jacobins kidnapped her husband during the night? Please, sir — this way.

*

A room — barred windows — a few chairs — a cot — the wife on a couch.

HUSBAND
Enters
I wish to be with her alone.

VOICE
From behind the door
My husband would be angry if…

HUSBAND
Irritated
If you please, my good woman!
He closes the door and approaches his wife.

VOICE FROM ABOVE THE CEILING
You've clipt God in chains. One of us already died on the cross. I'm another God, and I too find myself among knaves!

VOICE FROM BENEATH THE FLOOR
Heads of kings beneath the guillotine — with me begins the peoples' liberty!

VOICE FROM BEHIND THE RIGHT WALL
Bow down before your lord the king!

VOICE FROM BEHIND THE LEFT WALL
The comet winks already on the welkin. The day of doom approaches!

HUSBAND
Maria… do you recognise me?

WIFE
I have pledged my troth to thee unto the grave.

HUSBAND
Come on — give me your hand. We're going.

WIFE
I cannot rise. My soul hath left my body and is settled in my head.

HUSBAND
Let me help you.

WIFE
Grant me but a few more moments, and I shall be worthy of thee.

HUSBAND
What?

WIFE
I prayed for three nights straight, and finally, God heard my prayer.

HUSBAND
I don't understand you.

WIFE
From the moment I'd lost thee, there came upon me a great change. "O, Lord my God," I cried, beating my heart, holding a candle against my breast and doing penance, "send down the spirit of poetry upon me." And on the third day I became a poet.

HUSBAND
Maria!

WIFE
Henryk, now thou wilt despise me no more! I am filled with inspiration… Now thou wilt not abandon me of an evening.

HUSBAND
Never, never! —

WIFE
Cast thine eyes upon me. Am I not thy equal? — I grasp all, understand, give out, win out, sing out. — Seas, stars, storms, sieges! Yes, stars, storms, seas — ah! what is it I've forgot — sieges. Take me to war! I shall embrace war and sing war! corpse, shroud, blood, wave, dew, coffin —

> Eternity around me swirls,
>   And, like a bird, unto eternity,
> Azure wings do I unfurl
>   And, flying, faint into the press
> Of the black waves of nothingness.

HUSBAND
Curses! Curses!

WIFE
Embraces him and kisses him on the mouth
My Henryk! My Henryk! How happy I am!

VOICE FROM BENEATH THE FLOOR
Three kings I killed with these two hands — ten are left — and a hundred priests howling at Mass.

VOICE FROM THE LEFT SIDE
The sun has lost one third of its brilliance — the stars begin to hobble in their courses — Misfortune! Misfortune!

HUSBAND
For me the day of judgement has arrived.

WIFE
Uncloud thy brow — Thou makest me sad again. What is it that thou lackest? — I have something else to say to thee.

HUSBAND
Tell me, what is it? I will do anything…

WIFE
Thy son will be a poet, too.

HUSBAND
What?

WIFE
At the christening, the priest gave him his first name — poet — and the others thou knowest — Jerzy Stanisław. It is I who have caused this to happen. I blessed him, and added a curse — he will be a poet. Ah, how I love thee, Henryk!

VOICE FROM ABOVE THE CEILING
Forgive them, Father, for they know not what they do.

WIFE
That one suffers a strange dementia, no?

HUSBAND
The strangest.

WIFE
He knows not what he speaks, but I shall proclaim to thee what would hap, should God go insane. *Takes him by the hand.* All of the worlds hurtle downward — then zoom upward again — each man, each worm cries out "I am that I am" — and at each moment they perish one by one — comets and suns sputter to black. Christ will not save us now — He hath taken his cross in hand and flung it into the

abyss. Dost hear how that gibbet — the hope of millions — smashes against stars, breaks, splits apart, flies into pieces, ever lower and lower — a thick simoom gathering from its particles? The Most Holy Mother of God alone still prays and the stars of her crown have not yet abandoned her. But she too will go the way of the entire universe.

HUSBAND
Maria — surely you'd like to see your son?

WIFE
I have pinned wings upon his back and sent him amongst the worlds, so that he should imbibe of all that is beautiful and horrible and sublime. He will return one day and bring you joy! Ah!

HUSBAND
What's wrong?

WIFE
Someone has hung a lantern in my head — it swings — intolerably!

HUSBAND
Maria, my darling, be well! As you once were!

WIFE
Poets aren't long lived.

HUSBAND
Help! Help!

Enter Doctor's wife, with women.

DOCTOR'S WIFE
Pills! Powders! No, nothing thick, only liquid medicines. Małgorzata — run to the medicine cabinet! This is all your fault, sir! My husband will flay me!

WIFE
Farewell, Henryk!

DOCTOR'S WIFE
It's… the Count himself!

HUSBAND
Maria! Maria!

He takes her into his arms.

WIFE
I'm all right… I'm all right… I'm dying at your side… *Her head droops.*

DOCTOR'S WIFE
Look how red she is! The blood has rushed to her head.

HUSBAND
But this will pass, right? She'll be all right now!

Enter Doctor — he goes over to the couch.

DOCTOR
It has already passed. She's dead.

PART II

You mixture of mud and fire.

—Goethe

Why, O child, are you not skipping rope, playing with soldiers, squashing flies? collecting butterflies? rolling on the lawn? stealing candies? bathing your grammar with tears from A to Z? King of flies and moths, friend of Punchinello, little demon — why are you so like the angels? What do they mean, those blue eyes of yours, sunken, though alive, full of memories, though but a few springs have tousled your hair? Why do you lean your brow upon your little white fists and — it seems — dream, and, just like a flower encumbered with dew, your forehead is encumbered with thought?

*

And when you blush, you flame like a hundred-petalled rose, and, unwinding your curls, you reach into the heavens with your sight... Tell me: what do you hear? What do you see? With whom are you speaking? — For then your brow is furrowed with wrinkles, like little threads unravelling from an invisible spool. In your eyes a spark burns which no one understands... Your nurse weeps and calls out to you, thinking that you hear her not; your friends and family call to you and think that you recognise them not... Only your father falls silent and looks about moodily, while a tear wells in his eye and falls — somewhere.

*

A physician takes your pulse, counts the heartbeats and says "It's his nerves." Your godfather brings you cakes, pats your back and prophesies, "You'll be a proper citizen of a great nation." Then a professor rubs your scalp and says, "Here's a head for physics!" A beggar to whom you gave a penny says "I see a lovely missus for 'ee an' a crown in 'eaven, lad." A soldier, skipping stiffly to attention, smiles, "Your orders, Colonel!" A gypsy gazes long at your left palm, then at your right palm — and can read nothing there whatsoever. Moaning, she goes off, declining to take your coin. The mesmerist puffs into your eyes, dances with his fingers — and curses — for he himself was becoming entranced! The priest who prepares you for confession — kneels before you as if before a holy image. Then comes the painter. And when you got upset and stamped your feet — he painted you a devil, and placed you in his Day of Judgement amongst the outcast spirits.

*

Meanwhile you grow in stature and beauty — not with that childhood freshness of milk and berries — but with the beauty of wild, incomprehensible thought, which lights upon you, perhaps from another world. For although your eyes often seem to be fading; although your cheeks darken, and your chest is sunken, everyone, whosoever lays eyes upon you, stops a moment and cries out, "What a lovely child!" If a flower, withering, possessed a soul of fire and heavenly inspiration, and on each petal, bending towards the earth, was burdened with angelic thoughts instead of drops of dew, that flower would be your image, O child of mine. Thus perhaps were the flowers before Adam's fall.

Cemetery — Husband and Orcio before a mausoleum with Gothic pillars and turrets.

HUSBAND
Take off your hat and pray for Mother's soul.

ORCIO
Hail Maiden Mary, full of grace, Queen of the heavens, Lady of all which blossoms on the earth, in meadows and streams…

HUSBAND
Why are you changing the words? Pray for your mother as you were taught! Pray for your mother who, ten years ago, died at this very hour.

ORCIO
Hail Mary, full of grace, the Lord is with thee. Blessed art thou amongst the angels, and each of them in passing plucks a rainbow from his wings and casts it at thy feet. And thou dost tread upon them as if walking upon the waves of the sea…

HUSBAND
Orcio!

ORCIO
But the words come of themselves, writhing, and they hurt my head so, Daddy, that I have to let them out!

HUSBAND
Get up then. A prayer like that won't reach the ears of God. You don't remember your mother. How could you love her?

ORCIO
I see her lots of times.

HUSBAND
Where, darling?

ORCIO
In my dreams. I mean, not when I'm really dreaming, but when I'm just falling asleep. Like the day before yesterday.

HUSBAND
My child! What are you saying?

ORCIO
She was very white, and skinny.

HUSBAND
Did she say anything to you?

ORCIO
It was like she was walking in a place where everything was pitch black — I couldn't see anything but her, 'cos she was all white. She said:

> I wander every place
> And creep into every space
> There, where the worlds' last orbit lies
> And where the angels' singing fills the skies
> And for thee I gather
> Shapes and matter
> Of thoughts and inspirations wild —
> For thee, my darling child!
>
> And from the higher forms of life
> And from the lower sprites of strife
> Colours and shades,
> Sounds and rays,
> For thee I scrape a trove,
> For thee, my dearest kin
> For then indeed thoul't win
>   Thy father's love.

See Daddy? I remember it — word for word — Please, Daddy, I'm not lying!

HUSBAND
Steadies himself against a pillar of the mausoleum
Maria! Do you want to destroy your own child so that I should have two souls on my conscience? … What am I saying? She's in Heaven somewhere… quiet and peaceful… just like before… The poor boy's only imagining things.

ORCIO
I hear her voice even now — but I don't see her.

HUSBAND
Where? — From what direction?

ORCIO
As if she were by those two trees — where the light of the sunset falls.

> Upon thy lips I'll shower
> Colour, sound, and power.
> Thy temples bind bright
> With a ribbon of light
> So that, with a mother's love I might
> Awaken in thee
> All the beauty
> Of the earth and realms above,
> In thee, my dearest kin,
> So that thou might then win
> Thy father's love.

HUSBAND
Do the soul's last thoughts accompany her as she leaves the body, to remain with her even after she arrives in Heaven? Can a soul be happy, holy, and demented all at once?

ORCIO
Mama's voice is getting softer — it fades over there past the wall of the mausoleum now… There — there — she's still repeating:

O thou, my dearest son,
For thus thou shalt have won
Thy father's love.

HUSBAND
God! Have mercy on our child! Although it seems as if in your anger you've destined him for insanity and an early grave! Lord, do not rip reason out from your own creatures! Do not abandon the temple, which you have built for yourself! Look upon my anguish and don't give this angel over to Hell. You gave me the strength to suffer the flood of thought, passions and feelings, but him — you've given him a mind like a spider's web, which the least thought shreds! O God, O Lord God!

I haven't had one day of peace for the last ten years. You've sent hundreds of people to me, who've congratulated me for my happiness, wished me more, and were jealous of me. You've showered upon me a hail of pain and phantasmal images, and foresight and dreams... Your mercy fell not upon my heart, but on my head. Allow me to love this child in peace, and let there be peace between the Creator and His creation. Darling, bless yourself and come with me. Eternal rest, O Lord...
They exit.

*

A walk — ladies and cavaliers — the philosopher — the husband.

PHILOSOPHER
I repeat — I am absolutely, positively convinced that the time is coming for the emancipation of women and Negroes.

HUSBAND
I believe you're right.

PHILOSOPHER
A great transformation in human society — both in particular and in general — from which I deduce the renaissance of the human race through blood, and the destruction of old forms.

HUSBAND
You really think so?

PHILOSOPHER
Just as our globe straightens itself or leans on its axis as a result of a sudden revolution.

HUSBAND
See that rotten tree?

PHILOSOPHER
The one with the young leaves on its bottom branches?

HUSBAND
Right. What do you think — will it stand for many more years?

PHILOSOPHER
Do I know? A year, maybe two.

HUSBAND
And yet today it pushed out a few fresh leaves, even though its roots rot away more and more.

PHILOSOPHER
And — ?

HUSBAND
Nothing. Only — it'll soon tumble down, and be given over to flames and ashes, for even the carpenter won't have a use for it.

PHILOSOPHER
What are you talking about?

HUSBAND
This is your own image, that tree; your image, an image of your people, your age, your theories.

They walk across.

*

A mountain chasm.

HUSBAND
I toiled many years to arrive the very end of all knowledge, delight and thought, and discovered nothing but the charnel vacuum of my heart. I know all feelings by name, but there is no desire, no faith, no love in me at all. Only a few forebodings circle in this desert, concerning my son: that he will go blind; concerning the society in which I was raised: that it will fall apart… and I suffer just as God rejoices: alone, in myself, for myself.

VOICE OF GUARDIAN ANGEL
The sick, the hungry, the despairing… Love your brothers, your poor brothers, and you will be saved.

HUSBAND
Who speaks?

MEFISTO
Passing by
At your service. I often like to entertain travellers with the gift that Nature's bestowed upon me — I'm a ventriloquist.

HUSBAND
Lifting hand to hat
I saw a face like yours once on an engraving somewhere…

MEFISTO
Aside
The Count has a good memory. *Aloud:* Praise be…

HUSBAND
For ever and ever, Amen…

MEFISTO
Disappearing between the cliffs

... to you and your inanity.

HUSBAND
Poor child! For his father's sins, because of his mother's insanity, he is predestined to eternal blindness. Unfinished, without passion, living but a dream, the shadow of an angel flying by, cast on the earth and erring in his evanescence. What a great eagle has arisen over the very spot where that man disappeared!

EAGLE
Greetings — greetings!

HUSBAND
He flies toward me — all black — and the swish of his wings is like the rush of a thousand bullets in war.

EAGLE
With the sabre of thy fathers, fight for their glory and sway!

HUSBAND
He spreads himself above me... With the gaze of a rattlesnake he sucks at my pupils... Ha! I understand thee!

EAGLE
Never give way! Never give way! And thy enemies — thy base enemies — shall be ground into the dust!

HUSBAND
I bid thee farewell among the cliffs where thou vanishest! Come what may, be thou a lie or the truth, victory or my undoing, I shall believe in thee, harbinger of glory! O ages past, be my support! And if your spirit hath returned to the bosom of God, let it tear away from thence, and enter into my body, that it should become my thought, my strength, my deed.
He spurns a snake.
  Away, base reptile! As I have cast thee down, as there is no pity for thee in all of nature, so will they tumble down before me, and no one will mourn their loss! No fame shall be theirs; no cloud will pause in its sailing to cast a glance upon so many sons of this earth, perishing together!

They first — then I shall follow.

O immeasurable azure, thou who envelopest the earth! The earth is an infant, grinding his teeth and weeping; but thou tremblest not, hearest her not… Thou sailest on into thine infinity.

Mother nature, be my health! I go to transform myself into a man; I go to struggle with my brothers.

*

A room — husband — physician — Orcio

HUSBAND
Nothing's helped him. You're his last hope.

PHYSICIAN
The Count does me a great honour …

HUSBAND
Tell the doctor how you feel.

ORCIO
I can't tell you apart from the doctor anymore, Daddy. Sparks and black threads fly around in front of my eyes… sometimes I can make out a small snake… then a yellow cloud… It flies up, falls down, and a rainbow spurts out of it… It doesn't hurt at all.

PHYSICIAN
Stand in the shadow, Jerzy. How old are you?

HUSBAND
He's just turned fourteen.

PHYSICIAN
Now, turn to the window.

HUSBAND
Well?

PHYSICIAN
Beautiful eyelids, clear white eyes… The veins all in order, the muscles strong. *To Orcio.* Laugh at this, Jerzy. You'll soon be as healthy as I am. *To husband.* There's no hope at all. Take a look at his pupils for yourself. They don't react to light at all. Complete attenuation of the optic nerve.

ORCIO
It's like fog covering everything — everything.

HUSBAND
You're right. It's open — grey — lifeless.

ORCIO
I see more with my eyes closed than I do with them open.

PHYSICIAN
His thought's poisoned his body. We have to watch out for catalepsy.

HUSBAND
Takes the physician aside
Anything you want — half my fortune!

PHYSICIAN
Disorganisation can't reorganise itself. *Takes his hat and cane.* I have to go now and remove a cataract. Your humble servant…

HUSBAND
Please — don't leave us yet.

PHYSICIAN
Perhaps you'd like to know the name of the illness?

HUSBAND
There's no hope? No hope whatever?

PHYSICIAN
In Greek it's called "amaurosis."
Exit.

HUSBAND
Embraces his son
Do you see anything at all?

ORCIO
I hear your voice, father.

HUSBAND
Look through the window… Look at the sun, the fields…

ORCIO
I see a whole troop of figures between my pupil and my eyelid… faces I've seen, familiar places — the pages of books I've read.

HUSBAND
Then you do see?

ORCIO
Yes — with the eyes of the soul. The others are dead.

HUSBAND
Falls to his knees. Pause
To whom do I kneel? Whom shall I blame for the wrong done to my son? *Stands*. Let us stand, rather. God laughs at our prayers, and Satan at our curses.

VOICE FROM SOMEWHERE
Your son's a poet. What else do you want?

*

Physician — godfather

GODFATHER
What a great misfortune, to be blind.

PHYSICIAN
It's so unusual at so young an age.

GODFATHER
He always had a pale complexion. And his mother died so ... well ...

PHYSICIAN
How?

GODFATHER
So... you understand... without a full deck.

Husband enters.

HUSBAND
Please forgive me for summoning you at such a late hour, but for several days now, my poor son has been waking up around midnight, walking, and talking in his sleep. Please, come with me.

PHYSICIAN
Yes. I'm very interested in such phenomena.

*

Bedroom. Maid — relatives — godfather — physician — husband.

RELATIVE
Shh!

SECOND RELATIVE
He's up, but he doesn't hear us.

PHYSICIAN
Please, don't speak.

GODFATHER
Such a strange thing!

ORCIO
Rising
O God — God!

RELATIVE
How slowly he walks.

SECOND RELATIVE
With his hands crossed on his breast.

THIRD RELATIVE
He doesn't even bat an eye… He hardly opens his mouth, yet his voice is sharp… drawn out.

MAID
Jesus of Nazareth!

ORCIO
Away from me, darkness! I was born a son of light and song — what do you want of me? What do you demand of me?
    I shall not give in to you, even though my sight has flown away with the winds and chases on somewhere in space! It will return someday, enriched with the rays of stars, to rekindle my eyes with its flame.

GODFATHER
Just like his mother! Mumbling on about God knows what — this sight speaks volumes…

PHYSICIAN
I concur.

NURSE
Blessed Mother of Częstochowa, take these eyes of mine and give them to him!

ORCIO
Mother mine, I beg thee… mother mine, send unto me images and thoughts, that I might live inside myself — that I might create a second world within me equal to that which I have lost.

RELATIVE
What do you say, brother? This calls for a family council!

SECOND RELATIVE
Wait… Be quiet…

ORCIO
Thou dost not answer me — O mother! Do not abandon me!

PHYSICIAN
To husband
I am obliged to speak the truth.

GODFATHER
Yes — an obligation, and a virtue in a physician, counsellor.

PHYSICIAN
Your son's senses are in a tumult. This, coupled with an extraordinary nervous sensibility, often gives rise to a state of — so to say — sleeping and wakefulness together — such as we see before us now.

HUSBAND
Aside
Dear God, behold! He thinks to translate me Thy verdicts!

PHYSICIAN
A pen and some ink, please. Two grammes of cerasis laurei, etc. etc.

HUSBAND
You'll find them in the other room, Doctor. I would ask all of you to retire, now.

MIXED VOICES
Goodnight — Goodnight — 'Til tomorrow…

They exit.

ORCIO
Waking
They wish me goodnight. Speak of a long night rather, an eternal night, perhaps, but not of a good night, not of a happy one.

HUSBAND
Lean on me. I'll help you back into bed.

ORCIO
Father, what does all this mean?

HUSBAND
Cover up and sleep well. The doctor says you'll get your sight back.

ORCIO
I feel so bad… Some voices disturbed my sleep.
He sleeps.

HUSBAND
May my blessing rest upon you. I can't give you anything else: neither happiness nor light nor fame, and the hour will come when I shall have to fight, to act, along with the few against the many… Where then will you find yourself? Alone and among one hundred chasms, blind, weak…a child and yet a poet… a poor singer with no one to listen to you… Beyond the edge of the world, with your body still bound to the earth. O unfortunate! Most unfortunate of the angels, my son!

NURSE
At the door
The doctor asks to see my lord the Count.

HUSBAND
My good Katarzyna, stay with the little one.

He exits.

PART III

He was administered to, because the simple minded fool requested a priest, after which he was hanged, to the general satisfaction of all.

—Report of Citizen Caillot,
Commissioner of the Sixth Chamber,
Dated 5 Prairial, Year III.

To song — to song!

Who will begin it, and who will sing it to the end? Give me the past, clad in steel, flowing with a hussar's plumes! I call Gothic bastions forth before your eyes; I cast the shades of holy cathedrals above your heads. But that's not it. They will never be again.

*

Whoever you are, tell me: what do you believe in? It's easier to cast away one's life than to find a faith, to awaken a faith, in oneself. Shame on you, both small and great, shame! And yet despite yourselves, despite your pettiness and squalor, your heartlessness and brainlessness, the world spins on toward its goals, pulling you along, hustling you before itself, toying with you, tossing you around, tossing you away… The world waltzes on, couples disappearing and appearing, falling away because it's slippery — because there's a lot of blood spilled about — blood everywhere — lots of blood, I tell you.

*

Can you see those crowds milling about the gates of that city among hillocks and nurtured poplars — the pitched tents — the boards set up here and there, long ones, covered with meat and drink, resting on stumps and poles? The cup flies from hand to hand, and where the lips touch it, there a voice is pulled forth in threat, oath or imprecation. On it flies, stumbling, circling, dancing, yet always full, loud, shining... amongst thousands. Long live the cup of drunkenness and comfort!

*

Can you see how they wait impatiently, muttering amongst themselves, readying themselves for uproar — all of them squalid, with the sweat of toil on their brow; with unkempt hair, in rags, with sunburnt faces, with hands creased from labour? These hold scythes, those shake hammers and rasps... Look! That tall one is resting his weight on a great axe... and that one twirls an iron ramrod above his head; further on beneath a willow a little boy's cramming cherries into his mouth, gripping hard in his right hand a long awl. Women have come along as well: mothers and wives, hungry and poor as their men, withered before their time, without the slightest shade of beauty remaining them... their hair caked with the dust of the well-tramped road... the frocks on their bosoms ripped and torn... In their eyes something is fading, something gloomy, like the mockery of sight... But then they come alive: the cup flies from hand to hand, everywhere. Long live the cup of drunkenness and comfort!

*

Now a great murmur has arisen among the masses. Is it joy, or despair? Who can distinguish a single emotion in the voices of thousands? The one who has just arrived has climbed up on a table, jumped up on a chair and now he quiets them, addresses them. His voice is drawn out, sharp, and clear — you can make out each word, you understand them all... His gestures, slow and easy, accompany his words like the music of a song. His brow is high and expansive, without a single hair on his skull — all have fallen out, knocked out by thought... the skin has dried to his skull, his cheeks, yellowishly squeezing in between bone and muscle, and from his temples downward a black beard rings his face like a wreath. There is never any rush of blood, never any change of colour in those cheeks of his. His motionless eyes are fixed upon his auditors... Not a moment of doubt or confusion is to be seen. And when he lifts high an arm, stretching it out, straining it intensely above them, they bow their heads. They look about to fall to their knees before this benediction of triumphant reason — not love… Away with the heart, away with superstition; long live the word of comfort and slaughter! —

*

He is the incarnation of their fury, their passion, this ruler of their souls and enthusiasm; he promises them bread and money; their cheers grow, expand, burst out on all sides: "Long live Pankracy! — bread for us, bread, bread!" And at the feet of the speaker, leaning on the table, stands his friend, or comrade, or servant.

*

His eye has an eastern look to it; it is black, with long, shadowy lashes. Loosely hang his arms; his legs sag, his body weakly slopes to one side… On his mouth, the grin is somewhat lewd, somewhat malevolent; on his fingers there are gold rings. He too cries out in a raspy voice — "Long live Pankracy!" The speaker turns his glance toward him momentarily. "Citizen Convert, a handkerchief, please."

*

Meanwhile the applause and outcry continue. "Bread for us, bread, bread! — Death to the lords, death to the merchants — bread, bread!"

Rustic shed — several lamps — an open book on the table — converts.

CONVERT
My villainous brothers, my vengeful brothers, my dear brothers, let us suck at the pages of the Talmud as at a milky breast, a life-giving breast flowing with strength and honey for us, and for them — bitterness and poison!

CHORUS OF CONVERTS
Jehovah is our Lord, and no one else! He has scattered us everywhere, winding us around the world of the venerators of the Cross, our masters proud, stupid, illiterate, like the folds of an immense reptile. Let us spit thrice to seal their doom — thricely may they be accurst!

CONVERT
Let us rejoice, my brethren. That Cross, our enemy, undermined, rotten, now teeters over a puddle of blood, and once it falls, it will never rise again. Now only the bluebloods defend it.

CHORUS
The labour of ages is consummated, our labour sad, painful, dogged. Death to the bluebloods! Let us spit thrice to seal their doom — thricely may they be accursed!

CONVERT
On freedom without order, on slaughter without end, on conflict and malevolence, on their stupidity and pride we shall establish the power of Israel. We've only this handful to deal with — only this handful of bluebloods to topple into the abyss; then we shall sprinkle over their corpses the dusty ruins of the Cross.

CHORUS
The Cross, our holy sign; the water of baptism has joined us to the nations; those who held us despised ones in contempt, the despised, have been duped into believing in our love!

The freedom of the people is our law — The good of the people our goal — The sons of Christians have believed the ruse of the sons of Caiaphas!

Centuries ago our fathers put our enemy to torture — We shall torture Him again today and He will rise no more from the dead!

CONVERT
A few moments more, a few more drops of viper's venom, and the world is ours, ours, O my brethren!

CHORUS
Jehovah is our Lord, and no one else. Let us spit thrice to seal their doom — thricely may they be accurst!

A knocking.

CONVERT
To your labours, all! And thou, holy book, away, so that the glance of the accurst should not defile thy pages. *He puts the Talmud away.* Who is it?

VOICE FROM BEHIND THE DOOR
A friend. Open the door, in the name of Freedom.

CONVERT
Brothers — to your hammers and ropes.
Convert opens the door.

LEONARD
Enters
Excellent, Citizens, to see you all at the ready, sharpening your daggers for the morrow! *He moves closer to one of them.* And you — what are you doing there in the corner?

ONE OF THE CONVERTS
Plaiting nooses, Citizen.

LEONARD
You're thinking, brother! He who doesn't fall in the battle from steel will end his life dangling from a limb.

CONVERT
Good Citizen Leonard, is everything made certain for tomorrow?

LEONARD
He who thinks and feels most powerfully among us calls you to a meeting. He will answer your question himself.

CONVERT
I'm on my way — and you, don't leave off from your tasks. Yankiel, you're in charge of them.

Exits with Leonard.

CHORUS
Ropes and stilettos, clubs and sabres, work of our hands, arise to their destruction! These shall kill the bluebloods on the field of battle, hang them up over gardens and copses… And later on, we'll kill and hang their killers! Those held in contempt will rise in their ire, clothing themselves in the glory of Jehovah; His word our salvation, His love, destruction for all. Let us spit thrice to seal their doom — thricely may they be accurst!

*

A tent — bottles and wineglasses strewn about.

PANKRACY
Fifty people were going wild here just a few moments ago, exclaiming "Vivat" at each word that tumbled from my lips. Did even one of them understand my thoughts? Or comprehend the goal at the end of the journey, those who raise such a bluster at the start? Ah! servile imitatorum pecus!

Enter Leonard and convert.

PANKRACY
Are you acquainted with Count Henryk?

CONVERT
O great Citizen — I know him to see him, rather than to speak to him… Once only, I recall, during the Corpus Christi procession, he yelled at me, "Out of the way!" and shot at me the haughty sneer of a lord… for which I vowed to him, from the depths of my soul, a noose.

PANKRACY
First thing tomorrow morning you will go to him and tell him that I desire a personal interview. A secret one — day after tomorrow, in the evening.

CONVERT
Will you give me some people? A good handful? Because it wouldn't be prudent to go alone.

PANKRACY
You'll go alone, with my name for a bodyguard; the gallows, upon which you hanged the baron the day before yesterday, at your back.

CONVERT
Oy vey!

PANKRACY
You are to tell him that I will come to him the day after tomorrow, at midnight.

CONVERT
And if they lock me up, or beat me?

PANKRACY
In that case, you'll be a martyr in the people's cause.

CONVERT
Everything, everything for the freedom of the people! *Aside.* Oy, vey!

PANKRACY
Good night, Citizen.

Exit convert.

LEONARD
What's with all this tarrying, these half measures, these deals and midnight talks? When I swore to obey you, and adore you, I took you for a hero of drastic necessity — an eagle flying straight to its goal, a man who lay his own fate, and that of all his people, on one card.

PANKRACY
Quiet, child.

LEONARD
But everyone's ready — the converts have forged weapons and looped nooses; the crowds are roaring, begging for your command. Give the command; send forth the spark that looses the lightning, the flame that swells the thunderbolt!

PANKRACY
The blood's rushed to your head. Quite natural, considering your age. And since you don't know how to control it, you call your impudence enthusiasm.

LEONARD
Think of what you're doing. In their helplessness, the aristocrats have locked themselves up in Holy Trinity and await our approach like the blade of the guillotine. Forward, master! Forward without hesitation, and it's all over for them.

PANKRACY
It's all one. They've lost their strength of body in delight, and their strength of mind in idleness. Tomorrow, or the day after, will see them toppled.

LEONARD
Who is it that you fear? What holds you back?

PANKRACY
No one. Nothing but my own will.

LEONARD
And I'm supposed to trust it, blindly?

PANKRACY
Verily I say unto thee — blindly.

LEONARD
You are betraying us!

PANKRACY
As every song has its refrain, there's treason at the end of every word you say. Keep your voice down, 'cos if someone were to overhear us…

LEONARD
There are no spies here, and anyway, so what?

PANKRACY
So nothing, save for five bullets in your breast for daring to raise your voice in my presence *Moves closer*. Believe me — do yourself a favour.

LEONARD
All right — I admit it — I got carried away. But I'm not afraid. If my death would serve as an example, if it would add some courage and strength to our cause, just give the command.

PANKRACY
You're alive, full of hope and deep belief — the happiest of people. I don't want you dead.

LEONARD
So what are you saying?

PANKRACY
Think more, babble less, and someday you'll understand me. Have you sent to the magazine for those two thousand rounds?

LEONARD
I sent Dejec with his division.

PANKRACY
And have you put the shoemakers' subscription into our strongbox?

LEONARD
With unfeigned enthusiasm they contributed — every one of them — they collected one hundred thousand.

PANKRACY
I'll invite them to supper tomorrow. — Have you heard anything new about Count Henryk?

LEONARD
Such is my contempt for the bluebloods, that I don't trust anything I hear about them. Races in their decline have no energy — shouldn't have — couldn't have…

PANKRACY
And yet he's gathered his peasants and, assured of their devotion, is preparing to lift the siege of Holy Trinity Castle.

LEONARD
Who is able to defy us? After all, in us the Idea of our Age is incarnate.

PANKRACY
I want to see him. To look him in the eye, penetrate the depths of his heart… to draw him to our side.

LEONARD
A dyed in the wool aristocrat! On the lip of the grave…

PANKRACY
But a poet, too. Now, leave me alone.

LEONARD
Do… I have your forgiveness, Citizen?

PANKRACY
Sleep in peace. Had I not already forgiven you, you'd have been sleeping in your grave.

LEONARD
So there will be nothing doing tomorrow?

PANKRACY
Good night, and sweet dreams.

Exit Leonard

PANKRACY
Hey, Leonard!

LEONARD
Returning
Citizen Leader?

PANKRACY
Tomorrow night you'll accompany me to Count Henryk's.

LEONARD
Sir.
Exit.

PANKRACY
How can it be that this one man stands in my way — me, the leader of thousands? His forces are weak in comparison with mine: a few hundred peasants who trust blindly in his word, attached to him with the love of tamed beasts… Miserable. A miserable nothing! Why is it I so desire to see him, to beguile him? Can it be that my spirit has come across its equal that it thus pauses a moment in its progress? This is the last obstacle before me on these plains. We must burst through it, and then… O thought of mine, art thou not able to deceive thyself, as thou deceivest others? Shame on thee! After all, thou knowest thy goal: thou art the thought, the mistress of the people! In thee the will and power of the masses have come together, and that which is crime for others

is thy glory! Thou hast given a name to a people base, unknown, and faith to a people without feeling. Thou hast created a world in thine imagined likeness, a new world, and yet thou wanderest alone, and knowest not who thou art… No, no, no — thou art great!
Falls into a chair, deep in thought.

*

A grove of trees — canvas hung from the branches — in the centre, a meadow upon which a gallows stands — little huts — tents — campfires — barrels — crowds of people.

HUSBAND
Disguised in a dark cape, with a red cap of freedom on his head, enters, gripping the convert by the arm.
Remember!

CONVERT
Whispers
My good lord, I'll take you round — I won't betray you, on my honour.

HUSBAND
If you so much as wink or wiggle a finger I'll blow off your head. I'm sure you can understand that I don't give a damn about your life… since I'm risking my own.

CONVERT
Oy vey! You're gripping me with talons of iron! What am I supposed to do?

HUSBAND
Talk with me as if you knew me — as if I were an old friend who just joined up. What sort of dance is that?

CONVERT
The dance of free people.

Men and women dance about the gallows, singing.

CHORUS
Bread, money, wood for winter hearths, rest on summer afternoons! — Hurrah! — Hurrah!
> God had no mercy on us — Hurrah — Hurrah!
> The kings had no mercy on us — Hurrah — Hurrah!
> The lords had no mercy on us — Hurrah — Hurrah!
> Today we give our thanks to God,
> Our thanks to kings and bluebloods too,
> For all the dung they've made us chew
> > Hurrah — hurrah!

HUSBAND
To girl
How happy you are! How becoming is the blush on your cheek.

GIRL
Yeah — we've waited long for this day to dawn! Afore, it was hands red with the washin' of plates an' the polishin' a' forks — an' never a good word did I hear, for all the scrubbin' I did. Now it's my turn to dance, my turn to eat — Hurrah!

HUSBAND
Dance, citizen! Dance!

CONVERT
Whispers
Good my lord, have mercy on me! Somebody might recognise you. Let's get out of here!

HUSBAND
If somebody does recognise me, you're a dead man. Onward.

CONVERT
Under this oak tree, that's the Lackey's Club.

HUSBAND
Let's move closer.

FIRST LACKEY
I did in my old master a'ready.

SECOND LACKEY
I'm still lookin' for my sweet baron. To your health!

VALET
Citizens, hunched over shoetree in sweat and misery, polishin' boots, clippin' hair — we've come to recognise our rights all the same. Health to the entire club!

CHORUS OF LACKEYS
To the health of our president, who leads us on the path of honour!

VALET
Thank you, citizens.

CHORUS OF LACKEYS
From the foyers, from our prisons, all together, with one strong push, we've broken free. Vivat! Don't we know the idiocy and whoring that goes on in the bluebloods' salons? Vivat! Vivat!

HUSBAND
Whose voices are they — harsher and wilder, crying out by that clump of trees on the left?

CONVERT
That's the chorus of butchers, my lord.

CHORUS OF BUTCHERS
Poll-hammer, cleaver — them's our weapons, the shambles is our life! It's all the same, capon or count, swine or seigneur, we put to the knife.

 Children of strong-arm, children of blood, we look with impassive eye on weaker, on whiter. Well and good, whoever hires us: be it the bluebloods to slaughter their cattle, be it the people to slaughter their lords.

 Poll-hammer, cleaver — them's our weapons, the shambles is our life. O, the shambles, the shambles, the shambles!

HUSBAND
These I like — at least they make no pretensions to honour or philosophy. Good evening, madame.

CONVERT
Good my lord — say "citizen" or "freed woman!"

WOMAN
What's 'at supposed ta mean, "madame?" Tfu, tfu — you stink of stale clothes.

HUSBAND
Pardon me. Slip of the tongue.

WOMAN
I'm just as free as you are — a free woman. An' because it's the people what freed me, in return I give my love to all…

HUSBAND
And it's the people what've given you that ring and that amethyst necklace…? Ah! doubly benevolent people!

WOMAN
Nah — I nicked these gewgaws afore my lib'ration, from me husband, me enemy — enemy of freedom, 'e was, who kept me on a leash.

HUSBAND
I wish you a pleasant stroll, Citizen. *Moves on.* Who is that strange soldier, resting his weight on that double-edged sabre, with a death's head on his cap, another on his chain, and a third on his breast? Is that not the famous Bianchetti, the condottiere of the people after the fashion of those old condottieri of the lords and their governments?

CONVERT
The very same, my lord. He and his joined up with us just a few weeks ago.

HUSBAND
And what is the general musing on, may one inquire?

BIANCHETTI
See that space between the sycamores, Citizens? Take a good look. Up through there you can see the castle. With my glass I can even make out the walls, fosses and the four bastions.

HUSBAND
Difficult to take.

BIANCHETTI
Thousands and thousands of kings! One might steal along the ravine, undermine a bit and…

CONVERT
Winking
Citizen general…

HUSBAND
Whispers
The firearm beneath my cape's been cocked…

CONVERT
Aside
Oy, vey! *Aloud.* So, what've you thought up, Citizen General?

BIANCHETTI
In thought
You may be my brothers in freedom, but not in genius. Everyone will learn of my plans… after my victory.
Moves off.

HUSBAND
To convert
Kill him. That's my advice. Because that's the way all aristocracy gets its start.

CRAFTSMAN
Curses... Curses!

HUSBAND
What are you doing there under the tree, poor fellow? Why do you cast your eyes about so wildly, so moodily?

CRAFTSMAN
Curses to the merchants and factory directors! I wasted the best years of my life — When other fellows were out chasing girls, winning fame on the battlefield or sailing the open seas, I was slaving away in a cramped little space in a silk manufactory.

HUSBAND
Down the cup that you hold in your hand!

CRAFTSMAN
I haven't got the strength... can't even raise it to my mouth. I was hardly able to crawl here on hands and knees, and now I won't see any dawn of freedom rising for me... Curses to the merchants who sell silk, and to the bluebloods who wear it. Curses — Curses!
He dies.

CONVERT
What a repulsive corpse...

HUSBAND
You coward of liberty! Citizen Convert, look well upon that lifeless head awash in the bloody rays of the setting sun! Where are your fine words now, your promises: equality, perfection and happiness for humanity?

CONVERT
Aside
May you croak just as quickly as he, and may your own dogs tear you into pieces! *Aloud.* Let me go now. I must give an account of my mission to you.

HUSBAND
Tell them I took you for a spy and that's why you were detained. *Looks around.* The echoes of the feast are dying away. Before us now are only pines and spruces, bathed in the sunset. —

CONVERT
Clouds are gathering above the trees. You'd better return to your people. At any rate, they've been waiting for you a long time at St Ignatius Ravine.

HUSBAND
Thank you for your tender concern, your Converted Grace! We go back! I want to have another look at the citizens in the dusk.

VOICE FROM AMONG THE TREES
A son of churls wishes the sun a good night.

VOICE FROM THE RIGHT
To your health, old enemy, who chased us off to toil and pain! When you rise tomorrow, you'll find your slaves at meat and goblets. And now, wineglass, go to hell!

CONVERT
A group of peasants are on their way here.

HUSBAND
But you're not going anywhere. Stand behind that dead tree and keep your mouth shut.

CHORUS OF PEASANTS
Forward, forward, to the tents, to our brothers! Forward, forward, beneath the shadow of the sycamores, for a nice night's sleep, a nice evening's chat… There's girls there, and slaughtered oxen, that once pulled ploughs, waiting there for us.

FIRST VOICE
Gotta pull'm, gotta drag'm — an' he just snorts an' digs in 'is 'eels… Fall in step, you — now!

VOICE OF LANDOWNER
Children, my children — Mercy, mercy!

SECOND VOICE
Gimme back all the days I slaved for you for nothin'!

THIRD VOICE
Gimme back my son, what your Cossacks beat to death!

FOURTH VOICE
Your peasants drink your health, my lord. Beg your pardon, my lord.

CHORUS OF PEASANTS
This vampire sucked our blood and sweat — but we've got'm now! — an' we won't let him go. By the devil, by the very devil I swear, you'll die up on high, up on high as befits a lord, elevated above the common rabble. Death to the bluebloods, death to the tyrants! An' for us, the poor, the hungry, the worked to death: food, and drink, and sleep. Their corpses will be like the sheaves on the harvested field; like the chaff in the thresher, thus the embers of their castles! Forward! By our scythes, axes and flails, brothers, forward!

HUSBAND
I couldn't make out his face.

CONVERT
Maybe it's one of my lord's friends, or relatives.

HUSBAND
I've got nothing but contempt for him, and hatred for you all. Someday, poetry will gild all of this. Onward, Jew, onward!
They plunge into the bushes.

*

Another part of the grove — campfires about on the hillocks — groups of people with torches.

HUSBAND
Below, stepping out from behind a tree with the Convert
The branches here tear my cap of Liberty to shreds. Now, what sort of hell is this, with ruddy flames, rising amidst these two walls of forest, these two crowds of darkness?

CONVERT
We've lost our path searching for St Ignatius Ravine… Back into the bushes, 'cos here Leonard's celebrating the services of the new faith.

HUSBAND
Coming forward
By God, closer! This is what I've most wanted to see! Don't be afraid — no one will recognise us.

CONVERT
Easy — be careful!

HUSBAND
Everywhere ruins are strewn about, ruins of a colossus, which stood for ages before it fell — pillars, bases, capitals, quartered statues, decorative flourishes… which once wound about ancient vaults, now tossed about on the ground — Here a shard of coloured glass from a smashed window sparkles weakly at my feet — the face of the Mother of God, was it? — It flashed at me out of the darkness and again receded into the shadows: Look — here's an entire arcade, an iron gate covered in rubble… The gleam of a torch blazed forth up there — I see half a knight asleep on half a tomb… Where am I, guide?

CONVERT
Our men had a bloody job of it for forty days and nights in pulling down this church — the last one on these plains. We're just now passing through the churchyard.

HUSBAND
Your songs, new people, sound bitter to my ears! Black figures behind, before, along both sides, push forward and both melt and shimmer, hastened by the wind, fluttering about like living spirits.

PASSER-BY
I greet you both in the name of freedom.

ANOTHER
I greet you both, by the death of the lords.

THIRD
Why do you drag your feet? The priests of Liberty have begun the song!

CONVERT
No way to avoid it; they press us from all sides.

HUSBAND
Who is that young man standing on the rubble of the sanctuary? Three fires burn before him, and his own face seems to flame among the smoke and the glow, while his voice intones insanity.

CONVERT
That's Leonard, the inspired prophet of Liberty, and around him stand our priests, philosophers, poets, artists, and their daughters and lovers.

HUSBAND
Ha! So that's your aristocracy! Which one sent you to me?

CONVERT
I don't see him here.

LEONARD
Give her to me, that I may press her to my lips, to my bosom — Give me my beauteous one, my independent, free, liberated one, denuded, stripped free of all superstition, chosen from amongst the daughters of Liberty, my bride.

MAIDEN'S VOICE
I hasten to thee, my lover.

SECOND MAIDEN
See, I stretch out my arms toward thee! I have fallen, weak; I crawl to thee amongst the cinders, my lover!

THIRD
And I have passed them by, through ash and ember, fire and smoke, to approach thee, my lover.

HUSBAND
Her hair undone, with heaving bosom, she clambers upon the rubble in passionate bounds.

CONVERT
Same thing every night.

LEONARD
Come, come, my delight, daughter of Liberty, who tremblest with divine fury. Inspiration, embrace my soul! Listen, all — I am now about to prophesy…

HUSBAND
She bows her head, and faints.

LEONARD
We two are the image and likeness of the human race liberated, risen from the dead! Behold: we stand upon the shards of ancient forms and symbols, of an ancient God. Glory be to us, who have torn apart His members, of which there remain nothing but dust and ashes. We have vanquished His Spirit with our arms; His Spirit hath become nothingness.

CHORUS OF MAIDENS
O happy, happy the bride of the prophet! We stand here below, in envy of her glory.

LEONARD
I proclaim a new world — and bestow the heavens upon a new God. Lord of freedom and delight, God of the people, may each victim of

our vengeance, each oppressor's corpse, be an altar unto thee — The age-old tears and suffering of the human race will sink in an ocean of blood. From now on, the life of man will be happiness, and equality his law, and whoever invents any other laws shall receive in exchange but a noose and a curse.

CHORUS OF MEN
The edifice of exploitation and pride has crumbled. Whosoever picks up even a tiny stone from the rubble, shall find but death and a curse.

CONVERT
Blasphemers of Jehovah, three times I spit for your destruction.

HUSBAND
O eagle, keep thou thy promise, and on their prostrate necks I will raise a new Church of Christ!

MIXED VOICES
Liberty — Happiness — Hurrah! — Hey! — Huzzah! — Hurrah! Hurrah!

CHORUS OF PRIESTS
Where are the lords? Where are the kings who not long ago walked the earth in crowns, with sceptres in their hands, with pride, and anger?

MURDERER
I killed King Alexander.

SECOND MURDERER
And I King Henry.

THIRD
And I King Emmanuel.

LEONARD
Go now, fearlessly, and murder without scruple. For you are the chosen of the chosen, the saints among the most saintly; you are martyrs, the heroes of Liberty.

CHORUS OF MURDERERS
We go, in the dark night, stilettos gripped in our hands — We go, we go.

LEONARD
Awaken, my beloved.

Thunder.

LEONARD
Now then, make answer unto the living God. Raise your songs on high; everyone follow me, as once again we make circuit of the dead God's temple, grinding its rubble beneath our heels. And thou, raise thy head aloft — arise and awaken!

MAIDEN
With love I burn, love for thee and thy God, spreading my love about the entire world, burning — burning…

HUSBAND
Somebody's run up to him… He falls to his knees, rolls about in convulsions, babbling and moaning.

CONVERT
I see him — yes, that's the son of a famous philosopher.

LEONARD
What is it you wish, Herman?

HERMAN
O High Priest — anoint me a murderer!

LEONARD
To priests
Give me the oil, the stiletto and the poison. *To Herman.* With the oil once reserved for the anointing of kings I now anoint thee, to their destruction. The weapon of ancient knights and lords I now place in thy hand, and on thy breast I hang a medallion full of poison. There,

where steel reacheth not, may she burn and consume the bowels of tyrants. Go forth and destroy the ancient generations in all the four corners of the world.

HUSBAND
He's risen and now he makes for the hills, at the head of a band of men.

CONVERT
Let's get out of the way.

HUSBAND
No! I want to see this nightmare through to the end.

CONVERT
Aside
I spit on you, three times!
To Husband
Leonard might recognise me, my lord — look at the knife that dangles from his neck!

HUSBAND
Cover yourself with my cape. What women are they who dance before him?

CONVERTS
Countesses and princesses who have left their husbands to embrace our faith.

HUSBAND
Once they seemed angels to me… The common rout has completely engulfed him now… He's lost in the crowd… Only by the dying music can I tell that he's moving off. Come with me. We'll see better from over there.

He climbs up on a fragment of the wall

CONVERT
Oy vey, oy vey! Everyone will notice us.

HUSBAND
Now I see him again… Other women throw themselves at him, pale, demented, convulsed. The philosopher's son froths at the mouth, shaking his stiletto. Now they've reached the ruins of the northern tower.

They halt… dance on the rubble… tear apart the remaining arcades… scattering sparks on overturned altars and crosses… A fire blazes up and sends aloft great pillars of smoke. Woe to you all — Woe!

LEONARD
Woe to those who still bow before the dead God.

HUSBAND
The black-clad clowns turn again and speed our way.

CONVERT
O, Abraham!

HUSBAND
O eagle, surely my hour has not yet arrived?

CONVERT
We're done for!

LEONARD
Passing by, he halts
Who are you there, brother — you with the proud stare? Why do you not join with us?

HUSBAND
I've been hastening to you from afar at the news of your uprising. I'm a murderer from a Spanish cénacle and have just arrived today.

LEONARD
And that other one there — covered up in your cape?

HUSBAND
My younger brother. He's made a vow not to show his face until he's killed at least a baron.

LEONARD
And you? of whose death do you boast?

HUSBAND
I was ordained by my brothers just two days before leaving home.

LEONARD So, who's your first target, then?

HUSBAND. You, if you prove us false.

LEONARD Brother, you could use my own stiletto for that! *Takes it from his belt.*

HUSBAND
Takes out his own
Brother, for that mine own will suffice.

VOICES OF THE PEOPLE
Long live Leonard! Long live the Spanish murderer!

LEONARD
Show yourself tomorrow at the tent of our citizen leader.

CHORUS OF PRIESTS
We greet thee, guest, in the name of the Spirit of Liberty! In thy hands lieth a portion of our salvation. He who fights without cease, murders without weakness; he who day and night believes in victory, will have that victory at last.
They pass by.

CHORUS OF PHILOSOPHERS
We have led the human race out of its childhood. We have torn truth from the womb of darkness. You, fight for her, murder, and expire.
They pass by.

PHILOSOPHER'S SON
Comrade brother, I drink your health from the skull of a saint! Till we meet again…

He tosses the skull away.

GIRL
Dancing
Kill Prince John for me.

SECOND GIRL
And Count Henryk for me.

CHILDREN
Please, sir — C'n you get us the head of a 'ristocrat?

OTHERS
Success to your stiletto!

CHORUS OF ARTISTS
On the ruins of a Gothic sanctuary we build our new temple: no images, no statues; instead of ribbed vaults, long, stylised knives, pillars with capitals of eight severed heads, and from the summit of each pillar blood-clotted locks of hair. One white altar, and on it the cap of Liberty. Hurrah!

OTHERS
Come on, come on, it's almost dawn.

CONVERT
They'll be stringing us up! Look — there's the gallows.

HUSBAND
Keep quiet — they're going away with Leonard; they're not even looking at us. One last time I want to take it all in, grip this chaos with my mind, as it emerges from the flood of time, from the bosom of darkness, for my destruction and that of all my brethren. Whipped on by the frenzy, carried off with despair, my thoughts circle about, in all their strength…

    God, grant me now the power, which once Thou didst not withhold from me — and in one word I shall enclose this new, huge world, which doesn't yet know itself — But that word of mine will be the poetry of the future.

VOICE IN THE AIR
Ooh, what a part you're scripting. You the leading man?

HUSBAND
Thanks for the advice. The dishonoured ashes of my forefathers will be avenged! May these new generations be damned! I'm caught up in their whirlpool, but it won't pull me in… O eagle, eagle, keep thou thy promise! And now, come with me to St Ignatius Ravine.

CONVERT
It's almost daylight — Not a step further!

HUSBAND
Just find me the path, then I'll let you go.

CONVERT
In the fog, amidst the rubble, shades and ashes, where are you dragging me? Spare me!

HUSBAND
Forward, forward! The last songs of the people are dying away behind us. Here and there a torch burns down to ash… can you not see the shades of the past amongst these exhalations, these dew-soaked trees? Can you not hear their mournful voices?

CONVERT
The fog covers everything… We're descending lower and lower.

CHORUS OF FOREST SPIRITS
We weep for Christ, for Christ exiled, Christ tortured! Where is our God? Where is His Church?

HUSBAND
On, on to the battle, to the sword! I'll give Him back to you; on thousands of crosses will I crucify His enemies.

CHORUS OF SPIRITS
We guarded altar and holy image, bore the echoes of bells on our wings to the faithful. Our voices were in the sounds of the organ, our life in the shine of cathedral windows, the shadows of her pillars, the shimmer of the holy cup, the blessing of the Body of the Lord. Where shall we go now?

HUSBAND
It's getting brighter now — their forms melt away in the rays of dawn.

CONVERT
There's your road. There begins the ravine.

HUSBAND
Hey! Jesus and my blade! *He tosses away the cap after stuffing it with money.* Here — for a souvenir — the symbol and the signified.

CONVERT
Now, you've also sworn, my lord, to stand between me and the one who sent me, when, tonight at midnight…

HUSBAND
An old nobleman needn't repeat his word. Jesus and my blade!

VOICES IN THE BUSHES
The Virgin Mary and our blades! Long live our lord the Count!

HUSBAND
For the Faith! Come hither! Farewell, Citizen. The Faith! Come hither! Jesus and Mary!

*

Night — bushes — trees.

PANKRACY
To his people
Lie prone here, with your faces to the grass — Keep quiet, and no fires, not even a spark to light a pipe. At the first shot you hear, up and

hasten to my rescue. But if you hear no shot, then stay here where you are, until sunup.

LEONARD
Citizen, I beg you once again…

PANKRACY
Glue yourself to that pine there, and… muse.

LEONARD
At least take me with you! He's a nobleman, an aristocrat, a liar!

PANKRACY
Making a sign with his hand that he should stay where he is
The old nobility sometimes keeps their word…

*

A long chamber — portraits of ladies and knights along the walls — in the distance a pillar supporting a shield with a coat of arms — the husband sits at a little marble table, upon which are set a lamp, a couple of pistols, a sabre and a clock — facing it is a second table, with silver goblets and a pitcher.

HUSBAND
Once, long ago, at just such an hour, amidst threatening dangers and thoughts similar to my own, Brutus saw the genius of Caesar appear to him.

And now I am awaiting a similar vision. In a moment, before me shall stand a man without a name, without antecedents, without an angel guardian, who has emerged from nothingness to begin a new epoch, perhaps, unless I can thrust him backwards, back into nothingness.

O my forefathers, inspire me with the spirit that made you lords of the world! Cram into my bosom all of your lions' hearts; wreath my brows with the gravity of your temples, and Faith in Christ and His Church, a blind faith, implacable, seething, which was the inspiration of your earthly deeds, and hope of your immortal glory in heaven — May this light upon me today, and I shall murder and burn my enemies! Me, a son of one hundred generations, the last inheritor of your thought and hardiness, your virtues and your errors.

Twelve o'clock strikes.

HUSBAND
Now I'm ready.
He stands

SERVANT AT ARMS
Enters
My lord, the man you are expecting has arrived and waits without.

HUSBAND
Show him in.

Servant exits.

PANKRACY
Enters
Greetings to Count Henryk... That word "count" tastes odd.
He sits down — tosses off cape and cap of Liberty, stares at the column on which a coat of arms is fixed.

HUSBAND
Thank you for trustfully accepting the hospitality of my home. I drink your health, according to the ancient custom. *Takes goblet, drinks, hands it to Pankracy.* Into your hands, my guest! —

PANKRACY
Unless I'm much mistaken, that old red and azure symbol over there is called a coat of arms, in the dead language? There are ever fewer such symbols on the face of the earth these days. *Drinks.*

HUSBAND
With the help of God, soon you'll be seeing thousands.

PANKRACY
Takes the goblet from his lips
That's your old blueblood for you. Always so sure. Proud, obstinate, blooming with hope, but... penniless, weaponless, soldierless, threatening me with his bugbears like the dead man in the fairy story, accosting the carriageman at the cemetery gates. Believing, or pretending to believe, in God; 'cos it's hard for him even to believe in himself... But, show me the lightning bolts sent to your defence, and the divisions of angels sent you from Heaven!
Drinks.

HUSBAND
Go on, laugh. But atheism's as old as the world. I expected something new from you.

PANKRACY
Go on, laugh. I have a faith stronger and larger than yours! A moan torn by despair and pain from the bosoms of thousands upon thousands. The hunger of the craftsman, the misery of the peasant, the dishonouring of their wives and daughters, the humbling of humanity beneath the yoke of superstition and insecurity, a humanity accustomed to playing the beast of burden... this is my faith. And my God for the present; my thought, my power... which will distribute bread and glory to the people for ages to come.
Drinks and tosses cup away.

HUSBAND
I have placed my trust in the Lord, who gave my forefathers the right of rule.

PANKRACY
Whereas all your life *you* were the devil's plaything. Ah, let's leave all that to the theologians... if a pedant of that stripe can still be found hereabouts. Let's get down to business.

HUSBAND
What is it you want of me, saviour of the nations, citizen-idol?

PANKRACY
I come, first of all, to get to know you. Secondly, to save you.

HUSBAND
Quite obliged for the first — let's leave the second to my blade, thank you.

PANKRACY
Your blade — is glass. Your God — a dream. You've been condemned by the throats of thousands — thousands of pairs of arms wind you about. A couple acres of land is all that's left you — hardly enough dirt to cover your dead bodies. You can't hold out for twenty days. Where are your cannon, your armour, your food... and, when it comes down to that, your courage? If I were you, I know what I'd do.

HUSBAND
I'm all ears. See how patient.

PANKRACY
I, then, if I were Count Henryk, would say this to Pankracy: "All right — I'll disperse my petty little army — I won't attempt to lift the siege at Holy Trinity, and in exchange you will allow me to keep my title and my possessions, the entirety of which you guarantee me by your word." How old are you, my lord?

HUSBAND
Thirty-six, citizen.

PANKRACY
Fifteen more years, then — 'cos such people don't live long. Your son is closer to the grave than to the cradle... one exception will do no harm to the general rule. So, be the last count on these plains! Reign in the home of your ancestors till you die. Have their portraits painted and their arms carved — and don't waste another thought on those miserable fellows. Let the sentence of the people be carried out upon the heads of the scoundrels. *Pours himself another goblet.* To your health — the end of a long line of counts!

HUSBAND
Your every word is an insult. It seems that you're trying to turn me into a slave for your triumphal procession. Stop it, for I can't pay you back; the providence of my word protects you.

PANKRACY
Aha. Honour, knightly honour, makes its appearance on stage at last. A withered rag amidst the flags of humanity. O, I know you — I've sounded your depths. Full of life, you ally yourself to the moribund, 'cos you want to fool yourself, to believe in caste, in the mouldy bones of great-grandmama, in the word "Fatherland" and all that claptrap… But in the depths of your soul you know that your brothers deserve the punishment that's coming to them… and after the punishment, the oblivion.

HUSBAND
And you and yours deserve something else?

PANKRACY
Victory and life. I recognise but one law before which I bow my head, and by this law the world is spinning ever faster, in ever widening circles… and that is your destruction. It calls to you now, through my mouth:
    "Mouldy, verminous, full of drink and food, make room for the young, the hungry, the strong." But — I wish to save you — you alone.

HUSBAND
And may you die like a dog for that pity of yours! I too know you, and your world. Amidst the shades of night I watched the dancing of the mob, upon whose necks you climb upward, and saw all the old crimes of the world dressed up in new clothes, swaying to the rhythm of a new dance, the end of which, however, hasn't changed in one thousand years: dissipation, gold, and blood. But you were nowhere there to be seen. You didn't deign descend amongst your children, 'cos in the depths of your soul you hold them in contempt! A few minutes more, and if your reason doesn't abandon you, you'll hold yourself in contempt as well. Don't torment me any further.
He sits down beneath his coat of arms.

PANKRACY
My world's not spread itself wide yet — I agree. It hasn't yet grown into a giant, because it still needs bread and comfort, but the time will come! *He stands, goes over to Husband and leans on the pillar with the coat of arms.* The time will come when it will know itself and say "I am." And there will be no other voice in the whole world that might answer back "I am."

HUSBAND
And then?

PANKRACY
From this generation, over which I brood with the strength of my will, the final tribe shall emerge — the greatest, bravest. The earth has yet to see such men: free people, lords of the earth from pole to pole. And the earth herself shall be one city flourishing, one happy home, one workshop of happiness, riches and industry.

HUSBAND
Your words lie — but your face is unmoved, pale, unable to feign inspiration.

PANKRACY
Don't interrupt; there are people who have begged me on their knees to speak such things to them, and I have been niggardly of my words.
    There God resides, who now will never die; God, torn away from all shades and curtains by labour and the torment of time. Vanquished in Heaven by his own children, whom He once flung to the earth, for they have now looked about themselves and found the truth: the God of humanity has revealed himself to them.

HUSBAND
And to us, centuries ago. Humanity has been redeemed by Him.

PANKRACY
Some redemption! Two thousand years of misery since His death on the cross.

HUSBAND
I saw that cross, blasphemer, in ancient, ancient Rome! At its feet lay the ruins of greater forces than yours: one hundred gods, similar to your own, wallowing in the dust, not a single one daring to raise its wounded head in His presence, and He stood aloft, stretching His holy arms east and west, bathing His sacred brow in the rays of the sun… it was obvious that He is Lord of the world.

PANKRACY
Old wives' tales, as hollow as your plaster shield. *He strikes the coat of arms.* But I read your thoughts long ago — if you really wish to reach into infinity, if you love the truth and have searched for her sincerely, if you are a man after the manner of men, not in the image of nurses' lullabies, listen — Don't throw away this moment of salvation. Tomorrow there will be no trace of the blood we both of us will spill today. I'm telling you for the last time: if you are that, which you once seemed to be, arise, abandon your home, and follow me.

HUSBAND
You? Satan's younger brother! *He gets up and paces.* Vain dreams — who will realise them? Adam died in the wilderness, and we won't get back into Eden.

PANKRACY
Aside
I've wriggled my finger right beneath his heart, and touched the nerve of poetry!

HUSBAND
Progress, the happiness of the human race… I myself once believed… Ha! here — take my head, if only… it come true… One hundred years ago, two hundred… a mutual agreement could still have… But now, I know… Now we need mutual slaughter, 'cos now it's only about a switch of places.

PANKRACY
Woe to the vanquished! Don't hesitate! Repeat "woe" after me and… vanquish along with us!

HUSBAND
Can it be that you have searched all the trackless wastes of Destiny? Can she have stood before you in visible form at the flaps of your tent and blessed you one night with her gigantic palm? Or did you hear that voice in the daylight, when everyone else slept in the heat and you alone watched, thinking, that you threaten me so surely with your triumph, a man of clay like myself, and slave to the first best bullet, the first best swipe of the sword?

PANKRACY
Don't fool yourself with vain hope. No lead will scratch me, nor iron touch, as long as one of you opposes me in my work. And what happens after, that doesn't concern you.

The clock strikes.

PANKRACY
Time mocks us both. If you're tired of your own life, save at least that of your son…

HUSBAND
His pure soul is already reserved for Heaven — and on earth, his father's fate awaits him.
He lets his head droop in his hands, then rises.

PANKRACY
So the answer is no? *Pause.* You're silent — thinking — good. Let him meditate, who totters on the lip of the grave.

HUSBAND
Go! Far from all mysteries which, from the edges of your thought, have now sunk into the depths of my soul! The world's beastly flesh belongs to you: flatter it, smear it with your gore and wine, but presume no further. Begone! Away from me!

PANKRACY
You slave to one thought and her shapes, Sir Pedant, poet, shame on you! Look at me: thoughts and forms are wax in my fingers.

HUSBAND

No use. You'll never understand me. Because every single one of your fathers has mixed his dust with the common mob, like a dead thing, not like a man of strength and spirit. *He raises hand toward portraits.* Look at these figures — the very spirit of Fatherland, of home, family, a thought inimical to yourself, written in the furrows of their brows, and whatever was in them now lives in me. But you, fellow, tell me — Where is it your land lies? In the evening you stake your tent on the ruins of someone else's home; at sunrise you strike camp and wander elsewhere. You've not found your own hearth yet, nor will you ever, as long as one hundred repeat with me "Praise to our fathers!"

PANKRACY

Oh, sure — praise to thy fathers and grandfathers on earth as in ... Yes, there's quite a lot to look at around here.

That one there, the Subprefect, liked to shoot at women among the trees, and burned Jews alive. — That one, with the seal in his hand and the signature, the "Chancellor," falsified records, burned whole archives, bribed judges, hurried on his petty inheritances with poison — To him you owe your villages, your income, your power. That one, the darkish one with the fiery eye, slept with his friends' wives — that one with the Golden Fleece, in the Italian armour, fought — not for Fatherland, but for foreign pay. And that pale lady with the black locks muddied her pedigree with her squire — while that one reads a lover's letter and smiles because the sun is setting... That one over there, with the doggie on her farthingale, was whore to kings. — There's your genealogies for you, endless, stainless! — I like that chap in the green caftan. He drank and hunted with his brother aristocrats, and set out the peasants to chase deer with the dogs. The idiocy and adversity of the whole country — there's your reason, there's your power. — But the day of judgement is near at hand and on that day, I promise you, I won't forget a single one of you, a single one of your fathers, a single scrap of your glory!

HUSBAND

You're wrong, shopkeeper's whelp! Neither you, nor any one of yours would have lived were it not for the grace of my fathers which nourished you, the power of my fathers that defended you, and them.

In time of famine they gave you grain; in time of plague they founded hospitals, and when you'd lifted yourselves up from the levels of the cattle you tend to that of children, they gave you schools and churches. And during time of war they left you at home, knowing that you're not made for the battlefield.

Your words dash themselves against their glory and shatter, just as, long ago, the arrows of the pagans did, against their breastplates. These words of yours can't even stir their ashes — they die away like the howling of a mad dog, racing about frothing until he croaks beside the road. And now it's time for you to take your carcass from my home. My guest, you leave a free man.

PANKRACY
Until we meet again, on the battlements of Holy Trinity. And when you run out of powder and shot...

HUSBAND
Then we'll meet at sword's-point.

PANKRACY
We are two eagles. But your aerie is shattered by the lightning bolt. *Takes up his cap of liberty.* Crossing this threshold, I cast a curse upon it befitting ancient trash. And you, you and your son, I devote to destruction.

HUSBAND
Hey, Jakub!
Jakub enters.
See this fellow past the last of my pickets on the hill.

JAKUB
So help me God!
Exits.

PART IV

Bottomless perdition.

—Milton

From the bastions of Holy Trinity to the summit of each mountain, to the right, to the left, before and behind, a snowy mist, pale, immobile and silent lies — the nightmare of an ocean, which at one time had its boundaries marked by those black, sharp, torn heights, and its depths in the unseen valley. The sun has not yet arisen.

On a naked granite island stand the turrets of the castle, driven into the cliff by the exertions of ancient labourers and grown into the rock like the human breast of a Centaur's torso. Above them, a banner flies, on the highest point, alone amidst the grey heavens.

Slowly, the sleeping range begins to wake — the rush of winds is heard on high, the rays of the sun squeeze themselves below — a spark from a cloud rushes over this sea of exhalations.

Then, other voices, human voices, mix in with this ephemeral storm and, borne on the misty billows, jostle against the foot of the castle.

The abyss is clearly seen amidst the regions that crumbled about its lip. —

Black it is, there in the depths, black with human heads — the whole valley is spread with human heads, like boulders on the bottom of the sea.

The sun appears, from hill to cliff, lifting itself in gold; the clouds melt in gold, and the more they disappear, the better one hears the cries, the better one sees the crowds flowing there at the bottom. —

The mists have lifted themselves from the mountains and now they expire in the azure vacuum — About the Holy Trinity valley are strewn the glints of flashing weapons, as the people draw thither as if to the plain of Judgement on that final day.

Cathedral at Holy Trinity castle.
Noblemen, senators, and dignitaries sit along either side of the nave, each beneath the statue of some king or knight — behind the statues there are crowds of aristocrats — before the main altar in the rear the archbishop sits on a gilded throne, with a sword in his lap — behind the altar stands the chorus of priests. — The husband stands in the narthex for a moment, then begins a slow procession toward the archbishop, flag in hand. —

CHORUS OF PRIESTS
The last of Thy servants assembled in the last church of Thy Son, we beg Thee, on the honour of our forefathers — deliver us, Lord, from our enemies!

FIRST COUNT
Look how pridefully he glances around at everyone.

SECOND COUNT
As if he'd just conquered the whole world.

THIRD COUNT
And all he did was sneak through the peasants' camp at night.

FIRST COUNT
Cutting down one hundred, he lost two hundred of his own!

SECOND COUNT
No, we can't allow him to be elected leader.

HUSBAND
Kneels before Archbishop
At thy feet I lay the trophies that I've won.

ARCHBISHOP
Take up this sword, blessed long ago by the hand of St Florian.

VOICES
Long live Count Henryk!

ARCHBISHOP
Take also, with the Sign of the Cross, command of this castle, our last redoubt. By general acclamation I appoint thee leader.

VOICES
Long live Count Henryk! Vivat!

ONE VOICE
I protest.

VOICES
Who said that? Kick him out! — Away with him! — Long live Henryk!

HUSBAND
If there is anyone among you who has something to accuse me of, let him come forth and not hide in the crowd. *Pause.* Father, I take up this sword, and may God see fit to grant me a quick death, an early death, if with it I do not save you all.

CHORUS OF PRIESTS
Grant him the strength, Lord! Send down Thy Holy Spirit upon him, Lord! Deliver us, Lord, from our enemies!

HUSBAND
And now, swear — all of you — to defend the faith and honour of your ancestors. Swear that hunger and thirst may drive you to death, but never to shame — never to surrender — never to relinquish even one of the laws of God, or your own rights.

VOICES
We so swear.

The Archbishop kneels and raises aloft the Cross. All kneel.

CHORUS
May those who falsely swear be burdened with Thine anger! May those who quake in fear be burdened with Thine anger! May those who betray be burdened with Thine anger, O Lord!

VOICES
We so swear.

HUSBAND
Takes up the sword.
And now, I promise you glory — beg victory of the Lord.
Exits, surrounded by the crowd.

*

One of the castle courtyards — Husband — Counts — Barons — priests — nobility.

COUNT
leading Husband aside.
So — all is lost?

HUSBAND
Not everything… unless perhaps your hearts give out too soon.

COUNT
How soon is too soon?

HUSBAND
While they still beat, it is too soon.

BARON
Leads him to another side.
Count, is it true that you've met with that horrible man? Will he have at least a drop of pity for us when we fall into his hands?

HUSBAND
Verily I say unto thee — no father of yours ever heard of such pity. It's called the gallows.

BARON
We've got to defend ourselves as best we can.

HUSBAND
Pardon me, Prince?

PRINCE
A couple of words in private, if you don't mind… *Takes him aside.* All of what you say is fine for the … common sort, but, between you and me, it's obvious that we don't have a chance of resisting.

HUSBAND
What remains us, then?

PRINCE
You were chosen leader, therefore, it's up to you to begin negotiations.

HUSBAND
Quiet! Quiet!

PRINCE
Why?

HUSBAND
Because your Highness has just uttered words deserving the punishment of death! *Turns to the crowd.* Whoever amongst you even mentions surrender will be punished with death!

BARON, COUNTS, PRINCE
All together.
Whoever even mentions surrender will be punished with death!

ALL
With death, death — vivat!

Exit all.

*

A gallery at the top of a tower — Husband — Jakub.

HUSBAND
Where is my son?

JAKUB
He's sat himself down on the porch of the old prison, where he sings prophecies.

HUSBAND
The Eleanor bastion must be more strongly manned. Go there yourself, and stay there. Keep an eye on the rebels.

JAKUB
It'd be worth it, so help me God, to hand round a shot of vodka to perk up the spirits.

HUSBAND
If you need, open up the cellars of the counts and princes too.

Jakub exits, Husband climbs several steps, stands on a flat terrace beneath the flag.

HUSBAND
With my eyes, and with all the hatred in my heart, I embrace you, my enemies. Now no longer merely with empty breath and queasy words will I fight, but with iron and the men who have put themselves under my command.

How good it is to be a lord, to be in command, to gaze, even from one's deathbed, upon the wills of others; those grouped about one, and one's enemies — you, sunken in the abyss, lifting your voices toward me as the damned cry out toward Heaven.

A few more days, perhaps, and both I and these miserable creatures, who have forgotten their great forefathers, will no longer exist. But whatever awaits us, these few more days remain, and I will use them to my delight. I will rule — fight — live. Such is my final song!

Above the cliffs the sun disappears into the long, black coffin of the nether shades. Bloody rays spill all about the valley. These are the prophetic omens of my death. I greet you sincerely, with heart more frank, more open, than ever I greeted the promise of happiness, delusion, or love.

For I have grasped the ends of my desires — not through base labour, nor guile, nor industry, but suddenly, unexpectedly, just as I had always dreamed.

And now I stand here at the border of eternal sleep, in command of all these who but yesterday had been my equals.

*

A room in the castle lit with torches — Orcio sits on a bed. Enter Husband, who lays his weapon down on the table.

HUSBAND
Keep one hundred men upon the ramparts. Let the others rest, after such a long battle.

VOICE FROM BEHIND THE DOOR
So help me God!

HUSBAND
You must have heard the shots — the echoes of our retreat. But be of good cheer, my child, we won't fall today, or tomorrow.

ORCIO
I heard it all, but it touched not my heart. The chaos came and passed away. Something else makes me tremble, Father.

HUSBAND
You feared for my life.

ORCIO
No, because I know that your hour has not yet come.

HUSBAND
We're alone. The weight has fallen from my soul for today. For there in the valley lie the corpses of our vanquished enemies. Tell me all of your thoughts — I'll listen, as I used to, back home, back in our old home.

ORCIO
Follow me, Father, follow me. Each night a horrible judgement is repeated…
He goes toward a hidden door in the wall and opens it.

HUSBAND
Where are you going? Who showed you that passage? It leads to dungeons ever-dark, where the bones of ancient criminals crumble to dust.

ORCIO
There, where your eye, used to sunlight, sees not, my spirit treads faultlessly. Darkness, lead us on to the dark!

Exits.

*

Underground dungeons — iron bars, manacles, instruments of torture, broken, lay on the ground. — The Husband, holding a torch, at the foot of a large rock upon which Orcio stands.

HUSBAND
Come down from there, I beg you.

ORCIO
Can't you hear their voices? Can't you see their shapes?

HUSBAND
I hear the silence of the grave, and the light of the torch illumines only a few feet before us.

ORCIO
Ever closer — ever more distinct — They bend beneath the low vaults, one after the other, and take their places in the depths.

HUSBAND
My damnation in your insanity! You're hallucinating, my child, and destroying my strength, just when I need it most…

ORCIO
My spirit sees their pale figures, serious, gathering for a terrible sentencing. The accused now comes forth, gliding like mist.

CHORUS OF VOICES
By the power invested in us, and because of our torments, we, once chained here, whipped, tortured, ripped open with iron, slaked with poison, buried under heaps of brick and gravel, now it's our turn to torment and to judge, to judge and to condemn, and Satan will take care of the punishment!

HUSBAND
What do you see?

ORCIO
The accused… the accused… Oh, he's wringing his hands!

HUSBAND
Who is he?

ORCIO
Father — Father! —

FIRST VOICE
With you the damnable line comes to an end. In you all its strength and passion are gathered, all pride, in order to perish.

CHORUS OF VOICES
Because thou hast loved no one at all, honoured no one but thy self and thy thoughts, damned thou art — damned for all time!

HUSBAND
I can't see anything, but I hear: from beneath the earth, above it and on all hands, sighs and laments, verdicts and threats.

ORCIO
Now he's raised his hand, like you, Father, when you're angry. And he beats back the accuser with a prideful word… Like you, Father, when you're contemptuous.

CHORUS OF VOICES
In vain, in vain — There's no help for him on earth, or in heaven.

FIRST VOICE
A few more days of negligible, earthly glory, the sort of which your fathers deprived me and my brethren, and your funeral will be without mourning bells, without the sobbing of friends and relatives, just as ours were, on this cliff of pain!

HUSBAND
I know you, base spirits, miserable wills-o'-the-wisp, floating about the angelic deeps!
Takes a few steps forward.

ORCIO
No, Father — don't go any farther — By the Holy Name of Christ I beg you, Father!

HUSBAND
Returning
Tell me — what else do you see? — Tell me —

ORCIO
That figure…

HUSBAND
Whose?

ORCIO
A second you… All pale… wrapped in chains… And now they're tormenting you — I hear your cries *Falls on his knee.* Forgive me, Father! Mother came during the night and commanded me…
Faints.

HUSBAND
Takes him in his arms.
Only that was lacking. Ha! my own child leads me to the threshold of Hell! Maria! You implacable spirit! God! and Thou, the other Maria, to whom I prayed so often!

That way leads to the eternity of torture and darkness. Back! I must still fight with men, before the eternal struggle begins!
Runs off with son.

CHORUS OF VOICES
Because thou hast loved no one at all, honoured no one but thy self and thy thoughts, damned thou art — damned for all time!

*

Hall in the Holy Trinity castle — Husband, women, children, a few old men and counts kneeling at his feet — the godfather stands in the middle of the hall — a crowd in the depths — armour hung up around, gothic columns, decorations, windows. —

HUSBAND
No! By the life of my son, by the sacred memory of my wife, no! For the last time, no!

VOICES OF WOMEN
Have mercy — hunger is burning through our insides and those of our children! Night and day terror gnaws at us!

VOICES OF MEN
There's still time — hear what the delegate has to say. Don't send the envoy away unheard!

GODFATHER
My whole life has been that of a good citizen, and I don't give a damn for your reproaches, Henryk. If I've taken upon myself the office of envoy, which I now hold, that's because I know the Age I live in and have recognised its values. Pankracy is a civic representative, if I may put it that way…

HUSBAND
Out of my sight, old man! *Aside, to Jakub.* Call up our division, here.

Jakub goes out — the women stand and cry — the men retreat a few steps.

BARON
You've ruined us, Count!

SECOND BARON
We revoke our vow of obedience.

PRINCE
We'll make our own terms with the good citizen concerning the conditions for surrendering the castle.

GODFATHER
The great man who has sent me to you promises you your lives, if only you agree to come over to him and recognise the direction in which the Age we live in is naturally tending.

SEVERAL VOICES
We recognise it, that we do!

HUSBAND
When you summoned me, I swore to die on these walls. I will keep my word, and you shall all die with me! Ha! You all still want to live! Ha! Ask your forefathers why they oppressed and lorded it over others! *To Count.* You — why did you exploit your subjects? *To the other Count.* And why did you squander your youth in cards and foreign junkets, far from the Fatherland? *To another.* And you — you licked the boots of those above you, and trod down those beneath you, under your heel. *To one of the women.* Why did you not raise your boys to be your defenders — your knights? We could use them now. — But you were in love with the usurers and the lawyers — ask them now to defend your life! *Stands and raises his arms.* Why are you all racing headlong to shame? What is tempting you so to debase your final moments? Forward, rather,

with me! Forward, my lords, towards the bullets and bayonets, not towards the scaffold where the quiet hangman waits, holding the noose fit for your neck!

SEVERAL VOICES
He's right — to the bayonets!

OTHER VOICES
But there's no bread left at all.

WOMEN'S VOICES
Our children — your children!

MANY VOICES
We've got to surrender — terms — terms!

GODFATHER
I promise you, no one will lay a finger on you.

HUSBAND
Moves over to the godfather and grabs him by the shirt front.
Ah, envoy whose sacred person is inviolate! Go hide your grey head among the tents of the Convert Jews and shoemakers, before I defile my own blood by shedding yours!

Armed division enters with Jakub.

HUSBAND
Go! Before I use that forehead of yours, furrowed with the wrinkles of vain study, and that cap of Liberty, which trembles at my words on that brainless poll of yours — for a bull's eye!

Godfather runs off.

ALL
Grab him — send him to Pankracy! —

HUSBAND
Just a moment, my lords! *Looks from one soldier to another.* You're the one I took hunting once in the mountains, if I'm not mistaken… Remember how I pulled you up when you were dangling from a cliff by your fingernails? *To another.* With you I ran aground on the Danube rocks. Hieronym, Krzysztof, you were both with me on the Black Sea… *To others.* I rebuilt your burnt cottages. *To others.* You escaped to me from a tyrant master… And now you must tell me: are you with me, or am I alone, with a laugh on my lips, that among so many bodies I couldn't find a single man? —

ALL
Long live Count Henryk — vivat!

HUSBAND
Give them what's left of the meat and the vodka. And then, to the ramparts.

ALL THE SOLDIERS
Meat and vodka — Then, to the ramparts!

HUSBAND
Go with them, and be ready to fight in an hour.

JAKUB
So help me God!

WOMEN'S VOICES
We curse you, on account of our infants!

OTHERS
On account of our fathers!

OTHERS
Our wives!

HUSBAND
And I curse you, on account of your baseness.

Exit.

*

The trenches around Holy Trinity — Corpses strewn about — burst cannon — weapons lying on the ground — Here and there a soldier hurries — Husband, leaning on the rampart, Jakub beside him.

HUSBAND
Sheathing his sabre.
There's no delight in winning through danger always, and when it's time to lose — that happens once only.

JAKUB
They retreated at our final volley, but they've regrouped down below and will soon storm us again… Oh, well. No one's ever cheated fate, not since time began.

HUSBAND
There's no more grapeshot?

JAKUB
No bullets, no grenades, no shot — everything's running out, at last.

HUSBAND
Then bring my son to me, that I might embrace him one last time.

Jakub exits.

HUSBAND
The smoke of battle mists my eyes — it seems as if the valley were lifting itself up like a wave before falling back again. The cliffs break into one hundred angles and cross one another — Such a strange order my thoughts are taking. *Sits on the wall.* Not worth being a man. Not worth being an angel… Even the foremost of the archangels, after a few centuries of existence, like us after a few years, felt a boredom in his heart and desired more potent strengths. Have to be God or nothing.

Jakub brings in Orcio.

HUSBAND
Take a few of our men, go from hall to hall, and drive everyone you meet to the ramparts.

JAKUB
Bankers, counts, and princes!

Exits.

HUSBAND
Come here, my son. Put your hand in mine. Let me press my lips upon your brow. Your mother's brow was once as white and soft as yours…

ORCIO
I heard her voice today, before your men moved off to fight. Her words floated as light as a fragrance, and she said, "This evening you will be at my side."

HUSBAND
Didn't she even mention my name?

ORCIO
She said, "This evening, I wait upon my son."

HUSBAND
Aside
Will my strength fail me so near the very end of my road? Don't let that happen, God! In exchange for one moment of courage, I will give you a whole eternity of submission as your prisoner!
Aloud. Son, forgive me for giving you life. We must part — do you know for how long?

ORCIO
Grab hold of me and don't let go… Don't let go… and I'll pull you along with me!

HUSBAND
Our paths now separate. You'll forget me among the angelic choirs. You won't sprinkle drops of dew upon me from on high... O Jerzy, Jerzy! — O my son!

ORCIO
What cries are those? I'm trembling, all of me! Ever more threatening... ever closer... The roar of cannon and rifles sounds... The final hour foretold crawls nearer.

HUSBAND
Hurry up, Jakub! Hurry!

A company of Counts and Princes move through the courtyard — Jakub after them, with soldiers.

FIRST VOICE
You send us to fight with broken weapons.

SECOND VOICE
Henryk, have pity!

THIRD VOICE
Don't drive us weak and starving, to the wall!

OTHER VOICES
Where are they rushing us? Where?

HUSBAND
To them. To death. *To his son.* With this embrace I'd like to link us forever, but I must go another way...

Orcio falls, shot.

VOICE ALOFT
This way, pure spirit, this way! This way, my son!

HUSBAND
Hey! This way, people! *Takes out his sabre and lays it on the dead boy's lips.* Clean as glass, just as before. The spirit has flown out with the breath. Hey! Forward — They're at sabre's length up here... Back, sons of Liberty!

Sounds of battle.

*

Another part of the fortifications. — Echoes of battle — Jakub sprawled on the wall — Husband hurries up, covered in blood.

HUSBAND
What is it, old man? Old, faithful friend?

JAKUB
May the devil repay you in Hell for your stubbornness and for my torment! So help me God!
Dies.

HUSBAND
Throws away his sword.
Well, I don't need you anymore. My boys have died off, and those, kneeling, lift their hands toward the victors and bleat for mercy! *He looks around.* They're not headed this way yet... There's still time... Let's rest a bit... Ha! Now they've clambered up the northern tower... New people on the northern tower... And they're looking to see whether or not they can find Count Henryk. Here I am! I am... but you won't be my judges... I've already chosen my road. I'm off to God's bench. *He stands on a ruined portion of the bastion that hangs over the abyss.* I see it below me, black, the regions of darkness flowing towards me... my shoreless eternity, without island, without end, and in the very centre, God, like an ever-burning sun... ever bright... shining, on — nothing. *He moves a step forward.* Here they come... They've seen me. Jesus, Mary! Poetry, be damned, as I shall be, for all time! Arms, cleave through these bulwarks! *He leaps.*

*

Castle courtyard — Pankracy — Leonard — Bianchetti at the head of the crowds — before them file Counts and Princes, with their wives and children, in chains.

PANKRACY
Your name?

COUNT
Krzysztof de Volsagun.

PANKRACY
You've said it for the last time. And yours?

PRINCE
Władysław, Lord of Czarnolas.

PANKRACY
You've said it for the last time. And yours?

BARON
Aleksander of Godalberg.

PANKRACY
Expunged from the book of the living — Go!

BIANCHETTI
To Leonard.
Two whole months he held out, with a miserable battery of cannon and rotten walls.

LEONARD
Are there a lot of them still up there?

PANKRACY
All will be handed over to you. Let their blood flow as an example to the world. *To the captives.* But whichever one of you tells me where I can find Henryk shall be spared.

DIFFERENT VOICES
He disappeared at the very end.

GODFATHER
I stand here before you as a mediator between you and your slaves: these citizens of much honoured families, who, Great One, placed the keys of the Holy Trinity castle in your hands…

PANKRACY
I know no mediators where I myself had to conquer. You'll supervise their executions.

GODFATHER
My whole life has been that of a good citizen — of which fact there are abundant proofs, and if I have joined up with you, it was not so that I should supervise my brothers'…

PANKRACY
Take the old doctrinaire windbag and string him up along with the others.

Soldiers surround the godfather and the slaves.

PANKRACY
Where's Henryk? Did none of you see him, alive or dead? A sack of gold in exchange for Henryk — even for Henryk's corpse!

A company of armed men descend from the ramparts.

PANKRACY
And you — Haven't you seen Henryk either?

COMPANY COMMANDER
Citizen leader, I was posted by General Bianchetti at the western flank of the ramparts just as we entered the fortress, and at the third turning of the bastion I saw a wounded man standing weaponless near the body of another. I set my men to try and grab him, double quick, but we didn't have time. The fellow descended somewhat lower, stood on

a teetering rock and looked about for a while with a demented stare. Then he stretched out his arms like a swimmer about to dive and jumped out strongly. We all heard the echo of a body tumbling down the cliffs… This is the sabre we found a few feet from where he had been standing.

PANKRACY
Taking the sabre
Blood on the hilt — and beneath it, his coat of arms. This is Count Henryk's sword. He alone among you kept his word. For that, glory to him — and the gallows to you. General Bianchetti, have your men destroy the fortifications and carry out the sentences of execution. Leonard!

He climbs up on the bastion with Leonard.

LEONARD
You ought to rest, master, after so many sleepless nights. Your face shows your exhaustion.

PANKRACY
No time to sleep just yet, child. We shall have finished only half of our task with their last breath. Look around you at these huge barriers that stand between me and my thoughts. These wildernesses must be peopled; these cliffs tunnelled through; these lakes connected, these lands parcelled out, so that twice as much life should spring forth on these plains where death now rules. Otherwise, the work of destruction will not be redeemed.

LEONARD
The God of Liberty will grant us the strength.

PANKRACY
What are you bringing God into it for…? How slippery it is here from human blood. Whose blood is it? Behind us, the castle courtyards… We're alone, and yet it seems to me as if there were a third person here with us…

LEONARD
That body, shot through…?

PANKRACY
The body of his faithful servant… a corpse… and that cap… the same coat of arms… Look, there — the rock overhanging the abyss — that's where his heart broke.

LEONARD
You're turning pale, master…

PANKRACY
Do you see that up there — high — up there?

LEONARD
That cloud? Above the sharp summit I see a cloud, oblique, upon which the rays of the sun are expiring…

PANKRACY
A horrible symbol is burning upon it!

LEONARD
You're just imagining things, surely — ?

PANKRACY
Moments ago, one million people were doing my bidding… Where are my people?

LEONARD
You can hear them cheering… They're calling for you… waiting for you.

PANKRACY
Old women and children used to jabber about this… that such a sign would be seen… but only on the world's last day!

LEONARD
Who? What?

PANKRACY
Like a snow-white pillar He stands above the abyss — stretched wide upon the cross, as if upon an avenger's sword! His crown of thorns is woven of thunderbolts!

LEONARD
What's wrong? What's going on with you?

PANKRACY
Anyone whose living eye lights upon the lightning bolt of His glance must surely die!

LEONARD
Your face is growing paler... more and more bloodless, by the moment! Let's get out of here! Let's go... can you hear me?

PANKRACY
Place your hands upon my eyes! Strangle my pupils with your fists! Protect me from that stare that grinds me into dust!

LEONARD
Here — is that better? —

PANKRACY
No use, your hands! They're like those of a spirit without bone and flesh... They're as transparent as water... transparent as glass... transparent as air! I can still see!

LEONARD
Lean on me...

PANKRACY
Grant me just a bit of darkness!

LEONARD
O, my master!

PANKRACY
Darkness! Darkness!

LEONARD
Hey, citizens! Hey, brothers! Democrats… help! Hey! Help — help — help!

PANKRACY
Galilaee, vicisti!

He falls into Leonard's arms and dies.

IRYDION

Et cuncta terrarum subacta.

— Horatius

...Aestuat ingens
Uno in corde pudor mixtoque insania luctu
Et Furiis agitatus amor et conscia virtus.

(*Aeneidos*, lib. X)[14]

For Maria. In memory of unique days, now fled.
And thus a familiar voice shall return to her, after many years.[15]

—Dante

---

14   Mottos. From Horace, *Odes* II, 1: 23 "And all the earth subjected." From Virgil, *Aeneid*, X, 870-873 in Robert Fitzgerald's translation: "In that one heart / Shame seethed again, and madness mixed with grief."

15   This does not seem to be a direct citation from Dante's works. It may refer to that portion of the *Purgatorio*, where Beatrice directly reveals herself to Dante for the first time. Overcome with joy and longing, Dante quotes his beloved Virgil: "I feel the stirrings of an ancient flame."

INTRODUCTION

The ancient world is coming to an end — that once was vital in it, now decays, uncouples and raves — both gods and humans rave.

And as Jove, the lord of heaven, so Rome, the lord of all below, perishes, raving. — Only Fate remains calm, unmoved, as the unrelenting *reason* of the world, which looks on from high above at the maelstrom of earth, and heaven.

Among this chaos I lift a song, which leapt from my bosom with force. — May the spirit of destruction come to my aid! — May my inspiration whirl and roll, resounding on all sides, like the lightning bolt, that thunders now above the ages of the past and hurls all life into the abyss — and then let it die, as he did, after achieving his deed. — A new dawn, in the East! But that no longer concerns me.

Where are those figures, who once strutted so proudly, so haughtily, over your seven hills, O Rome? — Where the patricians, with the sacrificial knife and spear in hand, with hearts full of mysteries, with the cloud of terror on their brows; the *patres familias*, the oppressors of the plebs, the conquerors of Italy and Carthage? Where the vestal, ascending the steps of the Capitol in silence, the sacred flame glowing in her palms?

Where are your orators, those masters of myriads of souls, towering above the billowing multitudes, the buzz of whispers and the tempests of applause? — Where the legionnaires, sleepless, gigantic, their faces bronzed by the sun, cooled by toil, lit up by the flashing of swords? — They have all disappeared, one after the other; the past has engulfed them like a mother pulling them to her breast. — No one shall tear them from the arms of the past!

In their place now there arise figures heretofore unknown; neither beautiful like demigods, nor powerful like the giants of titanic ages, but strange ones, shimmering with gold, their brows wreathed, with cups in their hands, with stilettos hidden in the nosegays they bear, with poison brimming their festive cups, dancing with convulsive jerks — as if life knew no bounds amidst the songs and groans, the jabbering of hyenas and the cries of gladiators. — Laughable, such a springtime garnished with blood and the fragrances of burnt incense! — Laughable, such a life! — Such a life is a passage merely; it creates nothing, leaves nothing behind, save a few cheers and the glory of a vain perishing!

The mob and Caesar — there's all of Rome for you!

Isis, mother of wisdom and silence, your two feet splashed with seafoam, your body covered with the dust of a long journey, it is a foreign speech you hear round about you — yet you stand on the Forum Romanum and from thence cannot determine, in your loneliness, in what direction lie the banks of the Nile.

From the hills of Armenia, from the lowlands of Chaldea, Mithras too, the Lord of youth and death, makes his way to Rome and has now taken his place in the subterranean pits of the Capitol; in the still of the night he waves his sacrificial knife above the bodies of his victims.

In Grecian porticoes, in the sweet shade of Corinthian columns, the son of the North stamps with his barbarian tread, — halting at times, and, leaning on his heavy battle-axe, to look about him with his blue eyes, hoping to catch a glimpse of Odin, perchance, the god of his Northern peoples.

Yet Cimbric Odin has not yet arrived — he can't bear to leave his pinewoods and bed of snow, his grey skies, and the choirs of Valhalla. — But just a little while longer, and he too will set off on a pilgrimage to Rome!

Forward, gods! Forward, peoples! — Your roads crisscross east and west, north and south. — Soon there shall be no place for you. — So go, onward on your gyres, to wander and later return!

So it is, usually, in the days leading up to death.

Forward, gods! Forward, peoples! — rave on until you are sated with raving — This will be your last madness, your last chase, you playthings of Fate, that Fate which has adopted the Cross as its scutcheon — All of you, sooner or later, will fall before the Cross.

From out of this panting, perishing world I shall squeeze one more thought — in which my love will be found, though she too is the daughter of madness and the harbinger of the end!

Forward in your madness, on in your dance, gods and people, wheeling around my thought — Be the music to her dreaming — the storm, through which she tears like lightning — for I shall bestow upon her a name, a shape, and though she be conceived in Rome, the day on which Rome falls will not be her last. She shall remain as long as the earth, and earthly nations, remain — but all the same, in heaven there will be no place for her!

*

Where are you, son of vengeance — with what dust are your remains commingled? — Your spirit, amongst what spirits does it tarry?

I have called forth the shades of the departed from the world of ruins — At night the senate assembled before me on the Forum — hunched spectres, weighed down by the memory of villainy... among these you were not to be found!

A gladiator arose from the subterranean passages of the circus and marched at the head of his fellows by the light of the moon — all still bearing their wounds — and in the dream of death their livid mouths repeated: *Morituri te salutant, Caesar...* But among them, I found you not.

On the Palatine, on that hill of ruins and blossoms, the dust of the lords of the world was recomposed for me — They flowed past me — their brows held together by diadems soldered with blood — Each bore upon his forehead the mark of damnation — The winds lifted the purple from their shoulders, and I saw the stars shine through the openings gashed in their bosoms by the stilettos of their murderers — but amongst them I saw you not.

Then I heard the singing and prayers of the martyrs of Christ. Their voices wafted up from the catacombs and ascended straight into Heaven — Amongst these was the voice of one woman, sadder, more beautiful than the others — a voice well known to you once, but now, alone, not united with yours.

Where are you, son of vengeance, son of my song! It is time now to resurrect and trample beneath your heels the corpse of this giant... you remember — so you once swore to do. You abdicated hope, faith, and love, in order to — just once, just once — cast your glance there, and then sink down among the millions...

The hour has struck. For there, where the eternal city once reigned, is now to be found but a broad, open grave, full of bones and rubble, wound about by crawling ivy and the curious. Arise! — Come! — I conjure you... I and a force still more terrible, from which I am unable to preserve you... But all the same I shall tear your name away from your body and it shall pass away with you into oblivion!

Begone! Away from me! — Not for you, my companions, these wild spaces... It is better for you to remain in the Roman Campania, at the foot of the Apennines. I shall go; I wish to look upon him once more before he dies, before he dies for all ages!

In this cave that lies amidst the glooms of the abyss, he lies stretched out upon a bed of marble, breathless, motionless in sleep, dreaming of nothing; and so he awaits his awakening — his promised awakening — terrible, that of the Judgment Day, which is closer to him than it is to the rest of the world!

Ancient rot shines round about like the eyes of sphinxes — a snake, with sun-brilliant scales, sleeps the sleep of the ages at his feet. His countenance is sad, tormented with fever; even so long a sleep has been unable to lave it with coolness.

The form of his body is like a Greek statue; such is not to be found on earth today — his legs, as white as Parian marble in their black buskins are lain upon a black coverlet — Here and there, beneath them, above them, mosses and ivies wind.

A white tunic covers his bosom — He grips the shard of a lamp in his one hand, while his sword, gnawed by rust, rests at his side — his other hand hangs down, dead — in a clenched fist, as if he had fallen asleep in despair.

And so he lies, suspended between sleep and death — suspended between the last thought that formed in his brain ages ago, and this one, which will awaken in him shortly; suspended between the damnation of an entire life and eternal damnation.

Before he awakens I will tell you his story.

*

In the Cimbric Chersonese, in the silver land of streams, your father once walked shoulder to shoulder, like a brother with the kings of the sea, although he had arrived from a far country, although he spoke a foreign tongue, Greek, and bore the face of a Greek demigod.

But the women loved him, and so did the men, for he knew how to sweeten long nights with tales, while during the day, he was the first to battlefield or banquet-hall. — The wild wastes of the grey ocean were to him a familiar highway — from the light of the stars of heaven he deciphered good weather or storm — he could toss the heaviest lance over the tallest spar, and his forehead never lost its calm composure when breasting the fiercest gale.

On land, his horn resounded far over valley and cliff. The bear was no match for him — and when he returned from hunt or foray he would lie down upon the mosses, upon the ferns, and, downing thick cups, he would describe the chase, the grappling, the looting… His home on a far distant shore was studded with ivory and gold — There his slaves, standing on the portico amidst its forest of fluted columns, gazed out at a sea sprinkled with islets sparkling like the stars, scanning for his return — but he was in no hurry, because he had taken a shine to the tones of the conch-trumpet and the songs of the priestesses of Odin… For he had allowed his youth to run riot on errant paths and changing fortunes in order to effect a great deed later on — and thus he lifted the cup to his lips, and drank to the health of old Sigurd, king of men.

"Grimhilda, daughter of Sigurd, my people have groaned in chains for ages now — and along with my own people, a hundred other nations have sat themselves down on all the shores of the southern seas, weeping on the shingle.

"To free them, I have need of the inspiration that glows in your bosom! I myself am descended of slaves, but I possess a vengeful spirit… My enemies are as strong as Titans — in order to undermine them and cast them down, I have need of your inspired breast! — O maiden sacrosanct to Odin, you shall enter into my household, you shall be the companion of my trials, and our children will bring my toils to fruition — and their deeds will stand for ages upon ages!"

Here your father grew quiet and, by degrees, embraced her with the power of his stare and silence — She, standing on a rock, gazed out upon the grey eternity of the sea, and with hair undone, with misty eyes, was powerless, possessed by love. No more would Odin's transom shade her; she had determined to abandon that altar and go, with the foreigner, to a distant shore.

"Hermes, our own warriors have never dared cast a glance upon my forehead — You have arrived like a hero descending from Valhalla and have called 'Grimhilda!' and behold: I must become your slave.

"I know your fatherland not; I know not your enemies. The country to which you wish to draw me, has never appeared before me even in dreaming, and yet I shall go, I shall go, unfortunate one, — shamed amongst all maidens — cursed by the anger of Odin... Permit me only to take my seat upon the holy rock one final time, and sing out my final song!"

*

Amphilochus Hermes walked beside the maiden on carpets of moss, on layers of granite, through the sacred groves hung with frost, amidst the roar of waterfalls — The pines crowded in from all sides; from among their company, here and there the skeleton of an old oak stood, crowned with mistletoe. — Higher up hung a bitter heaven, leaden — and a thousand wild meadows round about, beckoning to the wilds — but the Maiden trod familiar paths leading to the God, to whom she went to bid farewell for all time.

The leaders of the hordes, the lords of the lands, the kings of the sea, their sailors and companions stood in a semicircle before the statue of Odin, awaiting the priestess — Sigurd alone, a descendant of the Gods, the king of all, sat on the stump of a fallen pine and covered his brows with his immense hand — His breast swelled, panting beneath his fish-scale armour — but he was silent, and so were all the rest silent — one heard only the rush of the sea battering the cliffs beyond the pine-grove.

Grimhilda then passed among them, with her eyes fixed on the statue of Odin, toward which she trod in a terrible earnestness. The foreigner remained far behind, amongst his the own retainers, with his arms crossed on his Corinthian armor, leaning against a tree.

Beneath the overhanging vault of the cave, on a boulder carved with runic mysteries, the maiden sat down and, so it seemed, began to dream. The god of the northern tribes loomed above her, his beard and hair congealed with ice, powdered with snow; his eyes were glassy, disturbing, and in his immense palm he gripped a club covered with the bloody gore of victims, while on his chest could be seen the deep wound he caused himself, when, his earthly incarnation having run its course, he desired to return to the banquet-hall of Valhalla.

Her dream lasted long. Only after a long while she emerged from it, slowly; she raised her arms, slowly, and spoke in a voice still muffled and soft: "I recognise you, my lord, amidst your heroes. — Your spirit nears my breast in a black stream — it roars around me like a flood that tears boulders asunder. — I am there, amidst the eddies. — I am there, amidst the omnipotence of your anger — your power is mine — Listen to me, all!"

Suddenly, she threw open her eyelids and uncovered her burning pupils — she thrust her arms out toward the assembly and her hands trembled as if at the moment of death — In her voice was to be heard the tones twisted away from the speech of heroes ascended above the clouds, and who then, among the storms, hastened near, calling to their children:

"Why is it that you chase here and there, day and night, my brothers — Sons of my people, who is it that whips you on from the rear — Who is it ordered you to abandon the land of silver streams?

"The enchained giants have arisen from the snows beneath which they were to lie until the end of the world; they have arisen by half and, beating their shackles against the summits of ice, with greedy nostrils they snuffle the wind for the fragrance of blood carried from afar —

"Can you not hear the hammer of Thor, smashing helmets and breastplates, skulls and breastbones, to dust? — The laughter of kings resounds in the empty air — The spear of Horgiebruda hovers over the entire earth!

"Who can withstand you, O my descendants? — Onward, hasten onward toward the great city! There a banquet awaits you — there cups are foaming with the blood of your enemies! A place has been reserved there for each of you. — Sit you down there in glory, my sons!"

Suddenly, her voice dropped, and changed to a whisper — Her eyes cast about, searching for something in the realm of visions, something that swam about in front of her — Her mouth strained to pronounce a word, some word. — A word that was arising, growing from the depths of her soul, winding itself around her heart like a serpent, and like a serpent fleeing, showing, then hiding itself again… She chased it vainly, as pale as snow, unhappy, fainting — One moment more, and perhaps she might tear it from her breast, for her eyes were shining, her face bright with new raving:

"The city, the city resting on seven hills is aflame! — Precious minerals, transparent stones, melt and flow! Bodies melt into blood and flow! — A great fortress, and a great God has thundered down upon it!... Help, Odin! I shall die unless I pronounce your mystery fully, to the end — His name — who shall tell me His name?"

And thus your mother's head collapsed on her breast and her lips closed tight — the king who continually held his hand on his forehead, did not glance at his daughter even once, and all the others too stood there unmoved, for no one dared approach the sacred boulder...

And so your god went silent, woman, and you too grew silent for ages — Upon your lips, the silence of the grave — upon your brow, the iciness of death. But he, who promised you a different Fatherland, he would not abandon you — he moved out from beneath the shadows of the oak and, inspired himself, hastened toward you with heavy tread. A cry of outrage broke forth from the crowd; the kings of the sea beat their spears against their breastplates. The grey Skalds cried out a curse. But he had already passed the terrible boundary; he bent over you, gave you his hand and said:

"By the name of Rome, by the name of my enemies and yours, I call you back to life. Arise, Grimhilda!..." And turning away, he cried out thrice: "Rome!" — and the Maiden, awakened, arose; again she repeated the mysterious word, repeating it with a voice pregnant with farewell: silent and feminine — and thus she went off after the foreigner, as a wife goes, after her husband.

*

And soon your father, sleepy youth, stood on deck and, with a smile of scepticism, poured full libations into the sea in honour of Poseidon. After which, he turned to his seamen and said, "More strongly hold the sail, more boldly the oars, and the god of the trident will calm these waves."

Beneath their feet, each beam shivered like the body of a woman — off along the horizon, dark strata were massed — from their bosoms flowed billows now gathering in skeins, now parting in sinuous currents, as once the Python slithered before he fell beneath the arrows of the sun — Now and again the flow parted, only to join together again in froths of white — and in the roar of the wind one caught the sound, now of deep breaths, now of terrifying moans.

Beneath the deck-covering, held up by groaning wooden pillars, Hermes sat down on furs taken away from the Cimbric Chersonese and, in his calm voice, explained to the maiden the world to which she was drawing near. He described to her the island of vineyards and copses just off shore of a great land — it is there that he ruled over his plough-men and merchants, his house and his ships. — There was his treasury, full of riches and weaponry... and those weapons would come in handy some day! For in those parts the human race did not romp beneath the leadership of heroes... No, beneath a fashionable yoke, they flaunted their shame in gold, marbles and silks and licked the feet of the city that stood upon the shores of the middle sea.

That city once became the god of lies and oppression in the eyes of the world. Beneath its fatal inspiration brother rose against brother, son against father, traitor against fatherland, and, unconsumed itself for a space of time, it consumed all the kings of the earth! Here peace disappeared from the forehead of your father and he became like the storm that was tossing the ship.

"My own Hellas was once the soul of the nations — Her songs were the world's goddesses — She chased away the barbarians who once challenged her from the east, with the clash of swords and the thrum of her lyres alike.

"The fire of heaven, stolen from the gods, was given to her alone... Wretched she, who trusted that city of damnation! — The rabble from the middle sea sailed to her happy isles, to her myrtle-clad shores. They did not conquer her with swords, but spread around the poison of flattery, inebriating her with the false nectar of promises!"

At that moment, the clouds parted — the wind tore them asunder in the west, and a few stars peeked through the heavens. Hermes took but one look and, before they were covered again by the gloomy skies, called to the helmsman: "Bear starboard, bear starboard all through the night, and at this same time tomorrow we shall pass through the Straits of Cadiz!" Then, pulling her close to his breast, he renewed his account of his ancestor Philopoemen, one of the last who battled against the sordid city... After him there was to be one more barbarian king to take the field and, after thirty years of fruitless battling, to succumb at last to a self-dealt blow — And since that time, no third had arisen in defence of the land!

And thus he did homage to the great Mithridates in a moment of silent reflection. Then he returned to his sad story — to which she listened with unmoved, but burning eyes. "Grimhilda, your god allowed you to divine in inspiration what I conjured myself at times through hatred, through the surmise of hope, from the night of future ages. Let us rejoice then, daughter of kings — for that city of unrighteousness, after having murdered all of the living, all of the free, has now turned its weapon against its own breast!

"The treasures they have sucked from the breasts of the earth will in a short while no longer suffice them. Soon the weapon, grown heavy in their hand, will slide from their grip — through the clamour of slaughter and feasting, their last hour begins to sound. O my wife, laugh at these billows and gales, for it is not our fate to perish here; no, we shall participate in the grand destruction!"

At these words, the voice of the hero took on even bitterer and more sarcastic tones — He recalled the gods of Hellas, once powerful, in whom at that time hardly anyone believed — their oracles long grown silent. But their idols stood yet, for it is hard for an old world to unaccustom itself to the habits of its youth. All of the gods of the earth have made their appearance in the city of damnation. Some of them beautiful, like to the immortals themselves, being the work of Greek chisels — others monstrous, sprung from desert sands, and the summits of distant mountains… But he knew that there is only one God, who before all ages placed His hand on the whirlpools of chaos and conquered them for all time.

"And what is His name?" — asked the priestess of Odin.

"Destiny" — and at this Hermes got up and walked to the stern of the boat, because the storm had doubled in fury.

*

Do you remember the island of Chiara, on which you grew up with your sister, the divine Elsinoe? Do you remember the campaigns of your father, when he raised on his masts, not the triangular sails of Greece, but the elongated, barbarian ones, himself wearing a Dacian cap, with a Cimbric battle-axe in hand, as he stole out of the bay at night and set sail for the wilds of the archipelago?

All of the dreams of Jugurtha and Mithridates came alive in his soul, — his desires and his deeds flew ceaselessly toward the wild tribes. He wandered the Maeotian marshes, he erred about the deserts where the wind-legged steeds fly, he wandered the wilds of Sirte, where in the depths of Africa arrow-tips are tainted with venom… ever in search of the enemies of his enemy. He clasped the hands of savage kings, learning their tongues, embracing their weapons, spilling his gifts at their feet and fanning the embers of their lusts with the promise of delight and booty.

Then were the days and nights long and painful for your mother. But no slave, no foreigner, ever deciphered from her visage traces of her suffering; her voice never trembled when giving commands.

Only sometimes did she take both you and your sister by the hands and lead you through the long porticoes into the depths of the palace. And there in an alcove studded with conchs and covered in moss stood a warrior of stone.

His forehead was furrowed in immortal savagery; in one hand, he held the skull of a dead enemy, and at his feet were slabs of ice chiseled from Parian marble.

Before him your mother was wont to bow her head and muse on her former Fatherland: "O my Irydion, O my Sigurd, you shall never behold that land of silver, nor your grandfather, a king among men. — Behold: this god is sacred unto me — the terrible source of my vatic inspiration, the Lord of Valhalla, the never-conquered Odin." — And then, pressing her daughter to her breast: "Where is your father, Elsione, tell me: Where is Hermes at this moment? I hear the sweep of the wind and the mournful moans of the waves. His ship is there, among the eternal waters; listing, with shredded sails; or perhaps he finds himself tossed up on some godless shore… But no — he shall conquer the storms, he shall put off the wild-man, and return to us in the glory of a demigod."

And when the horn announcing an arrival sang from the sea, when it sounded again, closer, among the lemon groves, when, dripping with the dew of night, burned by the sun and bronzed by the rains, Hermes flung himself into his wife's embrace and his black eye, passionate, burned with the splendour of hope — then again the peaceful and happy days resumed on Chiara, and the priestess forgot all of her bitter forebodings. You two ran about again in liberty, in delight, over the lawns and among the flowers, on the shores among the seashells, throughout the marble halls among the tripods and incense, resting yourselves from time to time upon your mother's breast, or on your father's lap; and he, each evening, pronounced a blessing upon your heads as they nodded towards sleep: "Remember," he would say, "remember to hate Rome! And when you grow up, let each of you harry her with your curses — you, with fire and sword — you, with your inspiration, and the treason that only a woman knows…"

From time to time a proconsul or a praetor would arrive at Chiara, or sometimes it was the freedman of some Caesar come to enjoy your father's hospitality — at which times Hermes had long couches and tables set out — The wines of Lesbos coursed in streams — The voices of slaves were raised in song — slaves of the lyre, who sang the lays of old Homer. "Anacreon, Anacreon!" the Romans would cry. At which, with a sarcastic smile, your father would nod toward the singers while the Romans filled their cups to the brim, passing round fresh garlands, and when they began to mumble in drunken comraderie and joke, he would speak, as if offhand, about the deeds of the past; of the glory of the state won through the wars with the Carthaginians, and also of the Legions of Varrus cut down, the Spanish revolts of Sertorius — And he drank to the health of the Emperor, until the cup burst in his fingers!

*

Soon there approached the thirteenth anniversary of the day on which the priestess abandoned her gods. — Her voice grew wild; she summoned her children — Her eye grows wild when she pressed you to her breast — as she recalled her father, her sisters, the rulers of the people — And a half-spoken word of farewell fell from her lips. — Only before Hermes was her crazed raving humbled. "What is it that you lack, my Grimhilda, daughter of kings?" — "Have you not heard of the vengeance of the immortal spirits? — Only for a time was I lent you — At the edges of the world there lies an island bound in ice, yet upon it a mountain pulses with fire — There, a giant enchanted has already stretched forth an arm, extending a hand towards the abyss, into which he will toss the snowy skein of my life."

Hermes raised his hand above her forehead. The shadow of his palm, like a rivulet of peace, fell upon her brow and sank into her soul: "Behold that flaming sky, that sea of sparks, where your northern clouds and your useless gods gather — the star of Amphilochus protects you! She will not give you over unto the evil spirits." But even as he spoke, he felt a strange weight begin to constrict his own heart as well.

*

What cry is that rebounding off the interior vault, and shattering among the columns of the portico? The slaves hastened into the depths of the palace, where the chamber of their lord was located. There on the bed of porphyry lay the priestess, with the Greek leader of men standing at its foot, with bowed head. Beneath his foot he crushed a cup, on the brim of which a few last drops of the fatal liquor yet clung. — The slaves dropped their heads as well; they waited, they listened, and when he turned around, they shuddered: because for the first time in his life, a pain greater than his strength befouled his visage. He turned around — and commanded that his son and daughter be led near.

"Grimhilda! Now it is I who call upon your god! There, where amidst his heroes he sits on the highest throne, drinking blood; even there, may the curse of Amphilochus the Greek fly! O my wife, leave me not…! In vain, all in vain… Only a few drops remain! The entire cup of poison is churning in your bosom, O my Grimhilda!"

At this she lifted herself up, as pale as the image on the lid of a sarcophagus. "I saw him three times tonight — he descended from Valhalla like a black sea and called to me: 'O my priestess.'

"I saw him extend his iron-clad arms above my sleeping Irydion, and above Elsinoe asleep; I heard him in his might curse their earthly lives, should I refuse to go to him.

"Only for a while was I lent you. There beneath his feet lies a sacrificial knife and a black shroud, the funereal wreath of his priestesses. You will lay the one beside me; you will cover my face with the other when I die."

And sliding from the bed, she tottered toward him on feet of marble, her elevated figure leaning towards him, her arms stretched out in his direction, fluttering, as if she wished to disperse the shades of death, while the flutings of her white robes trailed behind her. She reached him, fell upon him, and he supported her with one encircling arm. Together they began to move toward the fane. He trod heavily, step by step, struggling against an unknown power. They stopped, and he cast his eyes aloft, like Prometheus on his rock, like Laocoon on the shore of the sea, flinging the misery of this world into the faces of the gods. But he would not lower himself to utter a moan; remaining silent, he pushed on with his burden. Destiny dragged them both forward.

Then did her glance fall upon your head for the final time, Irydion, there at the feet of Odin, she bade you farewell in the name of your grandfather: "Sigurd, be you for me the terror of the haughty — Elsinoe, my spirit will be with you always. Never forget the land of streams, and my god — O my children, it is for your sake that I die." Then did her lips grow deathly pale. Livid shadows broke across her face, and then she beckoned you, only again to cast you away from her envenomed breast.

Then, suddenly, her thought abandoned those present, and flew to other regions and times. There, her ancient father was sitting in silent brooding; there, the kings of the sea cursed her; she stretched forth her hand — she would prophesy, as she dies: "To battle, my brothers! Pitch your tents on the seven hills! You shall feast on the summit of the Capitol. There, far below, gnashing her teeth, weeping in chains, trod underfoot, shall lie Roma, Roma, Roma —"

And thus she fell before her god. Amphilochus lifted her in his arms — she wished to twine her arm around his neck — but her arm fell — and she sank down on her back, her hair flowing, falling ever lower, until her body slipped from his embrace, as stiff as if it were made of marble.

He knelt, and placed the black veil, the funereal wreath of priestesses, upon her brow, after which he rose, and wildly racing, cried out — "Slaves! Where is the battle-axe of the Cimbric Chersonese?" The slaves gave it him and, gripping it tightly, and tensing all of his mortal strength against the immortals, he moved heavily toward the idol. He raised the iron aloft, swung it thrice over his head like lightning, and with his fourth swing knocked over the god, his enemy, and trod him underfoot in the silence of despair!

*

Such is your inheritance, such is your past history, O descendant of Philopoemen, grandson of the king of men, sleepy Irydion! Then did your father abandon the house of his fathers on Chiara and with the urn of Grimhilda he sailed for Rome. Having lost her whom he loved, he hastened to encamp in the midst his enemies, and, at least, indulge his empty heart with the fullness of hatred.

And the day foretold, the day of destruction, now draws near its appointed time.

PART I

A hall in Irydion's palace in Rome. — From both sides, colonnades diminish in the distance — in the middle is a fountain and tripods, upon which incense is burning. — Irydion is seated beneath a statue of his father — Slaves are lighting alabaster lamps.

SLAVE 1
Amphilochus' son rests his head upon the dead master's feet.

SLAVE 2
On the cold marble, and he has fallen asleep.

SLAVE 3
Meanwhile, our lady his sister faints and weeps in the gyneceum.

SLAVE 4
By Pollux, I've heard rumours that the Heliogabalus' negros are to tear her from us this evening.

SLAVE 1
Peace to him — Let's go, my brothers, let's leave him be.

They exit.

IRYDION
They depart as quietly as spirits, respecting my soul at rest. O, father, as far as they and everyone else are concerned, I sleep. You alone know that I am wide awake, waiting.
He gets up and goes over to a bronze shield, upon which a dagger is hanging.
Dusk falls, the hour approaches. — They will be here shortly — at such an hour old Brutus had to put his own sons to death…
He pounds the shield.

Elsinoe — Elsinoe! — Ah! She approaches: like the spirit of misfortune. She has set a cypress wreath upon her brows… Her mother once trod so, burdened with the ire of Odin.

ELSINOE
Enters
Have the lackeys arrived? The chariot of perdition?

IRYDION
No, not yet. I wanted to pour into you, one last time, my father's spirit.

ELSINOE
Oh, my brother.

IRYDION
You know yourself that, in his insanity, Caesar has demanded that the Senate declare you divine, and has ordered images of you to be set up in the temples of the city. You know yourself that you are no longer my sister, no longer fair-haired Elsinoe, the hope of our house, the darling of my heart — you have now become a sacrifice for the suffering of many and the shame of your fathers!

ELSINOE
Yes… So you have taught me since my childhood, and thus I am ready. But not today, not yet, not tomorrow… a little later, after I pull myself together, after I've heard my fill of the wisdom of Masinissa and your own commands… After I've downed to the dregs the chalice of your poison!

IRYDION
Chosen one, prepare yourself for your destiny. We must hasten along the road we now already tread.

ELSINOE
Do you remember how we once played on the lawns of Chiara? How I loved you, my brother! I used to weave chaplets of rose and myrtle for you… Oh, have pity on me!

IRYDION
Woman! Tempt me not to mercy! Your pleading is in vain!

ELSINOE
And so my final appeal, my sorrow, is unheard. In days past, it was the custom to redeem oneself to people and the gods through death. Look: There is your stiletto, Irydion. Let us hasten to the vacuum, Irydion!

IRYDION
You blaspheme against the thoughts of my father. We must live and suffer in order that the great soul of Amphilochus may rejoice among the shades. O sister, in ancient times, one man's death alone sufficed for the salvation of entire nations… today the times are different… today one must even offer up one's honour! *He embraces her.* Today you will wind your brows with roses, and place a smile upon your lips, — O, my poor sister, rest your poor head here a space… Your brother embraces you for the last time in your father's house. Bid me farewell in all the beauty of your virgin freshness. After today, I will never again see you young — never, never again! He will poison you with his envenomed breath, he… but he will perish; do you understand me, sister? He will perish along with his entire nation!

ELSINOE
Today I rest upon your bosom, O brother, but later, upon whose?

IRYDION
These pillars tremble upon their bases; black shadows flit among them. Gods, let me not fall here, on the very lip of the arena! Masinissa, come!

VOICE FROM BEYOND THE COLONNADE
Whoever hesitates was born to empty words, not deeds. Such a one I greet with derision and depart from with disdain.

Enter Masinissa.

MASINISSA
Those sent from Caesar now near your threshold.

IRYDION
You, upon whose brow is written the word Strength — You, who stand at the edge of your grave, as exalted as you were in the days of your youth, breathe your strength into me at this prophesied moment!

MASINISSA
Where is the chosen maiden? Where the garland of flowers for the beloved of Caesar?
He tears away the cypress wreath from the brows of Elsinoe.
Today our great work is begun!

Enter from the depths of the hall handmaids in costly vestments.

CHORUS OF HANDMAIDS
As was Aphrodite, newly sprung from the azure waves of ocean, amidst the chaste sea-foam, amidst the fragrant zephyrs, so shall you be! We bring you roses, incense, and pearls! As was Helen in the hour of her ravishment, trembling in the arms of Paris, blushing and coloured with the flames of desire, so shall you be! We bring you roses, incense, and pearls!

IRYDION
Take her by the hand, old man.
He leads his sister toward the statue of Amphilochus.
Hear me, woman, as if I were about to die, as if you were never again to hear my voice. You are about to cross a hateful threshold; you are to live among the damned; you will give over your body to the son of turpitude — but your soul, let your soul remain clean and fragrant — shield her with your mystery; make her as unapproachable as the holy of holies, in which our mother was wont to prophesy!

ELSINOE
Woe, woe to the orphaned daughter!

IRYDION
Never allow Caesar to fall asleep on your breast — Never let him be far from the shouts of praetorians calling each other to arms, the whispers of patricians conspiring treachery, the thuds of the fists of the people

beating against the palace gates! Do this slowly, day by day, drop by drop, until you have enmeshed him in madness and sucked all the life out of his heart. And now arise. Bow your head.
He places his hands on her head.
Conceived in the desire of vengeance, raised in the hope of vengeance, destined to infamy and perdition, I here devote you to the manes of Amphilochus the Greek!

ELSINOE
The voices of Erebus flutter about on all sides… O my mother!

CHORUS OF HANDMAIDS
Encircling her
Why do your members shiver beneath their veil of white, beneath the ribbons of purple with which we bind your bosom? Why do you grow pale beneath the garland, which we have plaited to adorn your forehead?

IRYDION
Look! She faints, the unfortunate girl!

MASINISSA
No, she begins her new life now, as she must live. Do you not see how her lips, her foaming lips, are labouring?

ELSINOE
As I leave my father's portico, I take not my household gods with me, and my holy garland, immaculate, I toss amidst the ashes of my father's hearth. Condemned by my father, condemned by my brother… Never again shall I return; I go now to torments and an endless mourning! Mother! Hasten to Odin with prayers for your daughter! Hurry, mother! Beg not a long life for me. Inspiration, nothing but inspiration! This womb of mine will never bear mortal children, but the future itself will be conceived within my bosom! Roma will entrust herself to my love — Roma will fall into her last sleep in my embrace!

Enter Eutychian at the head of Ethiopians bearing gifts.

EUTYCHIAN
The thricely holy, thricely fortunate Emperor, Caesar, Augustus, High Priest, Tribune and Consul, sends his greetings to the son of Amphilochus, and to his divine sister he sends one hundred purple conchs, one hundred cups of amethyst…

ELSINOE
Inspiration, inspiration amidst torments!

IRYDION
It has come to pass.
He takes his sister by the arm and leads her to Eutychian.
Take the fair-haired girl.

EUTYCHIAN
A chariot of ivory awaits the daughter of fortune!

IRYDION
I give a dowry of fifty of my own gladiators to Caesar, for she likes to look upon their sport. Go — they go with you…
He strikes the shield again — the troop of handmaids and Ethiopians depart with Elsinoe.

CHORUS OF GLADIATORS
From the depths
Are we off to hunt beasts? Or to overcome your enemies? Or to defend your sister?
They enter.

IRYDION
My brothers all, Greek and Barbarian, ransomed by me from the maw of the Roman people! — be faithful to me until the day of looting arrives!

CHORUS OF GLADIATORS
We shall, until our bodies are trampled into the thick bloody sand — our wiry, naked, elastic bodies!

IRYDION
You hear them yet: their footsteps and their voices — after them. I entrust the head of Elsinoe to the protection of your short swords: and when you stand before the Emperor, bow low to him, your new lord!

CHORUS OF GLADIATORS
Death to him! — an early death!
They exit.

IRYDION
Ancient oppressors of the world — looters of Hellas — sons of falsehood and perjury, I have sacrificed an unhandled virgin to you. Immortal gods, wherever you may be, hear my prayer! May she be the penultimate offering tossed into the gullet of Rome; and I, from among so many wretches chosen from all corners of the globe, ripped away by threat and torment, forgotten after agony and death, let me be the last!

MASINISSA
Sigurd!

IRYDION
Do not address me by that name! Or give me first the kings of the sea, surround me with the people of my grandfather, and not a thread of the purple raiments of the Caesars will remain! But my road has been traced before me through the darkness… wherever I stretch out my arms, there I find obstacles like unto iron, yet mobile like serpents, and among them I crawl without being, without life!

MASINISSA
Place your hope and faith in the miseries and stagnation of people, for Destiny has placed you at the gates of a crumbling city… She has enwrapped you in crisis and decrepitude of which you yourself have no part — there will come a time for laments; someday, some later day … someday…

IRYDION
Ah! Shame upon these Nazarenes, who prefer to be slaughtered like cattle rather than to fight like men! It is they, they who hold me back!

MASINISSA
Alexian, the son of Mammea, goes down to them each day and holds counsel with their high priests. If you don't forestall him, he will tip the balance, sweep away Heliogabalus, and found his own Nazarene empire, and then Rome will last for ages upon ages!

IRYDION
No, by Thor! I swear that he will never become Caesar!

MASINISSA
The fate of Rome will be decided in the catacombs! Go — with their sign on your breast, with their blemish on your forehead, with their mysteries on your lips. Instill in them a thirst for vengeance upon behalf of their God still unavenged. Where are His altars? Where is His glory on the face of the earth? And when you will arm them, lead them, when you will place in their hands the forbidden sword, O, then, my son, my spirit will be with you!
He comes close and rests his arm upon Irydion's shoulder.
Do you remember the evening on which your father lay dying, when he called out, "Masinissa, I hand my son and my thought over into your keeping?" I bent over him then as I bend over you right now: O Hermes, there among the shades of the underworld, ask after Masinissa, and you will be told: he never abandoned the one you entrusted to his charge, never, to the very end! O Hermes, our spirits are linked as a trinity, and nothing is able to separate them.

IRYDION
That of which you speak took place at an hour just like this… Only, Elsinoe was with me, and wept in my arms!

MASINISSA
Today I repeat what I said then. Believe, and have faith until the end. Together on earth, together before and after the fall of Rome! O, my chosen child, I shall never leave you, never…!

IRYDION
Strong currents of energy flow from your desiccated breast. Give me your hand, Old Man. Yes! Together before, and after, the fall of Rome!

He sinks upon the chair before the statue.
It all took place at an hour just like this… The dying man's eyes burned like stars ascendant… and it was then I swore … Can you hear that mad hubbub? Caesar has opened his purses and spread sesterces among the mobs as largesse, and the mobs rejoice in their Caesar's delights —
He covers his head with his toga
Leave me alone with the hell of my heart!

*

A temple in the subterranean spaces beneath the Capitol. — A giant statue of Mithras in the depths — faint music is heard, fading — enter the chaplain and the soothsayers. — Heliogabalus is dressed in the robes of a high priest, with him is Elsinoe.

HELIOGABALUS
Now you have seen my power, fair-haired Grecian. I have conversed with the god of light and the genius of darkness, and the highest of the high priests of the Orient have stood amazed at my words, my sacrifice.

ELSINOE
The daughter of ice holds these soft, dissolute gods, drowned in clouds of incense and wound about by flutes, in contempt! Smeared in the blood of timid deers and infants! And the diamond sun that shines there on your silken breast is nothing compared with the sun of heaven, shining off the snows of the north…

HELIOGABALUS
You viper whom I love! What more do you want?

ELSINOE
Where Odin, the lord of my mother, sits forged of iron and oak, unmoved by rain and frost and winds, with a goblet full of the foaming blood of heroes — there from the south the cliffs break apart in armrests for his throne, and he, resting upon the rock, gazes toward the northern sea that breaks at his feet in floes of ice.
She takes off her garland of hyacinth and throws it at Heliogabalus.

Faded flowers, fly to that fainting blossom! The daughter of the Cimbric priestess will touch no down-filled cushion!
She moves away.

HELIOGABALUS
Remain for the mysteries of Baal! Remain, nymph! I am the archpriest! I am beautiful, the Delphic Apollo… There was a time when an entire legion acclaimed me Caesar for the smoothness of my cheeks. Nymph, remain! I command you! I am Augustus, Antoninus, Aurelius, the Lord of Rome, Africa, and India. Why are you silent? Why is your glance so cold and piercing? At your feet I have poured earrings and armlets, cloth of purple, expensive sapphires; I have set feasts before you, such as were never dreamed of by the lovers of Sardanapalus! You wander about in gardens more beautiful than the Elysian Fields… One hundred lions fought to the death before you yesterday! I have banished all my concubines; and yet you remain as unbowed as marble — radiant and cold!

ELSINOE
You annoy me, you annoy me, you child nourished with birds' brains. I have been in Valhalla, among my forefathers who sit on thrones, each with the grave of an enemy at their feet! The murmur of these words of yours has interrupted my thoughts, which were far hence — in depths unplumbed — What is it you want? What is it you ask of me? It's late now; the best time to summon my gods. Farewell, Augustus, Caesar, Aurelius…

HELIOGABALUS
O fair-headed one, most beautiful, most shapely, I conjure you, I beg you! Behold: I am all atremble; I die here before you! Ye gods and goddesses! In all of Asia none of you have created such a face, such a bosom, such eyes of azure!

ELSINOE
Quiet — the voice of my mother is piercing the winds!

HELIOGABALUS
I shall prostrate myself at the foot of the altar and kiss the toes of your white feet.
He approaches her.

ELSINOE
For me arms of iron are needed, and lips that sound the horrid songs of battles. Be off to your praetorians, you slave of praetorians!

HELIOGABALUS
Falls before the altar.
You cursed woman! You shall die before your time! Before all of the assembled people I shall have you crucified. O beautiful one! Listen! If Caesar is not enough for you, I shall give you Mithras as well! I shall ordain that you be entitled the Consort of Mithras! I can do all things...

Be with me one moment more... I'm better when you are present, even if you be distant. I am to be pitied: so young, and already surrounded by conspiracies and death! I am sick, sick, and all the riches of the world cannot help me. The blood of men and beasts, the aroma of incense and blossoms, are already unable to help Heliogabalus. Can you hear me? Do you want me to die of my fury? Nymph — Elsinoe! Here, next to one another, hand in hand, brow resting upon brow, let us sleep!

ELSINOE
Yes, sleep, until the centurion arrive to murder Caesar. Wretched one, tell me, where are your arms? You poor fellow, how can you hold the hilt of a sword with these fingers of wax! Wait — I shall go and inquire of my gods if any hope yet remains you.
She exits.

HELIOGABALUS
To the emperor! Help for the emperor!

Enter sorcerers, priests, Eutychian.

CHORUS OF PRIESTS
What has befallen the offspring of the sun, the lord of mystery and sacrifice? His lips are moist with foam, and the star of splendour has burst upon his chest — his eyes in their frenzy now seem to call for blood, and now for delight, only to grow weak again, and... call for eternal sleep.

HELIOGABALUS
The Furies shall tear apart my limbs... I know... I know...

EUTYCHIAN
Evoe Bacche! My student, drunk after your pattern, once conquered India, drunk...

HELIOGABALUS
Alexian shall press cold steel to my neck and whisper, "your throat, if you please, Caesar!" Defend me... Each of you will receive ten talents!

EUTYCHIAN
I'll be the first to run Caesar through for ten talents...

HELIOGABALUS
Have mercy on me! — The sun will avenge me!

CHORUS
Arise, divine Caesar — You are our lord, and the entire earth is subject to your will. The gods are inimical, jealous of your glory, and so they persecute you with these fatal visions. But they shall disappear in the eternal fire, in the light of most immaculate Mithras, as the cloudy wave does in the azure sea, as the body of Semele in the power of Jove!

HELIOGABALUS
Arising from the floor.
Your hand, slave... Who was it called you here? I want her, in my bed — Do you hear? — I want her body, trembling in my embrace! Otherwise all of you, however many of you stand before me now, will perish by the fangs of leopards!

EUTYCHIAN
Mehercule! I'm at least worth a lion.

HELIOGABALUS
Silence! I want none of your jokes today. Where is she?

CHORUS
Her figure hovers among dark shades. Her foreign god is fighting with our god!

HELIOGABALUS
Silence! listen…

ELSINOE
In the depths, on a stone covered with hieroglyphs.
I have consulted them all… At first, they were silent, seated on their thrones, each, as if having fallen asleep after feasting.
    I have consulted them all. One shook his black armour. One only awoke for a moment, to lift an unfinished chalice to his calm lips.
I have consulted them all — and there, where the chalice touched the lips, a drop of blood slid down and, falling through the heavens, fell upon my brows…

HELIOGABALUS
Speak, my divine one! I am not yet condemned, right? I shall not perish before my time?

ELSINOE
On your knees, everyone! The sentence of the gods thunders in my soul.

HELIOGABALUS
Genuflecting
Forgive me, great Mithras!

EUTYCHIAN
Genuflecting
Good night, great Mithras!

CHORUS
Genuflecting
May she perish, the foreign woman, O holy, thrice-holy, swift flying Mithras!

ELSINOE
And then I saw on the plains of the earth a man clad in iron and terror... His brow was as calm as the surface of deep waters. In his right hand, he held the sword of triumph.
　I knew him — though I did not comprehend... though I trusted not myself.
But his name was repeated by the winds of night, and a voice flew down from the summit of Valhalla: "He shall save Caesar."

HELIOGABALUS
His name, his name?

ELSINOE
Sigurd, the son of the priestess.
She moves away from the stone and nears Heliogabalus.
Grovel no more in the dust! Arise, and you, all of you, be gone!

They leave.

ELSINOE
Wretch! If it was required of you to mount the burly shoulders of the waves and ride them, like a horse without bridle... If you had to lay down upon the snow, surrounded by murders of ravens, gazing all night long into the icy eye of the moon... O, you wretch with your purple and your gods! But stop your shivering! Stop your despairing. The son of Amphilochus the Greek will deliver you from the maw of the waters.

HELIOGABALUS
Who? Your brother — Irydion — Yes! His black pupils scatter strange flashes of light. O, if this entire people had but one head, which I might cut off and send toppling to the earth with one axe blow! Then might I fall asleep on your bosom, in peace! Irydion Amphilochides! —
　He shall be my good genius — say it, once more!

ELSINOE
Give me your hand, boy, and fear not, as long as my gods watch over you.

She leads him out.

*

Another part of the palace of the caesars — a peristyle — in the centre, before the altar of sacrifice, sits Mammea, with Alexander Severus before her — in the depths, a porch separated from the rest by a narrow walkway.

MAMMEA
They've seen tears in his eyes a few times, but no one's ever noticed a smile on his face. His features, they say, remind one of Plato, but something more severe, austere, reigns on his brows. Even his worst enemies agree in this.

ALEXANDER
Day after day my heart is more attracted to his teachings.

MAMMEA
Trust my words — in them are found the only wisdom on the earth and the only hope after death.

Ulpianus appears at the porch.

MAMMEA
Rising
Is that you, Domitian?

ALEXANDER
It's he, my Domitian! The most beloved of all people, my childhood master!

Goes up and flings himself into his embrace.

ULPIANUS
Be of good cheer — and you too, Augusta, for I bring you fortunate tidings.

MAMMEA
Ah! How long you have been silent! With how many sad forebodings you've filled my heart! Glory be to the immortal gods, that they were not borne out in truth.

ULPIANUS
I did not write to you from Antioch, because I was afraid that someone might go through my letters. The closer I got to my goal, the closer I had to keep my counsel. And now, it seems that we are indeed near the long-desired end!

MAMMEA
Tell us, tell us!

ULPIANUS
Gazing around
These walls — deaf and dumb?

ALEXANDER
You may be bold! Look, I cry aloud boldly that my young life has grown sick under this yoke. Just yesterday, the imperator's dwarf, that hunchback Roboam, brought me a basket of poisoned fruit, which I kicked aside with my foot!

ULPIANUS
Don't get carried away, Alexian. Be patient a while yet. Let a shrinking humility be read in your eyes, and let your enemies call you a timid child.

Great things are worked by calmness of mind and solemnity of body. What would I have accomplished, had I fallen upon Antioch and Laodicea, upon Ephesus and Smyrna, crying vengeance, testifying before the gods that Heliogabalus is unworthy of the throne, unworthy even of life? I was in all those places, yet first I examined the crowds of the people and the legionary cohorts with a silent eye. I listened to each complaint with a seemingly indifferent ear, and only when I was certain that the seed of hatred was mature to bursting, that everyone was desirous of change, did I say within myself: "The time has come. One spark, and all of Asia will be aflame." Then did I approach the tribunes and quaestors and praetors, striking bargains with them — showing these the profits they could obtain, those the high offices, linking all these benefits of their own desire to your elevation. Then the news arrived that your brother had named you Caesar-consul. Intuiting that this favour merely covered a black ruse, I hastened to Rome immediately, bringing you, in the name of the legions, the promise of a more glorious fortune. Just allow a little more time to pass, and it is sure to strike the shoreline of our salvation!

ALEXANDER
Why should this be put off until tomorrow?

ULPIANUS
Because in Rome, the imperator is surrounded with people who love him for his naumachias, and with praetorians, who praise him for a profligacy worthy of a god. I know for certain that the people love their Caesar, until they murder him. I also know that the praetorians, who are encamped beyond the city, have long supported our designs.

ALEXANDER
The tribune Aristommachus has made it known to me just today that, at any moment, he is ready to risk his life for me and Mammea.

ULPIANUS
Aristommachus will be the one at the crucial moment… but until then, let him keep silent, if he can; at the moment, this is the only service he is able to render us. There are others, more prudent and capable than he. And the palace guard, the soldiers, scattered about the city, do you set them at naught? Are you unaware of the fact that, each day, they are bathed in Caesar's graces? Alexian, even the East doesn't belong to us entirely. — The Syrians have not forgotten that they knew Heliogabalus when he was a child in Emesa, and later, as high priest in the temple of the sun. At any rate, remember that he who rules, why, the very name "ruler" remains him long after the supports of his

power have begun to rot. What a power such a silly word possesses among the people!

MAMMEA
I don't deny the truth of your words, but hurry, as much as you may. For we are standing at the lip of the grave, surrounded by the envoys of his insanity and fury… at any given moment, the splotches of poisoning may appear on these cheeks, and this poor child of mine, this glory of mine, this my future, will crawl up to rest his head on his mother's lap and perish!

ULPIANUS
Yet today I will be in the tent of Aristommachus and at the house of Lucius Tubero. *Approaches Alexander.* Heir of Augustus, fear not that the Parcae will snip the thread of your life before you win rule over your people. No — the gods will be merciful towards this tortured city. But, when you do obtain power, beware the venom hidden beneath the tunic of Deianira, woven into the purple of the Caesars!

MAMMEA
Know you not that the last hope, and the last glory, of Rome are here to be found in this son of mine? I have taught him the love of man according to the thought of Plato, according to the words of Christ — he will extend a brother's hand to the misprised and oppressed!

ULPIANUS
Teach him also to extend a punishing hand toward the unruly and refractory! In all the bazaars of Asia I have seen Roman knights embracing freedmen like brothers. There from their curule chairs they rule the world, balancing the scales of commerce in their hands; from there do they send abroad runners with false news, in order to raise or lower prices; there do they confiscate the goods of others, and those who appeal to them, they thrust into black dungeons or nail to the cross. I have seen these things — and have turned my eyes from them in horror!

ALEXANDER
Thus the descendants of the great consuls, the dictators!

ULPIANUS
Today, their cruelty does us faithful service. I shall lead you to the throne over their necks, as if over the steps of a staircase. But when you sit down upon that throne, spurn that staircase with your foot, so that it may fall to pieces and be swallowed by the abyss; and for that, something more than just the teachings of Christ is necessary!

ALEXANDER
I know the labour that has fallen to my part. My nights are spent musing on the feats of Dacian Trajan. I shall either equal them, or I shall perish young!

ULPIANUS
Alexian, think also on the Republic, and muse upon the men who walked about in togas at that time. Ah! And what has remained us of their glorious example? Where is that Roman people, upon whose ears the words of the law fall more melodiously than the verses of Homer, the dreams of Plato? Where will you see in this city, today, a face unmarked by filth? Who will hear today the laughter of pure joy? All the foreheads are crowned with a grey unwreathed by deeds — the villainous old age of fear or boredom! Sorcerers, sophists, singers and dancers choke the Forum, and whole ages have passed since the day that Julius spurred his horse into the ford of the Rubicon. But it is difficult to return to the past. It was already too late for that in the days of Cassius. We can only pray the gods send us a lord, whose right hand will return youth to the state, and an iron rod to flash in the lictors' grip, instead of an olive branch!

MAMMEA
I knew both gloomy and holy people in the East. They said that better, new times were to arrive; that after so many miseries, a Caesar would appear who would recognise their God!

ULPIANUS
Nazarenes! Augusta, I have spent my life in thought on things human and divine, and I do not care for those moles, who tunnel porous our land!

MAMMEA
You have not yet shaken off blind superstition!

ULPIANUS
Capitoline Jove, heed not these blasphemous words. I am a Roman of the old type — I have come of age among these monuments of freedom and glory, though they had all vanished from the earth before I saw the light of day. A state, in decline and close to its fall, has given birth to these nauseating, scandalous people, but the repair of that state can only come about through their extermination! *Taking Alexander by the hand.* Only thus will you rebuild the city — by that, which first brought it into life: unfailing bravery, and devotion to the mysterious rites of our forefathers. May everything else, foreign gods and foreign peoples, perish utterly!

ALEXANDER
My mother respects the Christians, for in their laws are hidden troves of constancy and virtue. Gaze, Domitian, upon her eyes, bedecked with tears. She likes the Christians, for they support me.

ULPIANUS
So use them as a support, which you may knock away from you later. This is my final word on that subject.

Music is heard.

ULPIANUS
Syrian flutes! Can it be that the archpriest of Mithras is on his way to visit his beloved brother?

MAMMEA
No — every day at this same hour he descends to the Palatine gardens with his lover.

ULPIANUS
In the east I heard many convoluted stories concerning this Greek maiden. Those who arrived from Rome stated that it was her brother who grovelled and cajoled, and later vilely sold her to the emperor.

MAMMEA
And you believe that?

ULPIANUS
My grey hairs have long ceased to wonder at villainy, although my black ones still can't comprehend it.

MAMMEA
But you remember Amphilochus, ever since he arrived on the Italian shores back in the day of the great Septimius. You always recognised the unparalleled dignity of his carriage and his words — be that at court, or in his own palace. He always seemed a second Caesar!

ULPIANUS
True, but the memory of his eminence matters little here. For most often, the sons of great fathers grovel prostrate in the shame of abjection. The people and senate of Rome offer ample proof of that!

ALEXANDER
Nor will my words bear witness against the Greek, although I have never marked the open frankness of youth on his pale countenance. And yet, there is something noble in his entire carriage. I do not know what slumbers in the depths of his heart. I know only that neither fear, nor abjection, is to be found there!

ULPIANUS
How then do you explain this latest turn of events?

ALEXANDER
The blind will of inexorable necessity. Several times did the emperor come across Irydion walking with Elsinoe — several times their chariots arrived together at the Flavian amphitheatre. I myself saw at those times how the veins on my brother's temples immediately swelled, and how he dropped the golden reins from his hands, with which he drove his lions, upon sighting her. And by heavenly Venus herself, all those who were standing there, devoured her with their eyes as well, for they had never seen a more beautiful woman!

ULPIANUS
Long ago, when I would visit her father, no one's eye had ever lit upon her, as, according to the Greek custom, she lived apart in the gynaeceum.

ALEXANDER
I tell you, a second such will not be found in all of Rome! I was in the hall of Narcissus when Heliogabalus was waiting for her, on the first night of her abduction. Leaning on me, he ground his teeth and pinched my arm — he was at the time still favourably disposed towards me — I for my part shivered with indignation and pity. From time to time I seemed to hear the echo of a fray. Then the praetorian prefect hurried in — you know, the court clown, Eutychian — and whispered into the ear of his master: "The bright-haired one is on her way." Then did the dwarves of both sexes, the negro eunuchs and the Lydian flautists go out. "The bright-haired one is on her way" the emperor repeated, and started in excitement, but then a troop of gladiators in dark tunics entered the hall — none of them familiar to the court. My brother, letting his head drop, bit me out of fright. But Eutychian, with a loud laugh, declared that the son of Amphilochus was presenting these men to her sister and Caesar, as a gift. Then the ranks parted, and only then did Elsinoe appear!

ULPIANUS
In a half-faint, borne forward on the arms of her handmaids?

ALEXANDER
No. She stood in the middle of the hall and, of course, without the slightest token of fear, did us no obeisance. At first her head was bowed, but immediately she raised it, straightened her figure and lifted her brow, and looked upon us with such fiery eyes, as if she were the mistress of us all. Caesar beckoned her near, yet she deigned neither to move closer, nor to retire a step. Then he nodded toward us, and we all left the hall!

ULPIANUS
The old Hellenic blood, in which something of the divine yet remains... And her brother, is he often at court? Does he visit his sister?

MAMMEA
It is said that once he visited Caesar and stayed with him for a long time. But usually, he avoids people. He sits in his palace amidst slaves and barbarians, upon whom he showers largesse.

ULPIANUS
His father was wont to do the same.

MAMMEA
Luxury delights him not. Abundance deceives him not. And although it is obvious that he is tortured by some stubborn thought, he knows how to master himself, and be silent.

ULPIANUS
What if that thought were a lust to avenge the wrongs done to his sister? We must win his confidence; lead him at first in errant paths, and then at last tear the veil from the truth. Let his pride and treasure enter our service! But now tell me: how did it happen, that the monster suddenly turned from cruelty, having obtained his great desire? The influence that woman has over him is incomprehensible to me!

ALEXANDER
Eutychian bruits abroad, that she has not yet submitted to him. From the moment of her abduction she has kept herself closed within Agrippina's peristyle. Since then, there have been no more banquets at the palace.

ULPIANUS
Her secret will not endure long. He will murder her, and burn her at a stake piled with Arabian incense, paying for it by depriving the first best citizen of his life and chattel, charging him first with the crime of insulting his majesty. But first, perhaps he himself...

MAMMEA
No, Domitian, I do not want him to die as his predecessors did. The reign of Wisdom and Good must not begin with the murder of my sister's son. I tell you again: the age of Mercy is approaching. You will

remove him from the throne, yes, but you will have him borne off into exile, like a sleeping child!

ULPIANUS
You'd need a Nazarene for such a task. Not far from here, Brutus murdered his own father. And that thin soul? Heliogabalus is not to tread the path shaded by the troubled, great spirit of the first of the Caesars?

MAMMEA
Woe is me!

SLAVE
Enters
Irydion, son of Amphilochus, comes to greet Severus, the consul of Caesar, and his noble mother!

ULPIANUS
Right on time.

Irydion enters.

MAMMEA
Always with a cloudy front? Is it possible that divine Sophia is unable to make it bright with her calm rays?

IRYDION
Let that Roman who fell at Philippi tell you, Augusta, how much solace that divinity brought him. Anyway, the expression on my face is not my concern. My spirit, calm and cold inside, regrets nothing, desires nothing, and expects nothing. How is your health, Caesar? Do the gods attend to your prayers these days?

ALEXANDER
In point of fact, my wishes have been granted this very day. My most beloved Domitian has arrived from Antioch!

IRYDION
I greet you, consul. If my memory serves me well, you did not disdain the threshold of my father.

ULPIANUS
The words of Amphilochus yet ring in my ears. And the old man, who often sat by his hearth, does he live still?

IRYDION
Masinissa?

ULPIANUS
I believe that was his name. Your father came to know him in Getulian Sirte, as he himself was wont to say, on a hot day, when he had wandered far from the tiger hunt.

IRYDION
Just as in my father's time, he sits yet at our hearth.

ULPIANUS
I ask about him, because from time to time a strange thought of his, or a bitter word, gave me pause. Once he stated that Tiberius was the greatest of all the Caesars!

ALEXANDER
How can that be, by the manes of Antoninus!

ULPIANUS
His reasoning escapes my memory. But one thing I do remember is how artfully he marshalled his reasons, developing such wild ideas about the predestination of men, that I was struck silent, in horror.

MAMMEA
I never want to give ear to such a frightful orator!

ULPIANUS
But as soon as the bewitching influence of his intelligence left me, I calmed down, like a man who sobers after drunkenness, regaining

his own thoughts. For how is one not to curse those, who, instead of righteousness and justice, sow oppression among the people, handing them over to the scourges and axes of the lictors, simply because they refuse to act like beasts? Am I not right, son of Amphilochus?

IRYDION
Yes, and no. There are as many opinions and hearts, as there are souls.

MAMMEA
To Alexander.
Note the burning lip on that placid face, and the eye in flames!

ALEXANDER
Mother, I wish to speak to him openly and sincerely!

MAMMEA
Wait a bit yet!

ULPIANUS
And yet you yourself neither bind nor beat your slaves, although you have the right of life and death over them. Nor do you spurn the wretched Suevi, Dacians or Marcomani who beg alms in the city. At least, so it is said of you!

IRYDION
My mother was a barbarian!

ULPIANUS
And her son wants to convince me that he is an Epicurean!

IRYDION
By the Olympic Zeus, one does not pretend to be a Stoic in this day and age!

MAMMEA
Perhaps I shall not live to see better days — but he, and you, Irydion, are just passing through the golden gate of life. Youth, like a dream,

still flits above you and governs you — trust your sweeter inclinations. Neither he, nor you can yet fall into despair!

ALEXANDER
Give me your hand, son of Amphilochus. Misfortune, no less than love, binds people together. Let us be friends. And perhaps someday we will rejoice together!

IRYDION
I thank you, noble Romans! It is apparent that the gods have loved you above all others, since they have left hope in your hearts. But sooner or later the one and the same end will come to you and me — death, and oblivion!

ULPIANUS
To Mammea
He is either leading us astray by the arts of the Greeks, or Jove has moulded him from flimsy metal. *Aloud.* And if illusion should become truth? If the shadow, which covers the city, melted away like clouds blown apart by fortunate winds, and all that remained was the light of virtue? What then would you do?

IRYDION
I would offer sacrifice to the immortals in thanksgiving.

ULPIANUS
And so, would you not act to speed on the advent of that day? Do you understand me? We are playing at assumptions as others play at dice. We merely speak of improbabilities, so that the time, which weighs upon us, might fly the more swiftly!

IRYDION
I understand you better than you understand me.

ULPIANUS
And so?

IRYDION
By Odin, you have that day call on me, and I will answer him!

ULPIANUS
Remember what you've just said!

ALEXANDER
Remember!

IRYDION
I shall not forget this moment, Romans! We shall meet again, consul!

ULPIANUS
Where are you going?

IRYDION
A group of friends await me at the foot of the Aventine with a banquet, and some new songs of a Sicilian poet. I go to listen to them, so that the time, which weighs upon us, might fly the more swiftly!

ULPIANUS
Young man, you go to stifle your own soul in forgetfulness, on the breast of luxury.

IRYDION
Lucius Mummius has left us nothing else save luxury and death. I wish Alexander and Augusta Mammea long life!

He exits.

ULPIANUS
Gazing after him.
Who knows if you will be able to mould a supporter from such wax.

*

Another part of the palace of the Caesars — a long atrium with a pond in the middle — mosaics, frescos of fauns, satyrs and nymphs — on columns of jasper: stone turtles, scorpions and crocodiles — along the walls, figures of Venus and Bacchus — Here and there groups of courtiers — praetorians — dancers — musicians — dwarves — Eutychian, the praetorian prefect — Rupilius — Eubullus — his parasites.

EUTYCHIAN
Evoe Bacche! I shall be lacking in nothing, because what can ever tear me from Caesar? And yet I have no need of such guests at court. And today, the emperor wishes to see him. Today, he had me wait here upon him.

RUPILIUS
Eutychian, so like the Demi-gods…

EUTYCHIAN
Say rather: half divine. The emperor is all god; but after him, I am the first.

RUPILIUS
And so, half divine Eutychian, let us tear the light of day from him. *Dulces moriens reminiscitor Argos!*[16]

EUTYCHIAN
Evoe! Just please, leave off the Maro. Our forefathers back in Augustus' day knew nothing of art…
He is lost in thought.

RUPILIUS
Nothing whatsoever!

EUBULLUS
No idea whatsoever about what constitutes poetry!

---

16   Virgil, *Aeneid*, X: 782. "Dying, he remembers his sweet [fatherland] Argos." *Reminiscitur* is the present tense of the verb used by Virgil and Krasiński; which we replace with the hortatory subjunctive so that the phrase would make sense here (Krasiński calques it into Polish: *Niechaj dulces moriens reminiscitur Argos.*

RUPILIUS
Completely flummoxed they were.

EUBULLUS
Worse than flummoxed!

EUTYCHIAN
Agreed. We must direct his steps on the path that leads to Erebus. But for now, give ear to this song. The divine Nero composed it for his dwarves.

RUPILIUS
Ah, Nero! There we reach the summits of music and rhythm.

EUBULLUS
Born brother to the nine muses.

CHORUS OF DWARVES
We stand to the side, and high above us on the tower, our lord tunes his lyre, while at his feet the city of gods burns among the misty shades of night!

'Twas he that kindled the inferno. For he wished to see what the conflagration of Troy looked like, ages before. He could not live as mere mortals do! And so he cloaked himself in flame and became the lord of the drama, the lord of the fire!

Coaxed by the notes of his lyre, from hill to hill, ever nearer, among groans and roaring, the flames leap. Above the city, above the falling city, another Rome arises in the air. Oh, wild the thrilling rites in those pyramids of sparks, in those columns of hissing flame!

And we clap our hands in time to the beat, crying out with joy. The day of destruction has overtaken the elevated and beautiful. On the swells of Phlegathon, palaces and temples are borne away, and disappear. But nothing shall happen to us — we have been saved by the master of art and music!

PHILOSOPHER
Coming close to Eutychian

You, to whom it seems all things are possible; second god of Rome, deign allow the Neoplatonic philosopher Anaxagoras to lecture twice weekly in the Baths of Caracalla.

EUTYCHIAN
What are your principles? Which gods to you acknowledge? And when you lecture to the people, are you sober, or drunk?

PHILOSOPHER
My god is a Unity, conceived in and by Unity. My god is by necessity opposed to all that is disunited. Enclosed within himself, he contemplates himself alone.

EUTYCHIAN
Satis est — with such teaching you will not overturn the state. *To Rupilius.* Perhaps Tiresias in hell will give ear to him.

RUPILIUS
Or Cerberus, with his trinity of muzzles.

EUBULLUS
To Rupilius
Excellent Rupilius, you had me mark something down on my tablets, yesterday.

RUPILIUS
Read it aloud, my dear.

EUBULLUS
"Day after tomorrow, the gladiator Sporus, and the tiger Ernax."

RUPILIUS
O, thrice-happy reminder — O, great Eutychian!

EUTYCHIAN
What?

RUPILIUS
I make of myself an offering to you.

EUTYCHIAN
And I am grateful for it, by Isis, Anubis, and any other Egyptian scarecrow you may choose. But why?

RUPILIUS
I have transported from Mauritania a tiger of gold and ebony speckled, with the strength of two horses in his tail alone, and nostrils flaring for the scent of human blood. I have a gladiator, braver than all others at court; a man who sold himself to me from hunger, a real Crotonian. And so. I have invited all of my beloved to a banquet, and I have laid a wager with Carbo, four to one, that my Sporus will make short work of Ernax. But when the fates so constrain us, we must employ the gladiator in another fight!

EUTYCHIAN
Halt!
To the praetorians
Sing to your leader. Evoe! Flutes and lyres! (*To Rupilius*). Now, speak further.

CHORUS OF PRAETORIANS
Long live dice and wine, sesterces and roses! As long as the wine cup froths, as long as Plutus grins, our feet are for dancing, our hands ready for the fight. But let us have Negresses black from Sirte! Let us have ruddy German girls from the woods!

    We shall not chase after Parths and Getae as of old. Our fathers sleep in their tombs, and with them, their dull parades. Here, on our couches, here, our foreheads wreathed with myrtle, here in Rome we shall await our enemies, let them come! Then, from the embrace of our black-haired lovers, among the tinkle of wine glasses, we shall arise with our shields, to the sword, to massacres! But now Evoe! Long live dice and wine, long live sesterces, and roses!

EUTYCHIAN
And if it should not succeed, you will bear false witness?

RUPILIUS
Calling to witness all the gods of Chaldea and Syria…

EUTYCHIAN
Iacta est alea[17] — yet today —

RUPILIUS
Here comes our pale Greek.

Enter Irydion. He directs his steps toward Eutychian.

EUTYCHIAN
Oh, the shiver that suddenly shot through my spine — there is something hellish in those eyes. They say that his father was a black sorcerer.
He leans on Rupilius.

RUPILIUS
Drawing away.
Demigods are not allowed to fear.

IRYDION
I am here at the appointed hour. Eutychian. Let us go there, where you have been commanded to lead me!

EUTYCHIAN
Yes — in a moment, illustrious Greek. *To Rupilius.* What a man, what pride! Vae capiti eius![18]

RUPILIUS
To Eutychian
The waters of Lethe will cure him of his pride.

---

[17] "The die is cast." A phrase associated with Julius Caesar, when he crossed the Rubicon and thus instigated the civil war, which eventually led to his elevation as head of state. It means "there's no turning back now."

[18] "Woe upon his head!" from Demosthenes, *Oratio adversus Leptinem*.

IRYDION
All of you at the court of Caesar like to waste so much time. Let's go!

EUTYCHIAN
This way, noble Irydion.

They exit.

*

Another part of the palace of the Caesars — the summit of a tower, surrounded by a colonnade.

ELSINOE
Departing
I entrust you to the gods and to his strength![19]

HELIOGABALUS
Cruel one!

Enter Irydion; Elsinoe pauses.

ELSINOE
The moon is rising — the flames rage, the poison froths!
She disappears.

HELIOGABALUS
O, save me! Or if you can't save me, don't deceive me, don't pretend, confess your purpose straight out, and I will plunge this golden dagger into my breast. *He produces a dirk from behind a pillar.* Have you ever seen such emeralds?

---

19   In Polish: *Powierzam cię bogom i sile jego!* It is an odd formulation, in that she entrusts him to the "gods" (plural) and to "his" strength (singular). The two nouns are thus unconnected; the gods are one thing, the "strength" belongs to someone else.

IRYDION
How comes it that the divine Caesar debates a premature death, today?

HELIOGABALUS
Ha, my friend! You are mistaken if you think Caesar unable to kill himself. And if I am to drink down the Elysian Fields from this chalice? *He raises a chalice from a tripod.* One hundred divers drowned in the depths of the sea before one of them brought up this unparalleled pearl!

IRYDION
From that chalice we shall toast the sun, but beneath a different sky, among a different people.

HELIOGABALUS
Look me in the eye. You are not lying? Ah! Turn away those eyes! The gods have inscribed something in them — with a stylus of pure fire. Your mother was a witch! Come closer to the columns — hold onto the grating — and tell me, what do you see there down below?

IRYDION
The depths of the courtyard sparkles with precious stones, like to a black abyss sprinkled with shining stars!

HELIOGABALUS
I chose the topazes myself; the beryls, the sharp-edged chrysolites, the bloody onyxes. A full day and night they needed to pave that courtyard, and I did not depart, did not rest in sleep, until they had finished. And then I had them all put to death!

IRYDION
Whom?

HELIOGABALUS
The vile slaves! Why do you ask? They but preceded their master. Who in Rome ought to know that Caesar was preparing himself to die? There were only one hundred of them, and two boys. Ah! I shall not hand over my snowy limbs to the people. It is here that I shall

dash my head in my final leap. Let my blood seep over diamonds to Erebus!

IRYDION
What is it that threatens you so inexorably?

HELIOGABALUS
Alexian — what a repulsive name — Alexian! — May he perish before his time! Alexian! Thricely I devote his head to Hecate! It is he, he, Alexian, who weighs black thoughts and readies treason.

IRYDION
My sleepless eye is fixed upon him and his mother.

HELIOGABALUS
Don't interrupt me — and don't hinder him, if the air you breathe is pleasing to you. Listen, I have commanded you to be brought to me so that you would hear me out. My spies have informed me that he has been taking counsel of Ulpianus. They say that for several days now he has appeared to be paler than usual; that, sunk in distant thought, now he unbinds, now he smooths, his locks… And that Ulpianus who hastened here from Antioch, ha! Do you know what's in his mind?

IRYDION
I have often heard that he is a lawyer by vocation, and a good one.

HELIOGABALUS
You praise him — O ye immortal gods! — and I tell you that no conspiracy for the past thirty years has gotten underway without his participation! Domitianus Ulpianus: so sweetly the words roll off his tongue, yet he is an implacable Stoic, ever ready to kill the ruler, or, if that does not succeed, himself. He is a walking conspiracy; he eats and drinks treason — a living curse for any government. He is Damocles' sword suspended above my head — and you will praise him to my face! A lawyer by vocation, and a good one! Foh! Jupiter! I would not only put him to death, but the law itself! Tell me, what am I to do?

IRYDION
You are not to despair while all is yet quiet and calm. And if it comes to danger, you are to rely on me.

HELIOGABALUS
And if the signs betokening my funeral have already become apparent? If other, stronger gods have arisen against those of your sister? *Unrolls a letter.* Look — In this letter, Symmachus Niger describes frightful tokens which have appeared in the sky above the Danube: The rising sun surrounded by the holy train of Bacchus, and amidst the heads garlanded with ivy, amongst the hands bearing the thyrsus, the spectre of Alexander the Macedonian rose over the broad meadows. The armour on his chest was flashing — the same armour he was wearing when, after sweeping Darius aside, he went on to conquer India. The golden helm on his bowed head was aflame. Behind him came leaders long dead. The peoples of Moesia and Thrace fell prostrate before the passing chiefs and, when they had all passed, they crowded after them, following them to the very sea shore! There at last the shades of the dead dissolved in the air. *He leans against a column.* Hand me the Falernian… *Takes the cup.* Yes, Alexander Severus shall receive the state from the hands of the Macedonian, along with my life! Dii, avertite omen![20]

IRYDION
Can it have slipped your memory that the son of great Septimius once loved your mother? Perhaps you have forgotten that the spirit of the Macedonian dwelt in his divine breast? But now, when the hero who was the guardian spirit of your father arises from the grave to foretell your glory, your face drains of blood and you are in need of wine, consolation, the hand of a friend to stay you from fainting and falling to the earth. Shame on you, son of Caracalla!

HELIOGABALUS
No, no, it was at Alexander, that rising sun, that he turned his pale, smiling lips! Each face threatens my death, each voice: the people,

---

20   "Gods! May the prophecy not come true!" Krasiński may have taken this from Bulwer-Lytton's 1834 novel *The Last Days of Pompeii*. Latinists suggest that the hortatory subjunctive *Avertant Dii* is a more proper construction.

the senate, the praetorians, all of Rome! I feel it, you all are marching close, step by step, to tear me from my sweet mother earth! All of you, however many of you there are, mean to drag me to Hell!

IRYDION
Be of better mind. Can it be that in the eternal struggle of man with the city, man will never be permitted to win?

HELIOGABALUS
What is it you are saying?

IRYDION
I speak of your fates! You, the emperors, have all perished; some by the sword, others by poison, others still by their own hand, but all amidst shame and terror, betrayed by their confidants, damned by their enemies. Why must human matters follow one and the same pattern always? Up until now, Rome has colluded in conspiracies and murdered the Caesars — Let Caesar now be a conspirator! Let Caesar strike at his enemy!

HELIOGABALUS
Who? How? I see power there on your forehead, but I cannot comprehend it!

IRYDION
Can it be that these palaces, temples and circuses, this fortress, three times burnt along with its former god, are never to fall? Have you never heard of cities of the East, more beautiful and larger than this, which once were wonders in the eyes of the people, beloved of the gods, and today — they are buried by sandstorms while through their fallen arcades wander lonely hyenas, howling? Was Jerusalem, with her bands of fervid defenders, able to resist the fate that destroys all things? And yet she had her lonely god, as strong as Fate itself! Go and ask the deserts whence they arose! — And these hills, built up with marble and granite, are they immortal gods? Look at them and understand my words. — There is your Alexian, truly; there is your vengeful enemy, crouched at your feet, but swelling day and night to overthrow you. If you don't steal a march on him, woe to thee, O wretched babe, in

the embrace of a giant! *Grabs him by the hand.* Ignite the strong will that slumbers in your breast — this world that I show you: challenge it to a duel! Become that, which appears only rarely upon the earth: a Destroyer. And these buildings, drunk with the lives of thousands of men, these villas, spreading wide beneath the sun, these trophies and memorials and delights of the people we shall give over to scorpions and snakes as their inheritance from the human race!

HELIOGABALUS
Now I see! — At times I have felt this, desired this, myself. Ha! What glory for Mithras, when Capitoline Jove will bite the dust! — But whose arm shall undertake the task? Who will arise against the sacred fortress, against the eternal city?

IRYDION
The son of the priestess and Amphilochus the Greek.

HELIOGABALUS
Do you really think that any soldier will follow you or me at such a drastic moment? And the senators, and the knights, and, what is more, the entire people? — Fear the immortal gods! What has happened to you; what are you pondering, Irydion?

IRYDION
The rescue of Caesar, through the inspiration of the gods.

HELIOGABALUS
I am filled with fear. The genius of the city has overcome all — and I am to raise my hand against it!

IRYDION
So live on in terror until you die in torture.
He turns around.

HELIOGABALUS
Fulfill the commands of the gods, powerful mortal. I shall cover you in purple — I shall take the sandals from my own feet and bind them on yours — just support me always, never abandon me, save me from death!

IRYDION
You may be saved only by the scattering of the senate, the slaughter of the praetorians, and the transfer of the capital!
HELIOGABALUS
The senate I can deal with; I am still capable of that — but the rest?

IRYDION
Earlier in Cataline's days, and then during the late years of Nero, there were arsonists to spare. It's far easier to turn to ash what stands today, than to build in stone what is to be tomorrow. In any event, those who will stand on the smoking embers will still be called Romans. For many years a handful of palaces, debased to hovels, will be known as Rome. Leave that dear name to the decrepit children — but it will be a name only; the vibrant life, the consuming power, will no longer inhabit this place. Caesar, on the day of the great massacre I shall bring men to you myself, and stand at your side!

HELIOGABALUS
How? — What men? — Where are they?

IRYDION
You are not the only man whose days Rome has shrouded with deathly darkness. What of the slaves, and the gladiators, and the barbarians, and the faithful of the Nazarene prophet? You are at the head, but they stretch behind you in long hosts — both them and you the genius of Rome has devoted to a painful life and a shameful death! Let us therefore accumulate all of their misery in one great charge of vengeance; then the lords of the amphitheatre, and the soldiers of the praetorium, will not be able to keep pace with so many starving, passionate and furious legions!

HELIOGABALUS
Good... good... But, later, will they not turn on us and devour us themselves? Where might one turn in such confusion? Who will rein in their boldness? With what shall we slake the thirst of blood that inflames their breasts?

IRYDION
In the very first days, vengeance and greed shall get drunk on blood and gold among the flames of the city. But then their arms and their wills, heretofore united only in a common hatred of Rome, will loosen of their own accord, and each shall return to the superstitions of their faith or to the customs of their nation. Then, we shall draw the divided and weakened hordes behind us, to the East, with promises of still greater delight. And there shall they perish from the swelter of the unbearable sun, and from the excesses with which they shall glut themselves according to the age old use of conquerors and savages, while the rest of them shall dissolve and dry up among the peoples who love you, and confess to your deity. And therefore, onward without fear, onward in the silence of death! Otherwise, we shall never attain life!

HELIOGABALUS
Io triumphe! Along with Prometheus, you have invaded the porch of heaven, and brought down fire therefrom! *He claps his hands.* Oh, to build a new temple in Emesa[21] — Oh, to live among my pythons and prophets!

IRYDION
You shall found a young city in those places, where you have found life — free of sleepless nights, both arch-priest and caesar, like to the ancient demigods of the Nile. You will spend your sweet days amidst the fumes of aloes and myrrh, amidst the tones of kithara and flute. Wherever you shall turn your glance, there shall crawl your silent slaves, upon whose black necks you shall rest your feet. Whatever you desire shall be yours; whatever you decree to be forgotten by man shall perish in oblivion; whatever you decree to be remembered, shall be remembered. The great names of the past shall lose their lustre in the face of yours; and there shall be no longer senator nor lawyer there, to dream of Republics or gibe at your Chaldean mitre, or mock the hanging sleeves of your eastern robe!

---

21   Known today as Homs, a city in Syria; ancient centre of worship of the sun god El-Gabal.

HELIOGABALUS
Oh, those repulsive Quirites! As if their old toga, their fibula, their tunics were more beautiful! Mithras, hear thou my pledge: may I never attain unto thy sunbeams, may the genies of the night tear me limb from limb if I do not cast all the gods of Rome, enchained, at the foot of thine altar! Son of Amphilochus, what you advise, I acknowledge to be good and helpful. By Baal and Astaroth, we shall destroy this city! Just advise me further!

IRYDION
Have your treasure transferred to Emesa in secret. Divert the people with games, and the praetorians with largesse. Meanwhile, call into the city Goth mercenaries from the Vindelician legions, and Cherusci mercenaries from the legions along the Rhine. As they arrive, I will make myself known to them — my mother taught me the savage language of the north!

HELIOGABALUS
You forget the Italian legions stationed in Ephesus, in Tarsus, in Pergamum and Miletus…

IRYDION
Send a runner to the Praetor Varius, and order him to gather them all together and march off as quickly as possible against the Parthians. While they are busy with bitter fighting on the shores of the Caspian Sea, news of what has taken place in Rome shall reach them. Then the enemy shall capture some, while the others shall melt away, and still others will rush to join us and bask in the graces of your court.

HELIOGABALUS
Consider this carefully — they are valiant cohorts. And perhaps dangerous?

IRYDION
Fear nothing after the destruction of Rome. One can tread with impunity upon a corpse, once the soul has abandoned it. And we ourselves shall put to death the very soul of the state. We shall tear away the soul from the world and slaughter it!

HELOGABALUS
But what if Alexian should forestall us meanwhile? The city praetorians are muttering ever more; singing songs of his courage! Ulpianus shall draw the senate to his side. They shall awaken me in the middle of the night, and cut my throat!

IRYDION
You shall be first to pronounce "Salve aeternum" over their lifeless bodies. Only, trust not Eutychian in anything. Assume a cold and calm countenance; visit Alexian and Mammea, and when you converse with them, let your words be sweet, your glances tender and merciful. Whether they come to trust you or no, this will restrain them from decisive action, for a while.

HELIOGABALUS
Smile, ye gods! Mithras, chase the gloom from thy face! Venus, thou mother of erotic delight, stretch out upon the waves, surrounded by your flying sons! Bacchus, drink thou the health of Heliogabalus! Bring forth roses and Falernian! Come, you best beloved of all people, let us recline upon the purple. We shall drink and praise the gods for the destruction of our enemies! *He leaps into Irydion's embrace.* Receive this kiss from the lips of Caesar! Is it not true that my fragment lips and smooth brow are the very prototype of maidenly pulchritude? Come! Elsinoe and I shall rule the Syrian shores, there where the stars converse with men concerning the destinies of future ages.

They exit.

*

The garden of the Caesars on the Palatine hill. Elsinoe and Irydion, beneath the statue of Diana.

ELSINOE
We mustn't go any farther. I would not be able to return. But don't leave me yet.

IRYDION
I also must make haste. The last rays of the sun now spill their blood on the heights of the Amphitheatre, and I must yet visit the city praetorians before I return home.

ELSINOE
I'm not asking you to stay for hours, I ask only for a moment more. *She rests her head on the plinth of the statue.* Look at the face of the immaculate one. Look — her countenance veiled by the tunic of the dusk. Oh, I could love as she, when, among the silences of the night, resting upon a golden bow, she descended through the waves of azure to muse above Endymion asleep! But go now — ask the people what has become of your sister. "Between Poppea and Messalina," they shall answer, "they have erected her altar."

IRYDION
He who has devoted himself to the cause of the people should give no ear to their judgements. Do you know who the Nazarenes worship as their God? He, who for the salvation of His brothers willingly accepted the shame of the Cross! Oh Elsinoe, we have been dealt a fate similar to His!

ELSINOE
You're already dabbling with foreign faiths! You seek consolation among those, despised of the people! But you know Alexander; you know how Mammea has reared him; you have heard the prophecies of the elders, that he shall someday be peer to the divine Aurelius! Yesterday, I came across him in the porch of Deianira. He paused and looked my way; at first, his glance was uncertain, it trembled, but then it became stronger, more expressive. And at last, he turned it away in the silence of contempt.

IRYDION
He and all who live in this city shall be given over to death.

ELSINOE
No, no! It is not vengeance I seek! Call back your words, call them back!

IRYDION
Calm down, poor girl. Poor misfortunate one, how is it with you now? In your sudden paling, you seemed just now about to faint away?

ELSINOE
I'm better, better — Forgive me. The gods have not called me to such sorrowful wringing of the hands. Go. I too shall return, to where the Furies wait for me. I go to entangle my feet among the coils of the reptile who constantly dances around me. I go where premature old age is rewarded with debasement and torture. There, among convulsions of disgust — but shh, shh — you know the secrets of this virgin bosom!

IRYDION
Ah! You who just recently shone with a life so radiant, you dancing nymph of beauty — where have you gone? The tear that now slides down my cheek, I shed for you. But go now — remember the sentence pronounced by Odin, and endure to the end.

ELSINOE
Oh, my brother!

IRYDION
Cultivate the frenzy of the one we despise. Be the rot that eats away his mind and his life. *Vale!*

ELSINOE
May the shades of Amphilochus and Grimhilda be ever with you. *Vale!*

*

The hall of Amphilochus. Night. Enter Iridion and Masinissa. After them, the leader of the slaves.

IRYDION
What did he want, Pilades?

PILADES
He spoke not a word. He just sat down and determined to wait for you. According to the custom of your house, we gave him bread, and meat, and wine.

IRYDION
Have him enter.

Pilades exits.

MASINISSA
Beware this man.

IRYDION
Why?

MASINISSA
He comes to kill you. Here!
Hands him a sword.

IRYDION
If it is true what you say, this Carthaginian blade is too noble for such work. I shall crush his skull with the chalice from which Amphilochus was used to drink.

Enter Gladiator.

GLADIATOR
I would like to be with you alone, for a moment.

IRYDION
This is my trusted man. You may speak boldly in his presence.

GLADIATOR
My master said unto me: "Instead of struggling with the tiger, go and murder the Greek, and I shall set you free." But you are one hundred times more a man than he who sent me. *He throws his stiletto to the floor.* To hell with my slavery!

IRYDION
Who is it that sent you?

GLADIATOR
A new man; a villain and a coward. A cruel man, a usurer.

IRYDION
Ha! In other words, a Roman.

GLADIATOR
You have guessed it. Aetius Rupilius.

IRYDION
The court jester of the court jester. *He sets down the chalice.* I knew it. Look: your skull was to be caved in by this Corinthian work!

GLADIATOR
Oh, son of Amphilochus, I did not take terror of you. In the arena, I have ground bigger men, and wilder, than you beneath my heel. But I was hungry, and in your palace they gave me food; I was thirsty, and in your palace they gave me wine, and waiting for your return, I heard the voices of my brother gladiators bless your name. So now, be well. I go to die in the tiger's jaws tomorrow.

IRYDION
No, you shall live, and you shall avenge your slavery upon your masters. Hey, Pilades!
Pilades enters.
Give this man one hundred sesterces, and a tunic, and the iron ring such as those of my household wear. What is your name?

GLADIATOR
Today they call me Sporus.

IRYDION
Something proud can be heard in your simple words. The embers of some old fire glow in you, like the rays of a lamp flitting through the cracks of a sarcophagus. Once more I ask you, what is your name?

GLADIATOR
Once, the people and senate of Rome did homage to my forebears as they did the gods. But what is past, is past. My name is Lucius Tiberius Scipio!

IRYDION
You fantasise, slave. That clan died out long ago.

GLADIATOR
Yes, but only in the memory of my countrymen. The last of my line who was known to the people had his wife stolen from him by Nero, who, along with her, confiscated his palace in Rome, his names in Italy, Sicily and Africa, banishing him to the Chersonese. His son returned to the city a beggar, and from that time beggars we have remained. My father was a gladiator before me!

IRYDION
No one in Rome rescued you from your misery?

GLADIATOR
Who would aid an old patrician? Perhaps the great-grandchildren of our lictors, who are now wealthy men? Perhaps the emperor, the enemy of the past, the murderer of its monuments? My father, dragged by hooks from the arena, died in the spoliarium cursing the gods. Oh, may that city fall, who so abandoned the grandsons of its consuls! *He picks up the stiletto.* One word from you, and I shall go and kill Rupilius, that Roman of today!

IRYDION
To kill one man would be the frenzy of a child, whereas we require the death of thousands. Preserve yourself for a broader field of action, for work more worthy.

GLADIATOR
If such a day be near, the day of vengeance and pillage, I shall bring to you Verres, Cassius and Sulla — all of those with names as ancient as mine, today in misery!

IRYDION
All of them shall find shelter among these columns. From now on, my house shall be yours. Vale!

MASINNISA
Go. Pursue vengeance with your whole heart, and the Fates will not keep it from you.

The Gladiator exits.

IRYDION
I am winning, old man, winning! Ah! you ancient conquerors, who led my brothers, burdened in chains, alongside kings in fetters; you destroyers of Carthage, Corinth, Syracuse, behold! — The last of the Scipios has become the slave and instrument of a Greek! Having come begging food of him, and the journeywork of thugs! Ah, I have lived to see the fall of the damned, the proud! Masinissa, take this cup in hand, and drink the health of the Scipios!

He pours the cup full and hands it to him.

MASINISSA
To the long success of the Scipio clan!

He gives it back to Irydion.

IRYDION
Drinks and throws aside the goblet.
And may Rome shatter, as did this pretty jewel!

MASINISSA
Little by little we swell with the strength and will of others. We grow, Sigurd; but until we convert Nazareth to our faith, we shall be unable to succeed in the treacherous and victorious battle!

IRYDION
The old man, before whom they bend their knees and thoughts as if he were a God, long held his arms aloft toward the black

vaults, calling forth the Spirit and calling down that Spirit upon me, into me, his trembling hands stretched above my head, from which there dripped the water of mystery, while the crowd of his pale, wretched brethren sang out, repeating my new name: "Hieronymus, Hieronymus," and their voices stretched out like an airy funeral, unseen… and yet, in that song there were words of hope!

MASINNISA
And you have hung their symbol upon your breast?

IRYDION
I have.

MASINISSA
Pressing it first to your lips in humility?

IRYDION
I have.

MASINISSA
That is good. Now shall you split apart their hearts!

IRYDION
They have already begun to divide. Among the elders — those who passed through martyrdom, who say, as they claim, the heavens opened wide above them — I strove to raise the spark of enthusiasm in vain. They repeated the same words to me again and again, like a stream that beats against the same gravel: "forgiveness, forgetfulness, love for one's killers." But the youngsters, the newly anointed soldiers, slaves, barbarians, the pilgrims who have visited the deserts of Egypt, they feel a different boldness. Their eyes take flame at the mention of abuse and torment. Their hearts, at least, desire something here and now, on this earth. They first bless the evil that tramples them, but at last, when their blood begins to dance within their veins, willing or not I elicit from them a curse.

MASINISSA
You need a woman in order to incarnate the kingdom that is not of this world, among the passions of this world. They have adopted for adoration a daughter of childhood and premature age. From the plunder of fleshly delight they have invented a mysterious mist; before the handmaid of man they have bowed their heads. From among so many virgins who wither there in prayers and fastings, choose one and exalt her above their spirits. Make of her a mirror of your thoughts; may she reflect them and shower them about her, without knowing, without feeling what she does, but overcome, destroyed, by the power that reigns in the heart of man!

IRYDION
I know such a one — praised by all as blessed, made a saint before her time. And she likes to speak to me of the glory of the heavens…

MASINISSA
I have touched the string, and it has resounded! Is it not true that her eye is as black as coal, but as bright as a flame? And that she is the last of the clan of Metellus?

IRYDION
If you know, why do you ask?

MASINISSA
Never forget to praise her God, each of His wounds, along with each nail that pierced Him — fondle those nails with mournful tears. For she is in love with that crucified Body, with that Countenance, which she imagines beautiful, fading in the victory of love. She did not see them, when they were expiring in the hideousness of pain, in the silence of exhaustion, smeared with blood, and with the wind whistling through His hair! Listen: draw her thought from him to you. He is far away; He was once on earth, but now is not, nor shall He return. You live, and are at her side. You shall be her god! Alma Venus and Eros, speed our intentions!

IRYDION
Ah, who can plumb the mysteries of her being? Who can reach the fountainhead of her life? She lives among the darknesses of those underground wastes, seen but not comprehended, marked with suffering which makes her beauty the more beguiling. Phidias himself would be unable to eternise her form with his omnipotent chisel. And all this beauty she will take with her, with her last breath! I myself become weak in her presence!

MASINISSA
Why is it you hesitate, and doubt? She must become yours — Not for vain delight, but because my reason, because our work, demands her loss, just as a question demands an answer, just as one sound demands another to respond in echo. When her head comes to rest upon your lap, when her bosom trembles like that of any slavegirl, and her heavenly soul forgets its very self in the infernos of the flesh, then shall you find grovelling, faithful slaves in the catacombs, my son! Then will my spirit be with you, and vengeance shall become flesh!
He makes to leave.

IRYDION
Masinissa!

MASINISSA
What is it?

IRYDION
I beg you — Tell me as a friend — No, pass sentence as a judge — Each of my words, each of my affairs and my desires, since the time when I laughed as a child and unconsciously, gaily, first collided against the wrongs and shame of my generation, to this very day, recall them — count them up — do you understand?

MASINISSA
Why have your eyes clouded over, and your voice become rough, wild?

IRYDION
Is it not true that whatever was holy and pleasing for others, was always sacrilege to me? And have I not been faithful to the wild virtue that I swore to the Furies? Up until now — witness to the fact that I have never been even slightly stained with mercy or regret?

MASINISSA
All the same, where is the deed, the son of your hand? Up until now, it is but a babe swaddled in nothingness, while you are unknown and weak. On the day your deed is brought into the light, on that day, you begin to exist through it, and it through you!

IRYDION
Ah, in my breast, the gods have left something superfluous — I feel the venom that pulses in my temples and floods my eyes. Women call that venom tears! Tell me! Once, I was supposed to be a man?

MASINISSA
And so you are at this very moment, in this moment of wretchedness. You do not know that each of you is capable of becoming omnipotent by virtue of his own thought — inexorable and impassioned — but the enemy, foreseeing this, has hung a heart in your breast, full of piety, illusion — a baseless thing, which you cuddle warmly like slaves who acquiesce to their own shame. This is how he has divided you and tossed you low and afar. In this way does he reign over you, and no one shall knock him from his throne, although each of you might.

IRYDION
Of whom do you speak? Who is it that has made me wretched and unhappy? I know only of one murderer who slays each minute of my life — and her name is Rome.

MASINISSA
There is another Rome, which cannot perish! And she has placed her feet, not on seven hills, but upon millions of stars! It is not the mere human race, that vain thing, that she has annoyed; she has harassed and tormented many scores of tribes of great and beautiful angels! You men are but clowns, while they are martyrs, and at each moment,

while your deluded kind praise her, they in their wisdom and beauty cry out for revenge upon her!

IRYDION
What is it you foretell of me, you horrific, unsounded creature?

MASINISSA
War!

IRYDION
Where? When?

MASINISSA
After this Rome has perished! Everywhere your spirit is able to feel and think!

IRYDION
Endless, then? An endless war?

MASINISSA
I shall lead you to it myself. In the meantime, attend to your work here, in this vale of lunacy, poisoned by the enemy. Against him and his lackeys, you will one day turn your ireful brows in the fullness of reason!

IRYDION
But victory, will there be victory? Will I ever strip myself of my heavy armour, here, or on some other star? Will I ever lay down my head without the necessity of watching, free of danger, free, loved, loving, and happy?

MASINISSA
Ask no such questions before their time. Onward, gain control of the beast inside you; learn to be lonely on the earth as that God of theirs is on the summits of the universe; learn to suffer, as spirits more powerful than you suffer! Because before you attain that, which you may grow into, fire shall consume you a thousand times; death shall transform you a thousand times; and his anger will push you

away one thousand times. You shall be like a wave tossed beneath the heavens and lost in the abyss. But while a wave is a dead thing, blind and deaf, in you there is immortal feeling!

IRYDION
My spirit shall never bow low before any enemy, whoever he might be. It is late now. You will return in the morning — we shall speak again. Go now! It is true, true! I had no mercy for my sister; now shall I pity her, a stranger?

MASINISSA
Remember well my words: for the nations of this world shall pass away, but my reason[22] shall never pass away!

He exits.

IRYDION
Tossing off his upper cloak
Away — you weigh me down — *Tosses away his ring* — Away — you burn my hand. I wish I could raze the hair from my brows — they are not me; they trouble me. Where am I? Irydion, show yourself! You, Torment, who have taken up residence in this bosom of mine, emerge! Let me look upon you as you are, let me know you just once! *Takes down a stiletto hanging above a shield.* Tell me, you flame of night, you blue blade, are you able to suck me forth from my own chest? But forever, forever! — No, no, you too are an illusion! — Cato himself awoke after his sacrifice to find another caesar standing over him, rattling sword and fetters! *Tosses down the stiletto and treads on it.* You liar, who have deceived so many suffering souls with the vain promise of the void — I mock you — I, whether here, or there, shall be but a slave! There is nowhere that I shall find rest — Lie there in the dust, you false viper! *He wipes his brow.* How unbearable to him, who cannot perish… who perishes endlessly, while never perishing entirely! *He paces the room.* What a desert of silence and rest! — I alone am in arrears with my never sleeping thought. — Night crowns my forehead

---

22   Throughout his speeches, Masinissa uses the word *rozum*, which can also signify "intellect."

with a wreath of fevers and cares. — Thank you for such laurels. You cursed gods! *He stands near a statue.* Father! When I look upon your features, it seems that a holy promise meets my ears… Oh, unfortunate Hellas! You shall press me to your bosom. The victor speeds near — Romans are bound to the wheels of his chariot — their brows are broken on the axle as it flames round! Ha! I reck not unending torments, as long as that day, that one day, should present me with the chaplet of a conqueror! *He kneels.* But must I slay her, too? — Father, spare her — she does not suffer like the rest of us, for she has her faith, an unending future. Ah, it has been carved into my fate to murder the proud, to shove thousands of wretches into Erebus, to end the torment of those in agony. But to tear hope from the trusting? To destroy the radiant? *He leaps to his feet.* The son of Amphilochus is harried by witches, as once Orestes was! *Takes a lamp in hand.* Time to sleep — the blessing of the Lares rests upon this house. It is my city, my fatherland[23] — blissful, dear — a lucky star, certainly, shone above our crib!
He exits.

---

23   He says *To miasto to ojczyzna*, which in Polish can be an entire sentence meaning "This city is [a, my] fatherland." That sentiment would not make much sense in the mouth of a man who hates the city and state of Rome as much as Irydion does; most likely, it is linked to his musings on his home, which, since his father's time, has been an oasis of virtue in the corrupt city. So, far from both his mother's North and his father's Greece, hating the city he was raised in, his "city, his fatherland" is reduced to the area occupied by his house. "This home is my city, my fatherland; it is to this home that I owe my only allegiance."

PART II

The catacombs. A lamp hangs from the vault in the centre of the dungeon-like room. To the rear: two sarcophagi. Passageways lead away from each of them, and are lost in the distance. The walls are filled with grave-niches, arranged in tiers. Bishop Victor is present, as is Alexander Severus in a soldier's cape, hooded.

VICTOR
All the past ages up until this present day now have been the childhood of the human race. The nearer creation draws to the Creator, the more ardent burns the love that man bears Him, and his brother. Soon, there will neither be sword nor hangman to be found on the earth, and blessed is he who has come to believe in such a future today, and who works to speed on its advent!

ALEXANDER
Oh, that one day I might reveal to the world the work of righteousness, the promise of your lips!

VICTOR
My son, think not that you shall dream this vision to the end. For each man rides but a single wave that bears him upon the ocean of eternity — the strength of which may be stronger or weaker, but in any case, it flows on for a short time merely. Live, then, and pass away, like the rest of your brethren, acting according to the light that has been poured upon you. Be a comforter, so that some day you may stand as a chosen one to the left of Christ, looking on while others, inspired, bring to a conclusion, through those long ages, what you have commenced in love and humility of spirit.

ALEXANDER
May your blessing rest upon the head of Alexander. Soon, Caesar will be unable to deny him. *He bows.* Prepare them for the change, father, accustom them to my name! — This Mammea begs of you.

VICTOR
As I bless you now, may all of humanity some day bless you, remembered with love by the sons of the sons of your people. — Arise, anointed of Christ!

ALEXANDER
I hear footsteps — Father, in the hour of my struggle be my good genius! *He exits.*

Enter Irydion, in a praetorian's cloak, from the opposite side.

IRYDION
Praise be the Lord in heaven! *He sets aside his sword, spear and armour at the entrance.* May the weapons of earthly violence sleep at the entrance to His house!

VICTOR
I was waiting for you, Hieronymus. This morning, your servants brought the body of our beheaded brother to the mausoleum of Cecelia Metella. There, the assembled faithful received it of their hands. His funeral procession will be passing by shortly — Thank you, my son!

IRYDION
I merely did my duty. I come to you now from the porch of the Caesars. The faces of the courtiers there have grown pale with fright. The city praetorians are starting to turn against the emperor.

VICTOR
The face of the earth is transformed in its pride like the colour of the ocean — at every little breeze. But such things should not disturb the peace of the graves! Let us pray in the shadow of the palm of martyrdom, plucked by Athanadorus!

IRYDION
Father, a few words more, with your permission. After all, our future is in your hands. With but one nod, you might toss thousands upon the dish of the balance, and that side to which their numbers are added will be victorious!

VICTOR
In the unseen kingdom, I can fight against the prince of this world by prayer and sacrifice. And if all of you join with me in the presence of the Lord, I promise you victory!

IRYDION
But I am speaking of struggles near at hand, and of a sooner triumph! Father, we suffer like people, we live in expectation like people, and we also need to play a part in this world. Up until now, we have been oppressed by the power of the hateful ones, from all sides, so that we have preferred to die rather than to bow down before debauchery or worship falsehood on earth. But today, that which destroys nations has halted before the gates of this city — decrepit age and unbounded pride. Heliogabalus lacks the strength to keep his own people in check; Alexander is yet too weak to set up a new government, and the rest of the combatants will be destroyed in the coming struggle — between them both, would not each man who has come to believe in Christ, wish to tear the cross from out the bowels of the earth, and plant it in the Forum Romanum? Father — I see clouds of horror gather on your brow... Forgive me, that I burn with love towards my oppressed brethren — Pardon me, that I dared to announce that the time has come to strike at the very heart of paganism, Rome!

VICTOR
I listen to your words in sadness! I have poured the waters of baptism upon your brow in vain! In vain did I explain the world of the spirit to you. You have not comprehended my words; you have not cast off from you the old man. You have placed your hope in fire and the sword, a hope of salvation here and now. Heavy are your sins!

The strains of a funeral hymn are heard.

Can you not hear the hymns that now wind among these graves like the last thunderclaps of that storm, during which the One and Only Lord bowed His head, expiring? — Did He call the angelic hosts to His aid? Did He call out to His Father for vengeance?

IRYDION
And so, misery and debasement are to be our portion, forever?

VICTOR
You are led astray in your arrogance, as you call what is but a moment, an eternity! Verily I say unto you, that those who sleep in these cemeteries were only pilgrims in this world. That not only in the forecourts of Heaven, but also on these plains of suffering, Love will eventually triumph. Verily, verily, the peoples will bow before that Love, and there will not be a singe Caesar who will not prostrate himself before her! Are you not familiar with this?
He points to a sculpture in relief on one of the sarcophagi.

IRYDION
That is a Hellenic lute, the four-voiced strings of my fathers. — Lycaon Orpheus!

VICTOR
And just as he, according to the stories of your people, tamed the fierce beasts, so Jesus shall unite millions of souls beneath the yoke of the living Word. As you gaze at that earthly instrument, understand that swarms of souls are labouring in the heavens above, and that the note that resounded at the foot of the Cross still reverberates among the nations. He lives in and of Himself; he does not derive His power from the earth! (*He makes the sign of the cross on Irydion's forehead*). Believe, and sin no more! — I have corrected you now as a father, weeping over the missteps of his son. But later, should you repeat your guilt, I will admonish you like the pastor of this flock, and punish you like a judge among men!

CHORUS, *nearby*
>From the depths we cry unto Thee, o Lord!
>Receive upon Thy breast Thy martyr's soul,
>And grant him endless rest in Thy glory,
>For spurning earth, his hangmen he forgave!

The funeral procession enters, bearing the martyr's body on a stretcher. The severed head rests upon its breast. First come men in black robes; after them, women in white.

VICTOR
Give here the symbol of witness and torment, sacred on earth, as in the heavens!

They bring him the Prochristum,[24] which he takes in his hands and places upon the martyr's breast.

As you enter your tomb, I present you with your own blood, shed on behalf of the Son of Man; through it, may you arise on the Day of Judgement.

He kneels, and with him, so do all.

O Thou, who deignedst assume the form of wretches so as to redeem the wretched, take away from us our anger and fury and toss our sins into the depths of the ocean. And him, who has begun his second, and final, pilgrimage, deign receive and reward in Thy truth!

MAIDEN'S VOICE
Grant him the sight of Thy sacred countenance!

ANOTHER VOICE
Grant him a springtime, such as he never had here on earth!

IRYDION
And deliver us from the temptation of vengeance. —

CHORUS
Vengeance?

---

24   A small vial with the Chi-Rho symbol, containing the martyr's blood.

VICTOR
Fortunate they, who die for the Lord. — For they enjoy an early victory. *He raises his arms above the crowd.* Arise, and bear the body to the cemetery of Faustinus.

He takes his place at their head, and they move off slowly. Irydion alone remains behind. Near the exit, Cornelia Metella breaks off from the train of women.

CORNELIA
Why do you not join us?

IRYDION
I must be somewhere else this night.

CORNELIA
Where, Hieronymus?

IRYDION
There, where you would quake in concern of your soul's salvation, although from thence glory shall arise for your people.

CORNELIA
I know that something terrible is being prepared in the catacombs. Today, I saw your comrade, Simeon of Corinth. As he passed, he knocked against me, and did not pause to turn around, but went on with the pelt of a lion upon his shoulders, and his eye fixed upon the vacuum before him — in his eye rebellion smouldered, rebellion and a fierce inspiration. Oh, how unfortunate am I!

IRYDION
Why is that, Cornelia? Does not the pastor himself, our father, the judge of men, Victor himself — oh, what glory! — Does not Victor repeat day in and day out that you are first among all your sisters, and that the mark of election already shines upon your forehead? What more can be desired in this world?

CORNELIA
I hear something strange in your voice, my brother.

IRYDION
It merely seems so to you.

CORNELIA
Ah, and are you the same person, with whom I knelt in the catacomb of Euphemia? To whom I taught my prayer — Hieronymus, is this you?

IRYDION
It is I, sister.

CORNELIA
I offered up so many prayers; I fasted so rigorously, through so many days and nights!

IRYDION
And so shall you reign one day in the heavens. Who would doubt it, Cornelia?

CORNELIA
Oh, it was not for me I did so — No!

IRYDION
Then, for whom?

CORNELIA
For one of my brothers…

IRYDION
For one of the brothers —
He draws near her.

CORNELIA
How terrible you are!

IRYDION
Tell me the truth— tell me his name. Whoever he may be, he shall be yours. But hurry, woman: not much time is left us. Later there will be no time for promises before a Cross, and I wish to unite you both, send you both far away, that you may live together — in happiness — in the Thebaid— Speak! Ha! an earthly love has crept into the soul of the chosen one!

CORNELIA
You are mad!

IRYDION
His name? — Your one and only— that brother of yours?

CORNELIA
Hieronymus! But as he was before — not him, who glares so wildly, who stands before me now, out of his senses. Apage! Apage!

IRYDION
Quiet, you beautiful, happy girl. Behold, I am once again as calm as before.

CORNELIA
And as sweet as before?

IRYDION
Humbly I stand before you.

CORNELIA
Before the Lord!

IRYDION
At your feet I shall kneel and invoke the name of Christ, again and again.

CORNELIA
Promise me that you will not mix in with the others. That you will not don your armour for earthly violence, violence condemned!

IRYDION
You poor girl, you do not know what you are saying.

CORNELIA
So you won't?

IRYDION
I am to lead them.

CORNELIA
Woe is me!

IRYDION
Have you not heard so many of the saints declare that the time is near? Do you not recall the words of Him who, in departing this world, promised to His own that He would return and ascend His throne? And did not his favourite, on the isle of Patmos, say again that Babylon was to fall, and that the just would recline upon her ruins?

CORNELIA
Someday, someday — but not today!

IRYDION
Today, my sister! Now, or never!

CORNELIA
For just such thoughts, just such words, Victor excommunicated Eudorus.

IRYDION
And for just such thoughts, just such words, the Romans nailed Eudorus to a cross.

CORNELIA
Go to the bishop, confess to him, ask him, like an obedient child…

IRYDION
I am able to become like a child only in your presence, and only for a brief moment, which then passes forever like a wave. Beyond the scope of your vision I shall wade through blood — and where my steed passes, there grass will never grow again!

CORNELIA
You blaspheme!

IRYDION
No, I merely foretell the triumph of your God!

CORNELIA
Was it such a triumph that you learned of Him? Did He not bless the weak on account of their weakness? Did He not promise the innocent the kingdom of Heaven, on account of their smallness, their stillness?

IRYDION
Such it was at the beginning, but today, sister, the weak have grown strong, and innocent babes have become men!

CORNELIA
Mercy, O Lord, have mercy on him! Let him not fall away here, before my eyes! Ah, what am I saying? Where am I? For did I not vow unto Thee, O Lord, my heart entire? — How gloomy it is here. — For the first time I tremble, here, among the dead — Who is here with us?

IRYDION
Lean on me.

CORNELIA
Yes, yes, you shall not take yourself away from my power — Grace will make your soul bloom anew with spring! I know that I was born to save you!

IRYDION
Neither you, nor anyone on earth shall tear from my bosom the desire that rends it. Even if God should not call us to the task, even if the aid

of the holy were not promised us, still would I commence the work! — Perhaps this is the last time I shall speak with you. You know all the deeds of my mother, but hidden from you are the great thoughts of my father. Take to your lips but a drop or two of the gall that eats at me — Listen!

CORNELIA
The last time... you will speak with me?

IRYDION
Listen!
He sits down at the front of a sarcophagus. Above, she leans on the same tomb.
On the morning of the thirteenth anniversary of Grimhilda's death, suddenly, my father called me to his side. For several days, an ill-boding paleness had befouled his cheeks. "My son," he said, "have them prepare a feast in the hall of Delphic Apollo. Today is the last day that we shall recline at the same table. The god of your mother pursues me, and before tomorrow's sun arises, I shall depart this earth." I was seized with fear, but I went to carry out his commands. He spent the entire day in conversation with the old man of the Mauretanian deserts. Their voices reached my ears like the last sword clashes of a battle drawing to a close. Then all grew silent, and both emerged and marched toward the banquet hall!

CORNELIA
A shiver, like the swipe of a reptile's scaly skin, slides down my back!

IRYDION
He took my sister in his embrace and then slowly pushed her away, saying "What your brother commands you to do, fulfill, out of love for me." He said nothing more to the weeping girl, but spilt a few drops of wine in libation and then lay down, to drink the health of great men from a cup crowned with myrtle. A freedman read *Phaedon* to him. He had one hundred slaves enter, and he manumitted them all. He responded to their thanks with: "As I have shattered your chains, remember yourselves — as much as it shall be in your power — to tear away the fetters that bind others. Whatever my son shall command

you, later, carry it out." Then he arose, as calm and beautiful as the evening slowly being enfolded by the night, yet still glowing with the purples of the sun!

A moment of silence.

And then, in the furthest chamber of the palace, that last night, which was to seal my fate, commenced. The flames of tripods shone around us — Masinissa cast incense upon them. The head of Amphilochus rested on the bosom of his friend, as life slowly ebbed away. All throughout we maintained an unwavering solemnity. Regret for interrupted designs lay bound in the depths of his soul. Suffering struggled in vain — the only sign he permitted it was the contempt seen on his lips. He died — as live the gods!

CORNELIA
I see him — I see him, but where is his guardian angel at this moment?

IRYDION
At that moment, he was busy creating the future, which he once longed to grasp himself, and now bequeathed unto me. "You shall never bend low your brow; you shall never lose faith in an evil hour, and in a good hour you shall never forgive. You shall never cease, but progress still over the corpse of him cast down in order that others standing might fall. You must never be sad or weak, for, as the moon in the skies, so the nations of the earth wax strong, only to wane. Today Rome nears its horizon, inching toward the lowlands of death." Thus did he teach, while from the silences of the night a life awoke by degrees — moment by moment the god of vengeance pressed upon him!

    At last, I made my vow before his holy countenance — He held his hand above my head — I vowed to taste no delight — to know no fellow-feeling, no love — to heed no pleas for mercy — but to live only to destroy, until my spirit should be joined to that of my father.

CORNELIA
Forgive him, Lord, he knows not what he says!

IRYDION
Then, from a chalice, Masinissa spilled the steaming blood upon my head and his hands, while the first ray of dawn shone upon the bed of the dying man. — "My Hellas!" he cried aloud in love, then looked about like one who triumphs, in an apotheosis of victory! In such inspiration, his earthly span coursed to its end. — Cornelia! Vengeance is my good — in vengeance I must live, and die!

CORNELIA
Upon whom would you wreak it? Hieronymus, who has sinned against him, against you?

IRYDION
Those have, who constrain you to wander about such places, which the living flee after burying the dead! Those have, who have abused your God a thousand times, and who have trodden underfoot all that was divine in the human heart! — Are you aware of the past? I shall explain it to you, as Christ the scriptures to his unknowning companions on the road to Emmaus. — It so happened, near the evening-time of the world — the blooms of the dawn had already withered, the fires of youth had died down on the Aegean shores — that, once more, in the North, the voice of free men resounded. And then all grew quiet. Then did there arise such a man, who said "I shall bring back the glories of the past, and those who destroyed everything, these shall I destroy." — Will you condemn him, daughter of Christians? He wished that the suffering should cast away their bonds, that those blinded in slavery should see and recognise again their paternal hearthside, that the deaf and dumb should hear and speak again their mother tongue. Was he not heralding the second coming of your God? John, alone and defenceless, once cried out in the desert, announcing the advent of the Son of Man. But such a Son as would be tortured and put to death. — My father was the precursor of him, who shall be victorious — who shall reign — in whom you put no faith, but doubted!

CORNELIA
Me?

IRYDION
Taking her by the shoulder.
Yes, when you reckoned that He should leave this earth to the pillaging of the Romans; when you thought that he would never be sated with your blood!

CORNELIA
He is lost, ah Lord! And yet a fire eternal, the flame of the cherubim, flashes in his eyes!

IRYDION
Believe! You cannot imagine what awaits me in the morning! I shall lead your people — just believe, and Jove shall tumble down from the Capitol, never to rise again.

Footsteps.

It is Victor, the unbeliever! — Remain! — I shall return in a moment.

He enters a dark passage.

CORNELIA
Kneels down.
Poor heart of mine, no, not mine — you heart unknown that beats so tearingly, lift up your prayers to Christ! O, Lord, Lord, hear Thy servant!

Never have I turned my eyes from Thy cross to rest them upon a mortal countenance — but now, O Lord, two eyes have burned themselves into my memory — his eyes, O Lord, his!

And like a prophet, like a saint, like an archangel he stands before me, and I give ear to his words, Lord, and wish to die.

She drops her face into her hands.

Lord, have mercy upon me!

VICTOR
Enters with a train.

"Whenever you shall gather in my Name, there shall I be in your midst." — Why did you not heed these words today? I saw neither you, nor Simeon of Corinth, nor many others. — My daughter, leave the paths of loneliness to the unrighteous; and turn away from them, as they stand bent over their graves, slyly conspiring.

CORNELIA
Oh, father!

VICTOR
Did you at least pray here, united with us all?

CORNELIA
I am praying now, father!

VICTOR
We're you alone?

CORNELIA
Father! I am alone —

VICTOR
You quiver like a dying flame. What has come over you, Metella?

CORNELIA
I search for my God, for my Lord, but cannot find Him.

VICTOR
The greatest saints have been visited with such moments of uncertainty — It is a sign that the enemy is near. Pray, and watch, for the spirit is willing, but the flesh is weak.
He makes to leave..

CORNELIA
Father!

VICTOR
Turns.
What is it, my child?

CORNELIA
Is it near dawn?

VICTOR
The night has just begun.

CORNELIA
And the Day of Judgement, father — is it near?

VICTOR
At each moment the Son of Man may call us before His face — Do you sense something?

CORNELIA
No — I am merely very weak — I just wished to know.

VICTOR
Still tonight in Elohim I will celebrate the Holy Sacrifice on your behalf. Your soul is sick, your body is exhausted with penances — Arise, fear not, and go to rest, go to sleep, my daughter!
He exits.

CORNELIA
Why did I not make the bishop stay?

Irydion returns.

I hear steps, light steps, the steps of a tempter. *Turns.* Ah, so beautiful! As beautiful as an angel! — Victor! Victor!

IRYDION
He cannot hear you.

CORNELIA
Throwing her arms around the sarcophagus.
Ashes of the saints, be my protectors this night!

IRYDION
What is it you fear?

CORNELIA
Can you not see how dark it is? Do you not feel how cold it is? It is as if everyone had died, and only the two of us remained behind — the two damned. The rest of them are in the heavens!

IRYDION
The hour of which I spoke to you pressed too heavily upon your heart!

CORNELIA
You are mistaken. Having pined for the palm of martyrdom, should I tremble in the face of my Lord's victory? No — no — but something's become unharnessed in my soul — something is eroding in my heart, something is breaking in my breast, Hieronymus.

IRYDION
A woman has no need of mighty acts; with one quiet prayer she may be redeemed. If she feels no strength moving within her, let her depart from me. Here our paths diverge. You shall once more be as peaceful as before. We shall meet again, someday, but not on this earth.

CORNELIA
You have spoken the truth. Come, my feet, bear this soul away, far away!
She tries to get up, Irydion gives her his hand.
Ah, again you pierce me — I cannot go —

IRYDION
Poor thing!

CORNELIA
Something immortal winds me around; two arms invisible, binding me!

IRYDION
I tell you for the last time: flee!

CORNELIA
No — as long as you have not yet given up the ghost in mortal error, so long are you my brother in the sight of our Heavenly Father.

IRYDION
I attest before you, bones of the dead, and before you, Mother Earth, I wished to save her, her alone!
He walks about the chamber.
Thus did my father once murder the soul of an innocent priestess — I am wound about by the might of wild fate.
He draws near her.
Cornelia! Cornelia!

CORNELIA
I am praying for you — Here, come kneel beside me. Put off your pride, and repeat my words…

IRYDION
Tomorrow, or the day after, my prayer begins. And it shall be a loud one, my sister, to the accompaniment of my enemies' groans!

A VOICE NEARBY
Hieronymus, to arms!

IRYDION
I'm on my way —

CORNELIA
That's him! — That's Simeon!

IRYDION
And further on, a thousand like him chafe in impatience, awaiting my coming!
He tears away her veil.
Shatter, you crust imprisoning my soul!
He pulls her to him in an embrace.
Lips, leave upon this pale brow the token of a better Destiny!

CORNELIA
Ah! Along with you I shall be damned, for age upon age!
She faints.

VOICE
Hurry! Hurry!

IRYDION
Picks up his helmet and sword, then returns and bends over Cornelia.
No — you haven't died.
Presses her to his breast.
Awaken, upon the hard armour of your husband;[25] awaken, Cornelia! — Masinissa, be damned if you do not repay me for her loss, with victory!

CORNELIA
Who is calling me?

IRYDION
The one, of whom it was said, "He comes to overcome the proud."

---

25 The line is more subtle in Polish: *Obudź się na twardym pancerzu męża*, in that the word "mąż" which in contemporary Polish is almost exclusively used to denote a man in a conjugal union, a "husband," in the formal Polish of Krasiński's time also carried the connotations of heroic "manhood." This meaning of the word can still be found in the term *mąż stanu*, "statesman." Given the erotic, romantic subtext of Irydion and Cornelia's relationship, I opted for the straightforward, contemporary translation, in hopes that the subtlety of the situation wasn't totally destroyed: after all, Irydion makes his confession of love to an unconscious girl.

CORNELIA
I see — I see Thee at last — and Thou hast deigned to rest thy hand upon thy beloved! Long, long have I waited...

IRYDION
Raise your head — pierce these vaults with the eye of your soul — There, the elect sing the hymn of triumph. Arise from the dead!

CORNELIA
O Lord, the glory of battles plays about Thy countenance! Thou art radiant in flashing iron! But Lord, where are Thy wounds? Permit me to bathe them with my tears!

IRYDION
Supporting her in his arms
Tomorrow, woman, the things foretold of the Kingdom of the Cross shall be fulfilled.

CORNELIA
O, disappear not among the dark shades! They said that Thou wouldst come; take me with Thee, now! Hast Thou forgotten Thy handmaid?

IRYDION
Poor thing — cease your weeping, your despair!

CORNELIA
Permit me to perish in Thy glory! I had already died, O Lord!

IRYDION
Raises her from the ground, passionately.
A few days more, woman. Meanwhile, call out to your brethren, "To arms, to arms!"

He exits.

CORNELIA
Have you not heard His last words? — He has set foot upon the earth again, and this time, a sword is shining in His hands! To arms! Bones of

the dead, priests, people of God, respond! Such was His command —
Follow me! To arms, to arms!

She exits in haste.

*

Another place in the catacombs — Simeon of Corinth, and next to him, a crucifix, a book, and a skull.

SIMEON
In one day to possess the world! Not this wretched globe, where gold flashes and iron clangs, but that immense world, that world of all souls, and to reign over them in Thy name, O God! Ah, that sea of brightness, that great thought spread wide before me — to swim to it over streams of suffering and abasement, cutting the gloomy billows with ever broader strokes! — O, Christ! Then I would conquer, in Thy name, everything, which is called the flesh. There, far below, lie deserts and rocky cliffs, and cities, from which resound the cries of monarch and merchant, and my spirit, an earthly reflection of Thine, hovering high above, shall press down on them in a unity of power. I shall make them grow silent, or pray — shiver in terror or jubilation — think, or fall asleep!

IRYDION
Enters.
I greet you, son of Hellas, my brother twice over!

SIMEON
At last you're here.

IRYDION
There is still time.

SIMEON
Did you meet with Victor?

IRYDION
Victor is an aged child, although he rule over us. He finds weakness sweet, and that weakness turns stubborn.

SIMEON
But I tell you truly — the flock will not head off into pastures unknown without the blessing of their Shepherd.

IRYDION
We will delay to the last moment — then, suddenly, we shall assault him from all sides with our desperate pleas. Caught unawares, he will either be paralysed with terror or enlightened by God's Holy Spirit!

SIMEON
I will throw myself at his feet, and the spark that will leap from my stricken heart will set his soul ablaze.

IRYDION
That soul slumbers deep inside him. Virtue has desiccated his face. But we must march ever forward whatever the case, never looking back. In this our salvation lies.

SIMEON
It shall be as you say. Can you hear that rumble of voices? They gather together, just as I commanded them to, where the consecrated graves border on the cemeteries of the old pagans.

IRYDION
Take in hand the unavenged, Crucified One, and carry Him before them!

SIMEON
Grasps the crucifix.
O how blind, how mean spirited I have been! Believing that unrighteousness must be borne meekly; that one must suffer one's way into Heaven! *He takes the skull in hand.* Behold these sunken brows — in these eye-sockets, the life of my life once shone! The bishop was to join our hands in matrimony. But the night before, a centurion broke in

and stole the innocent girl away from me, for the Flavian Circus — and this is all that was returned to me from the maw of the tiger! And how long did I struggle still against the lust to resist, as if against the devil himself. And yet, it was a living spirit, a holy one, that took possession of me by degrees! *He sets down the skull.* Rest, poor girl! Soon you shall arise to me, from the dead!

IRYDION
And so, to vengeance. Forward, to where the swarming bees hum!

They exit.

*

Ample dungeons — cenotaphs along the walls. Grave mounds here and there — Christians gathered with torches.

CHORUS OF YOUTHS
Wretched is he, of woman born. His days are of little consequence and fleeting; he is neither able to unpin his arms from the cross, nor tip the thorns from his brow. The dark shadows are his sisters, and his grave!

CHORUS OF AGED MEN
Holy, holy, holy, righteous are Thy judgements! Thou shalt elevate future generations through the torments of their fathers. The green of spring covers the piles of our bones, and the scarlet of power dost Thou spread before our sons!

CHORUS OF YOUTHS
Send us your comfortor — let him stand upon the high places, pressing down beneath his feet the necks of the proud, until the valleys are filled and uneven ways become straight.

Enter Simeon and Irydion.

Greetings!

SIMEON
In the name of the Father, the Son, and the Spirit — may hope be with you.

CHORUS OF AGED MEN
Simeon, Simeon, why does he who comes after you, who not long ago wore the robes of a catechumen, now dress himself in armour? Teach him, enlighten him: penance should be his breastplate, and sincere prayer his only weapon.

SIMEON
To Irydion
Climb up on this gravemound — speak for yourself, while I shall again conjure the spirit. A few moments more and I shall stand in him.

IRYDION
He who asks — let him not trust in his own wisdom, but let him look around him and recall the prophesied days of catastrophe that are to loom over the earth!

The age of meekness ends today, for the tortures of the righteous have overbrimmed the cup of suffering — there is no more room to be found in the graves. The very bones of the dead push you up, violently, toward the sweet blue skies!

He who lay in the dust, let him now arise. He who rejoiced in trampling our heads, let him now tremble. For the depths arise, and the elevated shall sink into the abyss!

CHORUS OF YOUTH
Son of promise, may the peace of the Lord be with you!

IRYDION
May the scorching bolts of the Lord be with me, and with you all! My inspiration has arisen from your wrongs — in the grace of the One God, Who is Three, my consolation has its beginning — and my strength, made stronger one hundredfold by your will, O, let it boil and cry out to God for vengeance!

Listen to me. The city is split in two this night. The son of luxury senses his throne trembling beneath him. The praetorians have turned their hearts away from him, and the people, like a sea uncertain what wind to submit to, wavers and is silent — but soon the heavy wings of the wind will fall upon it, and the hailstones of confused desires will pummel its waves. Look! visible darknesses gather above the capital that murders the prophets and the saints! All of the legions of Asia are up in arms. The Alemani are revolting on the Rhine. Caesar and Alexander ready themselves for the decisive struggle. The one calls upon Mithras, the other Stator, and whichever is victorious, shall be victorious with a curse for Christ upon his lips! Behold the sign given you — the promised slogan. Look, and behold — if only you wish it, you shall be free!

CHORUS OF AGED MEN
Who was it that gave power into your hands, and etched the word of God upon your brow? Where is Victor, father of the faithful, the anointed pastor? Will he say of you, "Behold the one awakened of God?"

SIMEON
Climbing up on another gravemound
I shall bear witness to him! *He lifts high the Cross.* Behold the Lord, above all pride, God, the victor nailed to the threshold of this mortal world! — You, who have no heart, stand there in your places like boulders cast upon the road. It is not for you that I speak. You, who do not desire that Jerusalem should emerge from the depths of time, grow old and be silent — It is not to you that I speak!

I only call upon those for whom He bore shame and endured mockery, until the very sun hid itself in the shades of night on account of His torments! And from the time of that horrid darkness, who has called anyone to account for the vituperation suffered by the Son of Man? — No one clothed Him, no one refreshed Him with cool water — All the nations of the earth, one after another, merely crucified Him anew!

CHORUS OF YOUTHS
Cursed be the worshippers of Moloch!

IRYDION
Let not the present moment slip by — Do not look upon it as you might a winged thing, that passes and disappears in the distance; as you might a lightning bolt that flashes, and expires in its flashing! No, everyone, together, in accord, stretch forth your arms, and embrace it! Press it to your hearts, O brothers! It is but a tiny thing now, this moment, and soon to pass — O, strike from it the spark of life, for verily I say unto you, in this tiny moment slumber long ages. If you but awaken them, they are yours!

CHORUS OF AGED MEN
The fire of prayer is snuffed in our breasts — the fogs of mystery float thick above us — Lord, deliver us from the seducer's temptation, Lord!

IRYDION
That is weakness — by the fetters of your fathers I implore you: Cast it away from you! By the flaming pyres of Nero, cast it away! By those sacrificed in the Circus I conjure you — grow strong!

CHORUS OF YOUTHS
Your voice is like a trumpet blaring — it calls us into the plains of the world — but our bosoms are atremble, our hackles rise! O Simeon of Corinth, speak — can you not see this?

SIMEON
I do see, with the eyes of John, who years ago beheld the Jerusalem of the elect. He is now sleeping in his grave, amidst angels inclining, and he shall arise, today or tomorrow, at which time I shall step aside. But now it is I who prophesy, who call!

CHORUS
His brow has tightened in furrows — the black cross trembles in his hands like a branch tossed by the winds!

SIMEON
The Spirit has gathered me up, lifted me aloft. I tread upon the ruins of the city — upon idols knocked down like clods of turf — golden eagles missing beaks, wingless, handsful of shattered weapons — purples like

linens spread upon the fields, wound about with the webs of spiders. Flames lick at the corpses — the braids of virgins are all undone, the long robes of consuls, caesars, heaped upon wagons that bear them away. *He falls to his knees.* O martyred God, inspire their souls as Thou hast mine own, and enkindle in their limbs the consuming flames of battle! *He rises.* The frothing waves of your prayers have crashed upon the shore of Heaven. The souls of the sons of men, murdered by ire, now stand around the altar upon which a flame burns eternally, before the footstool of the throne — And I looked upon Him, who reigns from the throne — He has counted them all up, and their number now completes the book of witness and death, which is now closed. And a voice thunders: "From now on, you will bear witness to me by living, by conquering!"

CHORUS
All kneel
Christ, Christ, our hearts are in turmoil, for we wish to rise again! Abandon us not at this moment of uncertainty! Grant us the revelation of Thy judgements!

IRYDION
Are you still uncertain, people of little faith? Lift up your eyes — Behold your Lord as He expires — See: His lips part for a final cry: "Father, why hast Thou abandoned me!" My brothers, and shall we too abandon Him again, today?

CHORUS
No. — No! —

IRYDION
Ha!
Turns around.

SIMEON
You turn pale?

IRYDION
There, at the turning of the barrel vault; there — at the very edge where light borders upon darkness…

ONE OF THE CHORUS
Someone nears us with light tread —

Metella runs in.

SIMEON
Greetings, virgin betrothed to eternal love. —

CHORUS
Whence do you come to us, at such a late hour, alone, your hair undone?

Metella halts at Irydion's gravemound.

SIMEON
To Irydion
Speak on!

IRYDION
Turning to Cornelia
Do you recognise me? Do you recall my words?

ONE OF THE CHORUS
Did you hear the screech of the holy woman?

OTHERS
Horrid; at this hour, the horrid has entered into our hearts.

IRYDION
Quiet! She is about to speak!

CORNELIA
Thou hast appeared and pronounced horrifying words — Since then I have been running, calling — days and nights pass, and I run, and I call — *Turning to the people.* To arms, to arms!

IRYDION
Through you, Masinissa, I am victorious! *To the people.* The soul of this woman has understood the mystery of the heavens more quickly than you. — Wash yourselves clean of your shame in the blood of the idolaters! *He places his hand on Cornelia's head.* Become now the living voice of the promised glory! Tear apart the curtains of the ages before the eyes of the people!

CORNELIA
I saw the armoured one amidst thunderbolts. He moved on, conquering, toward further conquests, and I was made immortal before his countenance!

CHORUS OF AGED MEN
Did you have a vision? And do you still gaze upon His fainting last moments? Respond, answer us!

CORNELIA
I see the armoured one amidst the thunderbolts. — The arrow that flies from his bowstring takes measure of the earth — He has covered himself in terror as if in the folds of a royal garment, and pale death walks behind him!

She flees.

ONE OF THE CHORUS
Among the standing throngs, among the torches, her hair rises and falls like the waves of the sea.

CHORUS
Where are you hastening?

CORNELIA
There, where the light does not reach — there, let my voice fly. To arms!

ALL
To arms! — To arms!

VOICE OF CORNELIA
Vanish, darkness! Ye lifeless rocks, tremble in witness to the Lord!

SIMEON
She has disappeared, carried hence by inspiration. Now, listen to my brother — Consider well the young man's words!

IRYDION
Whoever comes to Amphilochus' palace and pronounces these words at the threshold: "Sigurd, son of Grimhilda," shall receive sword and javelin, and a helmet of bronze. Remember: "Sigurd, son of Grimhilda."

FIRST BARBARIAN
There was a famous priestess in the Chrersonese —

SECOND BARBARIAN
Our fathers spoke that name, and trembled.

THIRD BARBARIAN
To the forests of Saxony, our brothers from the Northern sea arrived, mournfully intoning songs of her —

IRYDION
And she was my mother, and you are my brethren! *He descends and stands among them.* Give me your hands — We have left error behind us, but the errors of our fathers still bind the hands of their sons. Today, in Christ's name, be loyal to me!

CHORUS OF BARBARIANS
Son of Grimhilda, son of the lands of silver, accept the freely given and unbreakable faith of free men! No blue eyed, long-haired man shall betray you. We vow to you our flesh, as we have vowed our souls to our new God!

IRYDION
The grandson of the king of men thanks his brethren.

CHORUS OF BARBARIANS
Years ago, Herman initiated war with the southern sun. His sacred bones rest now in the black groves of Irminsul. Onward! Onward! It was there that, before the spirit of the wild wastes seized us by the shoulders and thrust us upon the wide paths of the earth, we first heard the songs foretelling the demise of that horrid thing called Rome — Onward! Onward! You shall be our Herman — under your command we shall destroy the palaces of the treacherous Italians!

Loud subterranean noises are heard.

SIMEON
Why do you take voice, earth, mother of dead flesh, not living spirit?

IRYDION
A judgement falls upon the city.

CHORUS OF AGED MEN
Simeon, Simeon! Do you not recognise the fearful echoes of the Lord's anger?

SIMEON
Verily, I bless the Lord and proclaim unto you His wrath! — Behold! The Almighty has arisen, and the depths cry out to Him for mercy! Behold! A trembling scurries over the rocks, the winds arise like hissing serpents — Hosanna —Hosana! — The graves of the idolaters are riven in twain. — The day of vengeance descends from the storm!

CHORUS OF YOUTHS
Hieronymus, keep your promise! The will of the One God has been revealed to us.

IRYDION
My treasures are yours. My blood is yours, to the last drop. Merely swear that you shall fix this cross upon the summit of the Capitol!

CHORUS OF AGED MEN
Woe to you all, woe!

CHORUS OF YOUTHS
We so swear, in the Name of Christ.

IRYDION
And that you will not rest, nor pray to Him, nor consume his Body and Blood, before you should affix that cross there!

CHORUS
No — No — No!

CHORUS OF AGED MEN
Flee, godless ones — the pillars are crumbling! The earth splits wide!

IRYDION
It is Rome that shall crumble.

OTHERS
Mind the torches!

SIMEON
After me! The One I bear with me once walked safely over the boisterous waves.

OTHERS
Fire! Fire!

CHORUS OF BARBARIANS
Let us stand toe to toe with the crowd. The sons of the northern ice will not perish here wretchedly among the offcast, sulphurus, unsufferable dust!

OTHERS
Back, back! Fire has erupted here!

IRYDION
This way — towards our graveyards, towards Elohim! — Ah! Fright has muddled your reason!

SIMEON
The rock sunds in reply — here at one plunge I have fallen at your feet.

IRYDION
Lean on me — this rock has never trembled yet.

SIMEON
Where are they, who were behind me?

IRYDION
They have disappeared. I have never seen such a night before. Where there were a thousand torches, now there smoulders but one, like a faint star.

SIMEON
And now it too has been snuffed, the one you were looking at… Ah — as has that one! And that one!

CONFUSED VOICES
Forgive us our trespasses — at the hour of our death, we beseech Thee, O Lord!

SIMEON
Stretch out your arms — Uplift your torch above this sea of shadows.

IRYDION
In vain.

SIMEON
Did you hear that rumble, which stifled the voices of the old men?

IRYDION
It is the living who call out — To me!

SIMEON
But those, who were beseeching the Lord a moment ago?

IRYDION
They are the Lord's concern now. To me! To me!

CHORUS OF BARBARIANS
We wandered lost — now among the darknesses, and now amidst the fires — lightning bolts harried us from all sides, but our hearts are beating just as coldly as they did before the storm!

IRYDION
Pass round the flame from torch to torch. I shall lead you out — I remember the road.

SIMEON
O! And now hear the deep voices — Those are our brothers who have made it to Elohim — Let us follow them!

VOICE FROM AFAR
Burn, earth, burn for the end of the world!

IRYDION
Did you hear that?

CHORUS
Let us lose no time — Onward!

IRYDION
Flee!

VOICE NEARER BY
To arms, to arms!

CHORUS
It is the father of lies, who lures you on to your destruction!

IRYDION
It is she!

SIMEON
I will not let you go —

IRYDION
Pushing him away
And who will lead them out, if I do not return? *He goes foward.* Father! I call to you! — May the flames of Erebus humble themselves before me!

VOICE NEARBY
And my chaplet shall be weft of immortal stars, at Thy side. —

IRYDION
Christ, God of her heavens, save the unfortunate girl!

It grows light — Fire beats up from below the earth. Among the flames — Cornelia.

CHORUS OF BARBARIANS
The helm of the fearless one shone forth, and then sank again in the darknesses!

SIMEON
Hieronymus!

CHORUS
Sigurd — Sigurd!

VOICE OF IRYDION
I am on my way!
He returns, bearing Cornelia in his arms.
Turn your faces away — bend low your torches. This way, this way, follow me!

CHORUS IN THE DISTANCE
Save us, Son of Man, and Rome shall be destroyed thrice over, thrice over consumed in flame, Rome, the enemy of the sacred peoples of the South, and the free peoples of the North!

VOICE AMIDST THE DARKNESSES
Sleep now, winds, among the dust of the ancient faithful.

Pillars of fire approach, and amidst them, Masinissa.

CHORUS OF SUBTERRANEAN VOICES
Behold! We have become like to the lamps of a quiet temple, O we torrid ones, we unfortunate wretches, victims of so many tortures, through so many ages!

MASINISSA
The time will come when the entire earth will be given over to you for fuel, but this is the end of your road today — Progress no further!

CHORUS
Victory! But a while, but a while we live by despair, by night! And the heavenly spirits ask:
    "Where is the earth, our sister?" And He shall ask, who saved her, "Where is my beloved?" And before their gaze, we shall shake out her ashes, beneath their stars!

MASINISSA
Calmly, quiet, my children. In this your eternity, it is but a moment more, yet still a thousand thousand human generations stand between you, and it!
    First they must waste their strengths, repulsing each faith, declaring them to be falsehoods, and smearing each denial in filth before at last they adore them! Until the dishes of humility and pride balance flat, until grey heads grow stupid, and strength — frenzy!

CHORUS
Until they perish!

MASINISSA
We shall bestraddle their thought — We shall create worlds for them, each further and further from the truth than the last — Thus shall we torment to death that spark in their soul, which they filched from the

upper regions. We shall enwreath their brows with the ignis fatuus of knowledge. We shall place in their hands paltry sceptres of air — We shall elevate them as masters of the earth!

CHORUS
And they shall perish!

MASINISSA
Walking among the flames
O faith, hope, and love! You Trinity, which were to last for ages! I have torn you to pieces in the hearts of the most beloved children of Your blessing! — No — with them You will not populate the devastated area where happy and beautiful swarms once seethed. You shall never obtain such sons. — You have extinguished the suns, Yourself, which once were Your glory!

CHORUS
May our thrones be raised, everlastingly empty and dead — May all songs of praise perish at their footstools!

MASINISSA
The extermination of those who come after us has begun this night. Just as once we, so shall they fall away from Him!

CHORUS
And they shall come to gnaw our crusts, and languish in our dark chamber!

MASINISSA
O, my Enemy! You know well that Their soul has erred since the world's very first springtime! — From now on, there will never be a day on which they will not argue about Your Names, Your attributes!

They shall kill and burn in Your Name — In Your Name they will rot and grow silent; in Your Name they will oppress others — In Your Name they will build, and destroy!

You shall be crucified both in their wisdom and their dullness, in their calculations and their frenzy, in the sleepy humility of their prayers and in the blasphemies of their pride!

There in the summit of heaven will You drink of that cup of gall until You curse them for all time. In the summit of Heaven, amidst Your power and might, You shall come to know our Hell!

CHORUS
Glory be to us, and to him, who still shines brightly in the fire of rejection, as once he shone with the rainbows of power! Glory be to us! Glory be to us!

MASINISSA
The scar of lightning on his brow he has covered with his palm. — In the depths of the abyss he nourishes his thought for the last days of the world! Glory be to him. And now, wrap me round, darknesses! Perish now in silence, my brethren!

PART III

A tent in the camp of the praetorians, beyond the walls. Aristommachus and Lucius Tubero in front. To the rear, on couches, Alexander Severus and Ulpianus, conversing quietly. Enter Irydion.

IRYDION
I come, Romans, in the name of your master. Rehearse your complaints; I will lend my ear to them all and respond to each according to the mind of Caesar.

ARISTOMMACHUS
If you are indeed curious as to our complaints, you ought to have come see us a year ago. Then we would have spoken with you. But today, Greek, he who has taken weapon in hand has laid aside his moaning. He who threatens, answers not — he commands. As you were coming to us, I'm sure that you saw all of our men, armoured, ready for marching! You will receive no other answer from me!

IRYDION
Is Lucius Tubero of the same mind?

TUBERO
Although my rash comrade is more fit for the ranks than the rostrum, Irydion, still I have but little to add to his words, at this moment. You need only remind the emperor that we had long submitted our requests to him in vain — that he did not deign build us the promised amphitheatre, nor did he dispense the well-deserved awards. And from me you will remind the emperor that my father lived in his bathtub until his throat was cut, and my sister's daughter lived too, until she was made to swallow live coals. You will rehearse to him the names of the senators whom, over the last three years, he sentenced to a loss of their honour, and a loss of their heads. You will tell him that once I had many friends and blood relations who enjoyed great prosperity,

while today I have no one, or, those that I do have are torn by the wrenching pains of hunger. And yet Eutychian lives, a few freedmen live on, and a few whores go about dressed in purple. And finally, you may add that he has brought shame upon a Greek girl of an ancient and honest house…

IRYDION
Takes up a tablet and stylus, and writes.

TUBERO
What is it you are writing, son of Amphilochus?

IRYDION
Your name, this hour, your death. Please, continue…

TUBERO
Thank you, Danaus! Yet, tell your master that if he hand over Eutychian, we shall break him on the cross, and we shall use all of his treasures to pay the wages of our soldiers. Tell him that if he immediately lays aside his consular power, and his tribunal and pontifical dignities, perhaps we shall yet allow him to live with his lover, sending him thence, whence he first dragged shame and misfortune to the city!

ARISTOMMACHUS
But let him hurry up about it, for tomorrow at dawn we shall be at the gates of the city, and an hour later — in the palace of the Caesars!

IRYDION
Is there nothing more, most noble Romans?

ARISTOMMACHUS
Taking his sword in his hand.
Only this!

TUBERO
For only that can pay back, in one day, the humiliations of many years!

ARISTOMMACHUS
Only this can slice the diadem from Caesar's brow, and knock the teeth out of the sarcastic smile that plays on the face of his trusted envoy!

IRYDION
You speak well — you have divined it — I laugh from the very depths of my heart to hear Romans speak of yokes and indignation and shame, with disgust!

You, whose fathers were transformed into a herd of cattle by Tiberius; you, whose fathers Nero held in contempt, although he himself was held in contempt by the very dust he trod upon; you dare to complain of abasement! You, the descendants of those who abused the entire world — Please, stop deceiving yourselves! Your clans, whether ancient or recent, were ever temples of baseness! Otherwise the streams that flowed from this city would not have made arid Asia, and Greece, and the whole wide world, as wretched as it is broad, from Hyrcania to Lybia to the deserts of the Jazygs!

Yes, yes, I laugh, Romans; but you have no idea what that laugh of mine portends. *He takes a step forward.* Now, if you don't lay down the sword immediately; if you do not fall at the feet of Heliogabalus; if you do not sacrifice one tenth of your number to his vengeance, woe to you all! Such is the message I bring.

ARISTOMMACHUS
Away with you! Return to the Syrian! Let him anoint his hair well with pommade in preparation for the banquet that awaits him — at the table of Pluto!

IRYDION
I have finished with you. For him there, I still have a word or two.
He draws near Alexander.

ULPIANUS *to Alexander.*
Turn him away with the silence of disdain!

ALEXANDER
I cannot!

IRYDION
Your brother thinks of you. He asks why you disappeared at night from the palace of the Caesars. He calls you back; if you will go, he will commute your sentence, from death to banishment.

ALEXANDER
Jumping from his bed, to Ulpianus.
No, once more no! There is something behind this — let me alone with him, I beg you. Draw away a space, my friends.

All exit.

ALEXANDER
Son of Amphilochus, was it the vindictive gods who spread such a cloud of confusion between us two? I cannot comprehend you — Do you not recognise me — Severus? Irydion, it was you, after all, who swore a hecatomb to Fortune on the day when she should make the dawn of justice to rise over Rome?

IRYDION
I repeat my vow to that same goddess. If she could bring me but a moment's justice, who knows but that in gratitude I might offer Rome entire in hecatomb upon her altar!

ALEXANDER
Son of Amphilochus, insult me not with equivocal words. For you owe me a debt of gratitude, that I do not believe my own eyes, although clearly, they testify to your perversity. Ah! I don't understand myself, why I always wished to trust you!

IRYDION
I thank you, Severus! If the fates had made me a man, and if I had wished to gladden my heart with the blessed gift of a man's friendship, it is you that I would have desired. But now, these bosoms of ours, which might have met in a friendly embrace, will confront one another only on the field of battle.

ALEXANDER
It is not too late yet — Abandon the tyrant! Peer out of the mist with which you have been engulfed and pronounce but one word of friendship, and I will never doubt of your faith. Irydion, where is your sister?

IRYDION
There, where fate has pinned her.

ALEXANDER
And yet she is as pure as are my thoughts of her. Irydion, I must detain you — she cannot suffer him. I read as much in her eyes — her unbearable torments — and you will fight in his defence?

IRYDION
Why must your days be so short, young shoot that you are? No trace shall remain of your flights toward the beautiful and the virtuous. You shall pass away like a sound unheard by man, known only to the gods!

ALEXANDER
Why do you fix such mournful eyes upon me? Ah! I have heard that once, somewhere, your mother bore a powerful god upon her bosom!

IRYDION
The inheritance of the good, from the hands of the base, is — punishment! Son of Mammea, your final hour draws near.

ALEXANDER
You hope to terrify me?

IRYDION
You are mistaken — I only announce the truth to you — If you lose, you shall perish at the hand of the conqueror. If you prevail, you will perish at the hands of those who today use your name as a battle cry.

ALEXANDER
Shame to him who would fret about death before it comes for him, or at the hour of its coming. Whatever the case may be, remain here at

my side. I shall extract Elsinoe from the tiger's maw, and Rome shall once more arise in the springtime of strength, armed with immortal lightning. — Why is it that you shiver? Can you find something bitter in these my hopes?

IRYDION
I remembered that I had come from Caesar to obtain your response!

ALEXANDER
Remind me not of him — But if the gods have granted you any spark of feeling, let it now ignite a firestorm on behalf of your sister's wrongs, and your father's memory! It was your forefathers, after all, who sang to the Persians that vengeance is the delight of the gods!

IRYDION
How innocent you are. *He takes his hand in his own.* I clasp your hand for the last time — the last — for both of us are standing at the lip of the grave, and before a third day dawns, one of us will descend to Erebus.
Exits.

*

A hall in the palace of the Caesars — peristyle, sculptures, costly vessels — In the centre, an altar dedicated to Mithras; in the depths, a curtain embroidered with costly gems hangs between two golden pillars. Elsinoe is dressed in imperial purple. Enter Irydion, helmed and in armour.

IRYDION
Where is the cursed one?

ELSINOE
In there — There his body lies upon violets, his soul upon the bosom of witches. I came out for a breath of fresh air!

IRYDION
Before he slept, did he speak of me? — Did you prepare him according to my instructions?

ELSINOE
He agreed to everything, sobbing and beating his brow. He called forth Eutychian, fell upon his neck, squeezed his hand, yet still he did not dare inform him that you would be taking command of the praetorium — He merely repeated his expectation that, with gentle words, you would convince the rebels to turn back from revolt. He then bade me direct my prayers, on his behalf, to the gods — Then he leapt among the flowers to lie there, though he did not rest, but grovelled like an anxious serpent.

IRYDION
It's time to wake him.

ELSINOE
Come with me.
She spreads wide the curtains to reveal Heliogabalus sleeping on piles of roses and violets.

IRYDION
Wait a moment! His lips part — perhaps he will say something…

ELSINOE
Cursed be those lips! Asleep or awake, quick or in the grave!

HELIOGABALUS
Iry, Iry, why hast thou abandoned me?

ELSINOE
He dreams of you.

HELIOGABALUS
Elsi, my Elsi, why hast thou abandoned me?

ELSINOE
Ah! The daughter of Grimhilda was never thine!

IRYDION
Touching Heliogabalus with his hand
Emperor!

HELIOGABALUS
Who calls? — What? — Where? *He starts.* Ah! It is you two! Ah! My roses and my beloved tripods! *He takes their hands and makes a few steps forward.* I was dying, when your voice recalled me to life!

IRYDION
What did you see that was so horrible?

HELIOGABALUS
It was horrid! As I fell asleep, it seemed to me that the people entire, and all nations, had shrunk into a helpless dwarf wrapped in chains; my foot, shining like a conch of transparent whiteness, rested on his head. My throne glowed with the light of Olympus — and Rome was flaming on all hands, just as you had promised. And there were no people anywhere, for I had crushed all of the living to death beneath my one foot!

IRYDION
And so the gods have sent you a happy omen!

HELIOGABALUS
Listen, listen! — Then it seemed to me that the dead had arisen from their mausolea — Tubero and Lucius Victor, the two Apuleas, and others, you know, all the others — and then at the horizon, suddenly, there appeared my father, Caracalla, his head wound about with serpents, holding human skulls in his hand… Gigantic he was, stumbling through the ashes. And then he fell, crying out "My son!" And then they all began to come in my direction; the dwarf laughed aloud and knocked my foot from his head, and they were coming, coming closer — Then you stood at my side and she, on the other side. Look — They come, they come, and with their togas draped over their left shoulder, while in their right hands they hold stilettos! Then you said, pointing at me, "Behold Caesar" — and Elsinoe said, as if handing me over, "Behold your murderer!" And one hundred naked lightning bolts flashed before my eyes — one hundred shattering thunderclaps fell upon, fell into, my breast! *He retreats and covers his eyes.* And then him again, him, my father!

IRYDION
Shake your head free of these deceptive grains sown in your senses by Morpheus. Now more than ever you must be in total command of yourself, and strong. For the praetorians have torn your insignias from their cloaks forever, and Alexander has sworn never to rest until your diadem should adorn his brows!

HELIOGABALUS
O, wretched me! Did you announce my entire will to them? Did you offer them the forgiveness, the largesse I promised them as a reward for returning to their loyalty?

IRYDION
It is not gold they desire, but your blood!

HELIOGABALUS
Embracing the altar.
O trinity of delight! O Chaldean lord!

ELSINOE
As long as you snivel before the altar of Mithras, so long will you remain in danger and the shadow of death. Pray to Odin, and the holy ravens he shall send will triumph over the eagle!

HELIOGABALUS
Your voice, Elsinoe! May I hear your voice at the hour of my death — May your arms wind round my chest like a fatal band — I loved you while I lived, although you never suffered me.

ELSINOE
Die not before death takes you! — Get up, and call Eutychian and your bodyguard. — Hand over your rule into my brother's hands, and in return, you shall receive victory.

HELIOGABALUS
Rising.
Ah, if only it still were possible…

IRYDION
No — no! — You must roll the dice of life and death upon the altar of Fortune! — This very night the city will be set aflame — Fear not — And those flames shall consume the songs on the lips of Aristommachus. Where are your treasures?

HELIOGABALUS
I sent a portion off to Syria — The rest are guarded by Eutychian.

IRYDION
Command that whatever remains be distributed among the praetorians of the court!

EUTYCHIAN
Running in.
O divine one, things are starting to go badly for us! The people have expelled the soldiers from the curial gates. The senators have forced their way into the curia; they have taken their seats there, and they debate — on what, sweet Anubis? On the death of the divine one!

IRYDION
Hasten, Caesar!

HELIOGABALUS
To Eutychian.
My old friend, give me your hand. Yes, all right, I shall lean upon you as of old. Together we burned incense in the temples of Mithras, together we drank; Ah! How delightful in the past it was to nibble parrot livers, and the lips of maidens burning with wantonness! But now, together, we must retreat before an adverse fate — Hand over your sword to Irydion — I beg you — You shall remain here at my side, and he shall be the praetorian prefect.

EUTYCHIAN
Who? Me? They seek my head, and he seeks my station! Without a sword, without a head, what shall be left of me? I seasoned Silvius' final chalice for you, and…

HELIOGABALUS
Silence! Hand it over!

EUTYCHIAN
Unbuckling his sword.
Greek, be not rough with my child. She has always rocked in a copper cradle here at my loins…

MESSENGER
Running in.
My lord, I come from the senate, where I had insinuated myself in disguise. Canuleus has just now proposed that you die the death of Nero, and that the throne be given over to your brother!

HELIOGABALUS
Ah! Ah! Just yesterday those same faces bent low to kiss my footprints!

IRYDION
Once more I say — Fear not! You, soldier, run through the lower floors and call together as many praetorians as possible. Have them wait for me in the atrium of Domitian. Then hasten to my palace. There you shall find gladiators at the ready, under the command of Scipio — Tell them to rush to the basilica where the senate has begun its deliberations, and as they go, have them call out my name!

MESSENGER *goes out.*

IRYDION
Son of Soaemis, I shall scatter those orators and broach the people like lapping waves! — But I will need something more to conquer Alexander!

HELIOGABALUS
Speak!

IRYDION
You have no time to declare me dictator pro tempore to the army and the people — Lend me your signet. Whoever looks upon it will

recognise me as your deputy, and will follow me, if only he be a loyal subject.

HELIOGABALUS
What? Know you not that the genius of Rome is etched on this stone? That the Emperor who entrusts it into the hands of another commits sacrilege?

EUTYCHIAN
Give it him, give it to Irydion! I shall remain at your side, and he shall be Caesar!

HELIOGABALUS
Mock not your lord and master! *Pulls out a dagger.* Behold this pleasantry — two edged and smeared in Gaetulian venom. I have the urge to sink it in your heart.

EUTYCHIAN
A dirk of gold! Your humble servant has never been afraid of gold…

HELIOGABALUS *rushes upon him.*

EUTYCHIAN
Wait! In the temple of Osiris it was foretold that Caesar will not outlive Eutychian by three days —

HELIOGABALUS
What is it that you say, my friend? Ah! Let me rest my poor head upon your shoulder — Give no ear to evil tongues. I have never stopped loving you!

EUTYCHIAN
As a drunken Macedonian his old Clitus…

IRYDION
I need a sign, a sign! —

HELIOGABALUS
Be gone! I shall not give you these golden serpents and this diamond god! You have all of my treasures, cups, silks… Enough, enough!

Cries are heard from afar.

IRYDION
Do you hear that? The triumphant hymn of Severus begins to sound!

ELSINOE
Respect the son of the priestess! Honour him and do his will!

HELIOGABALUS
O, Elsi! —

IRYDION
Did you hear the prophecy? — Your hand!

HELIOGABALUS
Take it from the hand of Heliogabalus yourself — No — Wait a moment more — Once I too fought with the Legions of Macrinus — It was a day of scorching glare. My silver chariot rolled over the corpses, and I tossed about javelins of gold — like to the rays of a second sun they were. Today, I'd like to repeat this… Ah! Can you see there, above the tripod? Ah! And now, there, behind the pillar! He, himself, beckoning me with his hand! He wraps himself round in the purple of his own blood! — Father! *He falls into Eutychian's arms.* It's bad with me, my friends — My breast is like a house abandoned. Grip not so hard my hand, Greek! You sin against my majesty…

IRYDION
Where power is, let the insignia also be! *He tears the ring from his hand.* Go to your slumbers. When the fires break out, I shall come and wake you.

HELIOGABALUS
Eheu! Now he is Caesar…. Lead me hence, Eutychian. You shall sit at the head of my bed. You shall polish my shield — In the midst of

the inferno I wish once more to see my reflection. Ah! I grow weak, I grow cold — Heliogabalus is sunk in darkness! Eheu! Eheu! O, Elsinoe!

ELSINOE
I hasten after you. —

EUTYCHIAN
Noble Amphilochidion! When you shall grind sand between your teeth, washing it down with your own blood, remember me! — I was a cook, in my youth.

The curtain closes upon him and the Emperor.

ELSINOE
And so it has come to pass. — I have given him frenzy for a final companion on the banks of the waters of Hell, where he now stands. — Speak; what else am I to do, my brother? For be it still tonight, or tomorrow morning, maybe, a praetorian will come and — perhaps flames will hurl themselves upon me, or perhaps my breast will itself disdain further breath, further suffering…

IRYDION
Keep watch over him until I return. Then you shall depart these corrupted halls, and go with me.

ELSINOE
And what will happen to him?

IRYDION
Neither his death, nor his continued life, means much to me. All that he was now flashes upon my finger; all that he is, is not worth a second thought.

ELSINOE
If that be true, come near me. Closer, closer — Can you hear my whisper, now?

IRYDION
What is it you wish, sister? Your hand trembles in mine; your beating heart thumps against my breastplate.

ELSINOE
Then may those eyes beneath which I withered be extinguished. Let the arms that wound about my neck fall away, like old, sick serpents. The lips which first touched my own — let them disappear in ashes!

IRYDION
On one pyre, at the same moment, both he and Severus…

ELSINOE
No, no! Allow me to say my last wish to the end. Irydion, I recognise the strength of your arm, and this is why I bring my final wish to you. Spare Alexander on the field of battle. Cast not the shades of death upon this Greek brow. He alone soothed my despair with his glance — he alone guessed…. Ah! Why do you turn your face from me?

IRYDION
Think not of him! He alone tears Rome from the embrace of my hatred! Can it be that the gods envied men on his account? — But sentence was pronounced upon him long ago.

ELSINOE
So, once more press your sister to your breast! — Do you not feel how this heart is beating? Before you return, it shall burst, son of Amphilochus. But remember: Elsinoe never demanded anyone's blood of you! Live on, all of you — Everyone — Even he, the Syrian; even that abominable one — let him live! As the sacrifice nears its completion, the virgin shall stain neither her white hands nor her snowy robes with gore. Ah, and she stood long before the altar indeed! Day and night her dreams, her desires, her springtime were all consumed into cinders! Look! Their smoke still rises through the air! — But the hour is approaching when the body too will be undone like the long bands of a coturnos — Nothing of it shall remain on the ground but a clutch of wormwood — and the spirit shall become a shade!

VOICES WITHIN THE PALACE
Forward! Fortune and Irydion the Greek!

IRYDION
Away with your womanish mourning, at the moment when Nemesis offers us the wreath of victory in her extended hand! Victory enters my soul — My life dances about those jaws, in those cries! I have been born at this very moment, and you are to die? Be joyful rather, and proud! What your father cried out for, what the long ages begged of the gods in tears, nears us now like a lightning bolt. Hear you not the thunder in the distance?

VOICES
Irydion, Irydion!

IRYDION
Be well!

ELSINOE
Go. You be joyful, you be great. And if ever again you are to sail the Aegean waters, toss a handful of my ashes upon the shores of Chiara!

*

The uppermost terrace of Irydion's palace, encircled with balustrade and statues of Greek deities. Masinissa is seated on an ivory chair. Behind him, Irydion's household and soldiers, barbarians..

MASINISSA
What else? Look again.

PILADES
Something is certainly going on around the basilica — but what it may be, only the Sphinx might guess. — From here, the Arch of Septimius Severus looks like a child's toy in a sandbox. Only the Capitol is large, so large!

BARBARIAN 1
Set up a branch of hazel at two hundred paces, and I will shatter it with my arrows. But that damned Forum is too far away!

MASINISSA
Although so many years weigh down my eyelids, and so many different suns have ruined the pupils of my eyes, still I see farther than you, young ones. — At this moment, the vulture of his helmet glides above the crowd — The unsheathed sword of Scipio precedes him — and following him are the black heads of all your brethren!

BARBARIAN 2
It flashed across my eyes once, too!

PILADES
Brethren, was it the dying echo of a thousand voices I heard? Or did it just seem so?

OTHERS
Listen! It thunders again!

MASINISSA
Nothing will happen to him — He has passed through, and disappeared in the portico. The gladiators have sat down upon the steps, and the mob, like a weary sea, laps against the foot of the structure. Ho! Verres!

VERRES
Here I am —

MASINISSA
How many men have you under your command?

VERRES
The son of Amphilochus has entrusted me with the slaves from Sition, and a company of Germans — those who came over to us yesterday from the Cisalpine Legion.

MASINISSA
As soon as Hesperus rises, you shall lead them to the Porta Collina. Wait there until you see the fiery column appear on these heights where we are now conversing, and then — beginning with the villa of Rupilius, set the blazes leftward, always progressing in the direction of the Forum.

VERRES
Put your faith in me as you would in Catiline!

MASINISSA
Ah, I trust the old patrician to drown the cup of vengeance to the lees!

VERRES
And then to fill it full again.

MASINISSA
Alboinus!

ALBOINUS
What does the son of the desert wish of me?

MASINISSA
You mean the father of the desert, rather. Where are your Heruli?

ALBOINUS
They have just returned, having blocked up one of the aqueducts above the city, as well as Galba's fountain and Manlius' spring within.

MASINISSA
This night your position will be at Nero's pool. Remember to fulfill the duty to which you are sworn.

ALBOINUS
I need no reminding of that. The village of my horde on the banks of the Rhine was burnt to the ground by Caracalla — He then impressed me into service, and today, finally, I reap the reward of my service! I shall thrust away even a blind old man, should he approach with a pail.

I shall refuse even a drop of water to the little child with outstretched hand!

MASINISSA
You speak well! The blessing of an old man will do you no harm!

VERRES
I pray you, look again — my heart aches with anticipation.

MASINISSA
It's empty now, everywhere. Only Scipio, galloping on a horse.

ALL
Where is he headed?

MASINISSA
Away from the Curia Hostilia. Now, at one leap, he disappears among the palaces.

PILADES
Perhaps our master needs our help…

MASINISSA
Hear you nothing?

ALL
No — nothing —

ALBOINUS
Some remnant of a sound swirls in my ear.

MASINISSA
Hoofbeats. Hoofbeats, I say.

VERRES
Something like that, something like that —

PILADES
Look! It's him — He's emerged —

VERRES
Now the obelisk and portico hide him from our sight.

ALBOINUS
He's pierced the temple through and through like an arrow —

MASINISSA
Scipio!

VOICE OF SCIPIO
Victory!

CHORUS
Long live the grandson of Scipio Africanus!

VOICE OF SCIPIO
On the stairs.
Waste no more time — the sun already sinks in pools of blood beyond the Tiber — It's time to drag the trunks and branches of cypress out of the cellars and, before the stars appear, make a pyre of them on the rooftop — *Enters.* — Verres, Masinissa, my friends, the senate is no more!

PILADES
And my master? Where is he?

SCIPIO
He's gone to the palace of the caesars, to oversee the praetorian guards. You'll see him here momentarily! *To the slaves entering with wood and jugs.* Here, in the centre — between Athenian Minerva and Diana of the Ephesians — Sprinkle each layer with aloes-bark and drench them with oil!

MASINISSA
I like your voice, Lucius! Tell us how you chased the brethren from their curule chairs.

SCIPIO
Iridion and I entered the curia together. The conscripted fathers sat there as in the good old days; the statue of Heliogabalus was tossed to the floor, with its head at their feet, their hands about its neck, and Volero the Elder rested his feet on its trunk and orated, as if he were Cato!

VERRES
That son of a merchant!

SCIPIO
He grew silent, when he caught sight of the Greek, for gloomy night sat upon Irydion's brow, as if the night of past ages were reclining there. Maximinus Uxor demanded by what right we profaned the threshold of the senate — in reply to which the son of Amphilochus leaned against the base of a column and, placing his hands on the Medusa that figures on his breastplate, commanded them: "Disperse now, and depart from the city!" A chaos of voices drowned out further speech. Ventidius, a priest of Jove, cried out for the lictors, while others leapt from their chairs, dagger in hand. Then, mockingly, Irydion took voice, icily: "In this tabernacle, where your fathers condemned Greece, I shall shame you, once and for all, if you heed not my words!" Volero rushed out from beneath the rostrum, but his stiletto slid off the Greek's armour, and he himself fell at the foot of Caligula's image, where, having broken his brow on a sharp corner, the good senator fainted away, gushing blood. The Greek hadn't even deigned unsheathe his sword. Turning to me, he said, "I give them over to you, Scipio," and he clapped his hands. At this our men took off the bronze doors, overcame the lictors, and rushed into the curia. The fathers backed down at the sight of their swords — whoever among them resisted, soon found himself stretched out at Volero's side. Those who could, escaped through side doors. As they ran, they called Jove to witness, while I, the victory at Zama, Verres!

VERRES
Ah! And I was not there!

MASINISSA
Be calm — For all that, you will sit you down to a better feast this evening!

CHORUS
Our master comes — We hear his voice —

Enter gladiators, and, following them, Irydion.

PILADES
O son of Amphilochus, you've returned to us, whole!

IRYDION
Rise, my good Pilades — I thank you!
　Ha! The pyre has been readied. All that is lacking is the shroud of amiantus for the ashes of Rome. I greet you all! Old man, have you given the orders?

MASINISSA
All has come to pass according to the wishes of my son.

IRYDION
Sits down beside Masinissa.
Let us rest awhile. Unlatch my helm, Pilades. Lucius!

SCIPIO
Sir!

IRYDION
Weigh each word well, so that you shall remember them, and nourish them like your vengeance! In the palace gardens the praetorians stood, in hope and terror — some drunk, others weaponless, still others without the insignia of their proper century. I allowed them to scream their fill, and when the commotion subsided, I raise my hand — at the sight of the signet, they comprehended the danger that loomed. The tribunes surrounded me with questions — I spoke briefly — The eunuchs of the Syrian carried in bowls piled with silver — and the most solemn oaths began to thunder from the mouths of all: "To the

last drop of blood; to the last breath," and so forth, all good for the day — and mouldy the day after. So go now and keep watch over them. I have told them that I shall send one of my own among them. For a token, take Eutychian's sword with you, and as an escort, take with you the gladiators of Elsinoe. — Keep them in a state of constant anticipation. Tell them that the maniples of Severus are already to be seen just beyond the walls. When the moans begin to be heard in the city, when the glow of the fires reaches the gardens, say, "The maniples of Severus!" They will not go out to meet their frenzied brethren — and if near morning someone from the city cohorts should arrive — at the start, deceive Alexander, invent whatever sort of condition you wish, then break the pact and swear it anew, until his patience be exhausted… and then fight to the last man. "Heliogabalus and Caracalla!" Let that be your deceptive battle cry — until you see the flames upon the summit of the Capitol and the flames in the Forum — for then you will know that the son of Amphilochus is near!

SCIPIO
And should the Syrian crawl forth from the depths of the palace and attempt to foil our plans?

IRYDION
My sister watches over the Syrian. At any rate, let him live until the end, for the praetorians will serve us only as long as breath remains him…

SCIPIO
And where are you off to?

IRYDION
Perhaps I will come to you again tonight. But now, hurry on your way. The dusk has already taken possession of the light headlands of the heavens.

Scipio exits.

IRYDION
It's time you were gone as well, Verres.

VERRES
With me, men!
He exits, leading several men.

IRYDION
Alboin, go along with them.

ALBOINUS
Until we meet again, Sigurd!
Exits.

IRYDION
To the slaves.
Shortly, you too must depart. But before you do, sit yourselves down to the banquet that has been prepared for you in the lower peristyle. Eat, and drink, one last time in my house. Tomorrow, it shall crumble into dust. And tomorrow you shall be wealthy, and free!

CHORUS OF SLAVES
You have been both father and mother to us — We are nourished with bread from your hand, while the bones of others like us are strewn about the circus and the barren lots. If any one of us does not return, seek not for him — for he has fallen on behalf of your glorious name, blessing you with his last breath.

IRYDION
Go now. And when you see this pile of cypresses blaze up, answer it from the temples, the baths, the city gates, with fire and smoke!

They exit. He rises and leans upon the pyre.

IRYDION
The closer approaches the hour, the more furiously races the blood in my veins. Are these darknesses not feigned? Has the eternal desire of my heart blotted the stars from my eyes? No — No — I see it now — this is the last night of Rome. Can you not see, Masinissa, how the men steal along there? On that side — do you see that lonely torch moving along the hills above the gardens? Ah — hear

the horses neigh — those are the horses of Verres. Hush! Hush, my people!

MASINISSA
The courtyards below us begin to empty. There are fewer and fewer voices to be heard… One more toast is raised…

IRYDION
My name shatters against the vault.

MASINISSA
And now, from the porticos, one after another, they go out, hunched over, silent. Then they disappear in darkness.

IRYDION
Everyone has kept his word — Everyone from the house of Amphilochus goes off to the destruction of Rome. The only ones I don't yet see are the Nazarenes! But Simeon swore to lead them here to me, himself, at the third hour.

MASINISSA
You haven't much longer to wait. Hesperus now stands above the Capitol, and the tresses of Berenice rise above the Sabine Hills.

IRYDION
O Night! Be not miserly of your clouds and winds! You shall have ages to shine brightly above these ruins! Time drags her feet, old man — time is what ails me!

MASINISSA
And me as well. But I have been waiting for the fall of my enemy longer than you have, and I wait in silence.

IRYDION
Ah — when you spoke just now, I thought I heard the voice of my father. Might it not be that, at such a moment, a living heart should begin to beat within the bosom of this image of Amphilochus, filling its veins hot blood? In the darkness, on that white chair, you remind

me of him. *Moves over to him.* His toga was arranged just so on the day of his death! Give me both your hands. Pronounce upon my head words of care, as if it were he himself speaking, before the battle-cry!

MASINISSA
May this my sign be on your brow until the end of time. With it, you shall endure such things as the stars above us shall never behold!

IRYDION
The city all in flames! — No — an inferno has erupted in my pupils. Where are they? Where are the Christians? It is ever darker, ever blacker and quieter down below, and ever windier above — and still they come not!

PILADES
Enters
You call me?

IRYDION
Not you — But wait… Are no sounds to be heard in the chambers underground? Do no footfalls approach from the direction of the catacombs?

PILADES
I am returning from the hall of Amphilochus. Nothing is to be heard anywhere.

IRYDION
Bring me a torch.

Pilades exits.

IRYDION
This cannot be — They shall be here, in a moment!

MASINISSA
And should they not come?

IRYDION
Take back those cursed words! Upon them all my power rests. At their head I shall rush about the city, reminding the Roman people of Brennus! My gladiators and soldiers won't suffice against the mobs. If they have betrayed me, I have already perished!

MASINISSA
Let them sing their recessional to the end. Be patient, my son!

Pilades returns with a torch.

IRYDION
Affix it to the pyre!
    I perish like Prometheus, in chains, one cloud away from the feasting hall of the gods. — Why are you so silent? Speak, Masinissa! Long live Hellas!

MASINISSA
I am silent, because the appointed hour is now passed, and at this moment I heard the wings of the passing hour, every feather of them, whistling past in flight, accompanied by laughter. Now, nothing can be heard.

IRYDION
In spite of the Fates, in spite of men, let my father's will be done! *Tears away the torch.* Glory to the land of Greece, glory! And you, threefold Hecate, deign accept this sacrifice…
    Ha! Who comes? Respond, black spectre! If you be my evil genius, come back later! You shall not restrain me now!

ENVOY
Peace be with you, in the Name of Jesus of Nazareth.

IRYDION
Yes, yes, go on! Where is the hermit? Where are his brethren?

ENVOY
Simeon calls to you in despair. The bishop has restrained at the threshold of Elohim all the armed men who were rushing towards the city!

IRYDION
Thank you, servant of the saints. Behold! I am cool — I shall not kill you. *He tramples the torch.* You alone, die! *To Masinissa.* Should any of my men return, have them sit down and wait!

MASINISSA
The dawn is still a long way off.

PILADES
Master, master, your helm!

IRYDION
To conquer, a blade suffices. To die, no helm is needed. Forward, Nazarene!

They exit.

MASINISSA
Rising from the chair and extending his hands.
O my city beloved, I bless you! O Rome, be of good cheer and calm within the shadow of these arms! Your villainy has saved you! Live, and oppress, so that the body might rot in torments, and the spirit doubt in God! *He disappears beyond the pyre.*

*

The Elohim tabernacle in the catacombs. Victor is standing at the steps of the altar. Behind him, priests and elders. On the one side — Simeon; on the other, Metella. Further: armed Christians, kneeling. A chalice and a cross rest upon the altar; the cross is adorned with roses, and stands amidst thuribles smoking with incense.

VICTOR
Like to nauseous billows of smoke, there shall be no trace of you, on earth or in Heaven! O! If your sleep could only be a sleep of stone, without consciousness, memory, or waking! But in the broad region of death you shall live where the vengeance of God beats down in constant bolts! You shall live thus, for age upon age! *To Simeon.* Begone! Flee as did the first murderer, from before the countenance of Jehovah!

SIMEON
Hear me out just once more!

VICTOR
Turn your eyes upon the woman here, whom I shall not address, as the hand of judgement rests upon her brow too. Answer me! Who was it killed her soul, exploiting still her flesh, that she might become a laughing stock among the living? Hear you not the voice of possession in the words formed of her lips?

CORNELIA
Why are you oppressing me, priests of my people?

CHORUS OF PRIESTS
Silence, daughter of rebellion! You were destined to be an angel, but you did not persevere unto the end. Damned you are, damned!

CORNELIA
"Poor thing," thus He spoke unto me. He knew that I was to suffer shame on His account. But, O Simeon, doubt not! He will come — My brethren, fall not away from Him — He will come!
    He has plucked me out from the midst of the flames, when they were disputing over my flesh — and from your midst too He shall pluck me. He will come; He will come!

SIMEON
Victor, hear me for the final time! I have always been obedient unto you — who will bear testimony against me? Have I not undergone a double martyrdom, once in the dungeons of Antioch, and again

in the agora of Tarsus? Have I not mortified my flesh in penitence, through long years in the desert? Have I ever trespassed against the Law, or scandalised my brothers?

VICTOR
You do so at this very moment, boasting like a Pharisee, damned as you are by the Son of Man!

SIMEON
I only speak the truth. Who among you has meditated more deeply than I upon the Lord's Passion? In whom was ever a more ardent love enkindled at the recollection of Golgotha? God Himself, in order to save the world, took on flesh, and we, in order to teach the world, have we not flesh as well? Up till now, we have been mere spirits. Where is our home, our church, our might?

VICTOR
You Corinthian sophist! Who is it you wish to confuse with your deceitful words? "My kingdom is not of this world." You have heard those words, have you not?

SIMEON
Why did I abandon my burning sands? There I loved only the Uncreated. Here, I cannot endure His creatures!

VICTOR
My son!

SIMEON
I am harried night by night, by a voice I hear — is this but a vain illusion?

VICTOR
Not long ago you were a chosen child of the Church, but today, you wish to crucify your Lord a second time!

CORNELIA
Bow low your heads! I hear the echoes of His second coming![26]

Irydion enters.

CORNELIA
Behold, the One whose countenance shines with eternal youth! *She casts herself at his feet.* I told them that Thou wouldst come, O Lord, Lord!

CHORUS OF PRIESTS
Begone, you heretic!

VICTOR
At this hour, the chalice of mercy goes dry in the hand of your angel.

IRYDION
I shall replenish it with Roman blood.
　Who here has sworn, and then failed to keep his oath? Simeon of Corinth. Who has cringed unto the dust and let fall the sword from his hand? You, brethren. And at this moment, in the city, nothing more is needed for Caesar and the city's gods to perish than the resurrection of the saints. Ha! Leave the old doddards among the graves! With me, now! There is victory — There you shall behold the star first seen by the kings on the day of Jesus' birth! — There you shall hear the songs of the archangels!

SIMEON
Hieronymus, Hieronymus, I stretch forth my arms to you, our hope!

CHORUS
Beseech Victor!

IRYDION
Father!

26　Krasiński coins the word *zniebozstąpienie* — or "Lord's descension" — from the word *wniebowstąpienie*, which signifies "the Lord's ascension."

VICTOR
This day you have lost your Father in the heavens.

IRYDION
Old man!

VICTOR
You shall not live to sport such grey hair as mine, you godless thing!

CORNELIA
To Irydion.
Forgive him, Lord — He knoweth not what he does! To arms, to arms!

IRYDION
You alone — For you have been abandoned by fate as well!

VICTOR
Sons of my people, behold! A sign will be given unto you, so that you shall mourn for your sins; so that you shall be saved by the intervention of your shepherd!

You, once first, now last at the Lord's table, draw near! I would place my hand upon your head!

CORNELIA
There was a time you loved the daughter of the Metelli. What do you want of her now?

VICTOR
Raising the chalice.
Humble yourself before the Blood of Christ!

CORNELIA
Turning towards Irydion.
I humble myself before the Lord!

The priests pass Holy Water to Victor.

VICTOR
O Holy Spirit, Who proceedeth from Father and Son, make of this frenzied heart Thy habitation once more!

Just as at the hour of your Baptism, so now do I bless your forehead, Cornelia!

CHORUS
Has the maiden fallen asleep that she thus closes her eyes and droops her head?

VICTOR
To the priests.
Bring her round — Support her with your arms.

CORNELIA
To arms!

VICTOR
Be quiet, unclean spirit who speaks through her frenzy! I bind thee with the Sign of the Cross! I command thee by the Name of Jesus! Liar, whatever thy name might be, whatever power thou mightest wield, begone from her; begone from here!

CORNELIA
I hear one hundred groans in my bosom, one hundred groans not my own!

VICTOR
Give way!

CORNELIA
Save me!

IRYDION
Come to me, my dear, come here into my embrace!

CORNELIA
Earth, cleave in twain! Hide me from his fatal glance!

IRYDION
Cornelia! My Cornelia! Mine!

CORNELIA
Where has she gone? Call her not by that name! For she believed in you, and she has died for all ages! She is dead! Ha! laughter, laughter rends the air! Black spectres surround you… Begone! Begone!

IRYDION
Back! Make way! Give her to me… Brothers, let us tear the maiden from the grasp of her tormentors!

CORNELIA
Whose voice is that I hear? I've heard it so often — Ah! She was simple once, and sincere! — She once loved you, and you were beautiful, yes, and you told her, "You shall be my glory."

VICTOR
Apage, Satanas!

CORNELIA
Come not near me — Flee my presence — See you not those black wings above him? Thousands of them! Where is my God?

VICTOR
Showing her the cross.
Here He is, daughter.

CORNELIA
Let me press Him to my lips. *Kisses the cross.* Forgive me, Lord, forgive me!

VICTOR
Dost thou renounce Satan?

CORNELIA
I do. *She collapses.* Brothers, he seduced her; he seduced you all!

CHORUS
Why have you grown so pale? Why can you not rise?

CORNELIA
The judgement of the Lord is now fulfilled in me — I die — But listen, listen: I die in the Lord! *Draws near Victor's feet.* Bless me, Father; Father, press me to your chest — I am afraid — I can no longer see you!

VICTOR
Be calm — Your sorrow has saved you!

IRYDION
Tear yourself from that heartless bosom! Cornelia, come here, to me!

CORNELIA
Ah! *Turns toward him.* I forgive you, Hieronymus; Hieronymus, pray — to Christ! *She collapses again.*

VICTOR
Can you hear me yet? Daughter, answer me. Cornelia!

CORNELIA
The aroma — of roses — of flowers…
She dies.

CHORUS OF CHRISTIANS
Father, intercede with the Invisible One on our behalf! What you loose on earth shall be loosed in Heaven — The one who seduced us grows pale now, himself!

IRYDION
Shame! Shame on you! Shall the words of a woman be your one faith? Was it on her command that you took iron to hand? And is it because these vile men have killed her that you now abandon my cause? You are as silent as stone — Shame it is that presses closed your lips; heavy shame! As heavy as the lid of a sarcophagus!

SIMEON
Look — I have rent my robes… Run me trough! Let my dream end along with my life!

IRYDION
Address me not, you slave of the aged! You are the one who gave her over into their hands! You, accursed!

VICTOR
I cast you out from among the sons of my people! He who touches your hand shall be polluted. He who pauses to hear you speak shall be excommunicated as well. Begone! Your name was Hieronymus!

Enter Envoy.

CHORUS OF PRIESTS
The Lord be with you. What news do you bring us, Julian?

ENVOY
Kneeling before the bishop.
Augusta Mammea would be remembered in your prayers. For at this moment her son has entered the city, and the battle begins in the Forum!

IRYDION
The hour has flown from me — I have been betrayed by men! *He tears a cross from beneath his breastplate and throws it down.* I return you the sign of eternal life. Look! See how it has shattered against the steps of the altar! Live on, you wretches!

SEVERAL BARBARIANS
Stay — True to our word, we shall go with you. Jesus will judge us later!

IRYDION
Call out: "Odin and Grimhilda!"
Leaves with them.

VICTOR
Pray now for Alexander Severus. He shall be emperor.

*

A street, with monuments, near the city walls of Rome. Soldiers carry in Verres, gravely wounded. In the depths, from time to time, refugees flit past.

VERRES
Your torch doubles, triples before my eyes — Read the inscription, Greek.

SOLDIER
Reads.
Diis Manibus Attilii Verris, bis consulis…

VERRES
Enough. Set me here at the feet of my great-grandfather, and bid me "good night," for although the day be near, I shall not behold the new sun!

From the other side, Irydion emerges from the catacombs, and passes through the ruins of a monument. Several armed men come in after him.

IRYDION
This dawn mocks me, mimicking the glow of an inferno. Undo the axes from your belts, comrades! *He moves a few steps forward.* Who are you there, resting among the graves?

VERRES
Do my dying ears deceive me, or do I hear the voice of Irydion, the Greek?

IRYDION
It is I, Verres. How goes it with you?

VERRES

Come closer — You know — You remember the signal that was to be given — I waited for it like a starving beast and, nothing, I saw nothing… and so I began, on my own, at last. Look past this pyramid, I beg you — There, there, clouds of smoke still coil upwards, there to the left. I stifled Rupilius in the ashes, and the people fell on us later, with "Long live Severus!" resounding loudly on all sides. I then received that which tears at my breast… It grows light, and Rome still stands, while I, last of the Verres, I fall beneath the scissors of the Parcae!
He dies.

IRYDION

Indeed, the last! Your efforts to revive him are in vain, my Greeks. He has but paid his debt to the Fates. Draw up now, you too, my Germans, and join together with the brothers I have led here.

Enter an escaping slave.

IRYDION

Stop! Where are you running from?

SLAVE

From the Forum Romanum! Now let me go!

IRYDION

I once gave you to my sister… You sang the verses of Homer to me from time to time… It was just yesterday that you pinned the fibula of my chlamys, in the palace of the Caesars! And now you recognise me not!

SLAVE

Ah! My noble master!

IRYDION

What news have you? And spare me no pain in the telling.

SLAVE
It's bad, very bad, my lord — Hardly had the first stars arisen in the night skies when, suddenly, from out of nowhere, it seemed, the legions of Severus cried out, horribly, and stormed the Palatine. Scipio defended the hill, furiously — I could hear his voice all night long, like the howling of a rabid wolf. You know, my lord, my post was outside the imperial chambers. Eutychian came and went, came and went, always deathly pale. Your sister came out once and called "Euphorion?" "What is it the divine Elsinoe desires?" But she said not one word the more. She went off slowly, beautiful, always beautiful... But there was a strange freshness upon her brow, as if it had already been splashed by the Stygian wave... Outside, the cries and the hubbub grew ever louder. Eutychian could bear it no longer. Hanging from the porphyry gate, he cried, insanely, "The Greek has betrayed us!" and again "The Greek maiden has betrayed us!" and then "The Emperor commands that the city be razed!" and "Forgive me, quirites!" From the other side, I heard Aristommachus speaking of rewards, of the generosity of Alexander, and when he grew silent, I heard moans from beneath his sword... He would rest, and again he would deceive our men with promises — At last, the praetorians rebelled. They would no longer heed tribune or centurion — the threats of Scipio flew about vainly in the air. Then the battle in the gardens died away; everyone rushed upon us in the palace. It was then, Master, that I went in to your sister, for I had sworn an oath to you, that I would defend her. Caesar lay there; his eyes were frenzied; he had pinned the high priest's earrings to his diadem; in one hand he held a sacrificial knife, and in the other, a cup of poison. But he could not bring himself to commit suicide, and he just lay there, groaning. Now, all you could hear was his slow, measured breathing, and then again he started singing a banqueting song. It was as if he were in the throes of a strange dream! Your sister was sitting near him on a golden chair, wrapped in purple, silent. Then the doors began to be burst open. The first, the second, the third... screeching, then splitting apart! Footsteps, voices, the clatter of weapons — I covered her body with my own!

IRYDION
Give me your hand!

SLAVE
Twenty spears pierced the curtain that separated us from the peristyle. They rushed in — Aristommachus at their head, crying "Pillage! Slaughter!" The emperor, like a tiger, leapt up... and then fell back, smothered in roses, covered in blood — a living wall of swords fell upon him... Later, I saw his hands, somewhere... and his head somewhere else!

IRYDION
And Elsinoe? Elsinoe!

SLAVE
It's bad, Master, bad. For when Alexander Severus entered, he cried at the top of his lungs, "Whoever touches the Greek maiden will not see tomorrow's sun!" But she herself, parting her robes of purple, stabbed herself with a stiletto. There was a flash of metal, and a spurt of blood — That's all I saw. Only a few more words remain etched in my memory!

IRYDION
Hold nothing back, nothing! The gods have carved my soul from stone!

SLAVE
"Irydion, Irydion, I shall not love your enemy!" And then, "I have fulfilled my duty! Now, mother, take me to your side!" I was pushed this way and that by the press of people. I tripped over the corpse of Eutychian, and I fled. I came across Scipio on my way out — he was retreating with a cohort of Cherusci — the only ones that did not go over to Severus — But here he comes now, Master!

IRYDION
O, sun, who risest so loathsomely, so brightly, tell me — Where is my sister, my poor sister?
Steps aside and leans against a tomb.
There in the west, bedewed with tears, the last mists of night pause yet upon the summit of the volcano! Elsinoe! Is that you bidding me farewell? Mother once said that the shades of the dead like to rock upon the dark clouds. Elsinoe!

Scipio enters with his cohort and stands over the body of Verres.

SCIPIO
You are the first of us to sleep, my brother! Let me once more press your clotted hand in my own! Sit tibi terra levis!

SLAVE
Look! It is he among the columbaria — where he wrestles with his pain.

SCIPIO
Who?

SLAVE
Can't you see? The son of Amphilochus!

SCIPIO
Ah, my leader! I waited for your fiery signal in vain!

IRYDION
I know.

SCIPIO
Fortune betrayed us on all hands.

IRYDION
I know.

SCIPIO
Ulpianus and Tubero are hot on our heels. What shall we do?

IRYDION
Turn and face them. A little more blood, a little more Roman blood, Scipio!

SCIPIO
There is no weakness in you. Your sword is other men's despair! Live on, my leader, for such were the patricians of Rome once, long

ago. It is better to die at your side than to be toppled in the Circus — Forward!

IRYDION
Let the scabbard fall away, like our departed hopes. And you, hilt, grow into the flesh of my palm. Death to Alexander! Forward!

They exit.

PART IV

The palace of the Caesars. Alexander Severus, Mammea, Ulpianus, courtiers.

ULPIANUS
And what else might you have expected of him? Did he not deceive us from the start with that cloudy gloominess of his? Later to rise up against us, inexorably, as clear as day? And again today he comes a-begging your grace, acknowledging you lord of Rome? All day yesterday he fought against us — burning two temples to the ground at night, propping up a losing cause more like the spirit of hatred than a mortal man — for from the gods' perspective, men love evil only to further their own goals, not out of love for evil in itself! My advice: have no mercy. You've shown him graciousness enough as it is, by sending him the body of his sister.

ALEXANDER
When she expired in my arms, her breast pierced, stifling her groans, I promised to pardon her brother. And with that vow of mine, her spirit departed from me.

ULPIANUS
Others may praise the emperor's generosity. I can call it by no other name than mere weakness. Our forefathers gave Junius the sobriquet of the Righteous, on account of his not pardoning his own sons — Look — He who pardons the vicious will one day punish the innocent!

MAMMEA
Hold true to your purpose. Mercy is the second purple of kings!

ULPIANUS
And, at times, the last!

ALEXANDER
Consul, we shall not alter our determination. Such is our will, today. Go and deliver to him the conditions, as we have instructed you. If you return with positive news from him, I shall turn to you all and, happier than Titus, exclaim "I have not wasted the day, my friends!"

ULPIANUS
And if I return with the shame of mercy spurned?

ALEXANDER
Then shall I be released of my vow — and you may begin your work of justice!

Exit Ulpianus.

*

The hall of Amphilochus. Elsinoe's body rests on a high bed. She is dressed in white robes and covered with cypress branches. Nearby stands a vessel with lustral water. There is an altar in the midst of the hall. A chorus of maidens and keeners. Pilades. Enter Irydion, leading his gladiators.

IRYDION
Where is Masinissa?

PILADES
I have not seen him since the moment you last saw him, master.

IRYDION
Masinissa!

CHORUS
Masinissa!

IRYDION
Twice has the vault alone replied on his behalf.

PILADES
The old man has betrayed you, master.

IRYDION
Don't say that! *He covers his face with his hands.* He, Amphilochus' friend? he, at whose mighty word even the tombs burst open! — No — No — He shall return. He will not abandon Sigurd! *He stands.* I've gathered you all together here, at the moment when the exhausted cohorts of the Romans draw back from battle, so that you might present your final honours to the remains of my sister. She was the first to fall, a sacrifice to our holy cause. Whoever respects me, let him hold her memory sacred. Whoever hates Rome, let him be eternally grateful to her. Whoever swore to die at my side, let him bless her soul!

He raises the cypress asperger and sprinkles water on the corpse. Everyone else approaches the bier, one after the other, and does likewise.

CHORUS OF WOMEN
Until the horrid ferryman, the son of Night and Erebus, receives you beneath his ebon sail, so long, O Elsinoe, will you still wander this side of the Styx. But now we place the golden coin within your mouth, as passage-payment to the ferryman. Receive now honey, and poppyseed, into your palm, with these to lull fierce Cerberus to sleep —
   A moment more, and you shall travel on to where the spirits of the dead crowd, like thick smoke coiling, like autumn leaves. You shall approach the bench of Rhadamanthus, you shall proceed toward tears and laments! — *Salve aeternum!*
   But your feet, touched by the flames, ephemeral, shall bear you farther on — you shall leave behind you the copper threshold of Erebus; you shall fly past the fiery river that coils seven times around Tartarus, to behold sweet light and green copses.
   There shall you find a soft and sad peace — there a chalice brimming with the waters of Lethe awaits you, and the shades of maidens who, like yourself, passed away before their time: petals that remain from flowers shorn. Go now, we place the golden coin within your mouth, the poppyseed and honey in your palm — *Salve aeternum!*

Enter Euphorion.

IRYDION
What news?

EUPHORION
An envoy from Caesar, a consul, requests an audience.

IRYDION
Let him enter!

Ulpianus enters, with the imperial eagles after him.

ULPIANUS
Just as you but lately came to me, enemy, so do I come to you today, as an envoy.

IRYDION
Just as you but lately answered me, so do I make answer to you today. "To arms!"

ULPIANUS
Alas, the same words have a different significance for different people. Your words then brought us victory…

IRYDION
Victory! — Has the triumphal chariot already passed down the Via Sacra? Has the statue of Fortune already held the chaplet above the head of the triumphant one? Has Alboin already been chased from the Viminal? Has Scipio retreated from the Aventine? Remind me — Who was it that last night reduced the temple of Faustina and the basilica of Emilius to ashes, while you looked on?

ULPIANUS
I have seen men sentenced to death shouting aloud and clapping their hands — just as you do now. Meanwhile, Alexander, like a child toying with an auspicious fortune, offers you peace, and pardon for your crimes…

IRYDION
Of lèse-majesté?

ULPIANUS
Have you not committed this?

IRYDION
The majesty you speak of was born but yesterday, while my crimes are as old as the heart of the first free man. What else?

ULPIANUS
The emperor requires you to leave the capital forever, returning to Chiara. But first you must swear an oath of fealty before the smoking entrails; you are also to hand over your partners in crime. If you accept these conditions, he who has the power to chain you in fetters and nail you to a cross will extend his hand to you at the moment of your departure, and forget the past…

IRYDION
Speak louder, Consul. *Turning to his people.* Have you heard these words, my people? The Emperor will return me to his good graces, if I but toss you all, beneath the lictors' rods, trussed up like cattle! What am I to do, my people? Shall we throw ourselves upon the mercy of the emperor? Would it not be pleasant to strike our brows against the ground at his feet?

You immortal gods, all you who drowse upon Olympus without the slightest concern for us mortals, laugh aloud, at least, at such a moment, when the son of Mammea sends a gift of shame to me, upon the lips of this lawyer of his! *Arises and approaches Ulpianus.* A scorpion shall sooner alight upon the palm of Caesar like an innocent butterfly, the bolts of Zeus will sooner beg his permission to tear through the clouds, than I shall set aside my sword and betray my brothers!

ULPIANUS
I shall not try to convince you. I merely fulfill the task that has been entrusted to me, by him who sent me. Of course: remain blind to the end, and huff and puff along with your handful of criminals a few days yet, on the broad bosom of Rome. Fight on in the memory of and for the glory of the master you chose for yourselves here on earth, and when at the head of your men you retreat into the

darkness of Tartarus, cry out still on the banks of the Styx, "Long live the Syrian!"And the triple throat of Cerberus will accompany your howling!

IRYDION
And such is the truth that you've discovered, you plumber of the hearts of men? The worm that writhes upon the ground, the dust that fell from beneath my cothurnus yesterday, have remained longer in my memory than he! Ask them and see if any answer you, "I knew the Syrian!"

PART OF THE CHORUS
We have ever served Irydion alone!

OTHERS
We are Sigurd's alone!

ULPIANUS
And the dead girl?

IRYDION
I sacrificed her myself. But not because of violent threats, nor on account of villainous promises! Insult not the sleeper, who never more shall wake! She remained pure beneath the tyrant's breath — she was more pure than all of your mothers and daughters!

ULPIANUS
For whom then do you fight, and against whom?

IRYDION
Old man, it is a long story!

ULPIANUS
Alexander Severus was always favourably disposed toward you.

IRYDION
And only a small portion of my hatred is directed at him.

ULPIANUS
Say then — Who is your enemy?

IRYDION
Tell this blind and deaf man, brothers — Who was it drove you from the beaten path of humanity and forced you to tread the paths of darkness? Who was it branded your foreheads with the sign of thirst and hunger, while you were still in your cribs? Who was it, in later years, who forbade you a woman's love and a warm bench at your own hearthside?

CHORUS
Rome!

IRYDION
Who was it, mortal herself, who set your sweetest hopes in mortal misery and abasement? Who was it sang the praises of Mithridates' son, when he raised his hand against his own father? Who was it spread a banquet before the traitors of the South and the traitors of the North? Who was it drained the cup of the world's misery to the lees?

CHORUS
Rome!

IRYDION
And who was it drank herself drunk with a nectar mixed of tears and blood, like the god of Hell himself?

CHORUS
Rome — Rome!

IRYDION
Do you hear? Now you know who I am.

ULPIANUS
A madman! From its earliest days, this city has flourished beneath the smiles of the gods! She became a second Destiny to the world! Do you not know that, with her broken wheel in hand, Fortuna, like a slave

woman, shuffles behind her triumphal chariot? Do you not know that the weak fall on their faces before her, that all that is stubborn and frenzied have vanished from the face of the earth? And you have arisen, of meagre strength and paltry means, a little child in fact! who would destroy this god, whose bolt thunders yet above the urn of Hannibal, and the graves of the Cimbri!

From here I see the place where your head will fall beneath the lictor's axe!

IRYDION
Before that happens, a Cimbric dart will fix itself in your breast, a Cheruscian axe shall split in twain Aristommachus' breastplate, and I shall fulfill the unbreakable vow I made to Lucius Tubero!

CHORUS
Before that happens, we shall drink blood from Roman skulls for all the wrongs we have suffered — And later, our descendants shall appear, and we from the vales underground will inspire and encourage them!

ULPIANUS
You will have no such descendants, for you are the last of your nations. Your frenzy and its penalty will add but one cornerstone to these hills.

IRYDION
And on it shall be chiselled the funeral inscription of Rome!

ULPIANUS
You paltry mortal! You are not capable of forestalling what has been decreed by immortal and sacred Destiny! Who was to receive the sceptre from its hands if not the city of perseverance, the city of deeds? Perhaps greedy, corruptible Africa? Or dissolute Seleucia? Or song-filled, playful Greece? No — power was born here, where the lyre was never strummed, where brows are encircled with stiff copper plate, not boughs of laurel. Here, where the souls of men have no room for rhythm or caprice! Here, where always has reigned one will, like to an abyss of seething strength, over which good sense and unwavering reason keep watch!

IRYDION
The martyrs of the nations are well acquainted with your good sense! The genius of Rome once stood at the threshold of Attalus with that word on her lips; winged, she set herself down at the old man's feet, flattering and seducing him, until at last she tore the deed to Pergamon from under his senile hand!

With that word on her lips, she arose at the Isthmian games, begged a hearing and praised the sons of Greece! With this word she has seduced the weak for all time, slaughtering men's souls!

Whatever wretch ever trusted her and her word agreed to his own fetters, abjured his home, his fatherland, glory in life and praise after death! And then did the Roman genius laugh and cry: "Now, there is a sensible man!" before spurning him from the Tarpeian Rock with her foot.

So you spoke the truth — Greece has never befouled herself with such reason! Her life was never a calculation; her hopes were never based on a foundation of lies! Latona's son took up residence in her land and sent forth his rays, Greek sunbeams, on all sides. Her brow, inebriated with thought, reclined upon the breast of Zeus, shaded by the aegis of Pallas, and springtime seas and countryside were her beloved footstool! Vengeance! Vengeance on her behalf!

ULPIANUS
Gaze but upon the arms of our might. Among the thunderclaps, when they strike, the glory of Athens, like the names Sparta and Corinth, sound no louder than the hum of bees dying off in the distance. These arms shall stretch out ever farther, from east to west; they cannot rest until the entire world leaps to its feet at the name of Rome!

IRYDION
Ah! So you wish to make green the lip of that ancient pit with newly-set ivy, so that the bones of your victims, the trophies torn from temples, and the swords stripped from hands by betrayal, should lie unseen in the depths! — It is your opinion, then, that you can dictate new strength to a tribe without honour and spirit, to send her sons out after new laurels! What blissful dreams you and your emperor share — like old men waiting for the day that their youth shall be returned to them — and that day will be the day of your death.

ULPIANUS
You ringleader of arsonists! Your breath infects the virtuous air! Crime still glows upon your brow, abandoned by the gods! The very sight of you sends a jolt through my ancient frame!

IRYDION
Father! Father, behold! A Roman shivers in indignation at my words of freedom! Speak on, Consul; tell me more: What have you made of the world that the gods entrusted to your hands? Your triumphal arches stand, and the well-tramped roads of the aediles — I see their stones inscribed with the blood and sweat of the dying! Ah! When the world stumbled into your embrace like a woman deceived, the musings of Plato were already rocking above it, and the wings of Carthage shone bright from Gades to Ultima Thule! — And now, what? Answer me, Consul — I hear the weak sighs of the Nazarenes from the dungeons — Here and there the distracted shades of a stoic or two, and a few words of Aurelius yet resound among the mournful groans of pain! Where have any olive branches sprung up more lushly than ours did, before our catastrophe? Where did your forebears lull the regrets of the defeated with caressing song and words of wisdom? O, I know: Augustus shut the gates of Janus, and the bought-and-sold lutenists played for him in the evening of his life; then did he call silent deserts, and cities pulverised to crumbled ruins, quietude and peace. Then, standing astride the graves of the nations, did you all sing out "Peace to the sons of men!"

ULPIANUS
As the pater familias children, as patricians the plebes, as master slaves, so did we, Quirites, receive provinces unto ourselves! — We conquered the world with iron, and we extend the law of iron over her yet today!

IRYDION
Try that one out on the gullible! Glance but backwards upon the valiant legions of the Republic: can you see how they head for the hills at the sight of the elephants of Pyrrhus? Or how they are humbled by the pitchforks of the Samnites? Look how they lie there on the shores of Lake Trasimine, like a fresh-mown harvest! Hear them cry out "Mercy!" and "Water!" in the valleys of Spain. Can you see them in the Hercynian Forest, kneeling pale beneath the sacrificial blade? It was

no flying bolt of Alexander's, nor was it that short sword of yours, but a poisoned cup, a handful of gold, a broken vow, some hypocritical advice and the kinship of traitors that helped you on in your creep towards power! That Roman eagle was hatched in the bogs, not upon the summits of the mountains!

ULPIANUS
In vain you shout, blasphemer! The rock you gnash your teeth against remains unmoved. It hears you not!
    So, you spurn the mercy offered you by your lord?

IRYDION
Who is my lord? I find no such lord worth following here on earth. Beyond the pyre the genii of death wheel, like a flock of birds of prey —They will tell me to whom I am subject! Here I had enemies only — and a few brothers, who served me faithfully — and one moment divine — as short as the clang of swords that shatter on impact — but sacred, sacred for all time!
    None among you shared in it, my comrades! That moment was me, and I her, entirely — The torch of vengeance blazed in this hand. The city lay at my feet, a consecrated offering cringing ever more quietly beneath the wraps of the night — Ah! Nemesis. —

He leans upon the monument of Amphilochus.

ULPIANUS
You grow pale!

IRYDION
My countenance is in need of your blood!

ULPIANUS
This is a warning sent you by the gods. One last time I remind you, in my office of messenger, that a sentence has been passed on your head. Time yet remains to beg mercy of the emperor — Rome forgives the humble!

IRYDION
And this is the moral you deduce from my words? Do not go — Stay a moment longer!

Euphorion, hand me the blessed cup. —

The snowy foam of Amphilochus' Lesbos I pour out upon thy feet — Accept the first fruits of my passing! — Now, brothers, drink, as did the men of Leonidas, before the fatal dawn! Drink, and be free of evil thoughts!

He approaches the smouldering altar that stands between the monument and his sister's pyre.

IRYDION
The guardian symbol of the state, blessed by the soothsaying of augurs, and the songs of the vestals, the symbol of the senate entrusted to the emperor, to thee, Father, I dedicate, and to thee, Mother Hellas!

ULPIANUS
Stop! Prevent the crime! Restrain him! Prevent the sacrilege!

If there be a Roman citizen among you, hear my voice! — Your life will be spared, I swear this upon Stater and Quirinus! Stop, you impudent man! That ring is inscribed with the secret name of Rome!

IRYDION
Did you hear that, my brothers?

He tosses the ring into the embers.

CHORUS
Euge! Euge! The Roman has covered his face with his toga — his breast swells with regret, and he dares not raise his eyes to us!

IRYDION
Before my lips close forever, I wish to pronounce my last will. Hear me, and curse the city!

CHORUS
Look! Is that the reflection of the flames, or is it a ray of light sent by the gods, that so beautifully bathes his face with silver?

IRYDION
Woe to the victors! As they wished to degrade us, it is degradation that will be imposed upon them! The child born in Rome, the old man dying in Rome, the Roman man in full possession of his mature body, all will share the same title — that of slave!

CHORUS
That of slave!

IRYDION
O primaeval Fate! Then shalt thou lift thy feet from off the heads of the gods to descend lower yet to the nether expanses, and lower still, to these Seven Hills, and here shalt thou be the Hag of their perishing! — So that they, who destroyed everything, might die before thy face, thou, who created everything!

CHORUS
Their nation will vanish — May their tongue be lost, for ever and ever!

IRYDION
But let their fame live unto distant ages — may the story of their oppression be inscribed upon their gravestone, to be read by future generations who will curse them, every day unto the end of the world!

CHORUS
The end of the world!

IRYDION
Now the time of prayer has come around. The altar flame has burnt out and the god of Rome is dead! Consul, you may now lift your eyes.

ULPIANUS
You have broken the peoples' laws and mockingly befouled the sacred rites — according to the custom of the fathers, I remove from thee

the protection of the law; I forbid thee fire; I forbid thee water! In exchange for thy head I grant freedom to the slave that brings it me, a monument near the Rostrum to the free man, and a place next to the consuls in the circus!

Godless ones! I await you at the threshold of the Mamertine Prison! — Condemned ones, I await you at the foot of the Tarpeian Rock!

IRYDION
None of them raises his hand against me — Be gone, old man! — Anger does not befit a grey head like yours.

Exit Ulpianus.

IRYDION
Your pyre has been prepared, my sister. — Take her up, and repeat after me the Ultium Vale.

*

A moonlit night. The temple of Venus across from the Flavian Amphitheatre. On the steps, praetorians, and Lucius Tubero.

TUBERO
What does this mean, that there is no sign of Aristommachus? The night had but fallen when we parted, and now the moon treads the upper reaches of the Amphitheatre. The peace of the arcades, broken in long shadows, troubles me; though I know not why. Despite the cool breeze, my face feels flushed — yet I have looked upon more desperate sights without foreboding or impatience. — O my soul, Lucius' slave, why do you rise up against your master today? *Paces about, slowly.* I have heard that one's spirit sends warnings by such strange unease, as death approaches. Thus it was for Brutus on the eve of his defeat; such prophetic signs occurred to Otho before the Battle of Bedriacum — Diespiter! But now cannot be the time for Lucius Tubero to die! The youngster depends upon my old virtue — On me alone — and upon Ulpianus, who holds on to the bit from the other side of Alexander's mouth. And if the lawyer was to fall from a German arrow, or by the hand of Amphilochus' son? Then…

Did someone make answer? No —A lion in the depths of the Circus waked, and roared — But that's... Something else... Mixed voices, horses neighing, a rumble! By Castor, who approaches?

Enter armed men in disorder, and after them, Aristommachus.

ARISTOMMACHUS
Help!

TUBERO
For shame! Caesar waits in the Forum for you to lead the Greek to him in chains, and here you come, running away from him!

ARISTOMMACHUS
He who states that Aristommachus ever turned coward is a liar! — Be he even the father of all men and all gods! My own spear has run through two centurions for turning their eyes from the fervent countenance of the Greek!

TUBERO
Whence this unexpected strength? Did he sow dragon's teeth and harvest new armed men from the sprouting seeds?

ARISTOMMACHUS
He is on his last legs, but those legs are tireless and furious. We were still proceeding along the slope of the Viminal when he commenced battle — Projectiles began to sweep down from the palace porch like lava — torches thrown, flaming arrows, boiling pitch. Three times I closed with him — Sparks showered from between my sword and his shield as thick as from an anvil in the Cyclops' forge — three times his mob repulsed us!

TUBERO
Let's go! The spoils I shall tear from the neck of the Greek, I promise to hang in thy temple, O Marspiter!

ARISTOMMACHUS
Take off that coat of mail — At this very moment, two scales have burst above your heart. —

TUBERO
Dii, avertite omen![27]

They exit.

MASINISSA
On the temple steps.
Birds of the night, nourished with the blood of the arena, weave yourselves into a chaplet above me!

You decrepit volcanic ruin, dreamt into a star of purity and grace by man, pour down your pale beams upon me!

Earth, provide what is necessary — Air, give me what you owe me, that I might nourish myself with blood and venom as once I did the eternal fires of aether!

But one night and one day more, and I and my son will abandon these parts!

CHORUS FROM THE INTERIOR OF THE TEMPLE
Beautiful and voluptuous, we greet our lord! Dancing above the helmets, we freshened our cheeks with blood of men's wounds, using the breastplate of your son for our looking-glass!

Beautiful and voluptuous, we caution our lord! With Orion's star, a mysterious spirit has arisen, circling the azure on a stream, encircling the soul of Irydion with all the quiet vibrations, all the sad waves with which it flowed — we crossed its current as we flew here!

MASINISSA
And did my son heed the promptings of the spirit?

---

27   Writing in the *British and Foreign Review, or European Quarterly Journal* of 1836, Sydney, Lady Morgan chides Edward Bulwer-Lytton for using this phrase in *The Last Days of Pompeii* as an English calque. She suggests that the proper Latin would be *Avertant Dii*. p. 495.

CHORUS
Whenever that voiceless thought touched his heart, he paled; his sword erred and glanced off the armour of his enemies, piercing none; in between these moments he fought like a fallen angel. Hasten, hasten to his side!

MASINISSA
Sickly souls of sainted women, wafting your sighs here from the far side of the grave, you shall not tear him from me! — It was not to harps of gold I trained his fingers through the long years — Not to songs of praise did I twist his lips!
He disappears.

*

The Forum. Torchlight. Alexander Severus, seated on the curule chair. Next to him stands Ulpianus, behind him, guards with golden eagles. Enter Aristommachus; after him, the wounded Scipio is carried in.

ARISTOMMACHUS
Divine majesty, by now Tubero must have taken the Greek. I struck left, and began battling with the Cheruscii, who were commanded by this fellow on the other slope of the Viminal. I pressed them at sword's point until they all began to cry "Long live Emperor Severus!" and to swear upon all the gods of the North that they had lost their wits after the death of Heliogabalus. This fellow stifled the mouths of two or three with his dagger, but soon all his men came over to us.

ALEXANDER
We thank our brave and warlike Aristommachus.

ARISTOMMACHUS
Now, back to Tubero!

He exits.

ULPIANUS
Your name?

SCIPIO
A dying man.

ULPIANUS
In that case, testify to the truth and become reconciled to the just gods with your last breath!

SCIPIO
Gods? Just?!

ULPIANUS
Answer me, in the presence of the Emperor. For how long has your conspiracy existed?

SCIPIO
For whole ages.

ULPIANUS
Joke not, slave! Did you have co-conspirators in other cities of our state?

SCIPIO
We have them everywhere!

ULPIANUS
Who among them is most noteworthy?

SCIPIO
You and Caesar. As long as you exist, so does our resistance.
He dies.

ALEXANDER
Stepping down from his throne.
Such people cannot be forced to anything by threat, or mercy!

ULPIANUS
They can, by fire and iron! You must learn how to step over the seething abyss without falling into it. Do not give ear to womanly voices — Do

not trust in the nobility of strangers. All of Rome is now concentrated in you. Be, therefore, as she is: strong and implacable!

*

An empty space near the fountain of Neptune. From below, one hears the clash of swords, and screams. Enter Irydion, in pursuit of Tubero.

TUBERO
Your eye, like to a hellish glow, has followed me all night long! Which of the gods has fashioned your armour? Your blows have had no effect on my courage, but my strength now faints dead away.

IRYDION
You have parried my blade for the last time.

TUBERO
Father Neptune, help me!
He falls.

IRYDION
Announce my near advent to my sister. *Kills him.* Vengeance! You sprinkle drops of blood on my tongue, whereas I would quaff whole oceans! Now my life seethes at full boil! The souls of my dying brothers pour into my breast! I have become a Titan! — And I must die — No — I do not want to die! *He bends down and tears away Tubero's sword.* Ah! Why do you harry me, unseen spirit? Christ — Christ — And what is that name to me? Be gone! Torment me not, Cornelia! Behold — I follow the silver pathways of the moon. Soon darkness will enfold the earth entire!

Enter Alboin.

IRYDION
Friend or enemy of Irydion the Greek?

ALBOIN
Once his comrade.

IRYDION
Have you grown pale from fear, or is it the rays of the moon?

ALBOIN
Scipio's body rests on the Gemonian Stairs!

IRYDION
While his forefathers haunted the summits of the Capitol!

ALBOIN
All the Cheruscii — to a man — have surrendered to Caesar.

IRYDION
Ah! My final moments have become so much the shorter! Come — Let us return to the palace. We will permit the Romans to enter the courtyard. There, Elsinoe's pyre yet smoulders — We shall perish in those flames: you, I, they, and my father's house. Forward!

ALBOIN
As long as but a spark of hope yet glowed, I served you faithfully. No less than you do I hate Rome. But now…

IRYDION
You slave of the eagle! Legionnaire of Caracalla — Do you too betray me?

ALBOIN
Not I, Fortune abandons you first! Bread calls me elsewhere. Do you hear the tribunes' voices? Caesar has set a price on your head, on the open market! *He pulls out his dagger.*

Irydion kills him.

IRYDION
Go to Hell! Sooner or later you will meet with Caesar along your road! *Exits opposite.*

*

An open space on the hill in front of Irydion's palace. Slaves, gladiators, soldiers with torches. To the side, the smoking pyre of Elsinoe.

SOME
Where are you running, Pilades?

PILADES
To the cellars, where the cypress and pine are piled. The master has so commanded!

OTHERS
Stop him! Tear that torch from his hand!

PILADES
Back! Dobn't come near me — Scatter! Do you not recognise me, brothers?

MIXED VOICES
Throw away that torch, and stand there, if you don't wish to die!

OTHERS
Down below there — The eagles of Aristommachus are already a-wing!

OTHERS
From this side, Tubero is advancing.

IRYDION
Enters.
Silence, my people. Tubero has lived through his last day. *He ascends the base of the obelisk.* What does all this mean? Battle-axes, breastplates, strewn on the ground? And you all stand there in disordered knots, as if you were at a loss for what's to be done? Brothers, one last time I call you to battle, after which there will be slumber, and everlasting quiet!

A moment of silence.

IRYDION
What does this mean? You turn cowardly eyes toward me. Your arms hang at your sides. The passing flashes borrow a pale, sickly hue from your bloodless faces! To arms!

ONE OF THE SOLDIERS
Chief, I have been fighting from dusk until the rising of the moon…

SECOND SOLDIER
Who remains at our side? Some lay lifeless in the dust, others are perishing in torment, still others have set themselves up better — by going over to Caesar!

OTHERS
Behold our wounds — We can barely stand on our feet!

ANOTHER
Aristommachus sank half his blade into my breast, before the iron snapped. Water — I beg you — Water!

IRYDION
Fire is all I can offer you!

ALL
Cruel man! Godless man!

IRYDION
Diomedes, your clan springs from Corinth. Can you wish to humble yourself before those who tore your homeland from you? And you Lasthenes, Glaucos, and you, Eutellus?

CHORUS OF VOICES
It's bad, it's a bad state we're in — We're sick and sad — What good are our torments to a dead fatherland?

IRYDION
Glory, you blasphemers!

CHORUS
Life, life, not glory!
Bread, bread, not glory!

IRYDION
Wretches! These ears heard your oaths! These eyes beheld your weapons covered in gore — You were brave men, once… But now, at the lip of the grave, when the end has come for you, the end common to all men — it is not despair, not fury, not fanaticism you display, but… vile shame!

CHORUS
The Emperor loved you, once. Throw yourself, and us, upon Caesar's mercy. There is still time, Irydion!

IRYDION
You think that you shall live long after obtaining Rome's pardon? I know that infamy will not shorten your days — but you shall be sent into exile, where the sands will devour your feet, where the suns shall heap live coals upon your heads. Perhaps they will slake your thirst with poison at festive banquets, or they will charge you, each day, with some new crime! — Those of you who enter his service will learn, all too soon, that their blood has been sold to their enemies. Those who remain in the city will die, slaving to pile a theatre in the name of the people. But all of you will perish, in a manner befitting sick base slaves such as yourselves!

ONE OF THE SOLDIERS
Why is it that you speak such evil of us, you who have betrayed us?

SECOND SOLDIER
You promised us victory — Keep your word!

IRYDION
Pilades! Strike down the one who holds you, and go on your way!

SOLDIER
A price has been put on your head!

SECOND
Brothers, let us take it, and present it to Caesar!

IRYDION
I throw away my shield — Come on, take aim! But your arms are shaking so, that you will not hit the mark!

Pilades himself is struck.

IRYDION
Ah, my poor Pilades!

PILADES
Your fate pains me more than this wound of mine, son of Amphilochus!
He falls and dies.

CHORUS
See you not those golden eagles, that imperial purple? Hear you not the trumpets of the legions?

IRYDION
Leaping down from the base of the obelisk.
Each of these swords has a throat to cut[28] — You, wretch, behold your reflection on the blade of Sigurd! But not one step closer! — Traitor, cower not beneath the iron of Tubero — Out of my way! Fold your hands in beggary, drop to your knees upon these stones! Pray to the Romans!
He passes through them and ascends Elsinoe's pyre.

CHORUS
Son of misfortune — May the blood of the fallen flow before you — May the curses of the living thunder behind you on the dark banks of the Styx!

---

28   *Każdy z tych mieczów gardło jedne przetnie.* An ambiguous line. "Each of these swords has one throat (i.e. mine) to cut," (in other words: "you are all cutthroats, not soldiers"); "Each of these swords has one [more] throat to cut," (your own, in despair).

IRYDION
Father, I die glutted with bitterness, and the shortness of my days! Father! Forgive not the villainous!

Masinissa appears next to the pyre.

IRYDION
Here you are, at last. Back, man! Your hour has not yet come — This belongs to me! Go there — there — Caesar will pardon you!

MASINISSA
Come with me, my son!

IRYDION
I know you not.

MASINISSA
It was I shielded you during the battle, though you saw me not. I supported you in your despair, but you saw me not. Now I come to save you!

IRYDION
Perish along with me, if there be any virtue in you.

MASINISSA
And if I am immortal?
Seizes him in his embrace.

IRYDION
What are you?

MASINISSA
God!

They disappear.
Aristommachus, Alexander Severus, Ulpianus and the Roman cohorts enter.

ALEXANDER
Where is the son of Amphilochus? Answer me, rebels!

CHORUS
He ascended his sister's pyre; his voice was heard once more, and then he disappeared — But we — We have lain down our weapons — We beseech you!

OTHERS
O divine one, Emperor, we wished to hand him over to you!

ALEXANDER
My pity has run dry.

CHORUS
Mercy! Be merciful to us! He alone was guilty! He seduced us, and betrayed us!

ULPIANUS
Vae victis! Lictors, approach!

*

The summit of a mountain. In the hazy distance, Rome — on the other side, the sea. Masinissa, with Irydion leaning on his shoulder.

IRYDION
O Thou, whom I adored on account of thy torments, Hellas, Hellas, wert thou, after all, nothing but a shadow? Cloud of my love, dost thou melt now, forever? Thy enemy, as before, stands unmoved, baring his marbles to the sun like the white fangs of a tiger! What am I doing here? A fever burns deep behind my forehead — my thoughts bore through me, like worms through a corpse!
He slides down upon the grass.

MASINISSA
Refresh your powers in the mist of the early morning. Drink in the cool air, the light.

IRYDION
Like the links of a chain, you fastened your hand upon mine and dragged me here — But a man has only one life to live, and my life is now passed. I perished yesterday.

MASINISSA
My son! Your task is not yet complete![29]

IRYDION
Torment me not — My father died in your arms, my sister perished in the palace of the Caesars, and my candle burns to its end here in your presence. Are you not yet satisfied? *He lifts himself up by half.* The girl I sacrificed to you was innocent — She disappeared into the air on groans of sadness — Her voice still resounds in my ears. I see her cross in the azure! Ah! If only her God were God above all gods — If only He were the truth of this world!

MASINISSA
What then would you do?

IRYDION
Dying, with this drowsy blade in my hand, I would call upon Him!

MASINISSA
Father, who art in Heaven, grant long years unto Rome! Forgive those who betrayed me, save those, who have tormented my motherland for age upon age!

IRYDION
No! Father, who art in Heaven, cherish Hellas, as I have cherished her! — O, tell me, in this my last hour, Masinissa, you, who deceived me, you who promised me so much, you upon whose breast my head

---

29   The original Polish reads: *Synu! zawód twój nie skończył się jeszcze!* The word "zawód," which we translate as "task," contains an untranslatable pun in the original language. It can mean "profession" as well as "disappointment, failure." In the mouth of the Satanic Masinissa, the word has as bitter irony — as all he is really concerned with is Irydion's damnation; he fully intends to "disappoint" him in the end.

in childhood drowsed to slumber — you, who at this moment stand above me, as if you could command the entire world — Speak! Look, Irydion's thoughts are chaotic — Quick! Speak now — Is Christ Lord of heaven and earth?

MASINISSA
You renounced Him yourself!

IRYDION
And so you bear witness to Him?

MASINISSA
As to an undying enemy... As one immortal enemy to another. Today He governs the old Heaven and the decrepit earth — But there are regions from which His name has been obliterated, as mine has been in Heaven. There exist worlds of limitless youth, labouring in pain and chaos; suns without light, future gods still enchained, seas still unnamed, swelling eternally toward happy shores! But He has finished; He has already sat down upon His throne and proclaimed "I Am," bowing His head! I do not deny Him — I see Him — My eyes, wounded by His splendour, turn constantly toward the darkness, toward my hopes! — From that darkness our victory shall come! — Make your choice!

IRYDION
A wealth of iron suffering blackens your brows — from among those furrows, show me hope! — No — No — You shall never rise from the gulfs of the ages! — You have deceived me, and destroyed me!

MASINISSA
Don't abandon me, as those villains abandoned you! *Pulls him up roughly from the ground.* Stand here above the chasm — behold the city you so hate! Do you know who will tear it from the hands of your brothers, when, according to Grimhilda's prophecy, they shall come to plunder Italy, pummelling her into clods of blood and furrows of ashes? Do you know who will catch the purple of the Caesars as it flaps through the air? The Nazarene! And in Him the treason of the senate, the cruelty of the people, will live on as an unobliterated

inheritance — His white hair, His heart as implacable as that of the first Cato — His voice only sometimes womanly and sweet — At his feet the men of the North will become like children, and He shall once more deify Rome among the nations of the world!

IRYDION
Ah! My desire was limitless; I laboured unstintingly to destroy, just as others have a limitless desire, and labour unstintingly, to love and bless, as death approaches, that which they loved during life! — Ah! — And now to me, dying, you foretell the immortality of Rome!

MASINISSA
Do not despair — For there shall come a time when the shadow of the cross shall appear to the nations as boiling pitch, and He will extend His arms in vain to press them once more to His bosom. One after another they shall rise up and exclaim, "We shall serve no longer!" — And then complaints and grumbling shall be heard at all the gates of the city; then again shall the genius of Rome hide his face and his lament will be never-ending — For only dust will be left of the Forum; only ruins will be left of the Circus; and of the Capitol, nothing will remain but shame! — Then shall I stroll among these fields, among the wild cattle and pale shepherds, the last inhabitants of Rome — and my battle on this earth will be nearing its conclusion!

IRYDION
My heart beats again — Ah! That day, is it still far off?

MASINISSA
I myself can hardly sense it!

IRYDION
O Amphilochus! And so your son was merely a dream — a mere shadow, reflected from a distant future — and as a plaything taken too early in hand, smashed to pieces by the Fates. *To Masinissa.* Depart from me — I shall surrender my soul neither to you, nor to any god — Here on this cliffside, staring into the eyes of Rome, I shall die as I have lived — in the loneliness of my spirit!

MASINISSA
O my son — Listen to me! The paleness of your cheeks I shall cast back into the face of death. I shall ignite a bonfire of strength in your heart once more. I shall grant you forgetfulness of the past — I shall grant you ignorance of the future!

IRYDION
Get away from me!

MASINISSA
I shall give you one thousand desires, and thousands of powers. I shall resurrect the forms of dead beauties for you — each, before she faints away again, will flame to ashes in your embrace: Helen of Troy, Idaean Venus, the daughter of the Ptolemies!
    In the transparent wave, in the ray of fire, in the black, hard earth, the breath of delight shall be yours!

IRYDION
Tempt me not!

MASINISSA
In distant lands I shall set apart a people for you, obedient at your palace hearth, and wild on the day of battle. Among spells of flattery, you shall fall in love with yourself, as once you loved Hellas. I shall inebriate you with the terrors of kingship, and the love of kingship, my son! Until I come, until once more I fix my sign upon your brow and summon you: "Time to renew the battle!"

IRYDION
Tempt me not! Or smash in ruins those vaults, each stone of which, I have cursed! Ha! If you be so mighty, step onto the field, at least once!

MASINISSA
For now, your request is a vain one!

IRYDION
And for now, you shall not be my master!

MASINISSA
Listen to me! Listen to me once more!

IRYDION
Weak spirit, among your treasures there is nothing for Irydion! As I die, I disdain both them, and you!

MASINISSA
And if I should destroy the ages for you?

IRYDION
What?

MASINISSA
If I were to pluck you from the rushing waves of time and place you on the soft shore, put you to sleep on the bosom of nothingness and oblivion — until the moment when I should take those bonds from you, and cast them to the earth? If I then were to awaken you, as you are today?

IRYDION
In Rome, after the passage of many years?

MASINISSA
Yes! So that your one desire might be fulfilled — So that you should tread her ruins and ashes underfoot!

IRYDION
But not when the flames will be consuming her — Not when the brethren of my mother shall sound their horns on the Seven Hills —

MASINISSA
When, then?

IRYDION
When the Forum will be nothing but ash!
When the Circus will be strewn with bones!
When the Capitol will be nought but shame!

MASINISSA
But then, my son…

IRYDION
Then I shall be yours. Swear!

MASINISSA
I swear to preserve your body. I swear to put your soul to sleep, and wake her again — By that, which He called evil, by the only good I possess, I do so swear! Now, your hand!

IRYDION
Take it, the wretched thing, which battled in vain!

MASINISSA
All of the powers of night, massed over thee, and the chasm, my mother, bear witness to thy oath! Dost thou renounce my enemy?

IRYDION
I do renounce Him — Ah! A groan of despair soars past my head!

MASINISSA
Pay it no mind!

IRYDION
Look! The rock — It has broken into the shape of the cross — and black drops — Ah! Drops of blood drip from it!

MASINISSA
Pay it no mind, my son!

IRYDION
A storm rises, strong, above the sea — Ah! Ah! — Someone calls me — There — Far off! — Father, can you hear?

MASINISSA
And now?

IRYDION
Silence.

MASINISSA
And so, together for all ages, without rest, without hope, without love, until eternal vengeance is effected!

IRYDION
Together — But see that you fulfill my earthly vengeance!

MASINISSA
It has come to pass[30] — Now, come along with me!

IRYDION
Where?

MASINISSA
To the banks of the lake, to the cool of the cave, beneath the grape leaves and chaplets of ivy — Where neither dawn nor star is ever seen, nor voice heard, nor pain or dream ever felt. — There you shall rest, until you enter into my kingdom!

IRYDION
Let us go! — Give me Rome, and you shall have my soul!

---

30   In Polish: *Stało się* — which can allude, ironically, to Christ's last words on the cross: *Consummatum est*, "it is finished."

CONSUMMATION

O thought of mine, you have endured whole ages! You slumbered through Alaric's day, and that of the great Attila — neither the clang of the imperial crown upon the hard brow of Charles, nor Rienzi, the tribune of the people, could rouse you! And the sacred lords of the Vatican — they too passed before you like shadows before a shade! But today you awaken, O thought of mine!

*

Today the sun scorched the wastes of the Roman Campania, and now over the edge of those wastes it sets gloomily. Above the wormwood of the sands, above the rushes of the bogs, above the lonely pines of the hills, above the cypresses of the vales, shadows are wheeling. The evening star, that goddess of ancient peoples, rises mournfully, and with her rising, here and there fall a few tears of dew. Only upon the waves of the sea does the seething foam yet frolic in the bloody glare.

*

There is swelter and silence aloft — nor cloud nor any breeze, yet the depths have moved, and the sea's purple breast groans toward the heavens with swelling billows. — He, who called the chasm his home, he, who promised much, has ascended the swirl of the waves and with a foot blacker than the night crushes his oceanic slave-women down. A glow beats from his figure, as if a second sun had arisen. From his shoulders the mist descends upon the far waters. On he comes alone, and, just as in ages past, with an immortal worry etched upon his brow.

*

And then he reaches the shore; the sea sighs in relief, and in the dusk, the tortured billows sleep again. On he goes — leaving his trace upon the Samnite Hills as he descends toward the lake. There, in the might of his spells, O son of vengeance! your life begins to awaken.

*

The snake that kept watch at your feet starts of a sudden, as if sensing the return of his master. The light gathers and grows upon his pallid scales — he unwinds his coils, and sparks shower from them upon the marble surface of your bed. He crawls to a high place and waits there now, like a glowing torch, in the rays of which the black boulders glimmer brightly, as do the scorched features of your countenance!

*

Suddenly, the sheen of sense begins to smoulder on your brow like a fata morgana above a gravestone — but soon from the threshold of the cave there sound celebratory voices, greeting you by name, once more raising the song of your life and, with each note, by one thought, with each rest, by one strength, you begin to resurrect. The knowledge of the years is given to you; knowledge of all the years that have passed since your falling asleep. Like the story of one single day, you behold the torments of Rome and the triumphs of the Cross!

*

They all, all roil about you in fiery colours — a clattering of hooves, a shattering of breastplates, the clang of bells and the echoes of hymns all sweep over you, as they swept over your slumber.

Dead bishops pass by in long ranks; before each walks a king bearing an open book upon his back. Over the Seven Hills: down and up, up and down, they wind in a perpetual round, back and forth. Angels hover over some of them, with chaplets swaying in their hands. — Others stand apart, with the symbol of salvation in their right hand, the sword of war at their side, and a cup of poison in their left!

*

And the closer you are to waking, the thinner grows the train, the softer the tread of the feet, the paler the features of the lords of Rome, and the more trembling their hands. And then, above all other singing voices, one resounds loudly, full of power and commanding — a voice which shall not reach the heavens, but which the earth echoes back from her innerest bowels. And that voice calls: "O my son!"

*

Then a flash falls upon the pane of the lake water, flashes upon the lawn of the lakeside, flashes upon the vault of the cave, and the bolt of life returning strikes you in the breast, and as you had been— young —as you hand been — beautiful — years ago, thus again you arise upon your bed! The first glance of your burning eyes meet with the pale face of Cynthia upon the Latin summits, and you reply — "I am!" Then does he gesture with his hand and lead you forth — No echo comes from footfall — Like two black clouds, your two figures sail above the black vales.

*

You stand upon the Roman Campania — and she has nothing with which to hide her shame from your gaze — The stars flicker like one thousand golden recollections and outrages. The black aqueducts, stretching toward the city, but finding the city not, have halted in their progress — the stones fallen from them are strewn about in funereal piles — there bindweed stretches, in dusty heaps — there the birds of night confer, and moan!

*

The son of the ages looks his fill upon it all, and rejoices in the justice of his vengeance. For him, each ruin is an award — both the depressions, the widows of amphitheatres, — and the swells, the orphans of temples — From his lithesome feet he shakes the dust and embers there, where the circus of Caracalla once reared; there, where the mausoleum of Cecilia, Crassus' wife, once stood.

And like a ghoulish cicerone, the street of ancient graves leads him to the gates of Rome. These open by themselves, without a single creak of hinge — they enter — The guards have suddenly fallen asleep, leaning upon their weapons. They pass through like shadows!

*

Their narrow road winds along the extensive walls and among the lonely chapels.

O night unique, O ultimate night! O night of my love — something sunny shines in your flashings — you tear apart the veil of shadows that hangs over each ruin — and, naked, fearsome to paralysis you seem to the enemy. Your moon fixes a ray of mockery upon the wretched houses and their wretched, sparse inhabitants!

*

In the arcades of the basilica stand two old men clad in purple cloaks. Monks bid them farewell with the name of Prince of the Church and Father — poverty of thought is etched upon their faces. They climb into a carriage pulled by black, sickly horses — behind them stand servants with lanterns, like widows bending over children perishing of hunger — and on the frames of the windows, and on the bars of the lower edges — the last remains of gilding! The groaning wheels have now passed on; slowly, the grey, bent heads have disappeared. — "Behold the heirs of the emperors — the chariot of Capitoline Fortune," states the guide, and the son of Greece beholds, and claps once his hands.

*

And now they ascend a steep slope lain with stairs, into an empty courtyard. In the midst thereof stands a statue of Aurelius astride a horse, his right hand extended into the vacant air. An emperor without any subjects — a triumphant warlord without a song of glory — and in the rear, the black background of the walls of the Capitol!

*

Near the Tarpeian Rock, with the fragment of a sword, the one who returned after so many years leaves his sign upon the brow of the best of the Caesars — And the clang of the Greek iron upon the Roman bronze spreads afar like the tolling of a funeral bell — the last tolling! And from above the summit of the fortress, it is answered by the mournful cry of an owl, while from a distant street, the howling of a dog wandering among other ruins makes reply!

*

Then along the Via Sacra, the path of triumphing emperors, over steps of granite and mud they descend into the Forum. The Arch of Septimius Severus is buried breast-high in the earth, while the last columns of the temples sink up to their necks, raising their capitals above the muck like the heads of the damned. — Still others have not foundered so; these stand tall, but lonely, as thin and meagre as skeletons.

The flowers and acanthus leaves of their capitals, which once shone so white, so unbearably white, ages ago, seem now the muddy bangs of vagabonds — today their half-split marble waists sift dust, as a fountain does droplets of water. — And at this moment of your triumph, you are unable to recognise anything, name anything!

*

There, beneath what remains of a portico, two wretches sleep beneath one ragged cloak — in the pallid light of the moon, their faces appear like two grave carvings. Little lizards slip in and out of their arms entwined — but as you approach, like autumn leaves they scatter before you.

Thus do you greet the last of the Roman people on the Forum; as you pass, you spurn them with your foot — and they do not awaken!

*

Your guide then points to a street lined with decrepit trees. There, the shadow of the Palatine stretches upon the ground; there, the quartered bodies of the gods lay strewn about, among heroes' sunken torsos of jasper and porphyry.

There, through the Arch of Titus, split and patched like a gigantic wound, they pass again into a brightly lit space — empty and mournful.

From there it seems to the one who had been raised from the dead that the Coliseum yet stands — but the old man merely laughs the louder and — takes him by the hand!

*

In the still arena, on the silver sands, among arcades transformed into wild cliffs, with ivy growing at their summits, with cracks running the length of their breasts, you give thanks to the Fates for the abasement of Rome!

Here was to be the end of your pilgrimage. From here you were to tread the road of countless millions who…

*

And everything you'd ever seen, everything you'd ever been, returns now to your memory. There was the throne of the Caesars — Through your mind now echo the trumpets and flutes, the applause and the imprecations — all that is lacking is the sun and the screen of purple that wound about the summits of the Circus — Only the pallid moon shines aloft, above the crowd of revived, passing, disappearing shades.

*

After their passing, there remains only the voice of a hymn once heard… That "once" was just yesterday — Yesterday, the Nazarenes perished here, their faces as peaceful as a summer eve — and here, today, at the place where they fell, stands a black wooden cross — silent, in the midst of the arena — and from its peaceful shadows the guide turns his gloomy countenance.

*

But in you a strange emotion wakes — Not pity for Rome, for her penance hardly covers her crimes — Not fear at your freely chosen destiny, for you have suffered too much ever to be terrified — Not regret for mother earth, for the love of life you'd forgotten in eternal sleep — but a memory of some maidenly face — a sort of sadness for that Cross that you once held in contempt — because you tried to sharpen it into a blade!

But now it seems to you that you no longer want to fight against it — it seems to you that it is just as weary as you are — just as deplorable as the fate of Hellas once was — and it seems to you, in the light of the moon, to be sacred — holy for all time!

*

But you do not abandon faith to your plighted word. You stand, and then go over to the old man of the desert. He shivers, for he has penetrated your soul. So, encircling you in a gigantic, gloomy embrace, he tears you away, step by step, from the sign of salvation. You tread slowly behind him, like your father on the day of his death!

*

And beautiful, lithe, with your black tunic and Achaean cothurni, you suddenly stop, and, stretching out your arms to Heaven, among the ruins you become like a swift sound, gigantic, which joins with a thousand other errant ones — and the remains of the Corinthian festoons sigh for you!

*

"Son! It is time — you have drunk down the potion which the ages distilled into your cup; no drop of it now remains. — Son! It is time — the dawn is not far off — and we still have a long road to traverse."

Groans are then heard from underground — where the bones of the martyrs sleep the long sleep — and groans are heard aloft, there, where hover the spirits belonging to Christ — but from the heights of the amphitheatre, above these mournful sounds, there resounds one voice, fulsome, a voice of praise!

*

And now there shines forth a bright figure of transparent whiteness — in which are concentrated all of the loves of the moon, like floating ribbons, now gathered, now scattered in the rays of light playing about two quiet, folded, angelic wings!

And you lift up your eyes toward that sweet face, and you recognise the old familiar features, features freshened by the dew, brightened by the breath of Heaven, and you gaze upon them like one who bids farewell to beauty, forever!

*

A voice calls the old man back to the foot of the Cross. For a judgement deferred must now be settled. Beneath the hymn of the angel, he bows his dusky brow and returns from the Circus gate — he gnashes his teeth and jerks at your hand and cries, "He is damned, damned! Who shall tear him from me?"

*

Here, at the foot of the Lord's Passion, with the dawn about to break, with the moon now sinking past the Amphitheatre, with the entire arena brightly lit with the flashing of wings, the music of an invisible choir resounds and the final, fatal struggle commences — the struggle for your devoted head!

*

And you, above the tempter and below the angel, you stand upon the steps leading to the Cross — there is neither fear on your brow nor prayer on your lips. — You are as you always were, alone in the world!

*

He, setting his feet upon the seething sands, his head sinking upon his scorched breast, argues his rights: "Immortal enemy, he is mine — he lived for vengeance, he hated Rome." But the angel, unfurling the rainbow of her wings, and shaking her golden locks, counters: "O Lord, he is mine, for he loved Greece."

*

And the air grows misty from the struggle of the powers — and you feel another death — Your life has become one great anticipation and scissure — fires burn your feet, and the flashes of Heaven pain your eyes — crowds tear at you from below, pulling downward, and other crowds pull you aloft — It is at this moment that hope divine is born in your heart; now fainting, now flashing forth like a spark, dying again so that all is black, empty, soundless, as in a vacuum, painful, bitter, unbearable, like despair, and weak — and base, like shame.

*

O hour predestined to every mortal, be gone from my thought! Father in Heaven! Once, and once alone didst Thou abandon Thy Son, so as never again to abandon any of Thy children! — No! — No work of Thy hands shall dissolve for all time!

*

Arise, O son of Greece — behold! The enemy has covered his face and the grand pile erected by the ancient people has been shaken to its core by his vain efforts — his gloomy figure faints ever more in the morning mist — he perishes, with his head leaning upon the Circus gate — his voice is now like the roar of distant waters. — The testimony of Cornelia, the prayers of Cornelia, have saved you, for you loved Greece!

*

Arise! Can you hear that voice, which thunders above the silence of all the spirits? At the first rays of dawn it descends like a lightning bolt and the aroma of all the flowers of the vale rise to meet it:

*

"Go north, in the Name of Christ — Go, and never cease your journey until you arrive at the land of graves and crosses — You will recognise it by the silence of the men and the sadness of the little children — By the burnt cottages of the poor man and the destroyed palaces of the exiled — You will recognise it by the groans of my angels that split the nighttime air.

*

"Go and live among the brothers I now give you — There shall be your new, second trial — for the second time you shall see your love pierced, perishing, while you yourself will not be able to die — and the torment of thousands will become incarnate in your one heart!

*

"Go and trust in my Name — ask not for your own glory, but for the good of those I now entrust to you — Be calm in the face of pride and oppression, and the mockery of the unrighteous — for they shall pass away, but you and my Word shall never pass away!

*

"After a long martyrdom I shall unfurl the dawn over you — I shall grant you what I granted my angels long ages ago — happiness — and that, which I promised to the people from the summit of Golgotha — Freedom!

*

"Go, and act! Although your heart will go dry in your bosom, although you will doubt your brothers, although you even may despair of me — act always and ceaselessly, and you shall outlive the petty ones, the happy and celebrated ones, and you shall resurrect — not from slumber as before, but from the labour of the ages — and you shall become a free Son of Heaven!"

*

And the sun arose over the remains of Rome — and there was no one to whom I could tell whither the traces of my thought had gone — but I know that that thought perseveres, and lives!

Author's Notes[31]

IRYDION

NOTES TO THE INTRODUCTION

The ancient world is coming to an end.
The present story is set in the third century AD. At this time, the Roman state was in agony, dissolution, disorganisation. Everything, which once constituted its life, which motivated its progress and being, was returning to nothingness, to eternity, in short: all was dying, being transformed. Three systems existed alongside one another: Paganism (already dead, but enlivened in Rome by all the religions arriving from the East; it was like a corpse, beautifully dressed, but stretched out already on its bier); Christianity (up until now rather bodiless, formless, oppressed, but growing among the people, challenging all the symbolic faiths of the past to to battle; and as far as philosophy is concerned: now chafing against it, now working in agreement with it); and the Barbarians, various, wild, restless like the sea during a storm. They also possessed their own myths, although the majority gave no mind to them once they set foot in Rome. Living from day to day in the Roman moLegions, they rebelled against the Romans in the northern provinces, while forcefully pressing into Italy from all sides, whether that be in armed attack, or as mercenaries in the hire of the state. Animated by some sort of unease, they were like atoms that someday are to collect together into one body. However, at this time they were without self consciousness and the higher faculties — they were blind, fearsome, like a force of nature. This was basic matter already in a state of ferment, ready to take shape and join together like a body to a spirit walking about the catacombs — to Christianity! The calm, which reigned before the great storm that engulfed Rome and transformed her into Christian Europe was accompanied by the last feasts of the

---

31   Notes translated in the footnotes of the play are not included here.

emperors, the inexpressible wretchedness of the people and the slaves in all sections of the state. Indeed, material superfluity and material misery always signify a great spiritual deadness, be that of individuals, or entire nations. It is the life of beasts on the very highest, or very lowest, possible level. Moral life seems to be asleep at such times, resting, in order to gain strength to rise anew and thunder aloud, later. In any event, the ancient world was rather a world of number and form than of the free movement of the spirit — for this reason, as it perished in convulsions, it had to wallow in its own matter — whereas our day and age, on the other hand, frolics spiritually.

Only Fate is calm, unmoved, the unrelenting reason of the world.
What the Romans called *Fatum*, and the Greeks *anangke*, was, according to Hesiod, the progeny of Night and Chaos. It signified predestination, a necessity higher than all the gods and all the spirits, be they heavenly or hellish. The ancients represented Fate as the figure of an old man grinding the earth beneath his feet, holding an urn in his hand, which contained the destinies of mortal men. Most often, however, understood in an ideal sense, Fate signified a divine unity, the final cause, mathematics, the *universum*, which no one could oppose.

The mob and Caesar — there's all of Rome for you! —
Under the emperors, the equality of all of his subjects was settled — before Caesar, all of the provinces of the state had been admitted to the ranks of citizenship, stingily bestowed by the patricians. The larger portion of the emperors came from the provinces. Trajan was a Spaniard, Heliogabalus a Syrian, Maximinus was a Goth, and so on. Rome, which strove to yoke the entire world beneath her rule, while remaining apart from it herself, like God after the creation of the world, was forced by necessity to spread open her gates before the peoples of the North and the South. Her egoism couldn't always maintain itself in that same, distant, lonely form — and as she didn't spread her individuality abroad, those she conquered tore it apart, piece by piece, each coming to claim its own portion. The art and philosophy of the Greeks first squeezed their way into the city, thus alienating a portion of the Roman spirit and arrogating it to themselves. In this way, a part of the Roman soul was destroyed. For great material egoism is strong, only as long as it is entirely material. To awaken a soul in it, and to destroy

it, is the same thing, for the nature of the spirit is an outward thrust, a spreading about on all sides — and sooner or later the material shell must crack open under its pressure. Further, Eastern stories, myths, ceremonies and spells arrived in Rome. Among the common people, this had the same effect as Greek philosophy had among the senators and patricians. The foreign myths and beliefs tore apart the egoistic symbol of the eternal Capital. Later, the palpable, visible effects of these unseen, moral causes became apparent. Rome became Greece, Egypt, and Asia Minor, rather than Greece, Egypt and Asia Minor becoming Rome. Barbarians took their seats in the Roman senate; all faiths and laws became mixed together in this *colluvio nationum*; all the ancient order and myths of Rome fell away in this disorganising agglomeration. The aristocracy completely died out, on the one hand because of the hatred of the emperors, and on the other because of an exhaustion of their natural vitality. By confiscating their goods or arrogating their testaments to himself, Caesar became their heir. In the same way, he concentrated in himself all of the rights of the priests and the people. What was in his advantage to destroy, he destroyed, gathering the strength of the destroyed into himself. But there was one thing, one unity that he could not destroy, and that is the people over whom he ruled. And so he found himself alone against them, and because the material strength, the strength of simple existence, was fixed in this second portion of the state — the people — from time to time he had to submit to them: flattering them with gifts, circuses, and so forth. But, except for him and the Roman people, nothing else existed any more in Rome.

To catch a glimpse of Odin, perchance, the god of his Northern peoples.

From the perspective of religion, the German tribes can be divided into two large halves. There is Germania, of which Tacitus writes, and in which the Suevi (Hermiones) dominate; these held to a religion of nature: they honoured the elements, trees, and springs. The goddess Hertha (*Erde*, earth) arose each year, arriving on a covered wagon from the far-off copses of the islands of the North Sea. Certainly, there were divers rites among the various local hordes, but generally speaking, their faiths were in a state of flux, confused, uncertain. Against this pale background strong colours first appeared with the invasions of hordes arriving from further north; hordes unknown to the Romans. Among these hordes a progressive movement had been initiated; a heroic one, based on revelations that can be termed religious. This revelation had Odin for a name. Stretching from Iceland, where later his religion was developed most boldly and strongly, the cult of Odin possessed the minds of people all the way to the banks of the Rhine. The Goths, the Saxons, the Gepids, the Lombards and the Burgundians were the generations of Odin, who believed in Odin's incarnation, as well as in certain codified rites and life beyond the grave. They believed in rewards awaiting them in Odin's palace in Valhalla, in a certain holy, earthly city called Asgard, from which their forefathers had descended, and to which they were to return, sooner or later. Their motive power arose from this form imposed upon their beliefs, from these myths. It was they who mobilised the Germanic tribes, up until now lying fallow in lower Germany; it was they who invaded the shores of the Baltic from Scandinavia, pushed down towards the Danube and overran all of Germania, brushing up in this way against the borders of the Empire. Their invasion from the north initiated chaos in Germania, which later fell upon Italy with a crash. Among the Goths, Odin's name was transformed into Wodan. For a while yet, the Saxons remained unmoved on the shores of the German Sea. The myths of Odin, in thumbnail form, are the following:

In the beginning, there was a giant named Imer. Odin, along with his brothers Vile and Ve, slew him. From his skull the heavenly firmament was made; from his flesh, the earth, and from his blood, the seas were fashioned. Another giant named Norv was the father of night. Night gave birth to day. Each of these were said to race an eternal round through the heavens on two chariots. Hrim-fax (frozen mane) was the name of the horse of the night; Skin-fax (bright mane) was the name of the horse of the day. There is a great bridge stretching from the earth to the sky: made of three colours, this is the Rainbow; it will be broken one day, when the evil spirits, after routing the gods in battle, will travel over it. The world is to end in an inferno. In the final battle, it is the evil spirits who will be victorious.

Odin is the god above all gods. He is given the sobriquet Alfader, which is to say "father of all," father of battles. He is also called Hor, Ianfchar and Thridi (Higher, Equal to the Higher, and Third — Trinity); he receives all heroes fallen on the battlefield into his palace in the heavens, Valhalla. They enter through 540 gates. Two ravens sit on Odin's shoulders. One is named Hugin (reason) and the other Munin (memory). Through their agency, he knows what is going on in the wide open spaces. The god Thor is Odin's son. He is god of war, and holds a hammer in his hand. This hammer became a symbol of victory, of conquest, among these tribes. There were goddesses, maidens of war, called the Valkyries. There were twelve of these, the most powerful among them being Frigga. Loki was the god of deception and evil. The gods of the heavens had enchanted his son, Ferris the wolf; in his role, the Scandinavian Loki is kind of a forerunner of Mephistopheles. The Amali and Balti were leaders descended from the gods; noblemen who led the troops in war. For the longest time, the Saxons remained a peaceful tribe. It was only when they felt themselves pressed from both sides — by the Franks from the West and the Slavs from the East — that they coalesced into a martial horde, in which Goths were the primary constituent element, and invaded England. On the other hand, the Goths, the Lombards and the Burgundians, were fain to subject themselves to leaders; it is among them that soldierly dedication, a soldier's unbreakable word, and the beginnings of the feudal system, have their beginnings. They were the first to set out on distant campaigns in search of gold and women. Such was their heroic goal — and from this grew the later poetic figure of Sigurd in the *Nibelungenlied* in whom intelligence and martial skill are combined — which in the Greek myths are divided between Ulysses and Achilles. From such an elementary revelation of Scandinavian religious form, then, arose their restlessness and vigour — a violent restlessness, a wild vigour, like a gushing fountainhead. The gloominess of the Scandinavian myths is indescribable. The only moral to be found among them is glory, the promised reward for bravery. In Valhalla feast the heroes, and among the courses these armoured skeletons arise and renew their ancient struggles amongst each other. In all the myths of Odin the influence of the nature of the North can be felt. One can sense a lack of hope, so to speak, an eternal despair united with savage, heroic manliness, a drive to always move onward, without a care should the end of the journey be horrific and fatal. The thought that the world will end in misfortune, and that at the end of the ages it will be the evil spirits who will be victorious, wheels about like the northern lights, hovering bloodily over the entirety of Norse mythology. Under this baleful sheen earthly warriors fight to the death, always chasing after danger. They seek oblivion, neither granting quarter to their enemies nor begging it for themselves. They live such violent interior lives so as not to dwell on what is without! Such a mother-thought, such a foreboding of the final destruction of all, simply had to incarnate itself in individual destructions; it simply had to create, from among these people, the Alarics, Geneserics and Attilas of history. Just as from its earliest beginnings Christianity has been a progressive movement of love, creation and unification, so the myths of the northern barbarians were a progressive force of destruction and unravelling. But when Christianity set itself at the hub of this wheel of events, and among these tribes, and began to exert an attractive force upon them, both the events, and the northern tribes, were transformed into an orderly, closed circle. After the consummation of the catastrophe, after the punishing of Rome, that torn material, which loomed so fatally everywhere, was vivified and came into being. Slowly, chaos was transformed into an organism; the love of the spirit was victorious over the resistance of matter. Our story has its beginnings still before the birth of the chaos and the creation. Irydion is only a harbinger of the coming chaos, and therefore of the coming life — for chaos was good for nothing else, really, than to become new life.

Morituri te salutant, Caesar
The gladiators, before the beginnings of their struggle, were wont to pass before Caesar and greet him with this formula: "Those about to die, greet thee, Caesar."

On the Palatine, on that hill of ruins and blossoms
The palace of the Caesars once stood on the Palatine hill. Today, one can see the ruins of the Farnese palace there, the foundations of which rest upon the ruins of the old imperial structure.

Wafted up from the catacombs
The catacombs are spacious underground dungeons excavated beneath the entirety of the city of Rome, stretching partially into the Roman Campania. Some have suggested that they stretch as far as the sea. These were originally ancient Roman cemeteries where the poor and the slaves were buried, that is, those who couldn't afford the costs of a

funeral pyre. Later, they became a refuge for the Christians during times of persecution. Today, portions of them are well preserved and may be visited. The greater part of them, however, have been filled in. Those that can be toured are made up of a great number of low and narrow warrens, sometimes spreading open into square or round underground chambers. The walls are set with the gravestones of martyrs; at this day, the remains of the martyrs are still being excavated from the catacombs.

In the Cimbric Chersonese
Thus the Romans named the Jutland Peninsula, as they used the general term of Cimbri for all the Scandinavian tribes.

In the silver land of streams
The barbarians themselves thus named the Chersonese, from the whiteness of its snows, and the streams that flow there.

Shoulder to shoulder, like a brother with the kings of the sea.
Among the Angles, Saxons, Norsemen and all Scandinavian tribes, their leaders were called "kings of the sea." Their lives were constantly taken up with oceanic brigandage.

Maeotian marshes (palus Maeotis)
The Sea of Azov.

NOTES TO PART I

Meanwhile… in the gyneceum
Among the Greeks, women had not yet arrived at the freedom they enjoy in Europe — something Eastern yet remained in their manner of life, and Greek women were raised in harems, called gynecea, from the word "gunaike," meaning "woman" — and from this they never departed until marriage.

Heliogabalus
This was the name adopted by Varius Bassianus, the son of Soaemias and Valerius Marcellus. It derives from the name of the god Halgah-Baal, or Mithras, of whom he was the high priest in Emesa

before becoming the Emperor of Rome. The history of Heliogabalus is the strongest proof, the clearest symbol, of the decrepitude of the world at that time. He ascended the throne at age fifteen, and died at eighteen, murdered by the praetorians. During this short space of time he enjoyed all the excess luxuries that power can afford a person.

He was never a young man; he was the incarnation of old age. It would seem as if the active past of Rome, the past full of Roman deeds, had left a vacuum in him, which nothing could fill. Two of his characteristic traits were: Ennui and Lewdness — the same things which often characterise aged men. For Ennui, Boredom, is a torment that arises from the sense of an eternal emptiness, and the vain desire to obliterate the same, while Lewdness is a labour of the imagination to invent something that might excite senses already dead. Passion is always strong and simple; it is a Synthesis, the poetry of the flesh. Lewdness, on the other hand, is a sophisticated thing, which is broken down into a thousand details — rather like prose, Analysis. Heliogabalus was unable to slake his passions, for he had none. His was nothing more than the desire to possess passion. Passion he searched for in all of nature, throughout all his domains, throughout his own person, constantly looking for the stimulation, the spark, which would ignite a bonfire in his breast. In such toil did he pass his unfortunate life. This is why everything that he did was mere caprice. Such a constitution in a young man would be incomprehensible if not for the fact that he was burdened down with the already fatal old age of the world in which he had been born. Heliogabalus was an old man because of the world that surrounded him, while being a young man in a physical sense — and from this there arose the eternal contradiction of impotence and desire.

This old man, this rotten individual at war with himself, this decrepit child, had been raised in Syria, a land of myths and sorcery, with a devouring climate. His grandmother Maesa was the sister of Julia (the wife of Septimius Severus). After the death of that Emperor, his wife's family, thrust out of power, was exiled to their fatherland, Syria. Maesa had two daughters, Soaemias and Mammea, the mother of Alexian, later known as Alexander Severus. Before his fourteenth year, Heliogabalus became the high priest of the temple of Emesa, in which the great god Halgah-Baal, otherwise Mithras, a Chaldean god, was worshipped, in whose person all the Eastern and Egyptian myths had converged. He was the symbol of the sun, recognised as a pure god, the highest and only god, a detached god, so to speak. This is why there were no figures of him in stone, save for a black rock in the shape of a cone, which served as his symbol. In this same temple other gods were worshipped: Baal-Phegor, or the materialised sun, as the power that gives rise to vegetation, and Gad-Baal, or the sun even more incarnate, a prophetic spirit — Phoebus-Apollo. There was Astarte-Baalis, the great goddess, the wife of Halgah-Baal, or the moon reflecting the light of the sun, nature vivified by the sun; Baalis-Benoth, or Venus, and Baalis-Dercoto, or the Greek Aphrodite, both of whom expressed nature incarnate, or woman. The death and resurrection of Adonis, or the symbol of nature abandoned by the sun in the winter and revivified by it in the spring, was celebrated in this temple. All Asia sent gifts of tribute here. The rites were performed with superhuman splendour and bestial bawdiness at one and the same time. It was there, above all, that Heliogabalus' thought developed. There his free will and all his strength were slain at the very threshold of life by fantastical scenes, far from worldly reality, through the influence of the dissolute, delightful climate. According to all material sources, he was a boy of unparalleled beauty. Rumours had circulated among the people that his mother had once been the lover of Caesar Caracalla, and that he was actually Caracalla's son. Now, the memory of that emperor was worshipped by the soldiers of the legions. Macrinus, the praetorian prefect, ruled Rome and hence the world after Caracalla's murder, but his hold on power was weak. Once, passing through Emesa, the legions caught sight of the young Heliogabalus. The legionaries were moved by his beauty and the memory of his father — to this must be added all the machinations and efforts of Maesa, who was unable to forget that her sister had once been first in all of Rome. It was she who led Heliogabalus and Soaemias at night from the temple to where the legions were encamped. There, the son of Caracalla was declared emperor. Ulpius Julianus, sent against these legions by Macrinus, was destroyed. In this battle, for the first and last time in his life, Heliogabalus gave a token of his bravery. Macrinus himself, hearing of the death of his son, leapt from a wagon during an attempt to escape and broke his arm. He was beheaded, and his head was taken to Heliogabalus. From that day dates his reign, that is, his constant dreaming up of ways to avoid boredom.

And so in order not to be bored, he transferred Halgah-Baal to Rome. He ordered all other gods and heroes, the Trojan palladium, Vesta and the breastplate of Numa to be carried into his temple. These became the lackeys, officers, proconsuls and harem of his god — and later he sought a wife for him. First he wed him to Pallas Athena. Then he divorced them and transferred Venus from Carthage to take her place — and she remained.

And in order not to be bored, he drove about in Sicilian chariots, kept flautists from Elis, bakers from Athens; he covered his floors with Lydian carpets, fumigated the air with Syrian incense, sent to Cyprus for doves, to Lydia for pearls, to the island of Melos for horses, to Cape Pilos for oysters, to the Hellespont for fish, to Minturno for crabs, to Euboea for pears, to Damascus for plums, to Rhodos for grapes, to Persia for oranges, to Palmyra for lemons, to Antioch for pomegranates, to Phoenicia for dates, to Naxos for almonds, to Tasos for wine with an apple aroma, and to Saprias for wine fragrant of violets, roses and hyacinths.

And in order not to be bored he hitched camels, lions and elephants to his chariot; he wore a long Median robe instead of the short, Roman tunic, and scandalised the Romans by wearing a diadem on his brow within the palace — for he dared not show himself thus before the people; he wore cothurni decorated with precious stones. He never wore the same clothes or shoes twice, nor the same ring. He bathed in gigantic marble bathtubs, in water infused with saffron and the most expensive scents. He slept on beds of silver, on mattresses of swansdown or partridge down; he drank from goblets of crystal, amber, onyx or gold. He changed the chaplet he wore with each course at each meal: during the first course, he wore a chaplet of roses; during the second: of violets; at the third course he donned laurels; at the fourth, a chaplet of narcissus; ivy at the fifth; for the sixth there was a chaplet of intertwined roses and papyrus, while for the seventh he wore a wreath of Alexandrian lotuses.

And in order not to be bored, he had them set on his plate the comb torn from a still living rooster, peacock and nightingale tongues, fieldfare and partridge brains, the heads of pheasants, canaries and parrots. As he progressed though the porticos of the palace or the palace gardens slaves went before him strewing rose petals and silver sand. Once he ordered ten thousand spiders to be brought before him, and another time ten thousand mice. Another time he had a yen to see ten thousand martens and cats. Once, after the conclusion of the games, he tossed among the assembled people snakes and basilisks. As presents to his parasites he sometimes sent the most expensive vessels, soldered shut, full of toads and bear cubs. He invited them to banquets in chambers, the false ceilings of which would open and rain down petals of violets, roses, and other flowers. At first, they would stretch out luxuriously beneath this rain of chaplets, but the rainstorm would never stop — more and more flowers would fall upon them, filling the room entirely, so that on the next morning their dead bodies, suffocated beneath passifloras and lilies, would have to be pulled out by the legs. At other times he had lions and tigers that he had pardoned from the arena brought in, to strike fear in the feasting senators, consuls and courtiers.

And so as not to be bored, he tried racing around the circus for money. He became a charioteer and collected the silver tossed onto the track by the spectators. Then he became a professional musician. It seems that, just like Caracalla his father whose great desire was to imitate Alexander the Great, Heliogabalus chose Nero for his model — that Nero who, before stabbing himself in some cave in the Roman Campania, cried out to his companions "See what a great artist dies in me!"

And so as not to be bored, he had Pomponius Bassus murdered, and, tearing his young wife away from the body, which she was bathed with tears, took her to his bed — sending her away at dawn, having already grown bored with her.

He also tried to see if a holy vestal, an unspoiled virgin, might amuse, entertain him. No one in all the ancient world had ever offered violence to a vestal — and for that one reason, the idea seemed to him more novel and more pleasant. He himself tore Aquilina Severa away from the vestal flame — sending her away on the next day, already bored.

He then arranged a naumachia, or water games, in the circus, creating for the occasion a lake of wine and wormwood water. The boats that took part in these battles were entirely plated with silver and gold.

Meanwhile, in the depths of his own palace, his doom was maturing, inexorably drawing close.

Mammea, the sister of Soaemias, had inherited from their mother Maesa a strong will, a sharp mind, and a desire to be elevated. While Soaemias had given herself over to all the spells, magical symbolism and dissolution of the East, for a long time Mammea had progressed along the path of Eastern idealism, Neoplatonic philosophy and the Christian teachings. She introduced her son Alexian to them as well. In his *sacrarium* (chapel), Alexian kept figures of Pythagoras, Abraham, Orpheus, Apollonius of Tyana and Christ. He ate only fruit and dairy products; he wrote poetry, and constantly read Seneca, Virgil and Cicero. Mammea convinced her nephew that, as the high priest of the sun, it was most fitting for him to concern himself entirely with supra-terrestrial rites, entrusting wretched, sublunary things to someone else. Heliogabalus was eager to acknowledge her reasoning as befitting his worth, and chose Alexian for the drudgery he was abandoning. Naming him Alexander Severus, he appointed him Caesar and consul. Then it was that the palace struggle began — at first covert, then in the open. Heliogabalus wished to refashion Alexander in his own image, and as Alexander did not give in, he grew furious at Mammea and Alexander's tutors. He sentenced Sylvinus to death, and banished the famous lawyer Ulpianus; he surrounded Mammea with spies. At last, he attempted to poison his cousin, several times even, although always unsuccessfully, for Mammea's sharp eye kept careful watch over her son. Then, he ordered the senators to deprive Alexander of the title Caesar, and to cast down all his statues. The senators paled, and dared not obey him in this. Enflamed and bribed by Mammea, the praetorians rebelled. Heliogabalus, the same person who, but three years previously, had challenged the power of Macrinus at the head of the legions in Emesa and had acquitted himself bravely on the field of battle, without armour or helmet, nearly naked, with only one sword in his hand, now, humbled, trembling, made his way to the camp outside the city walls and promised to respect and esteem his "brother" Alexander. Upon returning home, he began to plot how he might get rid of him as quickly as possible. Some time later, in order to dishearten the praetorians, he spread the false rumour that Alexander had died. And again rebellion broke out in camp, and again the emperor had to display his brother, alive and well, to the soldiers, in order to pacify them. But when, standing on a wagon, he spoke to them, leaning upon Alexander, he heard threats being tossed in his direction from all sides. Furious, he demanded that those who were guilty of such lèse-majesté be apprehended — which merely increased the tumult. Two parties emerged: on the one side, Mammea cheered on the soldiers, while on the other, Soaemias promised them rewards for remaining loyal. But Heliogabalus, overcome with fear, ran away — for the one time in his life, at least, he was not bored. Those loyal to him were cut down by the praetorians, and Alexander was declared emperor.

Long before this, Syrian soothsayers had foretold that their high priest was to end his life in an unusual manner — they constantly predicted that he would kill himself. With this in mind, he had prepared various instruments suited to the office: poisoned chalices, poisoned daggers, a courtyard lain with marble and precious stones beneath a tall tower. He wanted to season his death as he had seasoned his feasts, his games, his luxuries — but at the moment of death, at that one moment of strong feeling, not ennui, he forgot all about the long dreamt of and long prepared lubricities of death. Quite simply, and without further analysis, he hid along with his mother in the deepest secret recesses of the palace; in a place most unfitting for a Roman Emperor, of which even Nero would never have thought in his final, panicked moments. There the praetorians discovered him and put him to death. They hacked his head from his body, and then dragged his body, and that of his mother, through the streets of the city. They tossed them both into the latrine, but since the opening was so narrow, they pulled them out and flung them into the Tiber. Thus, the final sobriquet of Heliogabalus was: Tiburinus.

In him, all the myths of the East became incarnate — dead symbols existing merely in their vulgar forms; symbols once of deep, valid thought, but lost by then, forgotten — having become incarnate once more merely to disappear all the more surely and entirely from the face of the earth along with that man's death. It could only be so with Eastern symbolism. The purest thought could not assume a pure form in the East, because as soon as it became incarnate, it became subject to the laws of the nature of the locale, a nature that devours human freedom, incites to physical delight, ravishes to forgetfulness, and denies the spirit by virtue of its own beauty and might. Most historians look with contempt upon the short days of Heliogabalus. He has his worth as an individual, but not as an historical fact. For he initiated a period in which the victory of Christ became surer, day by day. Because of him, paganism reached its nadir; because of him it became apparent that paganism was rotted through, unable to bear any fruit, for in him it appeared in all its might, in all its breadth — and all in vain. In all that he did and represented, Heliogabalus is old age and death — he is the lack of spirit — he is matter in a state of decomposition. They say that he had been of unusual beauty; he was of such matter as is *a lightning before death*, as Shakespeare says.[32]

That the senate declare you divine
In Latin, *diva*. Usually, the emperors and their wives became gods through a senate proclamation. Idols and temples were then raised in their honour. For this reason, many Christians lost their lives, as they refused to toss incense upon altars burning before the images of the Caesars. After his death, the name of Antinous, Hadrian's favourite, was inscribed in the register of the gods through the *senates consultum* — and by the will of Hadrian.

I am Augustus, Antoninus, Aurelius
The names of the great Caesars, who had been elevated to places among the gods after their death, became titles for their successors, and the princes of the Caesarian line. And thus the emperors named themselves after Augustus, thus — Caesar. And so Heliogabalus, assuming the names of the best of the Caesars as honorific titles, called himself Antoninus, Aurelius, etc.

Evoe Bacche!
An exclamation voiced during dances on holidays dedicated to Bacchus. It signifies gaiety and comedy.

Mehercule!
"By Hercules!" A common Roman exclamation.

Peristyle
The peristyle was a sort of salon of the ancients. The large number of their houses consisted of rows of chambers, each coming after the

---

32   See *Romeo and Juliet*, V.3.90.

other in such a way that, by standing in the *vestibulum*, that is, at the (usually narrow) entrance, one could see all the way to the *viridarium*, or garden, which usually enclosed the house on the opposite side. Right after the *vestibulum* came the *atrium*, or courtyard, in which the slaves sat and guests of lesser quality were received. In the midst of the *atrium* was found the *impluvium*, in other words, a little pool of circular or rectangular shape in which rainfall was collected. This was surrounded by small bedrooms; the *impluvium* also admitted the light of day into the interior of the complex. Further on, the *tablinum* was located. This was a rather long chamber, decorated with the most representative decor[33] of the house, and behind it, at last, was found the *peristyle,* a square area usually surrounded by a colonnade, most often open to the sky, set aside for walks and conversations. Still further on was the *triclinium*, or dining room, connecting to the *viridarium* (in which it was sometimes actually located), where statues, flowers and shrubbery were placed. This entire row of chambers had the appearance of one long corridor, varied only by the walls, which either narrowed or spread out, with statues, frescos, and the altars of the household gods in the *atrium*, and those of other gods in the *peristyle* and the *viridarium.* The little rooms in which the slaves lived, those in which the masters of the house slept, the kitchen, the pantry and other such rooms were little more than recesses appended to this main corridor, which ran in their midst. Of course, in Rome and in the palace of the Caesars all of these sections of the house took on larger proportions, but the excavated ruins of Pompeii show us that it was only this main corridor, dedicated to the public functions of the house, the reception of guests, banquets, etc., which was large and beautiful. The rest of the house was made up of narrow little rooms with low ceilings — recesses, in a word.

The great Septimius
Septimius Severus, whose wife Julia was Maesa's sister (the mother of Mammea and Soaemias). After Septimius' reign, power passed into the hands of his son Caracalla. Then Macrinus, the praetorian prefect, ruled, and only after Macrinus did Heliogabalus become emperor.

---

33   Krasiński uses the word *kosztowności,* which usually denotes valuables.

Flavian amphitheatre (or Flavian circus)
Today's Coliseum, erected by Flavius Vespasian.

Divine Sophia
"Wisdom," in Greek (hence *philosophia*, or "the love of wisdom").

By the manes of Antoninus!
The word *manes*, or shade, signifies one's spirit after death. The ancients did not inscribe their gravestones with "to the memory of this or that one," but rather "to the gods-*manes* of this or that one," for example: *Diis Manibus Pueri Septemtrionis annor. XII. qui Antipoli in Theatro Biduo saltavit et placuit* ["To the gods-manes of a Child of the North aged 12 Years, who in the Theatre of Antibes for two days pleased the crowds by turning somersaults"]. This inscription, discovered in Antibes, we offer as an example that reflects all the frivolity of ancient Rome.

The arts of the Greeks
As in Virgil: *Timeo Danaos et dona ferentes* ["I fear the Greeks, even when they are bearing gifts" *Aeneid*, II:49).

Lucius Mummius has left us nothing else
Lucius Mummius put an end to Greece with the destruction of Corinth.

The Baths of Caracalla
Baths erected by order of the emperor Caracalla. Even in their ruined state they are impressive. In the ancient world, a bath was not so brief and insignificant an affair as it is with us today. One's sweetest hours were spent at the baths. These were buildings of many porticos, gardens, and libraries, adorned with masterpieces of art. When one emerged from the marble tubs, one was rubbed down with the most expensive perfumes and then enjoyed a pleasant walk, listened to the lectures of philosophers, or enjoyed various games and sports, or gymnastics. Sometimes, the baths also housed theatres and circuses.

Perhaps Tiresias in hell will give ear to him.
Tiresias, the famous soothsayer, was the son of the nymph Charycloe. Blinded by Juno, he was granted the gift of prophecy by

Jove. The ancient heroes would often descend to him in Hell, curious about the future and seeking enlightenment as to the mysteries of life.

A real Crotonian
The inhabitants of Kroton (Crotone) were famed for their strength and agility in wrestling matches.

Proh! Iupiter!
"Ah, Jove!" a common Roman exclamation.

Hands bearing the thyrsus
The thyrsus was a sacred wand, wound about with ivy and capped with a cluster of grapes. They were carried during games and holidays dedicated to Bacchus. The appearance of the spectre of Alexander the Great, noted here, is known to history.

Hand me the Falernian!
A famous Roman wine.

Can it have slipped your memory that the son of great Septimius (Caracalla), etc.
This speech of Irydion's is based on the fierce love in which Caracalla held the memory of Alexander the Great. Caracalla was quite a mediocre man, with iron caprices, so to speak, not an iron will. He was immeasurably boastful, full of a petty *amour propre*, suffering, it seems, from a mental illness. And yet he had been a brave soldier. He came to believe that he was a hero, created for great deeds by Fate. The one person, the effulgence of whose brilliant courage shone throughout the ancient world far and wide, was that of Alexander the Great — and Caracalla burned with the desire of winning similar glory. He imitated his hero in all things. His courtiers flattered him by stating that he was so similar in appearance to Alexander as to be his twin. He had copies of Alexander's armour, his helm, and his sword made for him; he even walked around inclining his head to one side, which was supposed to be characteristic of Alexander's posture. But he was not capable of being a conqueror and genius like his idol, so he comforted himself with drilling his legions; and since he was not able to conquer either Tyre or Babylon, he went

off to Alexandria, which belonged to him, and there, in the space of one day, he put one half of its inhabitants to the sword, deceiving himself with the pretense that this was a great conquest; that he was slaughtering his enemies, as once the Macedonian king had done. Fantasy had become reality for him to such an extent, that, at last, he convinced himself that the spirit of the Macedonian had become incarnate in him through metempsychosis, completely uniting him to Alexander the Great.

Sacred fortress
The Capitol, the *arae sacra, aeterna.*

The genius of the city
Each city, each state in the pagan world possessed its own genius, a guardian spirit, something like a guardian angel.

The lords of the amphitheatre
Thus was the mob of Roman citizens called.

Io triumphe!
An expression used in Bacchic songs.

Their fibula
The fibula was a brooch that fastened the toga or tunic at the shoulder.

Salve aeternum!
A formula used during funerals; a song intoned while bearing the body to the pyre. It is as if someone said in Polish: *Ty wprzódy nad nimi wyrzeczesz — Wieczny odpoczynek* ("Thou shalt say above them first — Eternal rest").

Vale!
A formula used by Romans at departing: "Be well."

New man
The *homo novus* was a Roman term used to describe a plebeian who found his way into office, or a man from a foreign city, who did not

enjoy the rights of a Roman citizen, but came to Rome and obtained such an office. Cicero was a *homo novus* (*un parvenu*).

He died in the spoliarium
The *spoliarium* was located next to each amphitheatre. Into it were tossed gladiators who had sustained mortal wounds in the arena.

Alma Venus
Alma, an adjective frequently applied to Cybele and Venus, means "she who gives birth to all" (*wszystkorodząca*).

NOTES TO PART II

The mausoleum of Cecilia Metella
It seems that a hidden entrance to the catacombs was found right next to this monument, erected by the triumvir Crassus, to his wife. It still stands in the Roman Campania, next to the church of St. Sebastian, from which one can descend into those portions of the catacombs open to visitors.

The Forum Romanum
This is the name of that large open area in front of the Capitol, upon which once stood speakers' platforms and curia, that is to say, tribunals, in which law cases were heard, and where the Senate sometimes debated. Stairs led from the Forum to the top of the Capitoline hill. There, to the left, above the Tarpeian Rock, stood the temple of Feretrian Jove, while on the right was found that of Capitoline Jove. The Via Sacra, or the Sacred Road of the triumphant, led to the Forum through the Arch of Fabian, and led out from it to ascend the Capitol through the Arch of Septimius Severus. Across from the Capitol, on the other side of the Forum, stood the temple and cloister of the vestal virgins, while closer to the foot of the Capitoline Hill were raised the temples of Fortune and Amity. The Rostrum was located in the very midst of the Forum, in an open space. The shape of the entire Forum was rectangular. Its sides were lined with rows of columns set before the temples and basilicas. The sight must have been quite splendid. In ancient architecture one does not find that spiritual

rapture one sees in the Gothic, but for all that, the solemnity of the flesh reigned everywhere, to the highest degree. A fitting symbol of ancient architecture would be an old patrician, unmoved, emotionally speaking, resting with his toga cast over his shoulder after having sacrificed to the gods. In ancient architecture, each fragment of a given building is rationally described, limited, perfectly finished. The ideas of measure and beauty are encompassed in a closed circle, so to speak. Imperturbability and unity are its chief characteristics, whereas in the Gothic, true movement, diversity and eternity come to life. One might say that ancient architecture is a spirit, completely incarnate in measure and matter, whereas Gothic architecture is matter toiling to become idealised, to become spiritual. This is why one is hard put to find a single completely finished Gothic church, while, on the other hand, pagan temples which are not completely finished in all of their parts are few and far between. And this is the reason that pagan architecture surpasses the Christian by a long shot as works of art, while Christian architecture surpasses the pagan insofar as thought, and soul, are concerned.

Those who sleep in these cemeteries were only pilgrims in this world [*w tych cmentarzach śpią goście tylko*; literally: "in these cemeteries sleep only guests"]

Above one of the entrances to the catacombs was inscribed: *Coemeterium est domus, in qua hospites dormire solent* — "The cemetery is a building, in which guests are used to sleep."

Lycaon Orpheus
The walls and sarcophagi of the catacombs were decorated with many symbolic carvings and paintings. In the early ages of Christianity, art was completely of a symbolic nature. And thus Orpheus, the first sage, poet, and founder of an association among the pagans, was used as an image of Christ. The same is true of the figures of Noah, Isaac, and the patriarch Joseph. Christ was also symbolised by a golden, three-armed candelabra; the vine was another Christian symbol. The lyre symbolised the cross, the palm frond: the triumph of heaven; God, the beginning and end of all things, was figured in a jewelled cross wound about by roses, with the letters Alpha and Omega hanging down from the arms on golden chains. The peacock was a symbol of

the Resurrection, and — sometimes — of Satan. The olive tree was a hieroglyph of eternity and peace. The cypress and the pine denoted death; the anchor: salvation; fish: people (according to the words Christ spoke to the apostles: *Faciam vos piscatores hominum* [I shall make of you fishers of men]). The dolphin symbolised the hopes of the departed, who had left this world for better regions. Samson, bearing on his back doors torn from their hinges, prefigured Christ, according to: *Tollit portas civitatis, id est inferni, et removit mortis imperium* ["He took away the gates of the city, that is, Hell, and did away with the dominion of death"]. Here *civitas* means, on the one hand, Samson's actual deed, whereas on the other hand, it symbolises the entire ancient world, which was nothing more than a conglomeration of cities, or structures egoistically enclosed within themselves, and fiercely oppressive ones, at that. And so Christ indeed delivers the death-blow to that old order, the composition of the entire ancient world, in calling people to brotherhood and freedom. (This proves that even the Christians of the first centuries felt called to a political vocation). Further on, the stag symbolised the apostles, the rooster — pastoral watchfulness, while the cross was always constituted of four types of wood: cypress, cedar, palm and olive.

The bring him the Prochristum
The Prochristum was an ampoule containing some of the martyr's blood. Placed upon his bosom as he lay in his tomb, it bore upon it the letters P. Ch., which (as its name signifies) means "for Christ." Even today the bodies of martyrs in the catacombs can be identified as such, in cases where inscriptions on their tombs are lacking.

Apage
Meaning "go away" in Greek, it was a formula used to chase the devil away from one's side.

Have you not heard so many of the saints declare that the time is near?
From the time of Christ's death until nearly the second half of the middle ages, the gloomy belief that the world was nearing its end, and that the final judgement was nigh, endured among Christians. The further on time advanced from the days of Christ, the weaker

grew this faith in the approaching end-times, or the more they were visioned as something to occur in the distant future. But in the first Christian ages, many of the faithful, especially mystics, hermits, and anchorites, expected the second coming of Jesus day by day. This conviction was especially prevalent in the East, in Egypt. From the very first, the Roman Church was rather more practical than ideal. It strove more to become incarnate in a certain shape and power, rather than tending to be dispersed from all form; still, even in the West there were many who believed in the imminent return of Christ. The greatest role in the grounding of this faith was played by St John, in his visions on the island of Patmos (his words are recorded for us in the New Testament book known as *Apocalypsis*). In the first age, and over the next several centuries, many similar books were written, containing other revelations and visions. More than one martyr, in his or her dying throes, saw the heavens opened, and foretold the end of Roman power, and thus the end of the world, and thus the second coming of Christ. For these reasons the deductions, hopes and desires of the first Christians on this topic were quite jumbled and tangled. Some were of the opinion that Christ was to return and establish His rule here on earth. Later, this faith came to be known as *millenarism,* for as the ages passed, people began to imagine that the final judgement would come about in the year 1000. During the English revolution of the seventeenth century, there was a certain political and religious sect that breathed new life into this faith. Others thought that this period of material testing would come to an end, along with the entire earth, along with Rome, all disappearing into thin air. The dead would rise, and the New Jerusalem promised by St John would appear in the heavens. This belief could also be based on some of the words of Christ Himself. Still others, who had been received into the Christian Church in the early ages, and who were still fain to understand things in a very material sense, desired that everything, both people and nature, should be completely transformed. Many of these people were influenced by their bitterness and suffering, having experienced abasement and injustice at the hands of the world. Each day, Christian formulas were repeated them: that his world of matter is nothing but illusion, that human life is a passing shadow, that there is another, higher, spiritual world — and each day they saw people facing death with a superhuman courage in order to get there. Such being the case, how could they not think that this second world would soon come about, destroying the lower world, and remaining, alone, in its place? And so they felt a vocation to overthrow the real world, which persecuted them. They still did not understand the moral truth: that thought always overcomes matter, just as a drop of water wears down a stone after the passage of many years. And so, as they saw no saecular power in their midst, they thought that Christ and His angels would come to their aid, so that in one day the Capitol would fall to pieces, along with the world — for there also existed such a conviction, such a faith just as strong as theirs, that the world would exist only as long as Rome herself stood. This, after all, is an exaggeration common to all people who cannot clearly imagine that the world might possibly go on living after the passing away of that, in which they were born and matured; that, of which they themselves formed a part. The Roman state was in fact nearing its end. What was to succeed it simply could not be foreseen by those people living in that state — and so, without any deeper consideration, they sentenced the whole world to death with their mistaken foreboding. It seems to me, however, that such was the faith only of the common people, never that of the head officers of Christianity. The bishops of Rome sensed that the teachings of Christ would yet become incarnate, on earth, in a material, universal rule. It is on such stories of the end of the world, the resurrection of the saints, and the destruction of Rome, that Irydion's conspiracy in the catacombs is based.

Where my steed passes, grass will never grow again.
These words are attributed to Attila, the barbarian chief.

A freedman read Phaedon *to him.*
The dialogue *Phaedon* concerns the immortality of the soul. It is this work of Plato's which Cato read before his suicide in Utica.

Cenotaphs along the walls
Cenotaph: Greek for tombstone.

Years ago, Herman
Herman is the Teuton name of the man the Romans called Arminius. He is the one who cut down the Roman legions led by

Varrus. The anguish felt by Augustus at this turn of events is recorded in his words, "Varrus, return my legions to me!"

NOTES TO PART III

Irydion takes up a tablet and stylus, and writes.
The ancients always carried around little tablets covered in a thin layer of wax, upon which they incised their notes with the help of a metal pen known as a stylus. They often carried this stylus hidden in the frontlet of their tunic, and they sometimes used it as a dagger. The greater part of the conspirators who assassinated Caesar entered the senate armed only with a stylus. Brutus stabbed him with a stylus as well.

We shall break him on the cross.
To the ancients, crucifixion was the most shameful form of execution. It is what death by hanging is to us.

From Hyrcania… to the deserts of the Jazygs.
Hyrcania was found along the shores of the Caspian Sea, near Parthia. The desert wilds of the Jazygs were found between the Dniepr and Don Rivers.

Hecatomb
From the Greek. A sacrificial offering made up of one hundred bulls. Figuratively, it describes every large sacrifice.

Vengeance is the delight of the gods.
An ancient Greek saying.

From the curial gates
The Curia signified any building in which a law court, or the Senate, was gathered.

Eheu!
The Latin form of *Alas!*

Hesperus
The evening star — Venus.

Drench them with oil
Napthta — a flammable mineral oil.

The victory at Zama
Scipio Africanus destroyed the forces of Hannibal at Zama.

Shroud of amiantus for the ashes of Rome
In order to distinguish the ashes of the human body from those of the pyre itself, it was customary among the ancients to wrap the body round in a shirt weft of a fibre made of asbestos. Such a fabric could be woven, and it was known as amiantus.

The maniples of Severus
On the battlefield, the Roman legions were arranged in three ranks. The first was made up of the *hastati*, the second of the *principes*, and the last, of the *triarii*. Each of these ranks was further divided into twelve maniples. Two maniples constituted a century, the commander of which was known as a centurion, and three maniples were called a cohort. There were at least sixty men to each maniple; sometimes, there were as much as one hundred and twenty.

The tresses of Berenice
This constellation of seven stars derives its name from the sister — and wife — of Ptolemy Euergetes, an Egyptian king. She had vowed to shave her head and hang her tresses in the temple of Mars as a votive offering for her husband's safe return from an expedition to Asia. She kept her promise, but her locks disappeared that same evening. Conon of Samos, the royal astronomer, swore at the time that he had seen Zephyr bear them aloft at the command of Venus. It was he gave the name Coma Berenices to the seven stars that shine next to the Lion's Tail (Denebola).

Reminding the Roman people of Brennus
Brennus, a Gallic chieftain, took Rome and slaughtered the Senate. Demanding ransom of the Roman people, he tossed his

sword onto the scale with the famous words *Vae victis!* — "Woe to the conquered!"

Threefold Hecate

Threefold, because she was worshipped as the Moon in the heavens, Diana on earth, and Proserpine or Hecate in the underworld. Her epithet was always *Dea feralis* — the "Fatal goddess."

If you be my evil genius

Among the ancients, it was popularly believed that each person had his or her own good, and evil, genius. Brutus was visited by his evil genius before the battle at Philippi.

Forgive me, quirites!

Quirites was another name for the Romans. It derives from the missile known as the *quiris*.

Sit tibi terra levis.

With this formula, the Romans bade farewell to the dead, as they turned away from the pyre or the urn. These words — "May the Earth Lay Lightly upon Thee" — were often incised upon tombstones.

Among the columbaria

A funeral monument for the less wealthy. Similar in shape to a dove-cote, with frames in which the urns were placed, it was known for this reason as a *columbarium*.

NOTES TO PART IV

The Threshold of Attalus

It is well known that the Roman Senate set aside the most beautiful provinces conquered from Antiochus the Great for Attalus, the King of Pergamon. When he was dying heirless, he was ordered to compose a testament, returning them to the Senate.

She arose at the Isthmian Games
Before Rome involved herself actively, and rapaciously, in Greek matters, the Roman ambassador declared publicly, during the Isthmian Games — and thus before a gathering of citizens from all the Greek cities — that, in consideration of the fact that the demands of the Macedonian king are unjust, and how beautiful and necessary the independence of Greece is, the Senate and People of Rome have promised to defend the land, with all their forces, from invasions by that ruler.

Latona's son
Phoebus Apollo.

The well-tramped roads of the aediles
Aediles were civic officers responsible for the building of public edifices, roads, bridges, aqueducts, etc.

From Gadez to Ultima Thule
Gadez is known today as Cadiz, and Thule is Iceland. The ancients almost always attached the adjective "ultima," or final, to the latter term, for they understood it as lying at the most distant edge of the world.

The distracted shades of a stoic or two.
The last word in the Platonic school of Greek philosophy was pronounced by the Stoics, who brought the ancient world to an end. The idealism of the ancient world was as incarnate in them as materialism was among the Epicureans. The Stoics were of great virtue, but that virtue was marked by impassivity. They knew how to die, but not how to live. Their first principle was contained in the imperative *apekho* — deny yourself; and so they denied themselves everything — casting upon the dying world a sad eye, without coming to its aid. Closed within themselves, doing homage to their pride alone, which they called their conscience, they ended up as moral egoists, full of an extraordinary egoistic nobility, but — they were not united into any group; they were not inspired by any spark of common, friendly intercourse. Their thoughts and prescriptions floated about the world of ideals, and were never adapted to the earth. For this reason, it is only

tales of their famous deaths have come down to us, nothing dealing with their lives. Emperor Marcus Aurelius was the purest, most beautiful, spirit among them. His maxims gave solace, for a long time, to a world ever more falling apart in the unharnessing of death — but they created nothing great or living. The stoic systems might be called a testament, by which the dying man hands on nothing to his inheritors, save a few sad comments about life. The stoics were the first to introduce the sickness called *spleen* to the world — later inherited by the British — the last crisis of which illness is suicide.

As the pater familias children, as patricians the plebes
As a Roman jurist might put it.

In the Hercynian Forest, kneeling pale beneath the sacrificial blade
Herman, or Arminius, surrounded the legions of Varrus in the Hercynian Forest and sacrificed the chief officers to the Germanic gods.

No flying bolt of Alexander's
In the history of Rome, nothing was ever elevated to the ideal — but for all that, there was never any nation on earth more *realistic* and *practical*. The Roman Senate practised unheard-of deception and villainy from its inception unto the end of the Republic. They got rid of their enemies, most often, through treachery (Hannibal, Jugurtha, Sertorius, the destruction of Carthage, Mithridatus), while deceiving their friends and allies in all possible ways (Greece, Asia Minor, Pergamon, Egypt, Gaul). The greatness of the city was founded upon weathering bad times, in the faith that Rome would remain standing, simply because it should, and upon an insolence that felt no shame. No Roman ever set off on a youthful, poetic, grand tour in the style of Alexander the Great — no civilising thought ever arose in their hearts as it did in the heart of Aristotle's pupil. Their guiding light was heavily materialistic. For this reason, they never attempted to conjoin peoples, they never attempted to unite the nationalities in harmony in order to create an organic whole; rather, they dispersed, exterminated, destroyed. The sentences of the Roman Senate constitute a primer of hypocrisy: we find therein endless testimonies to the gods, and repetitions of various prescriptions of virtue, justice and piety. In

the name of justice they deprived persons of their private property; they transformed independent lands into provinces or kingdoms which, when the kings died, they declared their own on the basis of the most laughably invented, and most shamelessly upheld laws. At the same time they clothed themselves in all the appearances of nobility, constantly coming to the defence of the weak and oppressed, so it would seem — only to shave clean the oppressed of the slightest bits of wealth and power that remained them. Treaties concluded in disadvantageous circumstances by leaders of the Republic were mere toys, for the Senate often refused to ratify them, on the basis that this praetor or that consul did not have the authority to make them in the first place — after which punishment would be meted out to the fellow in question. And then the war would be resumed, with Rome taking advantage of the respite, to the detriment of the enemies who had been deceived into losing time in this manner. The power of Rome was also a mere phrase. Their representatives at foreign courts would constantly lie, describing their power with the greatest cheek and pride. But it worked! Papilias Lenas kept the mightiest potentate of the East, Antiochus the Great, enclosed in a circle drawn upon the sand until he responded to his demands — and at the time Asia had hardly heard of the very name of Rome. In a word, Rome was never equalled in practical intelligence, but then again, no one had ever lied so barefacedly and continually to the world, no one had ever broken promises so basely, no power had ever wielded so gigantic a supply of bad faith. It is for this reason that the Romans remained so weak in the world of the spirit. They never invented, nor did they ever discover, anything at all. They had neither a literature nor an art of their own. Their intelligence, above all, was that of a legalist, a lawyer, a pleader. Their conquests are similar to trials carried out with great skill. Their final victory, their rule over the entire world, became the corruption and death of that same, entire world. Humanity began to rot under the foot of Rome. The unity of which the Romans dreamed was nothing more than a collection of mechanical atoms, not the organic vivification of a great, unified body. We inherited from them what they knew best: a codex of laws; besides that, nothing. For their writers are a mere reflection of Greek civilisation, which they simply imitated, and slavishly, at that. They were lords in the material world, but slaves in the world of the spirit. They suffered a self-inflicted punishment. They perished because they never comprehended any real political or social life; because they beat down, but never organised; they subtracted, without multiplying, they oppressed, but never liberated; they used strength to kill, but never to knit together with the spirit. When the time came for Rome to die, the empire looked around for the slightest spark of life that might transfuse its old veins with new life, but saw nothing around it but corpses lying at its feet — and these did not reawaken!

Euge! Euge!
An exclamation, such as "Look!" or "Ha!"

Rostrum
Speaker's platform

Ultimum vale
The final farewell at funerals

Diespiter!
Exclamation; otherwise *pater diei* — "Father of the day."

Father of all men and all gods
An epithet descriptive of Jove.

Did he sow dragon's teeth
In his quest for the Golden Fleece, Jason slew the dragon and broadcast its teeth — from which armed men sprang immediately from the earth.

Marspiter!
Exclamation; otherwise *Mars pater*.

Gemonia
A well, into which the corpses of criminals were tossed.

NOTES TO CONSUMMATION

The pale face of Cynthia
A name of Diana.

Screen of purple
During games, a screen or covering known as the *velarium* was pulled over the entire amphitheatre, as protection from the sun.

1846

It is January 1846. The setting is the Sister's salon, Warsaw, evening. Present are: the Ex-Chancellor's Wife and her three daughters, the Referendary, the Citizen. The Sister stands at the table, getting tea ready. An open piano stands in the middle of the salon; a light and some candles are set upon it.

SISTER
You don't take cream in your tea, Madame, am I right?

EX-CHANCELLOR'S WIFE
I can't tolerate cream, my dear little cousin. Just ask Cecylia. Well, go on, Cecylia, tell her. You remember how last winter, in Vienna, we were at Prince Metternich's and, by chance it happened that I didn't notice what was in my cup (there were so many important people there, such an elevated tone!) and I drank it up...

CECYLIA
Mother drank about half a cup...

EX-CHANCELLOR'S WIFE
Oh, Cecylia, not like that! You have to tell the whole story, my darling! That the Prince Arch-Chancellor himself was the one who handed me the cup, so I just couldn't refuse...

CECYLIA
And Mother began to feel ill, and besides the nausea, your face began to break out...

EX-CHANCELLOR'S WIFE
Maybe you should tell the story, Agata. Agata, you tell the story...

SISTER
And you, sir, always with rum?

REFERENDARY
If you would be so kind, my gracious lady. I fall at your feet in gratitude; and kiss the rim of the cup that your fingers have touched. Might I ask for use a tiny bit more of that rum? Just a drop, half a drop, really — O! Thanks, perfect. If I might speak frankly, I hardly touch the stuff these days — *votre très humble serviteur!*

CITIZEN
Nothing for me today, my dear lady. I can't seem to sleep well these past few nights, and tea would only make matters worse, I reckon. But why is it that you're not touching your tea? I hope you're not unwell?

SISTER
Actually, you're right. I'm not well.

EX-CHANCELLOR'S WIFE
What's that, my angel? My dear little cousin? What's wrong? It's true that you're looking rather poorly at the moment…

REFERENDARY
If I may be so bold in my, so to speak, blasphemy, I would say, my dear, dear lady that, when such a marvellously beautiful face is the subject of our concern, we oughtn't say "poorly," but "a tiny bit less gorgeous." Oh, no, please — don't go to any trouble on my behalf. I'll take, O, this pastry here. *Votre très humble serviteur!*

EX-CHANCELLOR'S WIFE
It's not uncommon for young widows to be… out of sorts. Pretty young widows, like yourself, little cousin, often don't feel quite right, and it's perfectly natural for that to be the case. So heed the advice of an old, yes, an old woman, for — comparatively speaking — I am older than you, little cousin, am I not? I'm an old woman by comparison. That's correct, isn't it, Cecylia? Cecylia, speak when your Mother addresses you!

CECYLIA
Certainly, old Mother...

EX-CHANCELLOR'S WIFE
Yet strange as it may seem, at a ball last winter at Archduke Franz's in Vienna I had a white dress on, completely white, and on my head a bright red turban, and on my front the Stern-Kreuz medal, which the Austrian Empress herself deigned to present me with, and — tell us, will you, Agata? No, you tell us, Julia, you tell us, after all, it was you who, once we'd returned home, told me that you had heard that the Danish consul — what's his name, Baron... Baron...

JULIA
Baron Helsinor, Mama.

EX-CHANCELLOR'S WIFE
That Baron Helshner, or whatever he's called, was surprised — and such a well-bred, polite man he is, entirely *comme il faut*, a famous diplomat — he was surprised that Polish women, even the mothers of three grown daughters, look so fresh and pretty — yet still it's true, there's no hiding it, I'm older, and quite a bit at that, than you, my little angel, my darling cousin... But that's not what I'm getting at. So, back to what I was saying before, the gentlemen here will certainly agree with me, isn't that true, my dear sirs? That you must, *il le faut*, find yourself someone handsome and wealthy, yes, wealthy! Because without money even the most intelligent person has nothing to show — Are you listening to me, my angel, my little cousin? So, handsome and wealthy and of course sensible, because that first husband of yours — please don't get angry! May God rest his soul! — he simply wasn't meant for you. I don't say he was a bad person, of course, may God receive him into His heavenly kingdom — but he was always bouncing about the aether as it was! His feet never touched the ground, a poet — and of course he died of consumption, because all poets, after all, are consumptive...

SISTER
If you don't mind, dear Aunt; let's change the subject.

EX-CHANCELLOR'S WIFE
It's always the same in this world. Young widows don't even want to entertain the thought, and yet, it never ends any other way.

REFERENDARY
When a moment, or two moments ago to be precise, your noble aunt invited us, and particularly, if I may be so bold as to assume, particularly encouraged me to take voice and offer my opinion, my completely unbiassed opinion, in this matter, my dear, sweet lady, I am therefore emboldened to suggest that days spent in solitude sooner or later end in melancholy. And thus I humbly assert that you should not, like a pearl, hide yourself in the ocean's depths, but among human society you…

SISTER
I must say I am surprised, Referendary, that you have decided to play along with the little joke begun by my noble aunt just a moment, or two moments ago, to be precise. Now, whereas I must give ear to my aunt, you will allow, sir, that the same does not apply in your case. I needn't, nor will I, listen to what you have to say in this matter. And so if you would be so kind, can you speak of something else? Let us leave our fate, that of each one of us, in the hands of God. The future is an abyss, and quite a black one, especially at this moment.

CITIZEN
Black, O, very black. You're quite right, Madame. Whenever I happen to walk in front of a church, it's not joyful wedding ceremonies that come to my mind, but quite different rites!

EX-CHANCELLOR'S WIFE
What sort, my good fellow?

CITIZEN
Funerals, my good woman

EX-CHANCELLOR'S WIFE
All men between twenty and forty are so gloomy these days.

REFERENDARY
Well, if I were asked to offer my opinion in the matter, I'd say that it comes from the widespread and ever wider spreading influence of French literature, which that independent and great, I say, critic of ours Michał Grabowski, characterised as *wild* and *raving*. Just take a look at the display windows of any bookseller in Warsaw, be that Gluksberg or Spiess or Merzbach, and what do you see on offer but more and more new translations of Dumas and Sand etc., etc. In this we find the essence, the embryo, the root of this universal gloominess, which, however before the Revolution had a savour pleasant and inviting, today smacks of illness.

SISTER
Surely Dumas is the author of "The Taking of Warsaw," and Madame Sand wrote that other work known as "The Citadel," which we've been hoping, these last fifteen years — maugre our ill minds and inflamed imaginations — that our Polish youth might take a liking to?

REFERENDARY
That's another matter, another matter entirely. Ah! It's true, these are difficult times. But just yesterday at a soirée at Madam Trusov's, the general's wife, I met with Senator Jurgiewicz, the Controller, who is often found at the palace, and he is a man — as you know, *Mesdames* — of sound judgement and, if I say so myself, a man of impeccable manners; you simply can't say that *he* has no heart; *enfin un homme de poids* — it's never yet been said of him that *he* ever informed on anyone or that *he* ever took a bribe; no, he never stole nor spied nor tattled — is it not true what I'm saying?

CITIZEN
And so? I admit it's true that no one has ever — yet — discovered that he's quite simply stolen, or informed on anyone directly — but, so?

REFERENDARY
He was very polite to me. I don't know why, but really, very, very nice — always calling me *mon cher*, taking me by the arm and leading me off to the corner or some to window-sill, where he would ask me for my opinion in the most complicated matters — governmental, administrative,

or financial. Now, he's a man who knows people, and I'm not talking about those of the sort of people who are servile towards Petersburg, trying to introduce the Russian language and finish off Polish so as to flatter the almighty Tsar; to persecute the Catholic religion and destroy the Code Napoléon or at least replace it with a new legal system — Not at all! — Of course, he'll puff up the Marshal when he can, although naturally, with all seemly delicacy, and it seems that he's in the Marshal's favour. The Marshal trusts him — trusts him sincerely. Of course, he can't praise the Revolution in his presence — that goes without being said — or anything else of that ilk, — what's true is true — but in all his behaviour and bearing there remains quite a lot of the Polish. Our ethnicity is rooted in him, deeply hidden, true, but firmly rooted. — Thank the Lord God that we've been blessed with such a high functionary!

CITIZEN
O my dear Referendary, you poet of panegyrics, please, in prose this time, tell us what that high functionary of yours entrusted you with yesterday, in that corner, at that window-sill.

REFERENDARY
I shall, word for word, as if you had been there yourself, sir. Well. As soon as he arrived at Madam Trusov's salon, right there, among the gathered people, I went right up to him to present myself. I was standing right next to him for maybe ten minutes, no more — and then he finished his conversation with Colonel Knoryng. He returned my bow, and when I addressed him, "*Votre excellence*," he interrupted me at once and, taking me by the arm, walked me around the hall twice, during a pause in the dancing.

CITIZEN
For God's sake, what did he tell you!

REFERENDARY
Not then — but later, by the window — because the mazurka was starting up again. So he took his place among the flowers that were piled up in rows between the stove and the window — you know, you've got to admit that when the General's wife is receiving, well, everything's done in splendid taste, simply *irreprochable* — well, then he leaned in

toward my ear, just as I'm doing now with you, Count, and he said, "You know what's come out of all the interrogations, *mon ami*" — "I don't, *votre excellence*." — "*Mon cher*, it seems that there's nothing nationalistic in any of this. Young students, applicants without a cent to their name, completely insignificant fellows; the Prince himself told me this just an hour ago." — "So," I said, "What's it all about, *votre excellence*?" — And he says "French Saint-Simonism and German communism — just please don't pass this on to anyone! — because, you know, you're the only person I'm entrusting this to." And when I said I wanted to learn something more about this from him, he walked away, gesturing, that I should remain there among the flowers by the window. So you see, ladies and gentlemen, it's just Communists at the bottom of it all!

CITIZEN
Communists who'd like nothing better than to see the peasants slit our throats. Because the lords and ladies are done with, by their own will, thanks to their devotion to some sort of dreams of social castes — and not to Polish aims and goals! — And you believe all this? — Only communists! — All of them, all of them who are being arrested constantly on the slightest of pretexts, paying with their lives, transported to Siberia or the Trans-Caucasus, and all for a forbidden book that happened to be found in their possession! — Or for an unguarded word — or for a bold glance cast towards the Marshal's carriage as it rolled past, or for not lifting their hats in deference to him! — No. What you've told us is a bald-faced lie. All of these young people are burning with vengeance, burning to rebel on behalf of their downtrodden country — In their veins courses the true, pure, free Polish blood, from father to son! — But Madame, you grow pale. What's happened? Are you all right?

SISTER
It's nothing — nothing at all — please, take no notice of me. Sometimes my colour fades like that, without warning, and for no reason at all. Maybe it's the sudden thaw outside, or perhaps I feel a big frost coming on, and it's this that affects my nerves, invisibly. Please, sir, go on, continue with what you were saying.

CITIZEN
Permit me to have a peek outside these doors, Madame. *Goes over to the doors and opens them.* No —
Nobody's eavesdropping. You know, Madame, I'm certain of the fact that that butler of yours, that other one with the blue eyes, the glassy eyes that, when he glances at you, it's as if he wanted to suck forth your very soul! — is in the pay of the police.

SISTER
I'm of the same opinion, sir. That's why I always tell him to sit there in the foyer, and not to approach until he's called by the little bell — otherwise not to enter. Please don't be afraid. He wouldn't dare eavesdrop, because he well knows that I often take a peek through those doors myself!

CITIZEN
Returning to his chair
So then I shall speak freely…

REFERENDARY
My good Count, my dear honoured Count, I beg you — speak more softly, please. — It's such an easy thing to compromise oneself, and others! The trained ear can catch a manly voice like yours from three rooms away! Who will vouch for that stove, that no one is sitting with his ear pressed near the pipe that leads to the chimney?

AGATA
I'd like for a person like that to jam his whole head in the pipe! And be choked by the smoke!

REFERNDARY
You may laugh at me, Miss, but one can never be too careful. Maybe the stove has no ears, but these days the walls are covered with them like wallpaper, the floors are lain with ears like slats of parquet, the carpets are woven of ears! Horrid, horrid! Let's talk of yesterday's concert, rather.

CITIZEN
But you're not going to snitch on us, sir, nor are we on you. But since you'd have it so, I'll speak more softly. — On my honour, therefore, I'll declare to you, ladies and gentlemen, that as far as my peasants are concerned, I have no fear of them whatsoever. They'd go to Hell and back for me. Just a month ago I called them all together. I wanted to abolish the corvée and replace it with rent. They stood there on the lawn before the porch, scratched their heads, and begged me to leave well enough alone. Because when there's a lean year, it's a good thing to be able to have charity from the lord, while if a rent system is in place, one has to struggle against hunger by oneself. — In short, they said "thanks, but no thanks." It's true, I tell you, that long ago I abolished their obligation of participating in public works and other types of non-remunerative labour, so their corvée isn't too much of a burden. And yet, all the same I'm going to have to replace it with a rent-system, because during the corvée I've got nobody to be out there making sure that the steward isn't thrashing the peasants or berating them with filthy language. And such things happen on my lands from time to time, although I myself try to keep an eye on things, and I scold, berate, and fire the strict ones. And what can be said of the others, who don't care, or don't want to understand, that this is a new age! — Completely new, I say, ladies and gentlemen! — Before 1830 the peasants didn't even dream of things that they discuss openly today in the taverns! — Really, really I say, we're in a little bit of a fix. — That damned government! O! Now they want to forbid us to promote sobriety! And a drunken peasantry is a satanic thing. And there are such landholders, who get their people drunk in the name of greater profits. They drink them to death. I know some such in my own neighbourhood who at the least provocation might have their throats cut, or their brains beaten out of them with flails. It's bad, it's really bad! The young boys are spreading various new ideas — peas and cabbage, a real jumble of hunter's stew. They're talking about an uprising! And with what sort of weapons? There's neither guns nor gunpowder nor an army! So it seems that the peasants want to form regiments — and fight like partisans — democratically. And God grant it! But right now there's such confusion. Here is the government — there is the peasant, and it's bad! For sure! But as I am a Polish nobleman, I swear that those youngsters of ours aren't giving a single thought to Communism! They are thinking only of Poland,

of the fatherland, of nationalism. They're ready for everything, it's true; they're in despair, that's also true, but how could it be otherwise? They're going to get rid of the Kingdom in a few months time, and we'll be Muscovites, not Poles. Another legal system, another religion. Our mayors will be deposed and replaced by chinovniks. There used to be eight gubernias, and now there's only five left; and we've already forgotten that they used to be called voivodships. Hell, it's bad! Referendary, you yourself, you won't try to tell me that it's not!

REFERENDARY
I'm terribly sorry, my Lord; I'm holding a ball of yarn for Miss Agata, and I have to make sure it unwinds properly… I beg your pardon, I didn't quite hear your entire dissertation. Miss Agata will witness to that, that I haven't…

AGATA
I hereby testify to the fact that the Referendary did not hear a thing. — But all the same you did, you did!

CITIZEN
I asked you if you did not agree, that among us, now, things are as bad as they can be.

REFERNDARY
A moment, a moment… Shall I now hold the other ball of yarn for you, my sweet young lady?

AGATA
No — I'd rather that you gave ear to the Count at the moment.

CITIZEN
It's so bad, that it can't be any worse.

REFERENDARY
O yes it can, it can be worse yet. For example, what if they replaced the viceroy with somebody else: Muraviev for example, or Bibikov?

CITIZEN
What difference would that make? They're all beasts.

REFERENDARY
But the Marshal…

CITIZEN
O, he's a pretty one, he is. There you have somebody to be proud of — the Marshal! He who orders his Cherkashes to arrest twelve-year old kids and parade them through the town to the guardroom! They ride in fine order, with their sabres and *handjar* daggers and pistols, on rearing horses, in their pagan robes, with their faces straight out of Hell, Muslims all, and among them a poor boy in a school uniform! But he walks on boldly, not crying, not trembling, no, not him: he cocks his hat to the side and skips along, as if he were on an outing — I've seen it with my own eyes. And who wallops the post-master with a closed fist when by chance there are no horses to be had at the station? And who, outside of a theatre, wallops a fellow cursing the bad weather, thinking that he was the object of the imprecations? And who was it, in front of all the nobles gathered at the races, who pulled a nobleman's son out of the crowd because of the French cut of his beard, and had him arrested and tossed into gaol and shaved it off? Well, Referendary, who?

REFERENDARY
Why wrap it up in rhetorical questions? You already gave the answer yourself, sir.

CITIZEN
And that Marshal of yours, he's topped Constantine now!

REFERENDARY
Not my Marshal, not mine at all — I don't defend him absolutely, only relatively, in the sense that it could still be worse!

CITIZEN
Worse? Maybe in Siberia or at the gallows. But even in Siberia or at the gallows a man would have a calmer heart, seeing that there is nothing more to hope for. He wouldn't feel anything anymore. What's to do,

only God knows. As I said yesterday to good old Chrzański: "You know what, major? Drink maybe, and drink oneself to death from despair." And he: "As God's my witness, I can think of nothing else." And so we went, both of us, to dinner at Mare's, and yet neither of us had a drop of wine. We hadn't a taste for it!

EX-CHANCELLOR'S WIFE
I think we need a gayer topic of conversation, to make things more pleasant! For see here, gentlemen, look how morosely my poor cousin is sitting. It's your fault, Count, you've deprived her of her good humour. Fe! My Lord, that was not very gallant of you!

CITIZEN
So what shall we gab about? Seventy tonnes are pressing down on my neck so, that my very bones are cracking, and you ask me, Madam, to skip about chasing flies!

SISTER
Please don't blame my aunt, dear sir. You've brought me great relief with what you've said!

EX-CHANCELLOR'S WIFE
Just please, please let's not return to that relief of yours, my darling angel, my sweet cousin! — *A propos*, you told me yourself that you're expecting Kęta this evening, who was to try out your piano. — What has become of him, that he's taking so long to arrive?

SISTER
These days, latecomers sometimes never arrive at all!

EX-CHANCELLOR'S WIFE
What?

REFERENDARY
If I might, as well, humbly ask you to explain your words, my dear lady?

CITIZEN
They're not hard to figure out. The dear lady is afraid lest the person she is expecting has fallen into the hands of the police. And perhaps they found on him the music of some patriotic song, which would slow down his progress all the more. — Everything's possible. — But Kęta is a careful man. All day long, he's busied with his music; he hardly sees anyone... Was that what you had in mind, Madame?

SISTER
Yes, and no. Because I really can't say that I've been thinking at all clearly for the past hour — for all that, I've been feeling deeply — and sadly. It seems to me as if something pernicious were taking place around us, without our knowing — but we're to find out about it in short order.

EX-CHANCELLOR'S WIFE
Fe! Spasms! Spasms, my little cousin! Call for an anodyne. The court physician of the King of Saxony himself once advised me to treat such symptoms with some powdered sugar and morphine. Right, Julia? Do you remember? Tell us, remember?

REFERENDARY
I am sure that you will be of my opinion, Madame — I'm certain of it! — when I say, what a talent that Kęta possesses! It's extraordinary! Ever since he returned from Paris, where he drank in with his eyes, or with his ears, rather, the thunderous tones broadcast through the heavens by the fingers of the greatest musical maestros of this century — bah, I would say, of all time!... Yes, ears, certainly, although the first expression, eyes, might also be appropriate... Eyewitness...

SISTER
He's so emotive, immensely so. And deeply Polish — the keys themselves weep tears of despair when he touches them — they weep and they moan, and they lift their prayers to God!

REFERENDARY
I've never heard Liszt. It was my bitterest misfortune to be in Lithuania when he was delighting Warsaw with his presence — thus I can't judge

his talent… Now, Thalberg I've heard, a bit, a little bit, a teeny-tiny bit… But you will agree, Madame, that I know a little bit about musical execution and *basso continuo*, in a word, about music? —And so I shall be so bold as to declare without fear of contradiction, this my opinion: Kęta stands just a little bit beneath Thalberg — a little bit — just a little bit, *Mesdames*!

SISTER
Higher by far, rather, for he plays patriotic songs!

REFERENDARY
However far it lies in my power, and indeed it somewhat does, I act as his patron here in town — he's given more than one lesson thanks to my protection. — He wasn't recognised for who he is here, at first. But I did my best to introduce him somehow into the very best houses.

CITIZEN
So he promised you, Madame, to come today for sure?

SISTER
For sure.

CITIZEN
What time might it be?

REFERENDARY
Let me check my Breguet, a truly perfect little piece, which I always carry about with me; ah! You see, my Lord: ten o'clock!

CITIZEN
The clock on the mantle says it's already ten thirty!

REFERENDARY
My Breguet is infallible!

CITIZEN
Someone's coming, I think.

BUTLER
Mr Kęta.

Enter Kęta.

CITIZEN
Speak of the devil!

REFERENDARY
Of the angel, rather. Or the nightingale, the most musical creature in the zoological kingdom!

KĘTA
I do beg your pardon, Madame, for arriving so late. You know that I am always most eager and prompt to serve you.

CITIZEN
You know, we had already begun to be fearful on your account.

SISTER
Terrified, rather.

EX-CHANCELLOR'S WIFE
I for one was not the least bit scared — Agatka, is that not so? Julia, you be my witness too. And Cecylia as well. For in the higher reaches of this world it's rather good taste to flirt by arriving late. I myself, along with my daughters, never arrive at exactly the appointed time. Whether it be Dresden or Vienna or Wrocław or Berlin, or when we take the waters…

REFERENDARY
Bonjour, Kęta — your hand, please! Bonjour, Kęta!

EX-CHANCELLOR'S WIFE
But now that Monsieur Kęta has kept us waiting so long without his presence, depriving us of his music, please, I beg you, sir, approach the piano; sit down and please do your best that we might heartily enjoy ourselves — for I tell you, Monseiur Kęta, in confidence, that up until

your arrival we had been tossing around the most horrible topics, *particulièrement* my dear little angel, my beloved little cousin — and so, we really need a lively tune. I'm sure that Monsieur Kęta knows all the waltzes of Strauss, is it not so? Sit down, sit down and delight us!

SISTER
Oh Auntie, allow the gentleman to catch his breath first and have a cup of tea — not too strong is it, I hope? — Wait just a moment, I'll add some water.

KĘTA
You are too kind, Madame, to remember your servant. Yes, I have heard a thing or two of Strauss. Who was it that asked for Strauss? I didn't quite notice…

EX-CHANCELLOR'S WIFE
Oh! Me, it was me, Monsieur Kęta, along with Cecylia and Agata and Julia — for they are always of one mind with me, always thinking and doing the same as I — we even dress the same!

KĘTA
Approaches the piano
And so, Madame wishes for something light, airy — dances and laughter, jokes and giggles? — At your service!

CITIZEN
What's this? — If that's Strauss, may my own peasants hang me!

REFERENDARY
Delicious — delicious — but that's rather a requiem. Bravo! Bravissimo! And not a bit of Mozart to be found, not even a single note. It's all his own! He's improvising, improvising! *To Kęta.* You are improvising, are you not? — On my honour, ladies and gentlemen, I declare that he is improvising! Bravo! Bravissimo!

EX-CHANCELLOR'S WIFE
I must say that you are a strange man, Monsieur Kęta…. Perhaps *vous voulez* that this divine little angel should fall into convulsions? — I'm

having a hard time keeping it all together myself, for my nerves are quite, quite delicate, and you are playing so beautifully, *on ne peut pas dire*, but you aren't really making our little gathering very pleasant. — Oh, those tones, dear St Joseph! — They remind me of the last funeral I attended, in Dresden, that of the Grand Huntsman of the Court, only there it was horns and reeds, not pianos… Do you know, sir, you're making me afraid!

KĘTA
And now no further, impossible! — Oh! Thus — just one more chord — perhaps the strings will snap — that, or the heart will break! — Amen!

SISTER
Why did you stop playing?

KĘTA
I hadn't the strength to continue! Later, at your request, I'll try to go on with it.

CITIZEN
Here, sit down, and enjoy your cup, at last. Any news? Pray tell!

KĘTA
The snow is blowing. The street lanterns are shining sadly. The wind whistles.

CITIZEN
Do you wish to keep some bad news from us, perhaps?

SISTER
What is this? What is the meaning of this? There is blood on your sleeve!

CITIZEN
There is! And on your vest, and on your handkerchief — you are not wounded?

KĘTA
I thought I'd cleaned myself up completely — that there were no marks left. For I didn't want to give you a fright, Madame. — No, it's not my blood — it's the blood of a poor man — Ah! I saw something horrible!

SISTER
Tell us, for God's sake! I beg you!

KĘTA
I left my house at seven-thirty, on my way here. — On Miodowa street I met with more numerous patrols of gendarmes on foot than usual, and mounted Cossacks in the middle of the street. One company no sooner passed, than another came by, flowing, riding up, passing by a second time. I thought "Something new must be going on." Not far from the Capuchin church I brushed up, in passing, against someone's overcoat — he stopped, we recognised one another: an old friend from school, today a doctor. He gripped my hand and said, "If you've got anything on you, hide it. Last night two lawyers and some fifteen students had their lodgings searched — they were all arrested and taken to the Citadel, except for three." And then he pushed on, and disappeared, just in time, because again there came the clatter of swords — another patrol of gendarmes was approaching. I pulled my hat down low on my brows, the collar of my coat up to my ears, and made room, so that they wouldn't shove me into the gutter. — They went on their way — and I on mine. Then, by the columns, again someone greeted me. I looked: it was a student from the gymnasium, the brother of one of my female students. "Two hours ago," he whispered, "I saw the arrestees being driven to the Castle along the Krakowskie Przedmieście — three fiacres and one coach, and on the coach box of each there sat a Cossack and a gendarme with drawn swords."

SISTER
Dear God! And did he not say who they were? Did he not recognise anyone? Didn't he hear, doesn't he know?

KĘTA
He hadn't the time to add a word to this — he slipped away and disappeared. And once again several policemen came along. Oh,

the bestial, vulgar way they talked amongst themselves! They didn't bother me, though, and I quickened my pace. Do you know, Madame, where Miodowa turns into Senatorska? Well, there I came across that *buduchnik*, who stands there with his halberd. I had to come near that scoundrel because I needed to give way to the sleds that were speeding from the direction of King Zygmunt's column. Now, a lantern was shining on each street corner there, so I saw everything as clear as day. This fellow with a great beard — a Muscovite — was speeding along, lashing the horses in a frenzy. Behind him, from within the sleigh, I saw the feathers of a military cap waving. From the opposite direction, to his misfortune, a hired sled approached, pulled by a couple of horses. He didn't have time to turn and avoid the accident, and the sleds became entangled. I heard the Muscovite roaring in Russian: *Let go, let go, you son of a bitch!* while I heard the voice of the Polish cabbie, "Certainly sir, right away sir, your Grace, General." And then again I hear in Russian: *You insurrectionist, you rebel, you Pole!* And the cabbie began pleading, "Dear God, *Nyet!* General, your Grace!" — he was trying to speak Russian, to disguise himself as a Muscovite. I then saw the poor fellow leap down from his box and extricate his runners from those of the general's sled with all his strength. Meanwhile, the general arose from his seat, cast the overcoat from his shoulder — all his medals and crosses were shining on his breast — and stretched his arm across to the left. By this time, the cabbie had separated the runners of the two sleds — if only he had hopped back onto his own and disappeared! But no! He obeyed the thunderous command of the Muscovite general, and leaving his horses alone approached the other sled. He took off his cap and bowed, apologising, kneeling down, and bending ever lower as he did so, almost lying prone before the general with arms outspread, grovelling, pleading to be forgiven for his transgression. The blood in my heart began to boil at that sight! But I did not anticipate what was to happen next. That bemedalled and befeathered bear roared once more "You Pole!" but the cabbie was silent — he just kept quiet, lying there, and — and then I heard a swishing sound and something flashed crookedly before my eyes — With all his strength, from above, bending over the side of the sled, the general whacked at the helpless cabbie's uncovered head down there on the snowy street! And again! And again! Never to rise from the cobbles again, that head. It patiently awaited a fourth stroke, the poor, shamed, silent head pulsing its black blood onto the grey snow. Then the general wiped his sword clean on the back of his driver and poked him in the back with the point of his scabbard. The bearded Cossack whistled, and the horses jumped furiously to life, speeding with the sleigh straight down Senatorska!

CECYLIA
Ah! If only I had him here, that general!

AGATA
I would prick out both his eyes with this needle!

JULIA
I'd only spit him in those eyes, but there would be Polish venom in my saliva, to burn out his pupils!

EX-CHANCELLOR'S WIFE
Mon Dieu, have mercy on us!

CITIZEN
Don't get up now, my dear Referendary! Don't get up now! You'll see: everyone will get his turn. *Hodie mihi, cras tibi!* Today the cabbie, tomorrow the Referendary!

REFERENDARY
That was an example of unheard of illegality — I'll admit as much!

SISTER
And so that poor man was killed there on the spot?

KĘTA
Not much life remained in him, but he was still breathing when we lifted him up. — I'm ashamed, ashamed to speak of this, Madame! O, you simply can't believe what terror reigns in the city! In our veins there runs, not blood, but mistrust — fear has found a lodging in the marrow of our bones. Please note Madame, that not I alone, but other passers by too had halted on the street. — The while the horrid scene was playing out, it's true, one couldn't say a word, but later, there was

nothing to prevent, nothing to oppose. And yet when that scoundrel drove away — can you comprehend it? — none of those present moved a muscle. Each of us stood there as motionless as a pole planted in the pavement. Meanwhile, in the middle of the road, all bloodied, the cabbie rolled about, moaning "Jesus, Jesus, Jesus!" Yet none of them, and there were many, dared to bring him aid. I was the first one who jumped out from among the columns on Miodowa — then the rest, in their dark overcoats and black greatcoats, all began to move near — but slowly, looking around, and in a deep silence. It seemed to me that I was ringed round by coffins, moving across the ground on their short ends —

CITIZEN
What was there to be afraid of, devil take it?

SISTER
Are you not aware of the fact, my Lord, that, in this land of ours, he who is touched by a Muscovite hand is already cursed? He no longer has any fellow countrymen, nor wife, nor child!

CITIZEN
Madame deigns to joke!

SISTER
It's a bitter joke, but true just the same!

KĘTA
I would gladly look upon the death of ten cabbies from the hand of ten generals, rather than such servility, such debasement! — In the end, we set him upon his own sled. I held him, supporting his head on my chest. One of the others gook the reins, and we drove him off to the St Roch hospital. On the way, my companion said not a word to me — nor I to him. It seems that each of us took the other for a spy. — When we arrived, we carried him into the first chamber — he had already fainted dead away — the surgeon just shook his head at his wounds. One of these was particularly deep, right on the crown of the head. Still, after he was bandaged, he regained his senses and seemed to be quite calm. — At any rate, perhaps now you see, Madame, why just

now I was more in the mood to bury the dead with this keyboard, than to play dances, even those of her beloved Viennese Strauss?

EX-CHANCELLOR'S WIFE,
Mon Dieu, when will they return, those good old days of happy parties and lively tunes?

REFERENDARY
I tell you, *Mesdames*, tomorrow I shall rise very early, before court is in session, and I shall go to the hospital and take the name of the wounded man, and I shall run with it to the president of the society of charitable works and I will recommend the poor man to him, warmly, very warmly. — That is, *nota bene*, if he survives the night, of course. — One must follow regulations, act legally — enlighten public opinion — spark some measured agitation in the manner of O'Connell[34] — Gentlemen, roll up your sleeves! — Let's get to work! — of course, within the bounds of the law, now...

CITIZEN
Why are you rubbing your palms together like that? What are you so delighted about? What is this you're dreaming up? Let's get to work? You and who else? With Peele and the House of Lords, since you want to fight with the power of the law on your side — against the lawless? What on earth are you talking about? There's only one thing to say here; otherwise, clench your teeth and shut up! Either that, or to grab a blade yourself and fight!...

REFERENDARY
Toujours des extrêmes, my dear Lord!

KĘTA
I suggest that the Referendary ask that cabbie tomorrow if this is a country ruled by reason and laws. — My God! And do you not know what happened day before yesterday, gentlemen?

---

34   Reference to Daniel O'Connell (1775-1847). Irish politician, who campaigned on behalf of Catholic Emancipation in Great Britain, working within the British Parliamentary system in order to effect the desired changes, which came about in 1830.

EX-CHANCELLOR'S WIFE
Mr Kęta always has some new, worse horror in store for us.

SISTER
Please, sir — tell us.

KĘTA
Well, day before yesterday, a name day was being celebrated in a home with which I am acquainted… It was the name day of the lady of the house… Now, I would have been ready to swear that there was no informer among the guests invited to the affair that evening — everyone there was either a relative, or a friend. After supper, during which the guests lifted more than one toast to the health of the woman of the hour, I played "Poland hath not perished yet" and the "Chłopicki Mazurka" on the piano.[35] Forbidden music was followed by forbidden poetry, and one of the young ladies there began to recite from memory that fragment from the Third Part of *Forefathers' Eve* known as "The Vision of Fr Piotr."[36] — But her memory failed her at one place, and she blushed beet red, then paled again; she stood there, unable to bring the poem to an end. At this, a young clerk got up from his chair and finished the poem for her, to the applause of all those assembled. And do you know, ladies and gentlemen, what happened, on the very next day, to this fellow, who knew Mickiewicz by heart?

CITIZEN.
What?

---

35   "Jeszcze Polska nie zginęła," otherwise "General Dąbrowski's Mazurek" (Józef Wybicki, 1797), is a Polish patriotic song composed in the revolutionary period following the third partition of Poland. It is today's Polish National Anthem. The "Mazurek Chłopickiego" (Karol Kurpiński, 1830) is similar in theme and significance, especially as it arose during the period of the November Uprising against the Russian Empire.

36   A reference to *Dziady* (*Forefathers' Eve*), the grand work of Polish Romanticism by Adam Mickiewicz (1798-1855). The "Vision of Fr. Piotr" is one of the three great mystical soliloquies of this part of the drama, during which the priest is given a vision of the "saviour" to come, who will first liberate Poland from the three Empires who have partitioned her, and then go on to free the rest of the downtrodden peoples of Europe.

KĘTA
The gendarmes came for him, at about two o'clock in the morning. They rifled through all his papers, and when they found a hand-copied *Forefathers' Eve,* Part III, among them, they dragged him off to the Citadel! It seems that the police already knew that he was the one who spoke the last words of the poem that the young girl had forgotten.[37] So, among us that evening there was a traitor! A Judas! May the Lord God remember that act of his on the day of judgement, just as the young clerk remembered the poem!

SISTER
Horrible!

REFERENDARY
And you are surprised, that the townspeople and the peasants around here have succumbed to a universal terror! — How is it possible not to be afraid? — In such a situation, fear, in my opinion, is the sign of a healthy mind!

SISTER
You can say the same thing about cringing. — God knows, not everyone has succumbed to that universal, as you put it, fear. God knows!

REFERENDARY
I beg you, gracious Madame, not to be angry with me — not to tear yourself out of your place so violently!

SISTER
But I am not angry, my dear sir. — I just want to walk around the room a bit — please take no notice of me!

KĘTA
I remember another peculiar incident…

---

[37] It is not specified which of the verses the girl stopped at. Had she got right on to the end before forgetting, the last line reads: „Sława! Sława! Sława!" ("Glory! Glory! Glory!")

EX-CHANCELLOR'S WIFE
Another incident! Another one! When will you have mercy on us, sir?

AGATA
But Mama — allow Mr Kęta to speak!

CITIZEN
Go on, Kęta.

KĘTA
I'd almost forgotten, but now, in connection with all this — I'll tell you what the doctor, my old school chum, related to me. It seems that about a month ago he was called to the home of a certain countess from the Podole region, who is spending the winter here, after obtaining — with much trouble — a passport from Kiev to Warsaw. I was told that she had to spend two thousand roubles for it, to the scribes in the chancellery of the Governor General there.

CITIZEN
It's always the same in those parts — what you can't get by bribery, you simply can't buy — and what you can't buy, you can't get — from the lowest official to the highest, you won't move an inch without greasing palms! — And now that custom has taken root among us as well!

KĘTA
When my friend arrived at the countess' apartments, he found her young ward there, an eight-year-old girl, no older than that, absolutely beautiful, but with a complexion like one of the dead — she hadn't a drop of blood in those pale cheeks of hers. The countess was concerned about her, but my doctor friend recognised immediately that she wasn't long for this world. She had heart pains, and headaches, all of which were symptomatic of an extraordinary disorder in a child so young… And despite this, wit and wisdom shone in her black eyes such as are not usually found in so immature a vessel. The words she spoke seemed inspired: she was always speaking of Poland, and the persecution of the Catholic faith in Russia. He wrote down some of the things she said. As far as treatment was concerned, he recommended baths and electromagnetism, but nothing helped. The little girl got

worse and worse. She seemed to dry up, yet all the while she grew and grew in wisdom. Then, just two weeks ago, he was awakened in the middle of the night and earnestly beseeched to return to the countess' lodgings. He jumped out of bed and sped there; when he arrived, he was met by the despairing countess, who led him to the little girl's bed. Now, as you know, ladies and gentlemen, doctors are trained to be bold in the face of human misery; stony-hearted, even — yet this friend of mine simply shivered from top to bottom when he caught sight of the little girl. Blood was flowing incessantly from her nose and from her mouth — yet she was strangely smiling all the same. He said — these are his words — that she looked like an angel, like a little martyr. Her eyes were shining with an unusual light; as she was dying, she cried out, "Just as in my case, blood will soon be flowing from the mouths of the Muscovites." He did all he could to stop the haemorrhage, but it was obvious that something had broken in her little heart. She gave up the ghost an hour later. At the very moment of her death, she called out again, in a strong, sharp, sonorous voice "Just like me — so they, and soon." What do you say to that?

SISTER
When dying children prophesy on earth, something is surely afoot with our great God in Heaven!

CECYLIA
Without a doubt. —

AGATA
God Himself — God! — Yes!

JULIA
Only let Him hurry up with those thunderbolts!

CITIZEN
Even were it to mean democracy!

EX-CHANCELLOR'S WIFE
My dear cousin, my dear little angel, listen, I beg you, I beseech you, please stop pacing back and forth like that! Can you not see how pale

she's become, gentlemen? — I don't like what I see there: look how she has crossed her arms on her chest and gazes, God only knows, where she gazes — Return to us here, my cousin, to us!

CITIZEN
To Kęta
As God is my witness — look! How marvellously beautiful she is, although sorrowful and pale…

KĘTA
To Citizen
Like a walking statue of the snowiest marble!

EX-CHANCELLOR'S WIFE
Can you hear me, *ma chère*…? Monsieur Kęta, play something! Maybe that will pull her out of this catatonic trance!

KĘTA
Rises to the piano
Strauss won't be of any help here!

EX-CHANCELLOR'S WIFE
Play whatever you like, Monsieur Kęta!

SISTER
What is that moan I hear? — Moan after moan — can you hear it too? They've taken them all — they're carting them off — they'll never see our daylight again. — The light of Siberia will be the last comfort in their lives. Ah! Is that you playing, sir? — How strange! — It seemed to me that a thousand fraternal hearts were breaking at this moment, and that their lament was trembling in the air, unable to arise to Heaven — because everything's so difficult — so difficult. —

CITIZEN
Be gracious, Madame. Please don't dream so blackly.

SISTER
Mr Kęta, you know, I'm certain that you know who it was that they carted off on those wagons to the castle today?

KĘTA
Their names — tremble in these chords of mine — their names are in my soul and in my fingers — but I cannot express them in a human tongue; I don't know the words to use! — I swear to you, Madame!

SISTER
Did you hear that bell? — A sleigh has come — someone's coming — someone, who will tell me what none of you will.

CITIZEN
Calm yourself, Madame — more than one sleigh is about on the street tonight, and they stop at many another house.

SISTER
I heard it, I heard it rightly — they're coming to *this* house! And now the footfalls of someone ascending the stairs. Are you all deaf?

KĘTA
It's my music confusing you, Madame. I shall cease playing!

CITIZEN
No, she's right — Now I can hear them too.

SISTER
They're coming — they're coming — do you know who?

ALL
Who?

SISTER
Whoever it is, his name is Misfortune!

A voice is heard on the other side of the doors.

[VOICE FROM BEYOND THE DOORS]
I tell you, let me in! — Do you not know that I am a friend of Madame's brother, and Madame herself! —

CITIZEN
Ah! It's Edward!

Enter the Neighbour.

SISTER
I knew it!

NEIGHBOUR.
                      […] *Here the text ends.*

FIRST PART
OF THE *UNDIVINE COMEDY*
(AN UNFINISHED POEM)

I

INTRODUCTION

Mountains in the environs of Venice — sunrise — Aligier and the Youth on a cliffside, the latter dressed in hunting garb.

YOUTH
Look, friend! Ah, the purples with which the god of day springs forth! If only man could be born like that, to rule the earth! Look! How that last, wretched little star now dies. Thus, they say, the tender heart dies before the flash of a genius — O, sun! Arise, come forth! Cast your glance into the vales, where the darkness still broods, and link the banks of those pale streams with bridges of rainbow! So fresh it is here — So good do I feel — So bracing, so sharp — So far can I see — I feel that no shot of mine will miss its mark today. The chamois who browses on the moss of that summit there — he shall not live to see the afternoon. Oh! The horns of our friends sound from the fir-topped summit — Come, let's go!

ALIGIER
I shall remain here —

YOUTH
What's with you today? Ever since the sun set yesterday, you've not spoken a single word to me. When we began our ascent of these cliffs at midnight, you walked the edge of the abyss in silence — alerting me to dangers only by gestures. And now that our hunt begins, when the very bark of the pines trembles at the coursing of our hounds, as

do the earth and the cliffs, and the spirit within us — you hang back? You don't wish to be with us?

ALIGIER
Do you not know that I am used to pray to the Lord at this hour?

YOUTH
So I'll wait.

ALIGIER
Do you not know that I am used to pray to the Lord alone?

YOUTH
Then tell me when I should return for you.

ALIGIER
This evening you shall find me here.

YOUTH
By the living God, man! Come with me. I beg you — come! I won't be able to find my aim without you. And we must reach that naked summit there. There crystals grow; there the wild goats balance their slender feet. — Come! — From there, so the hunters say, you can see the whole world!

ALIGIER
You can see it all from here as well!

YOUTH
How?

ALIGIER
By closing your eyes and humbling your soul before the Lord!

YOUTH
The horns sound again — Be well! Now: downward, then up again, into those clouds! Aligier! It really does pain me, that you don't want to come along!

He parts, quickly.

ALIGIER
Calling after him
Don't move on so fast and headlong! — Grip the branches as you go — For I see quite clearly... I see — Don't look back towards me — and have a care near the waterfalls!

Already he hears me not. On he goes, as swift as a bird in flight, as if gravity did not apply to him. Coltishly, carelessly, frolics the slender mortal child at the dawn of life, like to a spirit, who will never hear anything of death. — But neither do they know anything of life. Just like the aether, from which the azure is spun, the child may grow into a dark clod or a bright sun — or flimsy mist, the plaything of the breezes. He may become everything, or nothing! Elect of Heaven or victim of Hell!
He raises his arms aloft.

Heavenly Father! In these days, Thy roads upon this globe have been darkened. Thy face has been hidden in the clouds. Once more people seek Thee, but find Thee not. Thou dost rise — Thou shalt arise. But why do they look to the very zenith of the heavens? Why not to the horizons?

Heavenly Father! The moment of passage is a horrid dusk to their eyes, a horrid temptation to their thoughts, a horrid pain to their heart! If Thou dost not shorten it, many of them shall perish!

He kneels.

For him I pray, Lord, whose soul Thou hast entrusted to me. Hear my testimony on his behalf! Constantly, without being aware of it, he calls out to Thee, drawn to Thy Heaven. The embryo of all that is beautiful, Thy own spark, burns within the depths of his soul, yet the mists of the flesh wrap it around in obscurity. The spirit I guard seeks Thee through the fog!

He has not yet come to realise that Thou art not merely high above him, but that Thou dwellest within him as well. Forgive him, therefore, Lord, that he yearns for you elsewhere!

Behold, Lord, I am sad unto the death. For the period of his innocence is passing: his heart will soon be torn in the struggle between good and evil — which struggle is the unique, if frightful, mother of virtue. Think upon me too, Lord — have mercy on me, by having mercy on him.

He bows his forehead to the very ground.

I do not beg Thee, Heavenly Father, to spare him any of the trials of life — I know that, just like all those who have been exiled to this world, and who must pass through it in order to return to Thee, he too must be tested by falsehood when the hour of temptation strikes. Thy will be done — scourge him with the hailstones of pain — abase him among people — let them fetter his wrists — let his body suffer through martyrdom! I beg of Thee only so much: skimp him the shame of villainy — spare him the eternal night of the spirit!

For myself I beg this grace: to be allowed to warn him at the eleventh hour.

May this night hear me, as I conjure it in Thy Name — Let the exhalations of the vales and the mists of the streams arise before me, that I might weave supple figures of them, inspire them with the stuff of dreams, which shall not see tomorrow's dawn!

But in that slumber shall be Thy everlasting truth, and truth terrestrial as well!

And the one that I love shall some day recall Thy truth eternal, and for that, Thou shalt save him, O Lord!

A moment of silence.

YOUTH
Enters.
What's this? — Still in the same place, beneath the same fir, and still at your prayers? — Give me your hand — Stand up!

ALIGIER
Do you return so soon, Henryk?

YOUTH
Are you awake, or dreaming? I left you at sunrise and now — Look! — The sun now sets on that side of the sky, beyond the rocky headlands. So soon! Since I parted from you, I have thrice traversed the length and breadth of the Hevaldine glacier; I have stood upon the summits of these mountains, and thrice I sounded my horn from the ravine — You must have heard me?

ALIGIER
You're right — it's evening!

YOUTH
And so the day passed for you as if it were but a moment?

ALIGIER
Happy he, whose whole life so passes — It is a sign that he lives in eternity! But what's happened to you? What does that blood signify, there on your breast, and on the hilt of your knife?

YOUTH
I nearly saw my whole life pass by today — This is not the blood of fleet chamois or innocent fallow-deer. I'll tell you. But meanwhile, let us be on our way, for I sent the shooters ahead, and before we catch them up, it will be night.

ALIGIER
I follow you.

YOUTH
So, listen! I shot at a wild goat. It fell from the sheer rock wall, and tumbled down into the very depths of the chasm. So I called my Tyroleans, told them all about it, showed them where, but no one had been there, no one saw. So I had to descend into the canyon for the lost prize myself. Two of them went with me. We walked about, searched for a passage, descending lower and lower until we reached the dark woods, the great pine woods. It's quite black there, and such a whooshing! As if every tree were praying to God. So, on we go, and suddenly we hear a snapping of branches and twigs in the thicket right in front of us, no farther off than a shot. A deer? Perhaps a stag? I glanced at my gun — I'd neglected to load it — and at that very moment a bear emerged from the brake. He stood there, snuffling the air, and then he caught sight of us. My two companions discharged their guns at the same moment — the balls merely scraped his hide somewhere, effecting nothing more than to enrage the bear. He stood up on his hind legs and, roaring, began to come at us. Both of them screamed out to me and ran off — screaming yet, they began to scramble into

the branches of the nearest pine trees. I remained standing there alone — I don't know why, for what sort of glory can a man win in a fight with an animal? I don't know why, but I was ashamed to escape. My fathers never ran away from hunt or battlefield. I tossed my gun aside and pulled my knife from its sheath; by that time the shaggy king of the woods was already at my chest. He moved to embrace me with his arms, just like a man; he sunk his claws into my living flesh. I stabbed him in the chest, once, twice — he didn't fall until the third thrust, and I fell with him. but he was lying dead beneath me! When the shooters came up, I spat in their faces, and gave them the bear skin with the holes made by my knife — as a reminder of their baseness!

ALIGIER
The Lord saved you. Did you give thanks to Him for your preservation?

YOUTH
Perhaps not in words. But with all the feeling with which my heart was full once I had extricated myself; shaking off the shock and glad to be alive, I raised my arms to the sky!

ALIGIER
There are times when the Lord expects more of us than that!

YOUTH
Strange — I was not the least bit fatigued by it all. So fresh and sharp am I, and have been, since morning! Look, Aligier — so quickly we descend, that the cottages of the people must not be too far off — and here a maiden crosses our path. Hey! Good evening, my pretty thing! — Hey! Can't you hear me? You're not afraid, are you? Stop! And let me have those lilies of the valley you're carrying in your hand.

LITTLE GIRL
Passing
I shan't give them to you, but to him.

YOUTH
Why?

LITTLE GIRL
Because he looks just like that white angel who stands at the right hand of the Mother of God above the altar at our church. You're from other parts, for sure — You've never been at our church; you've never seen that angel. *To Aligier.* Good evening! Please sir, take these flowers!

ALIGIER
Thank you, child — Be happy, child!

YOUTH
Am I so ugly, little miss?

LITTLE GIRL
You're beautiful too, but not like an angel.
Goes off.

YOUTH
Let me have half of those flowers. I will keep them as a reminder of how the little girl thought the same thing of you as I did, when I saw you for the first time. She speaks the truth, the truth. It is not only that your face is more comely than mine, your spirit is more elevated, too. Aligier, do you remember the moment when we first met? It stands before my eyes as if it were now.

ALIGIER
Same for me. Because at that moment I became your friend.

YOUTH
O! I see that old building, in the halls of which a thousand of my peers would sit, as the teachers lectured us from their podiums — I see those staircases, spiralling like snakes, and that turning, that stony entrance, where you first appeared to me! I was a bold boy, was I not? Although immature and of slender strengths? I was coming from home — I strode through them all with pride seated upon my brow, conscious of their hatred — but then again, why? Unconscious! — They tightened

round me in a ring, an ever tighter ring, jeering "Little lord! Little lordling!" — as if it were a shameful thing to be able to point out where any given one of my forefathers had sacrificed his throat for the sake of the fatherland, and in which crypt of which church he rests. God! It was then that Hell was first born in this breast — the breast of a child! I gripped the iron handrail, while they tried to pull me down, by my legs, my arms, the folds of my cloak. And perhaps I would have been trampled beneath their feet, but you appeared at that moment — You descended from above, just as pale and slender as you are now, but with fire in your eyes. No one knew you — they had only seen you from time to time — but they remembered the look on your face! You raised your voice, and they fell away from me; like dry leaves they fell away from me — Give me your hand, Aligier! I shall never forget that moment!

ALIGIER
You may forget it, Henryk — But the words I said to you then, my first words to you — Them you must never forget!

YOUTH
Yes — I can still feel your hand in mine, and hear your voice: "They are unjust. You — be more than just. Forgive them in your soul and love them in your actions!" Then we went down together, and you, passing through them, repeated in a calm voice, "Shame on you all!"

ALIGIER
And from that day forth, we have been inseparable.

YOUTH
And so shall we be, until death. And from that day I've known that you are greater than me, and for that I love you!

ALIGIER
Until death, you say?
YOUTH
Yes.

ALIGIER
I shall die before you.

YOUTH
Don't soil this quiet moment with such foreboding! Let us rather drink in the gentle light with our eyes, and the warm air, inspired with the aroma of roses, with our lungs. Look! The sun's last rays on the snow of the mountains — that star that now rises above the cliff-tops is God's smile directed at us! And with you here, with you at my side, what else could we need?

ALIGIER
I say it again: I shall die before you.

YOUTH
You're not very nice. My father has already abandoned me in death, after all. My mother and my sister both sleep in the grave as well. And many of those among whom I grew up have passed away forever. Their graves in my poor distant fatherland dream of me. I alone remain, the last of my line — and you would leave me too, to go where it is better, rather than to remain here with me? No — no, Aligier!

ALIGIER
I feel the embryo of death in this my bosom — but can it be that you only know how to love the living, not the dead? My spirit will not die in you though my figure fly away. From heart to heart, thought sparks and catches fire. What I have desired, what I have prayed for, you shall execute: and I desired that you should be a man among men, and an angel among the heavenly spirits. You glance at these mountains, this sky, this evening, and would gladly halt the wheels of time exclaiming "Beautiful! Beautiful!" But just think, Henryk, what a miracle in this world is the soul of man, of which, whoever beholds her, must exclaim: "You are beautiful!"

    Grant your brothers just such delight. Be a masterpiece among them!

YOUTH
Are you composing your last will and testament? Leave off, Aligier! I don't want to hear any such thing! You've made the pure, clear sky gloomy at one blow— a curtain of sorts has fallen down before my eyes. Tell me — where are we? What does this mean? We were just now almost at the valley, weren't we? Even today when we passed by here together at the break of dawn I saw a cross here, somewhere to the right! Where is it now?

ALIGIER
Follow me.

YOUTH
Do you know the country better than I do? Oh — the moon has risen, the moon my old friend — he'll solve the riddle for me.

ALIGIER
So let's wait a bit.

YOUTH
By the living God! The brighter it grows, the less familiar this region looks, like I've never been here before. Once these mists disperse — Oh, there! There shines the road — No, that's a ribbon of mist along the meadows — Hey! Anybody there? Hey! Ho! Answer me! I'll shoot — maybe they'll hear us then?

He fires his weapon.

ALIGIER
The mountains alone have heard, and they make answer.

YOUTH
What a thunderous echo! Do you know how it is we've lost our way? It seemed to me that we were on the right path — That way, then, at once — do you see? The cliffs are trebled, even the sky itself is changed — There, a sea of clouds has flooded the canyon, and shines now like an unmoving glacier. Exhalations arise from it, winding and curling aloft so, that the head starts to spin. It's so dark, pitch dark — Oh!

Again the moon is bright, and so bright it hurts the eyes! — Aligier, I'm at sixes and sevens…!

ALIGIER
So, what are you waiting for? Follow me.

YOUTH
Left? Into that narrow gorge?

ALIGIER
That way my inspiration leads.

YOUTH
I'll go wherever you please: keep on looking, circle around, go up, down — it's all the same to me. We'll be erring like this until sunrise. I've never seen such a night. Who can be at home in it, except the wolf, heir to these wilds, or the chamois, the lady of the cliffs? Hey! Where are you? Answer!

ALIGIER
Right here.

YOUTH
The confounded mist billowed right up from beneath me, and darkened my sight — And now I'm floating up, toward those… sisters… Look! Is that not some old king on his throne, sceptre in hand? Behind him a gigantic snake stands guard — No — a dragon, rather — No, now it's a four-winged cherub and there, Oh! In the space between the cliffs — do you see? There a nation of shades hastens unto the Last Judgement! And what's this? What did I just trip against?

ALIGIER
Overturned gates leading into an old graveyard.

YOUTH
And just now the moon shone full, like a pale purgatory of souls above this cemetery of the flesh… Just a moment ago I was so brisk, lighter than air… And at this moment, I feel so heavy, I feel sick at heart.

Why? Where does this come from? Maybe the old corpses buried here have cast a spell upon me. If I were to rest upon this stone, I fear I'd fall asleep.

ALIGIER
Lean on me.

YOUTH
Good — For my eyes grow heavy, and I'd like to stay here.

ALIGIER
Just a little further! We're so close to that white chapel!

YOUTH
All right — It will be quieter beneath that roof than out here in the wind.

ALIGIER
So why do you stop? Go on!

YOUTH
God! Has my vision gone crazy from the venom of those exhalations? Or am I asleep and dreaming?

ALIGIER
What is it you see?

YOUTH
Your body has gone strangely sallow in the moonbeams — your eyes have sunken so — you've grown thin — and you seem to be growing older and older, and taller — Is this you?

ALIGIER
It is I, Henryk.

YOUTH
Only your voice is the same. It seems to me now as if a laurel wreath were flashing about your temples… It spins, it disappears, and appears

again… Bat it away! I'm afraid of you — I won't go a step farther — Sleep is weighing me down to the earth… I shall fall — Let me fall! God knows that I've seen a face like that — somewhere…

ALIGIER
Just a few more steps.

YOUTH
Where was it? Where? And I know that laurel crown, I know that subterranean fire in the eyes, brought here from another world! — There is a tapestry in the banquet hall of my father's house, gold, with silver stars… In my father's house…. Yes! And my father used to say, years ago, that that man had visited Hell and Purgatory, and had been in Paradise… Master, master, where are you leading me?

ALIGIER
Helping him into the chapel
Now you may sleep.

II

THE DREAM

It seemed to the youth that the figure of Dante then turned to him and said: "From there, where abide eternal Love and Reason, and Will, was I sent to reveal unto you the hell of this day and age. Cast off all dread, therefore, and where I go, you come and follow!" And like a pale pillar, the figure rose into the dark air, where he trod upon the misty exhalations, as if upon the waves of aether. — From time to time a meteor flashed and faded away beneath his feet, while a succession of grey dawns arose and flowed away, dying in the distance. And the soul of the youth grew very sad, for she did not know whither she was headed, but on she went into eternity, sensing, that that eternity was an eternity of evil.

*

The figure paused on the summit of a mountain, and then seemed to enter the mountain's depths. It began to grow light by degrees, and a swarthy dawn broke through the narrow embrasure of the rock walls carven on both sides of the path. Along the walls, to the left and the right, armed men, all dressed alike, all with the same expression on their faces, were in constant motion — Now they bent low, now they straightened up, cleaning the iron gun barrels, which they held in their hands. The figure touched the youth's eyelids with an ephemeral wave of his hand and said: "Look your fill — for here we have the entrance to hell on earth, in sooth." — And then he saw the souls of all these men. They were half-emerged from their bodies, leaning out of the flesh, unable either to enter fully within again, or to tear themselves completely away. And struggling thus, they wept: "Neither to live, nor to die is given us; where they command, there must we go — against God, we go; against our brothers, we go — woe is us!" And they wept inconsolably. The figure then halted and demanded of them: "Speak — What are you, and what are your names?". But the lips of those bodies made no response. "Where is your homeland?" And all these bodies lifted their eyes up in surprise. "Where is your home?" And among the myriad pairs of eyes, only a few let fall their tears, tears as of misty recollection. But the arms of all grew even more agitated; their motions became even brisker as they continually polished the gun barrels and sharpened the blades of their bayonets — until from above the speechless flesh all of the souls groaned out aloud: "We were still children when we were herded out into the world — They made us forget about ourselves, and kill others — Whoever resisted was shot himself, as a traitor, and so he fell — And now we no longer remember whence we arose, nor do we know where we are going." In response to this, the pallid figure said: "Long ago, when men set to the fight, they knew the cause they served, and why they had to die. They were like gods of war, while you are like cattle." And having parted the chain of the armed men with one nod, the figure of Dante passed through them, and continued on toward the east, which writhed in the depths.

*

The youth followed the bard into dark underground regions, when suddenly a flood of light spread out before him and he beheld black walls and iron bars, and iron rings with fetters sunk into the walls. In lamps of alabaster lubricious flames were dancing; the ground was spread with silken carpets. A great number of people were standing around one man seated upon an elevated chair. As white and slender as a woman, he turned the leaves of a black tome. Before him stood a cross of marble, huge, stretching up to the vault itself. Upon the cross was nailed an image of Christ. — The shade of Dante shivered from head to toe and said: "Among the ancient damned I never came across that sacred symbol. — They at least were unable to blaspheme God in God's own Name — but, behold and listen!"

*

The superior on the chair bent over, and, from beneath the foot of the cross, he pulled forth heavy bags of gold. All who stood there drew closer about him in a ring. They all stretched forth their hands — and the sweat of greed dripped from their brows. He, handing round their salaries, lectured them in a voice as squeaky and twitchy as the scrape of stylus upon looking glass: "Wherever you insinuate yourselves, be pleasant and sweet — In the homes of gentlemen of ancient manners, heap flattery upon pride — In the hovels of the impoverished, blandish their misery! Where husband torments wife, comfort her; where father is miserly toward his sons, loan them a penny or two! — Wherever the stronger oppresses the weak, become the defence of the oppressed, and all of their complaints and hopes, like buried treasures, will be openly revealed unto you! — In the presence of the gloomy and silent, begin to despair yourselves, and your cry shall awaken his voice! When you come across youths trembling impatiently for action, bind them immediately with fearsome oaths; fix mysterious weapons beneath their cloaks — for people are like ears of wheat: the fuller they are, the sooner are they milled! — And let your memory be greedy, sharp, eternal! Where the wind shakes the leaves upon the trees, turn your eyes toward the sound. When you come across a needle along your path, pick it up and bring it here — it is worth more than a sword, for where a sword is found, there the time has already passed! Love children and play with them. Like butterflies on flowers, on the lips of babes there sometimes sit the secrets of their families. Knowledge is the gift of all gifts. The bodies of all cannot fit in one gaol, but one head is capable of embracing the thoughts of all, and stretching over them like the eternal vaults of a prison!" — And all of those who had ringed him round, burdened with their gold, suddenly vanished like spectres.

*

From the other side of the dungeon a rosy tapestry was furled, and the iron doors behind it spread wide open. Two lackeys entered, dragging in a man dressed in rags by the arms. The man then straightened up and roared like a beast: "Give me some food! Give me something to drink! Yesterday my father died of hunger — This morning my mother expired — And I am burning up with a fever; I shall die tonight!" The superior nodded, and then an azure tapestry was winched up, behind which sparkled a table groaning beneath silver bowls and crystal goblets. The starving man lunged toward it, but he was restrained. "First, swear your fealty to us!" — "Food! Food! I will swear after I have eaten." At these words, the slender being on the chair laughed aloud and pointed to the crucifix, and the dying man fell to his knees before it.

*

And it seemed to the youth that the voice of the superior pierced the air like the hiss of a serpent: "By the Holy Trinity and by the Passion of the Lord, whatever I see, whatever I hear, whatever I deduce, I swear to bring hither — even if it be the groans of my brother, the sighing of my sister. If my friends or relatives conspire in anything, I shall reveal it, and may their throats be exposed to the executioner's blade! Should I hold anything back, may I perish myself, nailed to planks of wood, torn with pincers, burnt with fire and given poison to drink!" But the kneeling man refused to repeat those words, and fell to the ground crying out, "I am dying!" And the slender one responded, "Die!" and, crossing his arms, he waited.

*

Then, there fell a great silence, and it seemed to the youth that he directed a question to the figure of the bard: "Master! Where are the souls of these people, for I see them not, even though you have bestowed upon me spiritual sight?" And the figure said: "In the righteousness of God, there could be found no punishment severe enough for them. And so, thrust into an eternal contempt, they have become one with their flesh. Only they, among all, have been deprived of the sacred gift of life, and when their first bodies melt away, they will no longer exist anywhere." Then the starving man threw himself in the direction of the banquet prepared: "I shall so swear," he whispered, while sparks rained from his eyes, and the superior extended his hand to him, and set him once more upon his knees. — And he began to swear the oath! —

*

And a dream-image like to an angel, with veiled brow, looked down from the heights, and protected the crucifix with the embrace of his wings. And as long as the oath continued, the angel stood thus before the crucifix — but none of those present could see him. And when the final word of the oath had been expressed, when the starved body, arising, shuffled on, the angel's countenance was covered with a great swarthy shade. And he tore the veil in two, crying out, "One soul, Lord, has perished!" That cry pierced the heart of the youth through and through, and it seemed to him that he hung his head in unbearable pain.

*

When he lifted his eyes, all was dark. And through the shades of darkness there flowed pale graveyards, full of scaffoldings rising here and there, and bones unburied; they flowed on and on like the swollen clouds of the sky. Above them arose tatters of mist like autumn leaves, making a mournful sound, and all of these myriad voices mixed, and all of them complained of and accused the informers who had betrayed them — the sobs of women, the wailing of children, the resounding moans of men, all these voices, mixed together, were heard. And the shade of Dante spoke unto them, saying: "Your time will come, poor souls, and you shall enjoy a double eternity — your own, and that of those who destroyed you. For the spirit shall recoil from the vacuum designed for them, and it shall redound to you. Be of good cheer, therefore, misfortunate ones!" And saying this, he began to sob himself!

*

And once more he descended to the surface of the earth, to again enter in among the armed men, who now stood in ranks like rows of statues. The blare of trumpets and the tattoos of drums measured out their apportioned times and manners of life. Some moved off to rest, while others, like boulders, were fixed in their place. Others, taking aim at prisoners lying prone upon the ground, stood guard over them, their fingers ever on the trigger, the butts of their rifles ever at their breast, their eyes unmoving, their lungs taking in no breath. From time to time, from somewhere to the rear, somewhere to the sides, there resounded a gunshot; and the farther on the youth progressed in the steps of the bard, the wider spread the walls carven in the rock, reaching farther out into the open spaces, until each ran on in its own direction, to the east and to the west, as far as the eye could see.

*

And on they ran, as if they wished to encompass all of space. They grew in breadth, they grew in height, they clung to the horizons like a rim of stone; they paved the firmament with a vault of stone, until they formed one huge structure, as gigantic as the world itself: granite, grey, with no blue above, no green below. And in this world the youth caught sight of a spectral sun in the distance, far away, fixed to a curving cornice and shining with eternally diagonal beams — but their effulgence seemed rather the sickness of light than light itself; and in this swarthiness there walked about crowds innumerable, like to the nations of the earth — and the rumour of their speech, like to the roar of giant seas, beat against the walls of the world, and broke upon them.

*

The dreaming soul, the soul of the youth, asked, "Master, where are we?" And he replied: "In the temple in which, today, Humanity has taken up residence, but in which there is no God." And he went in among a crowd of people sitting at the entrance. Each had a little pit before him, as long and as deep as a coffin — and each bore on his head a lamp which, when he bent down, lit up the dark little pit, out of which they each drew tools appropriate to various crafts. — And each of them laboured with their hands, with flabbergasted stares, like those of the insane. And the youth looked upon some holding the head of a pin in their hands, and their brows were furrowed with deep wrinkles, as if they had spent all the years of their lives at the rounding of that pinhead. And whenever the hour of death, tolling in the distance, echoed from that immense vault, this one or that one would bow his head, and with a groan tumble into his pit. Then did their souls unbound become visible. They were like to blue clouds in the shape of cogwheels, stamps or siphons, and they arose and floated parallel to the earth, all of them going in the direction of that yellow, distant sun.

*

And at the sight of the bard these people arose, knocking their lamps together and crying out: "Whether you be gods or demons of which we had once heard — and it's all the same to us — Gold! Give us gold!" And they rattled like skeletons, with their hands outstretched. The pale figure of Dante flamed with the blood of anger and responded: "You mercenaries possessed!" And they fell prone to the ground like dead blocks of matter when faced with a spirit.

*

And again the figure flamed, but this time with the blood of inspiration, saying: "Would you even understand me, were I to prophesy future times to you? When still on the far side of the grave my body marched toward the tomb in the open brightness of the sunlight, there were such labourers on the earth too, and the banners of their guilds fluttered from the arcades of high towers. They hawked amaranth and all sorts of precious stone about the city markets — but a sword was sheathed, a rosary looped, at their sides; their hands knew how to manage the tiller on the swelling sea, and to build impregnable ramparts on the land. They took silver, and washed off the stain of that silver in the blood of battle! What shall such as you begin today — you with fingers as soft as wax, you whose lips have never formed a prayer! You, without strength on earth, and without hope in heaven, and all athirst for gold?" And a boy, as beautiful as an angel but withered before his time from toiling with his hands, crawled up, and, placing his head upon the feet of the apparition, whispered — "Have mercy on us! Each day we labour, and at evening we nourish the body, and on the morrow, again from dawn must we labour. We have no time to pray to God, we only have time to labour, to eat something, so as not to die — and no sooner have we eaten, but we must labour again, so as to eat — Have mercy on us!" And the apparition turned as swarthy as that boy wiping his feet with his hair — and raising aloft his eyes, he sighed: "The past shall not return — Child! Pray to the Father for the future, to the Father in the heavens!" And the boy went away, mumbling, "In the heavens, perhaps, but not on the earth." Those others, meanwhile, were gnashing their teeth, and wallowing about in the dust. — And the shade of Dante passed through them like a storm sweeping onward.

*

And in the midst of this world other souls stood leaning over a gigantic pit. Their faces, searching the abyss, flickered in the red glow — the earth round about shook with subterranean rumblings — and it seemed to the youth, when he drew near, that he was looking upon the bed of a dry lake, enclosed all around as if timbered with a circle of rocky, vertical walls. And it was black there in the depths from human heads, human heads swept about like storm-tossed waves; and there was a blood-red light from coals afire — coals smoking like the slag of a volcano — and from those depths there continually arose threats and curses!

*

As a mother will press her babe to her breast, so did the ghost of Dante embrace the youth with his arms, and thus did they fly down to the very depths of the dark pit. There, strange figures seethed and writhed — their faces were overgrown with shaggy beards, their sleeves were rolled up, their arms were livid with blue veins full of blood — here they piled up, and there they shovelled away — They crawled about on the floor of the chamber like snakes and then, in the flash of the fires, they jumped to their feet like men ready for battle. Around the closest fire knelt twelve, as brawny as giants. They had torn their shirts from their torsos; a thirteenth came up to them with a stiletto in his right hand and a goblet in his left. He said to them: "Now I shall consecrate you." The giants bowed their heads piously, and on their naked shoulders, upon which the reflection of the flames danced, the thirteenth carved bloody characters with the blade of his dagger. Not a single one of them groaned, nor did any tremble. The words "Equality" and "Liberty" bloomed on the back of each, at which the bard said, "See how he collects the blood that drips from his brothers' bodies in his goblet — each drop? Perhaps you assume that he shall preserve that blood as testimony to their torment, or that he shall display it to the people as an emblem of vengeance?" And the youth responded in a low voice, "Master, can it be otherwise?" And the voice of Dante's ghost resounded like a subterranean rumble: "Truly, that blood shall be sold to the merchants, on the spot and at the hour of the markets. So come along and have a look."

*

And as they went on, one of the black hosts began to cry out, staggering about the dying embers of coal: "Ah! Ah! and shall the vale of darkness always be our habitation? Shall we never find our way to the surface of the earth, to the tabernacle of the merchants?" And another host, fanning the sleepy embers to life with their hands, took up the refrain of the others: "To the temple of the golden sun, where one obtains sweet wines and savoury foods, and clothing that lays lightly on one's limbs — To the exchange, where by hazarding a man might amass power, from cradle to grave never wounding his hands with labour!" And a third host poured full flagons of oil upon the flames, shouting, "Let us have courage, and we shall enter the exchange of the nations! — After all, among us may be found breasts as hard as breastworks, and fangs like those of the predatory lion — We shall arm ourselves with long nails, since we have no swords!" Then all the gang clapped their hands and roared: "Although other tribes may resist us, we shall claw our way onto those flinty shores. One time only, just once, may fate place us in the paradise of the wealthy, and on their silken carpets! — For can it be better in Heaven itself, than it is for them on earth? — Just like them, therefore, let us be happy before our death too!" Then did that man with the dagger and goblet come among them, leading behind him the giants he had marked.

*

And a great number greeted him with a drunken outcry, demanding "When will you lead us out of here?" And he responded: "Wait just a bit longer; the hour will come." The giants raised their arms aloft; one heard the cracking of their bones; fresh blood spurted from their wounds, and an oath thundered from their lips: "On your behalf — victory, or death!" — And they followed their leader, traipsing in the direction of bright gallows, which stood in a long row, decorated with burning torches.

*

And beneath each gallows knelt a little boy, and both lawyers and those expert in letters were teaching them how they ought to curse the names of their forefathers. And those children dutifully repeated the curses in a murmuring chorus — and should one of them grow silent from fatigue, or burst out sobbing from disgust, the teachers would approach him whip in hand, at the sight of which, screening himself with his arms, he would resume his litany of curses. Like a grey pillar, the ghost of Dante stood near that long smudge of kneeling boys and listened. Then he cried out in a loud voice. The lawyers present grew pale and demanded: "Who was it that spoke?" And he, at that: "One of those whom you curse, you liars, you hypocrites, you, worse even than the basest of reptiles! Because you stand upright in the noble posture of humanity, and possess speech, as if of learned men!

*

"Gaze into my dead eyes — Will your hearts not break from shame? Do you know what freedom of the spirit is? Woe is you — You know nothing more than fleshly comfort!" And he called the children unto him, and, stretching out his hands over the nearest, and in the direction of those who were distant, he blessed them all, saying, "Believe not falsehoods — You are slaves, but the fathers of your fathers were free men in the simplicity of their hearts. Faith in God was a shield unto them, protecting them from the oppression of people. The freshness of spring bloomed within their souls; whether they inhabited a cottage in a vale or a castle on a high rock, they remained themselves. Loving, they loved; battling, they battled. Today as the world is wide, such love no longer exists; as the world is great there are no such noble causes to battle for, either."

*

And it seemed to the youth that one of the lawyers arose and approached the figure of Dante, with two guns in his hands — He had only eye, and he shouted: "Equality and Slaughter!" And his cap was at a rakish angle and on that cap was stitched: "The People." And coming on, he staggered, and as he came on he cocked the weapons and began a speech, rolling about his one eye and foaming at the mouth. But the figure of Dante interrupted him: That jabbering of yours is nothing but a vain sound, with no thought behind it; it is not by screeching, but by action; not by slaughter, but by the harmonious concord of all that the Republic stands. You are a beast, not a spirit, and before ten years have run their course, you shall betray your own people!" The eye of the orator flushed red with blood and, quaking with awestruck fear, he lowered the iron barrels of the guns, while the shade of Dante spoke thus to the youth: "Pass by this soul and spit on him in contempt! Among the waves of the sea, the noisiest are those which are to crash upon the sand: the bosoms of men are the waves of the world."

*

And the ground sloped progressively lower, and the light of the gallows shone on, but ever more weakly, until other little stars appeared in the depths, unmoved, like to the lamps that keep vigil in hospitals. And each of these lights was fixed above a bulrush mat, and on each mat there lay a woman, and this whole nation of women lay there, moaning, sighing, weeping. Here and there resounded the shriek of the dying, their last vocable. And once again the moaning, sighing and weeping resumed, which stretched further and further into ever deeper reaches of the underground.

*

One of those women arose on her mat at the sight of Dante's ghost, winding her loose hair around her hands and tearing at it; and the youth caught sight of her soul tangled amidst that hair, sliding from head to hands and from hands to feet with them in unendurable tossing. "Speak!" she cried, "whoever you are — and you other, too! Speak, men — Why was I pushed off the surface of the earth and into this pit? The while my flesh was comely I walked about in the rays of the sun, and people were good to me. But once I withered like a flower, like the most beautiful flower, they took me and flung me among the rotting things, in the darkness, where there is weeping and gnashing of teeth. — Men, when they grow old, are lauded by the young with paeans. While we, women, when we grow old, are made to lie down in the coffin even before we die — yes, many days beforehand! — We beg you, we bring our lament before you, we cry out to you, for those others are far off, they hear nothing. Then, we begin to die, and they are farther off still; they do not even come to bid us farewell. — And thus must we die." And while she was speaking still others arose, crying out "Justice! Justice!" — while others still beat their breasts, sobbing and cursing — and the streams of their tears flowed down their long tresses, dropping upon the earth with the dull rustling of rains in autumn. And the weaker or more tormented among them could hardly rise up before they collapsed anew; others who could only kneel crawled close on their knees; others yet, covering their faces with their hands, remembering how beautiful they once had been, approached the ghost, and from behind their fingers only their two eyes shone, the flames of which were slowly dying.

*

And then the youth caught sight of a few old men in long, black robes who, with an aspergillum in their hands, were flinging droplets of water on all of these women's heads, chanting in a gloomy voice. Some of the women bent their brows low and lay down again, quietly, upon their mats. Others, genuflecting, kissed the hands of the old men, whispering unending laments before them. — But the one who had first leapt to her feet began to tear at her hair with ever more violence, shouting at them: "Up there, on the earth's surface, men no longer heed you; instead, they say unto you: 'Go on! Spy on our dying women! When their souls are tearing themselves from the flesh, soothe their laments; when they curse us, stop up their lips, for their groans are unpleasant to our ears! Sometimes, when they resound in chorus from the abyss, they spoil our feasts or cast a pall upon our business dealings!' And so you go, you descend, you come — you teach us to die quietly. But I shall die crying aloud: I had a soul, I have a soul, whereas on earth they deigned only recognise my flesh! Judge then,

O God, Thou, who didst give me this soul!" And before the eyes of the youth, in a final convulsion, the soul of the woman tore herself from the tangles of her hair and went off into the dark space above the lamps, into a space resembling a bloody canvas pierced through by a thousand needles.

*

The bard passed on, deep in thought, but answering nothing, as if disgusted, until he came to a bed of white, which stood off to the side, at a great distance from all those others. There a lamp was burning, affixed to a marble pillar, beneath a crucifix, before which a woman dressed in mourning was kneeling, her back to Dante and the youth. The shade of the bard halted, and stood there in silence, as if sunk in a deep sadness.

"Master, who is she?" the youth demanded. And the shade responded — "Years ago, I saw only one such figure, on earth, only once. And later, another, up there in Heaven. When she turns her face to us, we will see who she is." — And he stood there, still, not interrupting the woman's prayer.

*

And then it seemed to the youth that he saw, next to the kneeling woman in black, a second woman kneeling, clad in white — She was identical to the other, except for this: instead of long tresses, she had two angelic wings, which were crossed silently, folded beneath her shoulders. And there were deep wounds on both of these wings, and in each wound was fixed a nail, so that the wings could not be spread wide. After a moment, both of the figures blended together, and once more it was only the woman in black kneeling there. At which the shade said: "She has finished her prayer, for her snowy soul has vanished from our sight," and he added, as if involuntarily, "Beatrice."

*

The woman in black then turned around and said, "She, who bore that name years ago, knew nothing on earth but Heaven, for she was snuffed in the first spring of her youth. She knows nothing but Heaven now that she has passed from the earth, for Heaven received her immediately! But no one has repaid me my first spring with a second — That is not my name!" And wringing her hands, she stood there with a bloodless face as white as alabaster.

*

But when the bard bound her, as with his divine authority, she began to speak thus: "I was born in a land flowing with milk and honey, which today is known as the land of crosses and gravemounds — They also call it the land of misery! There, up above, you have heard of me. But a thousand tongues had poisoned and torn apart my name, before it met your ears. At first, my parents called me Innocent, Beautiful and Happy! Later, I was named otherwise: Slave!

*

"For, as is the world's custom, while yet a child and a stranger to the love of man, I was given, or sold, in matrimony! Oh, weep for me, and for all of those my sisters, who neither knowing nor feeling anything yet, are given over, against their will, body and soul, to those who know everything, and have already felt all things — but whom knowledge did not endow with angelic brightness, but rather the decrepit cunning of Satans!

*

"I endured it all — for one can bear anything in this sad world except contempt. When such a dagger falls between two souls, the hilt in one heart, and the blade in the other, how can these two walk along the path of life together? Such as whom nothing unites but iron? How can they break their daily bread together, while yearning for the death that will divide them, as if it were a blessing? I said to myself: No — but I had to; I begged God that I might not — yet I had to — feel contempt!" Here she grew silent, and once again, still — with a bloodless face, as of alabaster.

*

And when the bard bound her anew, by his divine authority, she moaned and went on: "I shall not even answer God Himself, on the Day of Judgement. I alone know; I alone remember. As if it were today I see that palace — that road bordered by the aromatic lindens, the sun setting beyond them — I seem to be beneath those very trees, walking about as if in a lethargy — Didn't they all say back then, that something was in the offing? There, in the air smelling heavy of mown hay, some sort of premonition hovered, as when the plague is about to strike; as when many men are to arise, and take up arms to fight, and die! And my husband, slender and pale as a woman, walking about, too — waiting for something, for someone! Ah! Waiting with a smile on his face such as I shall never forget!

*

"People were gliding into the garden from all sides — relatives, friends, neighbours — He clasped their hands, making some sort of promises, vows! — And when the sun set, he asked them to set aside their weapons and sit down to confer one last time. Each of them did lay by his weapon, and then sat down on the lawn. He clapped — as a sign — and like to the hissing of a snake, he sounded his whistle — at which soldiers, from everywhere, appeared: soldiers, soldiers…

*

"Ask me not — I bore that man's name — I had sworn him fidelity, to the grave — I cannot betray him to you — as he betrayed his brothers to our enemies!

*

"And now my third earthly name: Shamed! Do you know why, people? Because despair tore my heart apart! Because there came a day when I was beloved — because on that day I believed in Beauty and Goodness, and Reason upon the earth — because I raised my head, already pale in death, and cried: 'O how good to grow to Heaven from out the grave!' — Because I truly loved!"

*

And now growing quiet, again she became immobile; her bloodless face as white as alabaster. And when the bard bound her by his divine authority for the third time, she said quietly: "Follow me!" and taking down the lamp from beneath the crucifix, she moved on, ever farther away from the women lying on their mats. The path twisted and turned through subterranean passages, through narrow dungeons, which stretched out suddenly whenever she should raise the hand in which she held the lantern.

*

Everywhere they beheld the same walls, weeping with humidity, beneath ever the same vault, low and stuffy — Then the rustle of her feet could no longer be heard. No breeze toyed with the flame of her lamp. The youth went on, although he was ever more sick at heart, weak and wilting. It was as if all the air were escaping somewhere, as if an invisible weight were crushing down upon his head — as if the blood had stopped coursing through his veins, and he seemed to hear himself cry out "I shall go no farther!"

*

Then, turning around, the woman in black spoke, her lamp above her head: "You cannot endure but one such hour, you, of the tribe of men, you, so strong and bold? Not one hour there, where all of my years must pass, and pass away? Begone then, go in peace!"

*

Then the bard demanded in a sad voice: "Where is he who loved you?" And she, lowering her eyes, replied, "He is there, where his manly fates drove him — He tore me free from the loneliness of the heart, and abandoned me in the spirit of loneliness. I loved him, and he deserted me." And she pointed to a distant stone shining white amidst the darknesses, and said: "There my soul, wrapped up in her own wings, lies buried. And this is Me, upon whom you gaze — mere flesh, which has not yet learned how to die."

*

And in a great sadness she fell to her knees, crying out: "O you, who know — tell me: shall it be like this, for us, forever?" And for the first time, she wept.

*

And resting his hand upon her head, the bard responded: "Up until now, you all have been like to the lilies of God, who grow, knowing nothing of their splendrous colours and aromas. But the day will come when you shall each be transformed into thinking roses. The reins of inspiration will fall from the hands of men and be given into yours. And they, prostrate at your feet, will beg of you but one song of sweetness — one prophecy of hope, one image of beauty — for their fate of unbearable difficulties and demanding acts will be a hard fate indeed, and a low one. But you, gazing upwards to God, will not glance their way; your ears will not hear their sobbing. Then will their hearts break as yours have, through so many ages!"

"Pronounce but one more word to me," the woman in black said, lifting a prayer to the bard with her eyes. And he: "Thus shall it be, until the hour of your second transformation strikes, and once more you shall extend your hand to them, and you shall save their perishing hearts with love. And for all time you shall be to them as sisters, their equals on earth as in heaven." And as the woman in black wept yet more copiously, he added: "Call back your soul and fear not — for if anything is to perish, the star of male praise will sooner grow dim at the judgement of God than the tear of one misfortunate woman dry up in vain."

*

And when the kneeling woman grew calmer, the apparition left her — moving straight toward the grave, leading the youth, and as they passed that white stone, he said: "Verily, she will die in these darknesses, here to rest — for the hour is but approaching, and has not yet arrived." And, blessing the grave, he went on, upward again from the depths.

*

Then through the aperture of the abyss, high, high above his head, the youth again saw the granite vault of the world. And the nearer they came to exiting the depths, the wider it grew in its swarthy light — From it, there seemed to resound the clamour of one thousand swinging bells, and the echo of steps, millions of hastening steps, and the groans of the stony floor beneath them! And when the shade of Dante stood on the lip of the abyss, and, with a gesture of his hand, pulled up the youth, who emerged as if he had been sucked up into a vortex, the latter caught sight of all the nations of the earth progressing towards the yellow sun, and, beneath that sun, a great platform, black, upon which thrones of a sort were shining in the distance.

*

Like exhalations harried by the wind, like streams rushing along their beds, like flocks driven, they hurried, one after another, all in the same direction. The sound of the unseen bells resounded all throughout the space, and old men and youths, women and children, all came up, passed by, passing away, all mixed up together; and the aged beseeched the young to halt for a moment, to take them along. But the young did not look behind them, did not want to listen — they ran! And pale maidens stood and wept, beseeching their brothers, their lovers, not to run away from them. But these too did not look back — they ran! And mothers with infants at the breast were passing, hastening onward, and suddenly, here and there, a child, jostled in the rush, would cry out and fall to the floor with arms outstretched, soon to be covered over by the crowds rushing in from all sides, and not a single mother paused or bent down — they all ran on! The youth stood over the little body of one of the trampled children and demanded, "Master! Has the hour of the final judgement struck?" And the apparition covered his face with his hands and said, "This is rather the hour of merchants' judgement — it's the hour of the Exchange, the markets!"

*

And having said this, he bore the young man on through the spaces of that world, unto the distant end, where is that sun and that platform, and it seemed to the youth as if he were hovering equally above the platform and below the sun — as if someone's wings held him there aloft — while the figure of his master clothed himself in great contempt and disappeared.

*

And that sun seemed to be made of gold, with artificial rays, while the platform was of black marble, with steps leading even unto where the shining thrones loomed. On those sat chosen merchants of the wandering generations of the East — wearing long robes, with grey beards, with a purple band encircling their brows. At their feet lay gigantic bags filled with tinkling metal.

*

At times, broken voices arose from those footrests, like insistent voices, begging, accusing. And the youth then realised that in those bags were hidden the souls of merchants, bound and weeping. And the more wretchedly, the more insistently they lamented, the greater grew the anger of those seated upon the thrones — they spurned the bags beneath their feet, stifling the voices of their own souls.

*

When the wretches grew silent, with slow and hoarse, grating voices, the enthroned began to consult amongst themselves, pointing at times toward the chaos of the peoples, who were drawing near from all sides, whilst above them, gigantic black mists, torn here and there with bands of ruddy brightness, were hanging. The youth saw that these mists were in the shape of the souls of all people gathered together, and that they flew together above the people, like blood flying through the air, or like melted granite: a blaze burning slowly to embers amidst great darknesses.

*

Beneath that glow, as if beneath an aethereal hell, the nations went on like loud ice floes booming on a river, like a thunderstorm. Now and then there resounded the cry of someone falling to the earth — the dull moan of the suffocated and trampled. One of the merchants arose from his throne, nodded, and then, below, some giant boulders split apart, dungeons gaped and, from beneath them, in ranks, soldiers, weapon in hand, began to emerge; there were bayonets affixed to their guns — in ranks three-deep they stood, on both sides of the marble stairs.

*

The noise and rumbling grew; moans and calls were heard — each class, each tribe, each mob wished to be first to press through these rows. The huge mass of thousands of arms, heads and breasts stumbled and tripped across one another, falling, rising — Now the bloody glow shone over them, and again it turned grey, livid, or dull in the air above. Like the funnels of the hurricane, like the elements of water and air at war with each other, they were nearing the platform stairs. The soldiers' weapons clattered as they pointed them in the direction of the myriads; then there arose a great silence, and another merchant stood up and cried out: "The markets are open!" and bells rang out together one more time, before dying away in the air.

*

Then the merchant inquired among the people for the events of the day just passed, and as the voices of the princes and wisemen who ruled the people made answer, speaking of quarrels and massacres, of discoveries and inventions, their accomplices stood behind them and took counsel and came to terms amongst themselves, and once more a great silence reigned. One could hear only the whispers of the merchants' voices in this world of granite. The aerial glow then grew pale, and all the souls of the people grew pallid as well, with anticipation!

*

After a few moments, a merchant-orator brought news of prices on earth — how much these had risen, and how much those had fallen. Then did a swell of applause, and curses, cries and weeping, arise from the many who had been holding their breath. Some of the mob lamented, "We shall die of hunger" while others cried "Long live the merchants omnipotent!" Some were dancing, screeching, "We've won! We've won!" and others: "O, merchants, O you, our only gods, have mercy on us!" And again all began to grumble and quarrel and fight and murder; again some fell, while others arose, treading on the backs of the fallen!

*

The youth beheld many corpses trampled in front of the platform, while the living began to ascend the marble steps, approaching them in orderly fashion, treading over the bodies. First came the princes, with sceptres in their hands and swords at their sides, surrounded by the grand bureaucrats of the nations. An archway of bayonets was raised above their heads, protecting them on their way from the steps of the platform up through half of the gigantic entrance — and there did the merchants descend to them, taking their hands in their own and leading them higher.

*

After them, all the industrious of the world began their climb: handcraftsmen and labourers, usurpers and hucksters; some of them carried products, others sacks of great volume, others still fluttering scrolls of paper marked with writings. These were made to halt when they reached the midpoint of the stairs, while a thunderous voice from above demanded news of each. And they responded with the names of their craft or their product, or their shop, or some number or other — for none of them possessed their own, human name in all the world.

*

Behind them, a train of bent and sad figures emerged from the black sea of the peoples, bearing in their hands or carrying on their backs strange swords, chain-mail and helmets. At this very moment, the youth heard a voice aloft saying, "Behold the last scions of the ancient nobility!" And turning round, again he saw the apparition standing behind him.

*

This train ascended the black steps until it reached the midpoint. There, they sat down on the wide marble stair. Then each of them set to work at their weapons with knife and hammer — pounding, tearing, breaking them. And the ghost of Dante said: "Behold how they pry out the Damascene gold and Persian turquoise from their fathers' shields — how they gouge the ancient diamonds from the maces and sabres, so as to carry off the last ancient glories as pawns to the merchants." And while Dante's ghost so lamented, they tossed down the pieces of the broken weapons, and there arose a frightful clatter from the helmets, breastplates, loop guards, discs and knuckle-bows that tumbled down the marble to shatter.

*

And these sons of brave forefathers arose and moved on, extending their hands to the merchants, hands full of gold dust and shining jewels, and as they went they begged in humble tones to be admitted among the princes and the traders. A sign was given from above that they be allowed to approach, at which they presented their thanks. Then, in raised voices they began to negotiate the prices of their valuables! Dante bit his lips until blood spurted, at which he cried in a funereal voice: "The hell of the ancients caused me less pain!"

*

He placed a hand — none too severely — on the youth's head, saying, "Remember..." But at this same moment he seemed to fade away again — he melted in the transparency of space — and was no longer there!

*

Now a gloomy, yet furious screech arose from the bowels of the earth, from the subterranean abyss, to soar over the heads of the nations and break against the platform. The princes and bureaucrats went momentarily pale, but the faces of the merchants were not affected — they merely laughed aloud, stroking their grey beards.

*

From that same direction some gigantic figures progressed through the very midst of the black multitude — they marched on to conquest, growing ever larger in the eyes of the youth until he recognised in them the consecrated twelve and their leader, the thirteenth, who led them, stiletto in his right hand and goblet in his left.

*

As he approached the platform, his face above the heads of the other people seemed to crackle with sparks, and wax in power. He led his men up to the first step, where he had them sit down and wait. Alone, asking no one's permission, pushing aside the soldiers' bayonets, he ascended the steps — huge, unhindered, flouncing his hair like the mane of a lion!

*

One of the merchants came down and led him up to the very summit of the platform, in the midst of the advisory ring. At this moment, it so seemed to the youth that the sparks suddenly went out of the eyes of the giant, and the ire of his brows seemed to soften. However, taking a place amidst the merchants, he cried out in a voice like a thunderclap: "For the final time I bring before you the summons of the maltreated, oppressed and wretched: Choose — an equal division among all, or your life!" And the martyrs left below applauded his words, while some voices from among the rabble repeated them — and the abysses echoed his voice, booming from afar!

*

The giant bent down, and threw his double-edged dagger upon the ground. Then he bent down even lower until his brow disappeared from the sight of the nations — and thus crouched, he sat down upon one of the trader-thrones and asked in a whisper: "Quickly — how much will you give today for this goblet of blood — A lot?"

*

And when the merchants named the price they had in mind, he responded: "That is not enough for this blood, today. Have you any idea what is going on in the depths? Have any of you ever dared descend to set foot there? At this moment, those who are gathered are clamouring in expectation of my return, scarring their own breasts with their blades, and tearing at their hair in fury! Today, after so many disappointments, if they are disappointed again, perhaps they shall rebel; perhaps I will no longer be able to appease them with flattery, oratory or promises, but with this dagger I will have to pacify them. And you would bargain with me! O merchants, lords of the earth! Are your continued days of bliss not worth a trifle more gold?" At which the merchants responded, "Are these not the same words we hear from you every day? Still, so that you might cease your griping, we shall raise our offer." And taking counsel among themselves, they offered him more. But he, again: "That is not enough for this blood, today!" And lifting high the goblet, he made as if to rise from the throne.

*

Then, one of the merchants unpinned a huge diamond from the purple band on his brow and said: "Here is a nail from the cross of Golgotha, which crystallised on the night in which your God expired. On the next morning, my great-great-grandfather pried it from the wood. Since that time we have kept it in our family. Speak — will this gem be enough for the blood of your brothers, today?"

*

The giant gazed — and then he lowered the goblet — and spilled from it all of the blood onto the black marble at the feet of the merchants, saying: "The nail is mine." And the Jew tossed the diamond into the empty goblet, and, as it fell therein, it gave forth a sound like to a moan!

*

Then did the leader of the consecrated arise, and took himself back to the nations of the world. As he descended he cursed and threatened until he came again unto his own, who arose before him and asked, "Well then? When?" And he in a proud voice replied: "Just come with me now; today is not yet the time — but the hour will arrive!" And leading them behind him, he parted the myriads and headed in the direction of the abyss.

*

Then the merchant-orator declared unto the nations universal peace and well-being on the earth; admonishing them that it behooves all to ascend and descend, to busy themselves with buying and selling. On the throne, above them, sat all the merchants and all the princes, while at their feet the train of nobles lay down on the marble, resting their heads upon the tinkling sacks, in which the souls of merchants were moaning — In their hands they gripped the jewels they had pried loose from the armour, and thus they lay there, unmoved, helpless, with furrowed brows, and large tears in their eyes! And all sorts of people, whole crowds, pressed over the steps, continually, now upwards, now downwards, like two opposing currents, and a hubbub of quarrels and compacts arose, while the myriad below was also abuzz, buying and selling as well!

*

And there was a gloomy rabble crying out that today they had lost their bread once and for all time — but no one gave ear to them. Whole ranks of people stood there, like ill persons, shivering from cold, and begging alms, but no one ever glanced their way. Trampled bodies lay about here and there, with lips still moving and rustling, "Help!" But no one extended a hand!

*

While this was happening on the earth, that glow of all the souls, pulsing with bloody flashes, grew more and more livid aloft. In the shape of hearts, one after the other breaking, all the fires, lights, and rays it gave off were smothered, and fell away. At last, catching onto the black cornices, like a black dome of smoke, it hung over the walls of the structure, and the yellow sun was dimmed thereby, and that huge structure grew dark all along the horizon, from its foundations to its apex. Amidst these nocturnal darknesses, only the merchants upon their thrones flashed with light. And the entire world was like one great, dark Exchange — and the merchants were like the kings of that world!

*

And all of these images began to overlap one another, to mix and to deform in the eye of the youth. Ever gloomier and ever thicker the apparition of the bard again began to grow, his face sad, but full of peace. And the youth heard: "Turn your eyes away from that Hell of the sordid!" With these words of Dante's, a refreshing cool, like a breeze in the nighttime, wafted over his brow.

*

The apparition took him by the hand and moved on ahead, over the clouds, white and silent, among the fragrance of unseen herbs. Here and there appeared the sapphire of the heavens. Little stars winked in the distance. Then, once more a great groan rushed out from behind the clouds and echoed among them, before dying away. But hardly had the first passed away than a second arose, and a third, and a fourth, at which the silver clouds dispersed like a bevy of spooked swans.

*

It seemed to the youth that he remained on one of these clouds, together with the bard, and that from this vantage point, as if from an elevated threshold, he were gazing upon a broad plain ringed by the pure azure, in which the full moon shone forth. It seemed to him that he saw before him, on those fields, a forest of slender and tall trees — pines they seemed to be, but strangely lopped — each having but two limbs and each standing upon its own mound. The groans did not cease; of course, they resumed, each shaking the air like a thunderbolt, they sounded like the wide-resounding cry of thousands of people at the moment of their death! The shade of Dante asked, "Can you see the Purgatory of these latter days?" At which the youth: "Besides these heavens and that wood, I can see nothing!" Then the bard, slowly lifting his arms, said: "You must accept from me a second gift of sight, for with the vision with which you saw through the sordid, you cannot behold the noble. But first, listen attentively to what I say to you!

*

"There is no such thing as death —there are only horrid dreams of death. The Lord never created it, nowhere; for everywhere, always, He is alive. Eternal death is something that one can only cause to oneself, becoming vile by one's own will. He who dies in such fashion possesses neither life nor grave. He degrades himself to nothingness, and destroys himself through iniquity. Perhaps, after the passage of millions of years, something of him will reawaken. But such a one will never be purged, nor shall he be resurrected. On the other hand, he who is to live again must be transformed, and each transformation, until it is perfected, bears the appearance of death. Such is the trial of the grave!

*

"Within it is abundance of mockery, and tears, and pain, and illusion. Individuals and whole tribes, humanity, and entire worlds must endure it — each immortal must touch upon it. Who has not endured it has perished forever! Be therefore like a lion at heart, for the shapes of these illusions shall be spread wide before you!" And placing his palm upon the youth's eyelids, he blew upon them with the breath of his mouth.

*

It seemed to the youth that the figure of a crucified man spurted from each pine of that wood. He beheld a great crowd of bodies, stretched, bleeding, trembling in the air — there were ever more of them. In the spectral light of the moon, crowds upon crowds of them appeared here, there, and farther on — some next to each other, some behind one another, stretching to the very horizon. The entire space was alive, loud, dying along with them. And the youth realised that this whole nation, hanged about in the torments of Christ, was his own — and his eyes filled with tears.

*

At which the apparition: "Turn not away, but look on, although it pain you sorely! In order to triumph over pain, one must experience it, to the dregs! — Note well how all the pines in this immense forest have been lopped with forethought and pruned into the shape of a cross! Note well: each is supported upon a mound of rubble — and that rubble consists of the dry bones of once vibrant churches and castles! And note still more: the spaces between each of these mounds is uniform — there are no bushes or undergrowth anywhere! As cities are built from quarried cliffs, so these woods have been reformed into one cemetery of torment. Only the most perfect torturer could so measure out pain, so organise death!"

*

The youth looked on once more, and it seemed to him that ribbons of mist, silvered by the moon, were winding round all those mounds, and although there was no wind, now they rose, and now they fell, alternately, as if in suffering too, disquieted. The youth realised that he was looking upon ranks of women and children, all clad in white, standing at the foot of each of the crosses. And he saw their hands, stretching up toward the treetops, like a multitude of white wings wishing to soar, but unable to do, and then falling to their sides in their infirmity. Then there began a trembling, prayerful song, which was stifled by sobbing!

*

And blood dripped and dripped upon those snowy crowds from above, and poured through them, seeping among the mounds; from there could be heard a growing rush as of streams in flood. And again it seemed to the youth that the apparition counselled him: "Turn not away from these melting thousands and the rivulets of blood! Now all the crucified are gripped by a fatal, current-like shiver. They cannot die, but they must be suffering unto the death, and you must witness it! I command you: look!"

*

Before he raised his eyes again, he had already heard a groan from thousands upon thousands of the crosses, thundering aloud — whilst all the trees from one end of the plain to the other creaked, and a wind arose from so many penetrating voices, which blew here and there! All of the bodies were as if gripped by a paroxysm of pain, trembling and twitching, each on his own cross — and just as a summer rain will fall after a lightning strike, so from all of these bodies there began to poor blood in more copious amounts. Slowly, this storm of torments passed; slowly, the plain grew silent; once more the bodies on the crosses grew still; order returned — silence reigned everywhere — but the sound of the blood was constantly to be heard!

*

And then a snatch of laughter tore through the air. The youth beheld, right below him, in the direction whence the laughter came, there on the open field, directly before the first row of the crosses, a huge black mound of ruins and embers, which stood there like the remnants of a city after a great inferno. From these layers of ash there poked forth splinters of cannon and broken weapons — and from the mound there arose thick smoke, winding about a giant, who stood on the summit of the ash heap.

*

The beams of the moon fell flush upon him. One could make out a crown of steel, as if wrought of fetters; one could make out a soldier's greatcoat, braided with chains and handcuffs. Instead of a sword, a leather whip hung from the loops of the chain, spilling down to the feet of that potentate. When the groan of the crucified ones resounded, he pricked his ears, listening closely, and when the sobbing of the women was heard, he responded by clapping his hands. The shade of Dante said: "The perfect torturer! Listen: he now begins to tempt them!"

*

And it seemed to the youth that the crowned giant then leaned down from above his mound, extending a hand in the direction of the tormented throngs, while resting the other upon his belt festooned with handcuffs and upon his whip, as if upon a sword, and he called out: "Deny the past and the future, your fatherland and your God! And as I commanded you to be nailed to the cross, so shall I command that you be taken down therefrom! I shall call my lackeys and they shall unpin you — and I will make of you a happy nation! I will give you food and drink, and all abundance. Your bodies will be healthy, and fresh; your wretched, punctured flesh will grow fat and sleek!"

*

But the crucified crowds made no reply. They did not even let out a complaining moan. But the blood was now sweeping past the first crosses in a broad current, and like the breakers of the sea upon the beach, so it crashed against the mound. In its falling, the youth seemed to hear the word *No*. The snowy crowds of the women made no response either. Only, when the wave receded from the mound, did they bend down and gather up their children therefrom, and whole ranks of these children, held aloft, cried out *No!* And hardly had these thousand little voices resounded, than a great brightness grew in the spaces all around, and the youth lifted up his eyes!

*

And there, high, high above, at the very summit of the nocturnal sapphire, it seemed that from the heavenly depths two milky ways began to descend, crossing one another and forming one giant, bright, white cross. Upon this cross was stretched a figure, it seemed, which floated into ever lower regions of the space, with both arms stretched out over the whole world. The arc they formed grew broader, more gigantic, moment by moment. And the youth saw a crown of thorns upon the brows of that heavenly Figure, a crown that seemed weft of crackling, yet silent, lightning bolts. And he saw what seemed to be three wounds in the hands and feet of the Figure, shining like three red moons — and constantly, there flowed rainbows of blood from them, and each of these rainbows, in falling, condensed into swarms of stars, scattered over the heavens, shining. And then, in glory and in blood, crucified and creating, lower and lower still floated the Figure, making the space beneath Him sunny-bright, until the two milky ways that bore the Figure became like two limitless hoops of silver, embracing the horizon from east to west and from north to south — until from the flowing blood a million stars came into being, forming a great veil of stars, covering His Body. And the eyes of the Figure shot out like two living lightning bolts, which did not burn out in the atmosphere, but went straight on, from heaven to earth, falling full upon the woods of the crucified.

*

And under this Divine glance, all of the pale and gory bodies were lifted up — all of the heads so similar now to skulls, with extinguished eyes. And it seemed to the youth that he saw the entire nation, tortured unto the death, floating in that sea of heavenly brightness, and he cried out, "Too late, too late!"

*

Then did the shade of Dante, who had been kneeling on the cloud, stand up, and cry: "Verily, verily, here we have the Purgatory of these latter days, for all the bodies on these plains are tormented, but the very Dearest, Hidden One watches over the soul of the nation Himself!" And because the youth began to weep and strike his breast, and would not be comforted, the master added: "Weep not for them, but for those upon the grey granite world, for there is Hell and corruption, and death adjudged, whereas here — there is only pain! And did I not tell you: the spirit resurrects through pain — there is no resurrection from iniquity!" And as he was saying this, the curtain of clouds parted, and everything — plain and forest, heavens, and the eyes of the heavenly Figure — disappeared.

*

It became ever more cool and fresh, and clear. The wreath smouldering on the master's brows began to fade away. It seemed to the youth that his open eyes again beheld the interior of a chapel, and fields, and mountains, and the rising sun — and he stretched forth his arms and called out: "O master, master, show me Paradise! That third, Paradise upon the earth!"

*

Dante's shade then took form once more and appeared fully amidst the flowing light. But his voice was different, as if coming from afar, as if he were returning thereth, to the glory from whence he had come. "Up until now, on that earth of yours, there has only been Hell and Purgatory. But the Spirit of the Lord has taken up residence in your bosoms — you are like chasms, but in your depths there secretly shines the hidden azure of Heaven. Awaken it in your core with faith, carry it aloft on the wings of sacred will, bring it out into the open — before you, above you, around you; encircle yourselves with it like the horizon, through the act of Love! Then that third, blessed region shall become incarnate upon the earth. But be carefully attentive: no other path leads to it — neither blind chance, nor the force of predestination, nor wanton caprice, nor any lying pride! And woe to the ages if the violence of the godless should make an attempt upon the booty of God's wealth! For the Lord your Creator has respected you so much, that He allows you even to wage war against Him, to conquer Him with your evil. But as soon as you should achieve such a victory, then the conquered All-Being should immediately elude your grasp, and you should find yourselves in possession of eternal emptiness instead; eternal death, eternal Nothingness. Watch carefully over the fate of your world!"

*

And fainting amidst the light of dawn, which silvered the air with its last traces, in ever wider rings, ever more transparently, like the eddies of waters in motion, like the breaths of calming breezes, like a passing dream, the figure of Dante went off through the spaces, into the distance, into the radiance of the sun, into the invisibility of endlessness!

Written in 1843

END OF THE INTRODUCTION

III

THE CATACOMBS OF VENICE

Carnival on the Piazza San Marco in Venice. To the rear, the church of San Marco and the Doges' Palace. Many maskers on the piazza and among the arcades. Enter the Youth, and the Banker-Prince.

CHORUS OF GREEK WOMEN
Eulaloe lana! We have fled the Archipelago — from the seraglio of the pagan pasha we have escaped! Can you see the fires in our eyes? Take away our masks, take them away! Eulaloe lana!

CHORUS OF VENETIAN WOMEN
On a black gondola there once rode a patrician and a well-born lady! — Roses, velvet and pearls, a sword, a guitar and a dagger, amidst the sighing wavelets!

There are still gondolas, roses and sighing waves, but where is all the rest? And alone, empty glides the black gondola along the waves with that wreath of roses!

CHORUS OF GYPSY WOMEN
Come here! Come near! Your future for a penny — for a penny, predestination! Just a penny, one penny is all we ask!

GYPSY WOMAN
Stay, young sir!

YOUTH
Why do you detain me, masked woman?

GYPSY WOMAN
Your hand — give me your hand!

YOUTH
Is it my destiny you'd read me?

GYPSY WOMAN
What crossroads are etched on this palm! Too much of everything: love — despair — suicide — storms — catastrophes — happiness — inspirations — frenzy. Beware of woman, beware!

YOUTH
Then let me go, that I may begin to follow your advice, with you.

BANKER-PRINCE
Perhaps, Count, you've never before seen such a carnival, in all your life?

YOUTH
Indeed, that's true! What a motley crowd! What a murmur, what cries!

BANKER-PRINCE
As soon as I received your letter of recommendation from Rothman and Co., that true monarch of the European market, just yesterday, I took it to heart immediately to serve your Lordship as a guide to today's celebrations. I have done well, have I not? You are enjoying yourself, are you not, my Lord?

YOUTH
What I most enjoy is this blue, without a mask; that sun without a mask; this air impregnated with the fragrance of violets, and the rain of rose petals that these freaks beat back and forth among one another! And that church with its rainbow of mosaics! And that band of lacy pillars with which that palace is wound about! And further on, that sea, like to a horizon-wide breastplate of silver!

BANKER-PRINCE
Let us go in under the portico — the best sort of maskers will be found there. There I will be able to show your Lordship some of the lights of our local society.

YOUTH
Alas, neither the sea nor these skies can be seen from there… but since you so wish it, Prince, let us go!

BANKER-PRINCE
You must have a passion for painting landscapes, your Lordship, since you so delight in air and water?

YOUTH
Not at all. But the eye of God flashes through them, especially in such a land!

BANKER-PRINCE
Aha! So that's the only reason! I see that your Lordship is an exalted soul. That is something common to youth, such vivid imagination! I was the same in my day, but I lacked the time to make such observations. I had to sit beneath my father's eye, morning to evening, at the counting house — or else we would never have achieved the rank of princes! But I was just the same when I was eighteen… Aha! one of my agents is looking for me; I beg your pardon for a moment. Well, what is it, Petruccio?

AGENT
Metals are holding at 102 1/4.

BANKER-PRINCE
Hold off yet, until they hit 103. Then, flood the market!

AGENT
And if they rise no higher?

BANKER-PRINCE
Doubt rather that the sun will rise, than to question me when I foretell a movement on the Exchange! An hour or two, and they'll be at 103!

AGENT
But Sir, if we flood the market with all we have, they say that the house of Pignatelli and Merecz will suffer — it might even fall.

BANKER-PRINCE
And for that very reason we shall do it! Be off now, to your tasks! *To Youth.* He's still very inexperienced. A new hire in my bookkeeping office. But he will learn. And I was once the same, when I was eighteen. Oh — do you see that harlequin?

YOUTH
Yes.

BANKER-PRINCE
That is my most trusted friend! A marquis, a Spanish grandee of the first order, chevalier of the Golden Fleece, Commendatore Monceni, the senior nobleman of all Venice!

YOUTH
The one with that elbow of a nose, his rags all jangling, and dragging a black tail behind him?

BANKER-PRINCE
The very same! How are you, Monceni! I recognised you, mask and all! Permit me to introduce you to my friend, a Count, from Poland, who came to me but two days ago, recommended by Rothman and Co.! Count, Commendatore Monceni! You must excuse me, your Lordship, I'm not adept at Slavic names, my tongue… But Monceni's already passed us by, in pursuit of that girl in the pink dominoes — I'll introduce you next time! — But what a beautiful and spry man he is, is he not? So elegant in that costume, half-harlequin, half devil!

YOUTH
Back in Poland, if one dressed up like that, people would say that…

BANKER-PRINCE
That…?

YOUTH
I lost it. And it was on the very tip of my tongue.

BANKER-PRINCE
Oh, tell me! I am so curious!

YOUTH
It's gone.

BANKER-PRINCE
But I beg you!

YOUTH
With your permission, then?

BANKER-PRINCE
Yes, I insist. It must be quite humorous!

YOUTH
You would make me say it?

BANKER-PRINCE
You must, my dear fellow! Tell me — what would they say of the most refined of our gentlemen, so humorously masked?

YOUTH
They would call him the degenerate son of dashing fathers.

BANKER-PRINCE
But why? He hasn't lost a farthing of their treasure — He's kept it all preserved to this very day.

YOUTH
They would say that as long as foreign mercenaries strut your squares with swords at their sides and pride on their brows, you ought not to dress yourselves up as harlequins, but rather to put on the hero, in silence, like the avengers of the old Republic!

BANKER-PRINCE
Ah, the varied characters of various nations! I see that your Lordship also has an exalted political soul — I was just the same at age eighteen!

Oh, and that one there — that monk with staff and sandals? — A local painter of the first rank — Good day, Arpeggiani! Don't forget now — you're to sup with me on Wednesday, seven o'clock sharp. You see, my dear Count, I am a great patron of the arts. Thrice weekly I invite to my table all the artists who excel with brush, bow, or rhyme. But what would you expect, your Lordship? He who has millions must be generous. Today the purse is what the papacy once was — *richesse oblige*. From time to time one must dispense largesse, ha ha. And I do, I do, so much so, that people have taken to calling me the Maecenas of this municipality; others say that I must be one of the Medici. And perhaps our families did mix up once, ha, ha, ha! Look to your left, Count!

YOUTH
To see...?

BANKER-PRINCE
Among those two rows of masks that just passed, you will behold the most beautiful woman in all of Venice. See? She walks toward us!

YOUTH
The one on the arm of that tall man?

BANKER-PRINCE
Herself, in a black dress, without a mask. It's too bad though, really too bad, that for some time now she grows so thin. Look her over carefully — *per Baccho!* What lines! What an eye! What a gait! The gait of a great lady!

YOUTH
Truly, there is something regal in it...

BANKER-PRINCE
And how!

YOUTH
My knees would kneel of themselves!

BANKER-PRINCE
My dear Count — do you feel faint?

YOUTH
No, no, but listen! At this moment I would like nothing better than to be a bunch of violets in your hands, that you might cast me beneath those feet!

BANKER-PRINCE
I see that your Lordship cherishes exalted feelings towards women, as well. I was just the same at eighteen. And thus I am obliged to introduce my dear Count to the princess. But there are no means to do so just now, as it is obvious that she is in a hurry, and moreover, the prince is at her side. And he is a gentleman, every inch a one, and to speak frankly, he is… he is…

YOUTH
She passes — She's passed away like a dream!

BANKER-PRINCE
How can I say it? He is… He is… an immensely serious man, and at the same time, immensely polite, but after a peculiar fashion. He's also very deep and wise — a grand figure — do you understand? I don't know how to explain it to you… He's a fearsome man!

YOUTH
How so?

BANKER-PRINCE
Just, for the love of God, don't repeat that to anyone, dear Count. You see, I am being quite candid and sincere with you — for you came to me recommended by Rothman and Co., and so I speak to you now as I wouldn't speak to anyone else who had come to me recommended by any other house with less capital, never, on my word of honour! But for all that, you must never betray me to anyone. Do I have your word of honour?

YOUTH
Look into my eyes. Do you see anything treacherous there? And you will be kind to note, Prince, that you have revealed no secret to me, nothing at all. You merely said that he is a fearsome man…

BANKER-PRINCE
And I have spoken too freely as it is! Let us move on, let us not stop here — Don't fix your eyes so openly upon them! They will say that it was not at her, but at him you stare! That you are taking his measure! God knows what lies people will tell!

YOUTH
But tell me, at last, who is he?

BANKER-PRINCE
He is Prince Rahoga, an excellent man. Come, let us turn the corner here, into the alley!

YOUTH
And she?

BANKER-PRINCE
Princess Rahoga — his wife!

YOUTH
His wife?

BANKER-PRINCE
Yes!

YOUTH
His wife — are you sure?

BANKER-PRINCE
Lord! What a question!

YOUTH
And so, you say, she is his wife?

BANKER-PRINCE
I do so say, I state again, I swear, as surely as twenty-thousand, six hundred and fifty one gold Napoleons, neither more nor less, repose at this moment in the drawer of my safe! The Count is distracted — why should that amaze you?

YOUTH
It amazes me not, it causes me pain!

BANKER-PRINCE
But why?

YOUTH
I am a strange creature — I do not like wives! Let us go on! I came across that aethereal figure once before. But where? Where?

BANKER-PRINCE
Certainly in Russia — She is a Russian.

YOUTH
Blaspheme not — Such a thing is impossible!

BANKER-PRINCE
She is not Italian, that I know. Nor is she German nor English. She comes of the Slavs.

YOUTH
She is Polish, for sure!

BANKER-PRINCE
That may well be — as a matter of fact, it is true! You are right, your Lordship. Indeed I now recall how it was lately said of her that she came into an inheritance in Poland, but in that Poland which is Russia!

YOUTH
How came it therefore, Prince, that you thought her a Muscovite?

BANKER-PRINCE
Is it not one and the same thing?

YOUTH
Just as atheism and religion are one and the same thing! Just as the clatter of your Napoleons, and the clash of Bonaparte's sword are one and the same thing, Prince!

BANKER-PRINCE
For us Italians there is no such distinction. We call every northerner a Russian.

YOUTH
What is her Polish name?

BANKER-PRINCE
That I cannot say.

YOUTH
The giggling of these masks is starting to grate upon me! Tell me whatever you know of her.

BANKER-PRINCE
Well, they say that some inheritance fell to her, unexpectedly, and that it lies adjacent to the great holdings that belong to the Prince in that country, somewhere near the city of Odessa. It was even said that this made the Prince angry!

YOUTH
Angry? Why?

BANKER-PRINCE
Here, make way for those running Mandarins! You see, it is said that the prince took her to wife without a dowry, although she came of an excellent house — the very sort with a coat of arms, and past glories, but which didn't keep their eyes upon their interests — not like us financiers — ignorant of the fact that the secret motor of the world is money! Yes, dear Count! Sometimes on sleepless nights, I ask myself

how God created the world without money! He had to have some capital to distribute… Are the stars his ducats? Ha, ha, ha!

YOUTH
Let us speak of the Princess.

BANKER-PRINCE
Well then, the Prince, who owns vast estates everywhere — in Austria, Silesia, Italy, and those near Odessa, was put out at the fact that she had come into an inheritance of her own.

YOUTH
I don't understand!

BANKER-PRINCE
You don't? It's as clear as mathematics. An estate brings with it independence, bestows strength, and even develops the memory, the will, the imagination! And all such gifts, which are divine to wives, are plagues to their husbands. He had, the Prince had, a reason to be angry, on my honour! Now, there's no way he can handle her as he did before. He can no longer walk all over her! He can no longer keep her under lock and key! She'd find herself someone to hack through locked doors! You see for yourself, Count, what money means!

YOUTH
What? And that's how he treated her? Oppressing her, tormenting her, imprisoning her?

BANKER-PRINCE
I've heard dark rumours, and they are credible ones, for he is jealous to a measure unheard of! An iron despot!

YOUTH
That Rahoga must be Satan himself!

BANKER-PRINCE
How inexperienced you are, my Lord! Please, I beseech you, keep your voice down! Don't pronounce people's names so loudly in public places. Have mercy!

YOUTH
I've said nothing that I would not tell him to his face.

BANKER-PRINCE
And perhaps that would be safer than to say it behind his back. For he might be inclined to forgive you such presumption, but if your words were to be repeated to him at second hand, he would be implacable.

YOUTH
So, all these present are his relatives, friends, servants?

BANKER-PRINCE
No — but perhaps they are something else.

YOUTH
Such as what?

BANKER-PRINCE
Just imagine, my dear Count — he is received at court in an extraordinary fashion — he is inexpressibly welcome there. Although he has no official appointment, the doors to the Emperor's most private apartments open themselves to him of their own accord, and where he enters, he reigns. Everyone present grows pale, everyone scurries at his nod!

YOUTH
Yet here there is no masked Emperor, no Viennese courtiers who, hearing my words, should rush off to inform on me. I see only orgiastic crowds in frenzied inebriation, Turks and Indians scampering about, gods and Pulcinellas!

BANKER-PRINCE
Draw your ear closer to my lips, Count.

YOUTH
I'm listening.

BANKER-PRINCE
You think there are no spies here on the Piazza San Marco?

YOUTH
What? The husband of that woman is — a policeman?

BANKER-PRINCE
Who would ever suppose such a thing? How? Did I say anything that would lead you to that assumption? Can the governor of the city of Venice be a policeman? But don't the governor and the Emperor himself read the police reports?

YOUTH
So who is this Rahoga? Stop tormenting me already, and tell me!

BANKER-PRINCE
I can't quite describe him more exactly, my Lord. He knows everything. He touches upon many things in the State, and he has a gorgeous wife, to whom I will do my best to introduce you. When shall I present you at her salon? For if I'm not mistaken, you've already fallen in love! Ha, ha, ha!

YOUTH
You do not understand my people at all. To you, our Polish fatherland is a place from a fairy tale. You have no idea what blooms that most trampled land of Europe gives forth, that land furrowed by the ploughs of catastrophe, and watered with the tears of generations! You can't imagine the bonds that link her native sons and daughters to one another. They may not know one another at sight, but when fate brings them together, they recognise each another immediately, as equals, stricken by the same immense suffering. It is enough that she is a Pole, and I am a Pole, and that we meet on foreign soil, for me to see in her my sister!

BANKER-PRINCE

Say what you will, my Lord, say what you will — I still affirm, you are in love! Ha, ha, ha! And you are well to be so, though it be a difficult case. You are quite right, on my honour! What a shape she has! What legs! Bravo! Bravissimo! Ha, ha, ha!

YOUTH

Prince! I must warn you of yet another national custom of Poland!

BANKER-PRINCE

Yes?

YOUTH

Poles were carefree and happy once upon a time, but the grave's made them gloomy — they don't like jokes. They endure them only the first time told; at the second telling, they reply with a warning, and at the third, either they, or the teller, perishes!

BANKER-PRINCE

But don't be cross, my Lord, don't be cross! How can this be? And with the recommendation of such a house! That of Rothman and Co.! An all-powerful house, well-grounded, eternal! It never crossed my mind to insult your Lordship, my dear Count! Your hand, I beseech you — I shall take you to the Rahogas whenever you like. Shall it be today? At nine, say? Will that do?

YOUTH

I tender you my deepest thanks, Prince, but let us set aside your graceful service for later. And at any rate, I can find my way to their house on my own, if I decide to go there.

BANKER-PRINCE

I am at your command, dear sir, whenever the mood strikes you, at any moment of the day!

YOUTH

With your permission, Prince, let us speak of other things. I see that someone else is chasing you.

BANKER-PRINCE
Another agent of mine. What is it, Gregorio?

YOUTH
A half hour ago, metals rose to 103. And I had the market flooded. Pignatelli and Merecz have fallen, and you, your Excellency, have risen!

BANKER-PRINCE
Excellent, Gregorio! I foresaw it all! Pignatelli and Merecz are truly down?

AGENT
That it is so, I swear on all the saints in heaven!

BANKER-PRINCE
O, I shall sleep well tonight! Return to the cashiers, Gregorio! *To the Youth.* But why are you so downcast, my dear Count? I'm sorry for it, truly I am! Of course, nothing can spoil my present good humour. Health seems to bathe me, from tip to toe! Ah, Shrovetide, such delicious fun! The city of Venice, the most beautiful in all of Italy! And so it is, your Lordship, on my honour! Enjoy yourself, Count, be wanton! Come to my home for supper! Come now, be a little more lively! Well? What do you say?

YOUTH
I hope that you will not be angry with me, Prince, but I must bid you farewell. I've had enough enjoyment for one day.
Exit.

BANKER-PRINCE
But I beg you, my dear sir, remain! Where are you off to in such haste, my dearest Count? — He's gone! Is he cross? I've never seen such an exalted soul all my life long. These Poles have sulphur and saltpetre in their veins instead of blood! He must be a Jacobin. I can see through a person at first glance — he's a Jacobin for sure! And I'm never wrong — A Jacobin! A Jacobin!
He disappears among the masked throngs.

IV

The Youth's apartments. A hall, with Moorish windows and an extensive gallery. Two candles are glowing on a table. Aligier is in the gallery; Jacob enters through doors in the depths.

ALIGIER
How wonderful and strange your heavens, O Lord! Rushing, whirling, alive and yet so peaceful! And how strange this Venice, Lord! In the balsam of the moonbeams, so beautiful, and so dead! But beneath that silver immobility, there are deep mysteries as well, and in them, movement, rushing, just as there are there, aloft! Thou knowest this Thyself, O God!

JACOB
Master, master…

ALIGIER
Is that you, Jacob?

JACOB
Who else, sir?

ALIGIER
What is it you wish of me, my Jacob?

JACOB
Well sir, the people say, sir, that the nation hereabout is not as honest as ours…

ALIGIER
There is some truth in that…

JACOB
And so I beg your Honour, this worries me. Because the night is well advanced, and my Lord the Count has not yet returned; it's crossed my mind — God forbid that something evil should have befallen him!

ALIGIER
He's been held up by the carnival somewhere — don't worry.

JACOB
Don't worry! As if I've had anything else from his Lordship than grey hairs from worry! He takes a pocket pistol or a dagger upon leaving the house, and with it, the brassiness to take on a hundred thugs! And when I say to him, sometimes, "Please your Honour, take your Jacob along with you," he gives me such a look as my stomach flops inside me. But he is a good man, a good master — it's just that he's so stubborn at heart. If only he liked the sunshine, you know! But he, ah he — I don't know if you've marked it — he grows fond of any old star in the nighttime sky, rather. And when the moon is full, then, brother, you can wait up for him until that moon falls from the sky! He's off wandering God only knows where, and doing God only knows what; who he's talking to and what he's saying, or crooning, maybe! That's all right once, or twice, or a hundred times even, but someday the chickens will come home to roost — you can bet your life they will!

ALIGIER
Shh! Hear that?

JACOB
A plop of paddles?

ALIGIER
The echo is coming from the turn of the canal.

JACOB
God's will it's him!

ALIGIER
A gondola — gliding just past the wall.

JACOB
Please sir, is it his Lordship?

ALIGIER
Wait — it seems to be — Yes! It is he.

JACOB
And I bet he's standing there, gawping at the sky, and not at the quick fingers of the rowers!

ALIGIER
You've lost your bet. He's talking with them. Go down and light the stairs for him.

JACOB
Praised be Jesus Christ!
Exit.

ALIGIER
Forever and ever, amen. *To Youth.* Lift up your eyes, Henryk. I stand here at the porch.

VOICE OF YOUTH
From below
I see, I see — Wait a bit! Hey! Jacob, don't lock the gate just yet — the waterman's coming up with me for a moment.

ALIGIER
Draws near the doors at the depth. The youth and the gondolier enter
Where've you been so long at play?

YOUTH
Just let me finish my business with this man. Your name?

GONDOLIER
Ambrosio. At your service, Signore.

YOUTH
Where do you usually stand with your gondola?

AMBROSIO
There, at the Rialto bridge, where your Lordship found me today.

YOUTH
And you are sure that the Prince lives at the Korners' palace, where you directed my eyes at those proud columns, shining in the moonlight?

AMBROSIO
Who in all of Venice doesn't know that?

YOUTH
You also showed me two sphinxes near the side door and said something about them — or about the door — I've forgotten.

AMBROSIO
I had the honour of informing your Lordship that it is through that door that the Princess usually leaves for Mass at San Giorgio's every Sunday morning.

YOUTH
Yes — that was it! You also said that the Prince himself never attends Mass…

AMBROSIO
I beg your pardon, Signore, but I know nothing about that — He certainly must, like every good Catholic, only at a different hour. I only said that the Princess always exits the same door on Sunday morning, and always gets into a gondola alone, which takes her to San Giorgio.

YOUTH
Pardon me — I was thinking of those sphinxes, and thus confused your words. Tomorrow is Sunday, is it not?

AMBROSIO
Without a doubt…

YOUTH
I'd like to have a closer look at those porphyry sphinxes. They look so grand, even in the light of the moon… What must they be like in daylight, which highlights each detail!

AMBROSIO
The experts swear them to be the work of Michelangelo himself!

YOUTH
Here — thank you for the trip.

AMBROSIO
This is ten times more than I and Beppo deserve for our service to your Lordship… By the Adriatic! Even the ancient Doges were not so generous!

YOUTH
These are my thanks for showing me the sphinxes — for I am an artist myself, of a sort. Return here with your gondola tomorrow morning.

AMBROSIO
We are your Lordship's humble servants.
Exit.

ALIGIER
You stand, and stare. Well, my Henryk? You do not even take my hand?

YOUTH
Ah, air, air! Come out into the gallery. I cannot speak here, where the candles are burning!

ALIGIER
I'm already standing in the full light of the nighttime sky.

YOUTH
Ah, those ribbons of bright waters, those circlets of bridges, those gondolas: as sharp as arrows, as black as coffins, as delicious as salvation after the last breath… Those azures and sapphires and the

stars that wink therein like so many eyes — that moon, burning me like the eye of the sun! — All of this came about through love, was it not so? Through the love that was before the world, and always shall be? And God, before He created the world, did He not love the as yet uncreated — and for that reason, creation is so awe-inspiring… Is it not so? O, Aligier, what with me, now?

ALIGIER
You have a fever.

YOUTH
Tell me, where was it, where might it have been, that I met her before? And meet her I did, as I live, I met her, surely! And so am I tormented — I flog my memory to the blood, yet I can't, I cannot remember…

ALIGIER
Her? What her?

YOUTH
What? Need I even tell you? Today, walking along the Piazza San Marco with that unbearable Banker-Prince, I suddenly caught sight of a figure I'd seen somewhere, once, already. They call her by her husband's name — Her husband is named Rahoga — but she is a Pole! What? Did you know nothing of my encountering her? That is a surprise! You so love me, Aligier, and yet you felt nothing?

ALIGIER
Ah, beware!

YOUTH
Of what? Of these incomprehensible raptures, which so conspire in me that I can almost touch the omnipresence of God in all things with my very fingers? — Oh, even in these moonbeams that creep towards me across the marble!

ALIGIER
Beware Rahoga, and his household!

YOUTH
Why?

ALIGIER
He's one of the most confirmed enemies of your Polish fatherland!

YOUTH
And is she as well? And so her angelic form is a mere illusion? A shining overcoating of flesh, tossed by the Creator upon the shoulders of a spirit unclean? A sacrilegious being? A Polish woman, who hates Poland? Such a thing cannot be! Come now, tell me the truth: graze not the flesh above my heart with the point of your knife — plunge it straight in!

ALIGIER
Have I said anything about her?

YOUTH
Oh, how good you are now, how merciful! How grand and holy in this moonlight — thus I've always loved you, and love you still! So you do not bear witness against her, only against him?

ALIGIER
Against him, alone.

YOUTH
All the better!

ALIGIER
What do you mean, "all the better," since he's her husband?

YOUTH
Her husband, and the oppressor of her brethren? What sort of husband is that? He is a torturer, rather!

ALIGIER
And so you rejoice in the fact that he is her tormentor?

YOUTH
No! But if he is a tormentor, then she is a victim — and a victim must be protected from her tormentor! Why do you crush your fist against your breast?

ALIGIER
My sick heart once more gives notice of itself — nothing strange there! As it beats, it jostles against the mistakes committed by those it loves, against their frenzy, against their perishing! And at this moment, it strikes against you, thumping against your error, your frenzy, and perhaps your loss!

YOUTH
Oh — And I am so happy; so strong do I feel! It seems to me as I gaze upon this night, that I've breath enough to visit all these worlds shining above, one after the other, and that I still might arrive at God's own threshold, with breath to spare…

ALIGIER
And yet, instead of the immortality of youth, a premature decrepitude crawls near you.

YOUTH
Me? Am I ever to grow old? Me?

ALIGIER
You, yes, and in short order!

YOUTH
How? Why?

ALIGIER
The mirage of Paradise that shimmers in the air before you will lead you to the doors of your enemy. And you shall pass through those doors without blessing them — cursing them, of course! And it's wrong thus to enter a stranger's gate when neither the hag of necessity, nor the angel of duty, pushes one through. And from that moment, your soul will begin to wither!

YOUTH
O, Aligier! you stand there leaning on the granite balustrade, your chin upon your palm, and you do not wish to look at me, while fat tears hang upon your eyelashes, O Aligier!

ALIGIER
So how can it be, your Lordship! — that a son of man can never be satisfied with such beauty as resides within his bosom! Eternity cannot sate his thirst, no — he must descend into the temporal and, by a mockery of a mistake, take earth for Heaven in his search for the latter! And that, from which all takes being, the Ideal, in its very name he becomes enamoured of everything, which is nothing to him! And so he shall abandon Thee, Uncreated Creator, for the sake of a creation that creates nothing! Only in two mortal eyes shall he read that Thou art — Thou, who art figured in the bas-relief of all the stars of heaven — Thou, who art found in every breath of history that rustles over the earth! One, amongst so many millions, he has discovered Thee otherwise! Ah, is it not true, Lord, that he has been Thou, Thyself? And what shall become of us, if we do not cleave unto him as brothers? O Lord, Lord!

YOUTH
You cast the first greys of age upon my hart, with this your horrid moaning!

ALIGIER
Ah, man — you have attained the Ideal twice over! The Frenchman, the German, the Briton senses God only by halves — none of them touches His wounds each day, in the martyrdom of his nation! They do not behold the wonder of His life each day, in the unbreakable carriage of their nation! There is your treasure! And what a jewel it is! Of pain and sacrifice, of merit and memory and hope and undying desire! And this is not enough for you? Will you still err about the worlds after an *ignis fatuus*? Will you still waste time and strength plucking flowers on the meadows, when you should boldly enter the ghast, dark wood rather, climbing over cliffs, striving ever upwards, through mists, bearing with you that cruciform treasure, clinging to the rocks by your very blood so as not to tumble into the abyss?

YOUTH
Ah — You did not behold the vision that was granted me! And I tell you, Aligier, that like all of Poland, she, that one Polish woman, is a limitless expanse of misfortune, disguised in unearthly grace! I've never seen anything similar to that passing image of my fatherland!

ALIGIER
Go on with your flattery, continue lying to yourself, you mortal baby! Summon before you all your passions and caprices, just as the Tsar his boyars, and let them counsel you: "O, high-born Lord, you are right! It is just so!" — until you make of your bosom a foyer full of base courtiers, who would convince you of your greatness, even though you be small; of your bravery, even though you are weak and wilting; of your freedom, even though you descend into possession!

YOUTH
Whence comes this bitterness?

ALIGIER
I am bitter because I see you in love with yourself, while you deceive yourself that you are in love with another — and thus you unravel your powers with your own hands!

YOUTH
And how am I to say unto the lightning that bathed me in its brightness, "Dark thing, you have no lustre?" Know you not that Spirits are drawn one to another in a mysterious and irrevocable fashion? Spirits, who perhaps knew one another, somewhere, in God, and who rediscover one another here, on earth? And who after death will be united anew? You do know this, better even than I!

ALIGIER
Perhaps I do, and thus I weep for you. Have you plumbed the depths of the laws that rule these errant spirits? Do you know how, when they melt into one another, sometimes they are torn asunder by a comet, which splits them apart and whirls them from their centre, to spin through the abysses of the universe before they are able again to approach the sun they abandoned? Have you counted up such

Purgatories? How many mournful unions there are among them? How many ever-breaking hearts? How many sinful figures, whirled by the vortices of despair, who vainly cry out through the darkness, "Forgive us, O Lord!"…?

YOUTH
Even from there would I snatch her up and bear her before the face of God!

ALIGIER
So you say, so you say, and so you know nothing at all, my Henryk!

YOUTH
What is it that you think that I desire? Grant me but a crumb of the sacred friendship you bear me in your heart — for this alone, that I might bring it some relief. This is all I ask. For, Aligier, ah! I repeat — I swear to you that I've never before seen such an expression of pain on the face of any earthly woman. Imagine the most immaculate marble, Parian, marble radiating light, with no inscription: and you shall say "A stone worthy of a Medici statue, alone!" And then you glance at it again and see: it is the lid of a tomb, beneath which is — death. Kneel then, and pray, and weep! — For such is She!

ALIGIER
Do not bother yourself with graves, when you know that your duty is to live, and spend your life in service to your brethren!

YOUTH
And what am I to do, when I am bid to love death? Nor pride, nor triumph, nor shrinking glory, but pain — here or there — be that the pain of my brothers, or that of one of my sisters. It is always sadness and pain that speak to me, that beckon me! Such is my destiny! Forever to be with them who cast at fate, and lose! For they must be hopeless, if they put their hope in me!

ALIGIER
How many such as you have I seen — and you are all the same! yearning, winged, irrepressible, flitting about the azure spaces like

human butterflies, each with his own bloom hovering at his side, until that bloom sheds its petals, and the butterfly its wings, and down they plummet, into the gravel, the sand, the dust — from the aethereal meadows unto the dust, the dust! How many such have I seen — and they are all the same!

YOUTH
What is this mournful tale that you address to the stars?

ALIGIER
The history of the reckless!

YOUTH
Of my recklessness? Mock me not — let it be, now. I'd rather you told me where it was that I've seen her before?

ALIGIER
Ah, you poor wretch!

YOUTH
What?

ALIGIER
I called you a poor wretch.

YOUTH
Why?

ALIGIER
Do you not understand my words? Do you not remember what I told you when we came down from the mountains into this city?

YOUTH
What?

ALIGIER
You've forgotten even that! And you are not reckless…?

YOUTH
No, no! But at this moment I have been searching for something with my soul entire — You know how, sometimes, the ear searches for a note it's lost, a note that does not return, while the sense of hearing, despite itself, strains after it, is persecuted by it? But I know what you're speaking of — repeat your words.

ALIGIER
I asked you if you remembered what I told you when we descended the last mountains and made for this city?

YOUTH
How could I not? You said that you are to introduce me into the company of the hidden yearning, in whom the spirit of the future is worked out.

ALIGIER
Are you ready?

YOUTH
At all times.

ALIGIER
Three days hence, at midnight, I shall lead you there. And there you shall behold with your own eyes all that happens on the earth, and you shall compare it to one earthly woman — to judge whether your place is with history, or with her!

YOUTH
Let's not speak of that now… Give me your blessing as you do each evening. I'm going now.

ALIGIER
For the first time in my life, my soul is chilled at your side.

YOUTH
You do not even wish to bid me a good night?

ALIGIER
There must be something fatal hovering in the airy spaces about you, when I feel this badly! Listen — Renounce her! — Give me your word that…

YOUTH
By the Living God, I shall do no such thing! Aligier, have you turned tyrant? I would hear nothing save her voice, nothing else — and this is to be forbidden me?

ALIGIER
Nothing else?

YOUTH
You will see for yourself and be convinced, believe me! To but hear her voice, to but receive the thought of that soul… No, nothing else!

ALIGIER
He believes so deeply, that "nothing else!"

YOUTH
And what would it avail you should you bend my will to yours by spiritual violence? To tear me from my duty? What is the end result of violence? Rebellion!

ALIGIER
I know this too.

YOUTH
Love me!

ALIGIER
I am sick at heart.

YOUTH
O God, I've not yet exchanged a word with her, and already I suffer on her account!

ALIGIER
Here — accept my blessing as you do each evening, the blessing of friendship. I do not wish you to suffer today, for you are soon to suffer so much!

YOUTH
Ah, thank you! Let me throw myself into your arms! Yes! And let my heart beat in time with your own!

ALIGIER
Watch out for yourself, though I do not think you capable of it, nor myself capable of watching out for you. Watch out for yourself!
Exits through the rear door.

YOUTH
Moving towards the door opposite
Maybe I've never beheld her before with my eyes... Maybe I've only felt her presence around me, like a current of power enveloping me... Until now I have at last beheld her and it only seems to me that, not for the first time, although it was the first time... with these mortal eyes... but not the first time for my eternal being! Who will tell me that we've never met before!...

V

THE CATACOMBS OF VENICE

SCENE I

A dark chamber in the cellars of a Venetian palace. Youth, Aligier.

YOUTH
The last rays of the moon have melted from these stairs — I can't see anything — I hear nothing but the rush of water overhead!

ALIGIER
Hold on to my hand — we must descend yet farther into the depths of the earth!

YOUTH
Are you not inconvenienced by this road? This staircase is in ruins!

ALIGIER
I know each stone and pitfall here. I know where the steps have crumbled into dust, and where they stand firm and solid — and it will soon grow lighter. Jump here, Henryk — Yes, good — Now come: slowly, watch your head — lower still!

YOUTH
How odd! Your health returned as soon as you disappeared from the surface of the earth! For that reason — God is my witness — these black caverns are now dear to me. I'd gladly remain here, long and without feeling the slightest discomfort, if only you were at my side!

ALIGIER
Perhaps, at one time, you would have made such a sacrifice on my behalf, but now — Oh, no! — For you have entered upon life, and he who once touches that billowy stream, must flow along with its current. But neither do I need such a sacrifice, Henryk. So strong am I, so healthy at this moment, that I want to, and must, transport you into the world of memory and intuition, into the world of humanity. In the morning, when I return to the surface of the earth, you will see me in the sunlight and say once more, "He is on his way out!" But now think not of that — strain your ears, peel your eyes, be conscious in every fibre of your being! We near the end of the stairs — Can you see that drop of light in the distance?

YOUTH
It is like a tiny dawn that strives to rise, yet cannot!

ALIGIER
Come!

CHORUS AFAR
You who wish to foretell, remember! You who would build the present and look upon the future from its summits, take first into the depths of your soul all of the days of the past. Because, although the events of time differ, as do their relative powers, there is but one eternal plan, one truth! She is a soul, one that swells wide the breast of the world, ever more broadly, ever more greatly! As a man awakens slowly from his sleep, so it is with humanity, through the ages. As that man awakens in the morning and his eyesight then grows sharper, his feelings more sensitive and sure until he can say "I am here," so it is with this earthly spirit!

YOUTH
Let us go more quickly, let us move nearer — the dawn grows and grows!

ALIGER
Listen — they sing again.

CHORUS AFAR

Each thought begotten in God, sent out from Eternity into time and space, as a portion of the truth, as a daughter of God, must suffer just the same as did the Son of God incarnate! Appearing among men, announcing a portion of Heaven — to be tormented, to bear her cross, to descend into the grave!

Some have died before their time, like sacred virgins. Others, in the fulness of their strength, fell like heroines; still others awaited their graves in humility, in misery, descending from the summits of life into its catacombs. But none of them died in the white robes in which they first alit upon the earth — Given vinegar and gall to drink, spattered with blood, thus they vanished!

But each was resurrected in the next life! Each was raised from the grave into another, higher form of flesh! You who wish to foretell, remember! You who would build the present and look upon the future from its summits, take first into the depths of your soul all of the thoughts of past days — For only thus, from those which have passed, as well as those which are to come, is the fulness of truth handed on!

YOUTH

More and more light! Where does it come from? Am I once more seized by the sleep of wonder?

ALIGIER

No — it is true that the ages shall begin to pass by like dreams, but not inside you this time, only without. Go on, and cease not your progress!

YOUTH

What a blinding, noontime brightness! And it grows so hot! Those buildings in the distance… I draw nearer to them, and they, as if blown on the breath of a soft wind, approach us!

ALIGIER

Do you recognise them?

YOUTH

I've never seen them before!

ALIGIER
Is it possible that humanity, at the breast of which you were nourished, has not provided you with the memory of the ages? Is it not possible for you to recognise the shapes that existed on this planet thousands of years ago, with the eyes of her spirit, fixed in your own soul?

YOUTH
I remember — I recall! Ah — the hanging gardens! And there — rising up high into the air, the tower from which to mark the courses of the stars! And there again a temple gigantic, wound about with arcades. What crystalline waters! And palms everywhere — the banks of the Euphrates! Babylon!

ALIGIER
And those dressed in scarlet, can you see them?

YOUTH
Gathered at the foot of the tower — the tiaras on their heads are dripping with gold, their robes are sown with stars — the clan of Chaldean soothsayers!

ALIGIER
Give ear, give ear!

CHORUS OF CHALDEANS
O Time, measureless, limitless; O Light! Immobile, calm, Forefather of all the lights that be — How far, how far it is to Thee! Thy first-born son Ormuzd and thy younger, rebellious scion Ariman are in constant combat everywhere, whether clothed in the hues of the rainbow, or in the heart of man. We have yearned for liberation, to be cleansed, to flame ourselves clean — to Thee! And the lower folk too, we have sought to tear from their darkness and lift towards the sun, toward the fields of Ormuzd! But now we sense that our strength is failing — now, as we read what is written among the planets of the nighttime sky — that a conqueror approaches, ah! A savage lord, ah! On his way here! Accompanied by men on chariots, accompanied by cavalry, accompanied by tramping boots! Our minds grow weak, our glory is transformed. Oh! Why must we be dying, we sons of the light?

CHORUS AFAR
You are not the light, yourselves.

CHORUS OF CHALDEANS
Zoroaster, who was sent by Ormuzd, promised us that Ormuzd would be victorious some day, and that Ariman himself, after the purging fires of penitence, would return to the bosom of universal Light![1] But these eyes shall not behold that event. It shall not occur today, or tomorrow! And so in vain, in vain, O sacred Brightness, were all our desires to become free, cleansed, to flame ourselves clean to Thee!

CHORUS AFAR
To live on, first you must be spilt out; first you must be trans-incarnated; first you must die!

YOUTH
What is happening to them, Aligier? A huge lightning bolt — like a crashing eternity — lights up the walls and gates, and the river too — It consumes everything! And how dark it grows again!

ALIGIER
Remain where you are — another age will soon be bathed in light before your eyes.

[*A chord is heard, strummed several times.*]

YOUTH
That chord, an insistent triad, gives me pain — who plays it?

ALIGIER
Turn your eyes to the right.

YOUTH
Each time it sounds, a gloomy sort of spring spurts forth. An invisible moan has arisen somewhere and soars aloft — I can make out the

---

1   One of Krasiński's mannerist coinings: *wszechświatło*. Perhaps "omniluminescence."

summits of three pyramids glowing over the desert… There is a black crowd of Sphinxes near a forest of obelisks… Is that Memnon who sits to the rear, beneath that light?

ALIGIER
Take note of the gate of the great pyramid!

YOUTH
A swarm of ghostly figures emerges from it, and each now sits upon a grave of granite.

CHORUS OF EGYPTIAN PRIESTS
The mystery of mysteries is preserved among us. We were first to acknowledge Thee, whose name is "Was and Is, and Shall Be." Like waves at the base of a cliff, so time and space mingle at thy feet! And over that confused swirl, the good Osiris, the evil Typhon and sad Arueris chase one another. And the eyes of mortals behold them, but not Thee!

Why is it, Thou Immortal One, that you escape us? It was our desire to slowly instruct the corrupt tribe of men in eternal truth, slowly to release the soul from the flesh, that she might joyfully ascend to her heavenly fatherland. It was for this reason we balsamed and preserved the flesh — all of our corpses — so that the people should become used to immortality!

Why now therefore is this tabernacle shaken? And its wisdom spilt out before its time? From the immensity of these pyramids and their twisting labyrinths dost Thou abandon us for other regions — Where the sun sets, there is Thy might transformed; there shalt Thou impend above more joyous peoples, and we here in our bitterness shall become desiccate, we, the eldest of Thy sons!

CHORUS AFAR
But His only sons you shall not remain. Younger that you are born.

CHORUS OF EGYPTIAN PRIESTS
O! Why must we perish, since we feel ourselves to be the messengers of God?

CHORUS AFAR
But you are not God yourselves, and He alone does not die in order to live again!

YOUTH
The moon's brightness grows and grows… And they are swallowed by their graves. And through the graves they fall deeper still! What is that immense moan that meets my ears, so sonorous and clear?

ALIGIER
The rising sun has grazed Memnon!

CHORUS OF VOICES ALOFT
From Egyptian darknesses, O mind of Man, we elevate you into the region of roses, myrtle, and azure — there, where Zeus achieved his victory over Typhon — Where the monstrous serpent was lain low by the darts of the Sun — Where the figure of Aphrodite is rocked upon the foaming seas — There, where the statues of Pallas are raised upon the heights!

    You shall be rolled up like a scroll, O desert! Away with you, pyramids! Bow down, obelisks, before the first true beauty! Here is wisdom, here is harmony — Here graceful Psyche searches for her Eros!

YOUTH
O how beautifully, how gorgeously, all is transformed! The shore so green, the sea so blue, the cliffs all clad in tunics of grape vines… I am inebriated with the aroma that hangs in the air!

ALIGIER
Look — Right before us, a snowy billow is taking shape; something is being formed. The light is labouring to produce a structure — and now a temple shines forth upon the Greek promontory: a temple of Parian marble — immaculate Eleusis!

YOUTH
I hear the strains of zither and lyre resounding therefrom, and new hymns are raised on high.

ALIGIER
Behold — the hierophant of the mysteries, the one there clad in white, with the golden sickle in his hand.

YOUTH
And that one, there?

ALIGIER
Which?

YOUTH
That one most beautiful of all, broad-chested, sublime, somewhat similar to Christ!

ALIGIER
The divine Plato!

YOUTH
Thus did my very heart make answer.

ELEUSIAN CHORUS
O soul, lost in the snares of the flesh, O virgin abandoned on distant shores, be cleansed, be cleansed and sigh, and yearn, and you shall return to the realm of forms, to your father and your mother Eimarmena!
    Behold, from beyond the drapes of the senses in which you are enshrouded, look! Such azure heavens, such flowery lands — one thousand reflections from each wave that crashes, a myriad of hues from each beam that falls — and multitudes of gods, from one God born, each moment!

HIEROPHANT
And all these earthly gods are but the powers of the God in Heaven.

ELEUSIAN CHORUS
And the earth, the sky, the mighty stars so beautiful, rhythmic and alive — What are these?

HIEROPHANT
Nothing but a shadow — the reflection of the Ideal!

ELEUSIAN CHORUS
And so, O soul, love the Ideal without measure!

VOICE OF PLATO
Love with unequalled love, and be consumed in the flames of that love! There, where is the Unbegotten, there alone is true beauty, immortality and rhythmic harmony! Know yourself, and with this knowledge arise upon a butterfly's wings, which shall carry you home — and your home, your family hearth, is the bosom of God, teeming with crowds of people — Eternal Ideas!

ELEUSIAN CHORUS
And yet although you bring us faith and hope, why do we remain sad?

VOICE OF PLATO
For you do not yet possess love!

ELEUSIAN CHORUS
Why must we begin to muse upon our nearing end? Like a statue crafted of ivory and gold by Phidias, our Greece shall be shattered — its fragments to lie among the ash and the dust!

HIEROPHANT
Your end-goal, O soul, is not to be found upon the earth!

ELEUSIAN CHORUS
And yet we regret, we so regret the loss of our Hellenic fatherland! And visible temples, and melodious games, and dreamt-of gods, dreamt up so wonderfully!

VOICE OF PLATO
Behold and love, and separate, to love anew and separate once more; such is the temporal trial of souls, until they love the eternal, eternally.

ELEUSIAN CHORUS
Shall no one appear to save us? Shall we never behold with mortal eyes the love we are lacking? Will we meet with such love only upon the fields of Heaven?

CHORUS AFAR
Be of good cheer, poor ones! The Well-Desired One approaches you now, upon the waves of the ages!

YOUTH
And now what? The same waters, but another shore — Other hills, and many caverns among them... No trace of people anywhere... Tall cedars, and here below, dates with their long fronds. Above the dusty hilltops a summit smoulders purple and gold. The sun must be sinking into the sea from that side. Aligier, what hermits are those, ascending by those paths? All of them, all of them, tending toward that summit!

ALIGIER
They are the first Carmelites. How many times have they greeted the sun, and bade it farewell, from those heights! How many times have they raised their voices in psalmodic prayer to the Lord, sensing the Lord — their robes of such thin linen, their harps so light — just as you see!

YOUTH
You speak as if you had been on these hills before.

ALIGIER
And now the world knows nothing of the Essenes! Of them, who watched long in anticipation of the victory of the soul over the might of the senses! You ask who they are! The prophets are always quickly forgotten; only the perfected Act is remembered!

CHORUS OF ESSENES
Father unknown! From the petty regard[2] of the world, which perishes from pride, we escape to Thee!

---

2   *Obliczność;* perhaps derived from *oblicze,* or "countenance," hence, something surface-oriented, trifling.

For Thy Spirit hovers over the watery abyss, and where the desert is still, there dost Thou speak!

With water from pure springs we wash the stain of sin from our brows. There are neither rich nor poor among us; we are all equals here, all brothers, all of us, Thy sons!

Have mercy! Like to these shores wrapped in darkness, our nation, and all other peoples, have grown pale, livid with filth and mire!

Send down pure thought upon them! May an inner fire consume and destroy all flesh, tossing it aside, like a handful of ashes! And He, once beheld by Thy prophets, Thy Christos, O, let Him descend!

YOUTH
They kneel… and their harps send up one loud massed cry, together, to the skies!

ALIGIER
Kneel down as well! And watch —

YOUTH
I can see nothing else… Even their spectral forms have melted into the night. And the sound of their harp strings, it fades as well.

ALIGIER
On your knees, I say!

YOUTH
Now I can see nothing at all — I can only feel your hand upon my shoulder. Why do you press me down so crushingly? Do you kneel as well?

ALIGIER
As I shall in that hour, which nears once again.

YOUTH
How can that be —?

ALIGIER
Ask not — just watch! Well, what do you see?

YOUTH
Ah — the hem of a garment, vanishing somewhere aloft, into that limitless light! Ah! Two feet, snowy-white, like doves, ascending into Heaven!

ALIGIER
And now look down below.

YOUTH
I cannot — My eyes have ascended into the aether, following that garment of azure — I have no eyes — Rest your palm upon my eyelids!

ALIGIER
Can you not see that tomb?

YOUTH
Thank you! I strained my sight so… O! Such beautiful, gorgeous angels there at the tomb!

ALIGIER
And there behind them, that woman redeemed from sin by love; that yearning, watchful, sister of sisters who first beheld His face after death!

YOUTH
I see flowers — lilies perhaps, or lilies of the valley — in her hand. She slips away, like a sigh!

CHORUS OF VOICES ALOFT
Flowing, endless time is parted. To the one side are days past, to the other, all days yet to come, and between them the incarnate Word, the visible Lord, a pillar of eternal brightness!

Sion, you hypocrite! Orgiastic Greece and oppressive Rome, where are you now? In vain you sought to restrain the tribes of humanity, in vain you would corrupt them, kill them! They have not perished! The Son of Man died, and the Son of God rose from the dead!

From this time hence no people who become a nation, who become a spirit, shall rot in the tomb! Hosannah, hosannah!

CHORUS AFAR
By soul and body, by spirit a Trinity, and one revealed God! Once the soul of but one tribe, He has become the body of one Church! — He shall be a spirit over Humanity united in one! Hosannah, hosannah!

YOUTH
Now the tomb of Christ fades away; the wonderful angelic forms are dispersed by the wind!

ALIGIER
Take my hand so you will not be tripped up in the darkness.

YOUTH
Ah, where is that garment of white fire? Where those feet? It is again so dark!

ALIGIER
The vault becomes lower here — bend low your head!

YOUTH
Where are we going?

ALIGIER
Into the Christian world! Into the second half of history. Toward the other trials that await Humanity!

VOICES ALOFT
Day and night we build the church upon the rock of Peter!

OTHER VOICES
Ages like days — for seven days they were building it, and on the eighth, it ruled the world.

OTHERS
For the living Word — Wisdom and Love — dwelt within it. The Holy Ghost resided therein!

YOUTH
Where are those flying voices?

ALIGIER
They fly before us to where we are tending. Now you may stand again. Here there is space to spare.

YOUTH
I seem to hear the rustle of many feet gathering somewhere, somewhere afar, directly before us.

ALIGIER
Your ears do not deceive you.

YOUTH
If only there were some light!

ALIGIER
Ten more paces — count them — and stop!

CHORUS AFAR
Like providential counsel from thousands of pendulous thoughts, like a great manly Act from many youthful desires — thus from the confusion of oppressions and persecutions, from the chaos of dreams and doubts and heresies, the might of Peter was raised on high. He, the first, the eldest servant of the servants of Christ on earth!

    At his feet lay the crowns and foreheads of kings — In the cradle of his palm infant nations were rocked!

    And he grows in body, treading over flesh!

    And it has come to pass!

    He has clothed himself in scarlet — He has become a magnate — He has become Roman. And now do the nations begin to grumble against him. So, give ear and watch, you who would know the Present and would behold the Future from its summits!

YOUTH
What a sight! So fearsome, Aligier!

ALIGIER
Thus, and not otherwise, appeared the plains of Provence during the days of the Albigenses!

YOUTH
Such a murder of ravens in the blue sky! And so many corpses among the olive trees — so many! And further on, charred pyres and skulls, and the last wisps of smoke!

ALIGIER
Soon you shall behold the living.

YOUTH
Is that a candle I see glowing suddenly in the depths of that cavern?

ALIGIER
The heretics often came forth from there, in file, from the bowels of the earth to greet the light of day.

YOUTH
What dry, gloomy faces… Cowls… Habits… Each with sword and dagger — Horrid!

ALIGIER
You behold their persecuted rites. They would stand in a semi-circle, confess to one another, while they placed their hands upon each other and invoked the Spirit in silence.

YOUTH
But how funereal — it is as if it were the last time they should do so.

VOICE OF A KNIGHT
I hasten from the great massacre — My horse is about to fall, and I after him! — The Romans surrounded us… Before the day ends, your end will come. Brothers, farewell, till we meet again — somewhere!

VOICE OF A WOMAN
The child at my breast — and my own bosom — were pierced through with a Catholic arrow. I cannot crawl any closer, brothers… Farewell, till we meet again, somewhere!

OLD MAN'S VOICE
My four sons were burned at the stake yesterday. The Spirit be with them, the Spirit be with you! I have walked here all through the night — and now I sit down, to die. Until we meet again, somewhere!

SEVERAL VOICES
When shall the promised Paraclete come?

CHORUS OF ALBIGENSES
Today, for us, for today we die! But, for the world? Only the Father in Heaven and the Son know that!

SEVERAL VOICES
And so we shall see no tomorrow here on earth?

CHORUS OF ALBIGENSES
We shall see fetters in dungeons, and axes on scaffoldings. Such is our tomorrow. We depart, leaving the perverted words of Christ to Rome — and Rome has united itself with the violence of the cruel worldly, and will oppress as the worldly do, until it shall be oppressed in turn!

SEVERAL VOICES
Christ made equals of servant and lord, man and woman, and the Church stones us for wishing to be free and equal!

CHORUS OF ALBIGENSES
The unfinished cup of life slips from our hands — Other lips will draw near its rim. O Knights Templar! Into your hands we entrust it! Accept it from ours. It is you who will cast down unrighteousness and violence — It is you who will greet the advent of the Spirit!

SEVERAL VOICES
Why hast Thou abandoned us, O Lord? For we are thy true sons, and Thou dost give victory to Thy stepchildren!

CHORUS AFAR
On earth he is an orphan, and no son of the Lord, who demands with impatience, for he knows not the Wisdom existing before all ages.
　　But truly they are but stepchildren of the Lord, who respond to impatient sighs with slaughter, for such do not know the Love existing before all ages.

YOUTH
Such moans! Moans thousand-fold! From all sides, riders rush in with lances — They trample and cut the people down like staves of wheat! Why do you restrain me, Aligier? We must aid them — help them! Upon the riders' princely helmets, their ducal coronets — the Cross — sweet Jesus! Thy Cross! Jesus and Mary! Everywhere the Cross, and everywhere beneath it — blood! A ring of flame has set the plain afire… It tightens, moves in tighter… My eyes are smarting from the smoke, and now I can see nothing more than this curtain of smoke, but behind it, I hear the gnashing of teeth, and cries — Psalms here and there, and O, that scream!

ALIGIER
That was, but is no longer.

YOUTH
What? Where? Some force magnetic has wrapped me round and oppresses me… My thoughts begin to flag, to rot… everything I see is like it were real — a lifelike life; a real death!

ALIGIER
O man! Can you not even bear to gaze upon a mere likeness of the reality that once swept away your brethren? — That is an ideal blood, and yet you pale!

YOUTH
For it is the blood of others, not my own!

ALIGIER
Turn towards me — The Provençal plain is no more. Look! A prison merely, and a few grave lamps, and the Grand Master sentenced… and his brothers who will follow him to the stake!

YOUTH
How many times, as I child, did I dream of that red cross on those white tunics! And I loved the order condemned, because it had been condemned!

ALIGIER
And now give ear to the words the old man pronounced on the eve of his death… That grey form of his will repeat them now!

VOICE OF GRAND MASTER
Knights Templar! Sons and brothers! the idea, was it not a holy one, from which a sacred act was to result? From sea to sea, from the east to the west, one Republic, the Kingdom of God upon the earth! As I bear witness to you, do you the same for me in these final hours!

    It was not unto error that I led you, after all, and although you will all perish, I did not deceive you! For were we not there, did we not live there, where Our Lord was born? Did we not hear His voice in the breezes blowing through Mount Olivet?

CHORUS OF KNIGHTS TEMPLAR
And in the moonlit night, passing near Golgotha, we saw His figure!

VOICE OF GRAND MASTER
Not crucified!

CHORUS OF KNIGHTS TEMPLAR
With stars in His hands, with stars at His feet, floating in the air!

VOICE OF GRAND MASTER
And though He did not speak to us with human speech, we heard Him — we perceived His thought! And since then we have known it is not so much one man, or one nation, or several nations, but all together which form the Church universal!

CHORUS OF KNIGHTS TEMPLAR
This we know, and bear witness to. There must be one fold, Humanity; one Shepherd, God enthroned.

VOICE OF GRAND MASTER
And today? What have we? Pope and king, king and pope, like two swords plunged painfully into one heart, the heart of the world! Everything, which should be united, is torn asunder. Heaven is cut off from the misfortunate as an escape beyond the grave, and present time is made miserable for the living — Heaven and earth blocked off, for ages! There is the Lord's will, here: the will of popes and kings!

CHORUS OF KNIGHTS TEMPLAR
And on earth as it is in Heaven — there should be but one will, one!

VOICE OF GRAND MASTER
Amen! But we shall not see its triumph; we have only enough time to submit and crumble into ash — and become immortal! O, such a shame, a shame for the ages! And everything had been made ready: all of Europe was trembling with yearning and hope! Brothers! Into the hands of the knights who shall remain upon the earth, but who will no longer be known by our name — into the hands of our faithful brethren, the Rosicrucians, let us pass the unfinished cup of life!

CHORUS OF KNIGHTS TEMPLAR
Into their hands, we entrust it!

VOICE OF GRAND MASTER
Amen! *Gloria Deo in excelsis!*

CHORUS OF KNIGHTS TEMPLAR
May they liberate all flesh… May ashes spark to life for them… May all metal ores become golden at their touch… May they reconcile the world, the inner with the outer, by the might of Miracle; May the Spirit be a Comforter, to them, and to all upon the earth!

VOICE OF GRAND MASTER
Amen!

ALIGIER
Night has engulfed them; time has swallowed them... Onward, with our chase after time, Henryk. Follow me. Onward, onward!

YOUTH
The pain of all transformations, the sorrow of all deaths, fall upon us this night!

ALIGIER
He who has not died all the deaths of Humanity shall not resurrect with all of Humanity's dawns. He who has not equalled the sufferings of mankind with his own, nor matched her endurance with his own patience, will not see the Banquet prepared for her from all eternity! When I say come, come!

CHORUS OF VOICES ALOFT
Above the ages we fly, we watch, we cry! — Woe, woe! The Word of God is in ruins! The Church is petrified, a rock, and the sea of the human spirit beats against it with one million waves, crashing, ebbing, and roaring beside it — The rock is here, the waves, there!

Woe, woe! The edifice of Europe is shaken! It has neither grown into cathedral nor imperial palace! Half priestly and half worldly, it neither stretches unto heaven nor is it set firmly in the depths of the earth! It will fall, and — such violence! Such pain and scission, such sadness and war!

Woe! Woe! Whether king or priest, or collective — all are in their triumph cruel! They struggle amongst themselves; they trample one another; there is ever less Christ in the world, ever less living spirit!

CHORUS AFAR
The child leaves his parents' home when the years of young manhood begin to seethe within him; only later will he return, as a stately man. It is the same with Humanity — and her home is God!

YOUTH
Can we not stop here? For the light now grows, only to show us someone else's death, surely!

ALIGIER
Why must you sadden me so?

YOUTH
The spirit is willing, but the flesh is weak!

ALIGIER
He alone is a spirit, my Henryk, who is able to conform both soul and body to his own will as he slips a soft glove upon his hand!

YOUTH
And yet more spectres stand before my eyes — I know not which, those of the body, or those of the soul… I seem to see, and yet I see not!

ALIGIER
You see, I assure you.

YOUTH
I greet you, round hats and black capes, from beneath which the swords flash! I greet you, forges and bellows, crucibles and hammers! It is you, sons of the Knights Templar, alchemists and sorcerers, who fretted the earth until the toppling of the throne of the Stuarts!

CHORUS OF ROSICRUCIANS
The flesh, if not of God — and it is — must therefore be God; and if of God, then it must be divine — and as a creation of the Lord, it lives for and sighs after the Lord! Peace to all flesh, so long cursed and oppressed. It wishes to rise, to shine as gold, to blossom as the alchemical rose!

Freedom and inspiration — such are our laws! Nature is our living, lovely sister! As Christ has redeemed us, so shall we redeem and ennoble her in our love. Peace to her and to all flesh!

CHORUS OF MASTERS
It's not yet time! Not yet!

CHORUS OF ROSICRUCIANS
And we are aged now, consumed with labour!

CHORUS OF MASTERS
First the yoke, wherever it oppresses, must be shattered! That of the soul burdening the body, or that of the body burdening the soul, in the Church, in the state, in Humanity!

CHORUS OF ROSICRUCIANS
And so it has been in vain that we trusted you — all of our flames are snuffed at once. No gold among the slag and cinders — mere ash floats off through the air, and we, as they, are dispersed! O masters, you have lied to us!

CHORUS OF MASTERS
It was sacred truth we spoke unto you!

CHORUS OF ROSICRUCIANS
For has not Mercury united sun and moon together in the house of eternity? Where is the philosopher's stone? Where, the spirits of the dead recalled among the living?

CHORUS OF MASTERS
Until the Kingdom of God reigns upon the earth, until the Spirit descends, there shall be no miracle! Prepare then the way of the Spirit, strive after righteousness upon the earth! Transform the social order! Unsheathe your swords and sharpen your daggers!

CHORUS OF ROSICRUCIANS
Oh, woe is us — we shall perish without having witnessed the consummation! Nor bloom nor gold are for us, not for us! Just like our ancestors, those great ones, tormented ones, those from whom we descend, we shall not drain the cup of life to the lees!

CHORUS OF MASTERS
Others shall take your places if you be of such little faith and palsied arm. Now is the time to spill blood — one's own, and those of others; now is the time to pulverise governments and strike the heads of kings from off the necks of the peoples of Europe. Now is the time to tear the body of the church with new pains, that she may know thereby that she lives, and awaken! A new age! A new task! So, onward!

YOUTH
O poor, pale shades! They unsheathe their swords, and these tumble from their grip. They bend down, they fall upon the earth, and with their hands they embrace their masters' feet. O! Nothing can aid a person when his hour has passed!

CHORUS OF MASTERS
You see yourselves that nothing remains of you but dust, sifting dust! Be not stubborn, do not hesitate. Say of your own will the words that spill the strength of the mysteries from the past to the future!

CHORUS OF ROSICRUCIANS
Into whose hands must we entrust the cup of life?

CHORUS OF MASTERS
Into the hands of your brothers the Masons!

CHORUS OF ROSICRUCIANS
Amen! And may they hasten the Kingdom by a thousand years — May faith and hope not desert their hearts in disappointment, as they have ours!

YOUTH
What a horrid death!

ALIGIER
Doubt and death are the harshest proving grounds of spirits — The last, by which death itself shall be vanquished. If not for their death, their merit would be lessened by a heaven entire! And without merit, without labour, how might one become oneself? How might one become immortal?

YOUTH
The masters have departed, and they lie there outstretched, their flames snuffed out above their bodies. Somewhere, I recall, I have seen Carthusians stretched out upon the floor of a great church…

ALIGIER
Peace to the departed! Let us follow the masters; turn not around — there is nothing but darkness behind!

YOUTH
I sorrow for the dead!

ALIGIER
You child! If you wish to find again the dead you've left behind you, never turn round, of course — look ahead! Look in front of you! They are there, trans-born,[3] alive upon the meadows of the future!

CHORUS OF VOICES ALOFT
Above the ages we fly, we watch, we cry!
 The Soul of the world is torn asunder, the Church is split, and everywhere, in Rome and in Augsburg, the Soul has done obeisance to the Flesh! The Church has bowed before the King!
 And the Body of the World does not, in one Spirit, mingle with the Soul — It has grown haughty. It wishes to live alone, of itself — It has sprouted one hundred heads, and wears a hundred crowns — Here a king, and there! Everywhere! And the name of Europe is… the King!
 Their thrones are firmly set upon the skulls axed from the necks of heroes! And each of these earthly deities has forgotten about the God in Heaven; that He is Omnipresent, and that Humanity is His daughter, the nations His sons, and that the sons must go on, searching for their mother, until they find her, and rest at her feet in joy!
 O nations! O you lights upon the earth! You grow dim and flicker to dark! From your petty remains empires will be moulded, corpses animated by the Galvanic spark of Government! And everywhere, Violence! Everywhere Force! — And everywhere, Rebellion!

CHORUS AFAR
Behold and consider! From the time of the Cross, upon which the Lord expired, there has been no more hellish a crime and no more ardent torture on this entire planet! There, God was murdered in man; here, Humanity is murdered in the Nation. But have faith — immeasurable

---

3 Another coining: *przerodzeni*.

Crime must be redeemed by immeasurable Good! From limitless torment, Life must arise whole; limitless Life in all!

YOUTH
O God, O God! From all directions — above, below, from all sides — lamps burst forth and are hung upon the walls; and everywhere: black fabric, drapes, silver eagles, everywhere, and a turmoil of crimson standards, transparent palls, fluttering in the air. Whose funeral might this be? That of everyone upon the earth?

ALIGIER
Indeed — the funeral of mankind!

YOUTH
The earth parts, and a catafalque rises from the depths. How high, how large it is, and a body is shrouded upon it!

ALIGIER
Those three, slowly ascending the steps of the catafalque, will tear away the shroud, and you shall see!

YOUTH
They seem like three dwarves in comparison to that gigantic figure — What is it they have in their hands?

ALIGIER
Sceptres — But topped not with crosses, but bayonets!

YOUTH
And on their heads, large pearls and coral beads?

ALIGIER
Yes, the congealed tears and blood of the people.

YOUTH
They've reached the top…

ALIGIER
They take away the shroud — behold!

YOUTH
An archangel, dressed in the white dalmatic of his own wings, stretching from his shoulders to his feet. A dead archangel — O God! His wings are pinned upon his breast with the hilts of three swords, plunged like three crosses into his bosom!

ALIGIER
And the Name above him, written in shining blood upon the air!

YOUTH
Ah! I'd like to touch that bloody rainbow with my lips! I must kiss something — I must — if but the ground before that Name!

ALIGIER
Stand up!

YOUTH
No, I wish to lie here, crosswise — for that is my Archangel, mine! And I know that he is not dead! Corpses do not shed such light around them. He is only sleeping! Through him God speaks to me, and will speak. I am of him — I am a portion of that Divine beauty! That holiness, that righteousness and that pain! This is my father and my mother — my everything! Why will you not allow me to rest in the dust? Don't pull me up like that!

CHORUS OF DWARVES
Replace the shroud! Replace it, replace it — he breathes! And as long as he breathes, there will be no order, no peace; we shall not harvest our grain nor fall asleep upon sheaves of human corpses!

YOUTH
You shall not sleep, not for a moment, neither here on earth, nor in the grave! You shall be immortal in disquiet and shame, as others are in joy and glory!

ALIGIER
Do you see how they tremble and quake?

YOUTH
And again they have covered my treasure, my omni-beautiful form!

ALIGIER
You have arisen, and now they wallow prone in the dust!

CHORUS OF DWARVES
When, O when will the heart in that bosom cease its beating, pierced by those three blades? Again and again we hammer at the sword-hilts with our sceptres, and still the heart pushes them back; and those wings — immaculate, however much blood we splash against them! What can this mean? Can it be true that someone's Spirit, and not blind Fate, rules this world?

CHORUS OF SUBTERRANEAN VOICES
Not true! Not true! Don't believe it! Don't even dream it! There is only the sentient flesh, and coincidental Hap, and Chaos. The thought of God is merely a fever of the flesh, while fleshly wisdom is calculation, order, power over the earth. From the death of many results the life of the few. And those few who live know how to kill! To kill is to harness chaos!

CHORUS OF DWARVES
Once more, peace enters our bosom.

CHORUS OF VOICES ALOFT
O Light of Heaven! O most transparent, most pure! Flow in from all hands, and like burly waves, bear him, O bear him hence, who sleeps for the time being!

YOUTH
Let me attach myself to those shades — let this flood of light bear me away as well, along with my Saint! Ah, Aligier, let me go!

CHORUS AFAR
From the day of the righteous one's death, the European world will never rest, until it too becomes righteous! Like a man who has had his heart torn from his breast, so shall all the nations be, without this nation! They live, yet are always lacking life! They are and are not, for they cannot be according to the intentions of God! And every people shall be in despair, and every king shall quake in terror! And the earth shall tremble beneath their feet, and they shall stumble over her, drunk with pangs of conscience!

YOUTH
And those three — where are they now?

ALIGIER
They were not borne away by the light; the darkness must have swallowed them somewhere!

YOUTH
Why did no bolt shatter them from above?

ALIGIER
Had they perished at once, they would not have been undermined by their own work, and this would have remained on earth after them, like an inheritance. The evil ones must become suicides by their own Evil! It is for this reason that the Lord lengthens their days, mocking them, merciful to us!

But now others approach. Can you hear those savage shrieks? Others, hateful to them yet awakened by them and equal to them, for the light which enlightens all, Christ, has also been extinguished in their souls — Look!

YOUTH
What great numbers! And how diverse the robes!

ALIGIER
Those first, who raise their swords aloft toward the steel vault, are pledges and apprentices. Then the master masons — can you see? — come after, bearing Bible, square and compass.

YOUTH
And those in priestly robes?

ALIGIER
They belong to the degree of the Chosen.

YOUTH
And those with the skull and bones, and the cross on their breast?

ALIGIER
Scottish cavaliers.

YOUTH
And those others, those few, the last, in their capes that seem to drip with blood?

ALIGIER
The highest illuminati masters; and their name: the Reborn.

CHORUS OF ALL MASONS
Mak benak! The flesh falls from the bone. *Mak benak!* Victory, or death! *Mak benak!* Freedom and equality!

CHORUS OF THE REBORN
The hour foretold approaches. Terror grips the globe entire. The frayed and rotting veil of the temple tears in two. Will you vow to be loyal to us, unto death?

ALL OTHER CHORUSES
We swore, we swear, we shall swear.

CHORUS OF THE REBORN
Today what's needed is hatred! The labour of hatred is the destruction of the hated! Will you destroy them without mercy?

OTHER CHORUSES
We shall.

CHORUS OF THE REBORN
Whole ages were spent dreaming of the soul, and nothing was effected. Let us begin with the body, crushed under endless oppression!

OTHER CHORUSES
From all flesh we shall lift the yoke!

CHORUS OF THE REBORN
What may be in Heaven, of this we know nothing. What is upon the earth we see, we feel, we suffer — It devours us and we become desiccate! So that the instruction of Christ might be realised, let us care less for those who bear the sign of Christ. They are liars, cheats! These we must topple, destroy, and moral respectability will become incarnate, not in the mouths of the few, but in the reason of all!

CHORUS OF THE CHOSEN
Reason is promised Humanity, Reason its only King!

CHORUS OF THE REBORN
So now defile before us! We shall direct you, and you — the fates of the peoples. Who is with us, belongs to us, and we shall treat him philanthropically! Who is against us is no man at all; he shall be to us as a beast, to be hobbled and bound, to be led and to be whipped, at last to be slaughtered, if such be required!

Now is the time of struggle. Now must the heart have no soft tissue! Thrones are but planks and glue, altars merely lime and rubble!

CHORUS OF ALL MASONS
Mak benak! Only the skeleton will remain of the old European society, and we shall clothe it with new meat, new skin. We shall build upon the ruins…

CHORUS OF THE REBORN
Of this, keep silent! Of this, only we are to know! In order for Solomon's church to stand, the old edifices must be toppled!

CHORUS OF MASONS
We shall tear them down! Topple them! Onward, onward!

ALIGIER
Let us follow them.

YOUTH
We must be near our own day and age![4]

ALIGIER
Ah, there at the far end, in the mists, where those rows of lamps are swaying, our own days flutter. But we are still divided from them by a flood of catastrophes, and one gigantic spirit!

YOUTH
Must we pass through that sea of blood and tears as well?

ALIGIER
We shall not enter it, not with mind nor heart nor footstep. But with our eyes we must — Do not recoil!

YOUTH
But if my eyes are not mistaken — Guillotines? As the marchers move on, more and more of them arise — a whole street of guillotines! And how long… how long… Now they set them all in motion, here, there, here again, and there once more, and everywhere the blades flash and fall! And beneath each flashing bolt a head is lopped! How many blades! How many severed heads! How can we pass through them?

ALIGIER
Lean on me.

YOUTH
And they — They move on, singing!

---

4   The original reads *Wszak już blisko nam do nas samych!* which could be literally translated as: "We are close now to our very selves." And this might be understood as the poet's criticism of his own society.

ALIGIER
Do you remember? When the soul is disgusted with the body, she escapes to the Thebaid, retiring from the society of man to weep over herself and to wither. But now behold what the body becomes, when it tears itself away from the soul! It grows frenzied, it murders! Here and there full love is lacking. There — suicides, here — murder, massacre!

YOUTH
I prefer suicides to murderers!

ALIGIER
Esteem rather the spirits of the living. For the hour of flesh and the hour of souls is passing, and the hour of the Spirit sounds! Those where but a prologue, the minutes leading up to this!

YOUTH
Command — or earnestly request — that these heads cease rolling here to my feet... Although each fades like a dream, I am sick, so sick at heart, Aligier!

ALIGIER
We must move on; we must proceed through this kingdom of rebellious flesh — If you do not pass through, I cannot save you. Ah! The foundations of the world tremble! Ages of suffering have swelled and swelled, slowly and silently, until at last the volcano has erupted! This happened once before — it had to — but, O Lord God, O Spirit supreme amongst all spirits, another such bestial day, another such crime, will surely not reoccur?

YOUTH
I am sick, I am sick — What disgusting maggots! What a range[5] of gloomy hangmen! And each stands by his own workbench! And those gory baskets, all of them full — and those grey torsos — and the pied clowns of the people, rollicking alongside with axe and spear and sword! And that column of marchers, always the same, singing,

---

5   The Polish word is *rząd*, which means "government" as well as "rank, file."

festive! They go on and on, tossing flowers amidst the mobs and corpses!

ALIGIER
Collect your thoughts — Note the expression on all their faces!

YOUTH
Terror seethes on their foreheads! Terror makes their hair stand on end! Terror spurts from their veins! Everywhere, Terror, an overpowering Terror, nothing more! O, shame eternal to you, who feared murder or death more than Terror! Only the blades neither tremble nor grow pale! They rise and they fall, ever the same! Ah, how red, blood-bathed, dripping and splattering — O my God! O my God!

CHORUS OF VOICES ALOFT
Woe unto these times! In the name of God, the kings once quartered one of the sacred thoughts of God, the Nation among Humanity! And now, in the name of Man, the people cut the throats of king and priest, and of all human authority! O woe, woe!

YOUTH
I thank you, airy spirits! Now I can walk down that street of scaffolds without falling. I have lost people closer to me than these — fathers and brothers; I have lost spirits that I loved! What have I to do with these? With my Archangel in the grave!

CHORUS OF MASONS
O Reborn ones! O supreme masters! There is nowhere now for us to go, no one left to kill! The workers' arms flag in exhaustion from the bloody work, and each of them now lies down upon his scaffold. Can you hear the heavy snoring of the hangmen above the whispering streams of blood?

CHORUS OF THE REBORN
Onward, onward!

CHORUS OF MASONS
But where? We know not. Two last guillotines stand here, but beyond them, there is only darkness.

CHORUS OF THE REBORN
Onward, ever onward!

CHORUS OF MASONS
But neither the lot of the flesh, nor that of the soul, has been bettered — Everywhere is waste and sadness, and the red mist arising from human blood gathers gloomily around us — we are blinded!

CHORUS OF THE REBORN
Can you not see a small path anywhere open before you? Is there not the slightest lamp flickering before you?

CHORUS OF MASONS
We see nothing — It is ever more dark around us, and in us as well!

CHORUS OF THE REBORN
Awaken the sleepers! Awaken the workers!

CHORUS OF MASONS
No one wakes; the headless dead lie about like so much timber and rock — and the living are in the same lethargy. How shall we begin? What? Behind us is death, deaf and dumb, and before us, Something yet unborn, something like Nothingness! Where have you driven us? Where are we? What are we? Where is God? Where is the earth, the heavens? Is everything but a dream, full of anger and pain?

CHORUS OF THE REBORN
Stop mewling like infants! Don't lie down in the shade of the gallows, stretched out along the cobblestones! Up, up on your feet! A few minutes more!

CHORUS OF MASONS
Mak benak! Our own flesh begins to drop from our bones! *Mak benak!* We too would rest — rest our heads, at least, upon these severed polls,

and lie down in a row along with the corpses, and sleep! And you, be damned! For you are able to scatter death around just like God, but unlike Him, you know not how to bring back to life, or to create! Be damned, be cursed, you impotent ones!

CHORUS OF VOICES ALOFT
And thus the Lord is merciful. Arise, all thoughts of the dead! All dreams of the slumbering, gather together! All yearnings of this generation, you immature ones, interrupted; you who desired, but were incapable, tear yourselves away and hover above this sea of blood!

YOUTH
Is the Last Judgement about to begin? Is my vision of Ezekiel returning?

CHORUS OF VOICES ALOFT
Hover, and mingle! Mark one another — interpenetrate — until you have become one Soul, one Will, one Act!

YOUTH
Something begins to flash from the heads, the breasts, the bodies of all; it flashes aloft and circles in the air, now glowing, now growing dim. Like birds of the night, a flock of these flashes flies in the air — I hear the rustle of wings, but cannot see any!

ALIGIER
Yes, upon the earth, the hearts of all who vanished now come alive and pour one into another. This is the first Resurrection! The second shall only be on the last day of Mankind, when each shall say of himself "This — am I!"

YOUTH
Where are the guillotines? Where, the scarlet puddles? Where is that entire people that lay there, strewn about below? Everything has evaporated into the air, like moisture after a summer cloudburst. Aloft, everything, like airy sparks! Embers, exhalations, hurricanes! Like snaky, electric currents! Where have we come? What sort of aethereal world is this?

ALIGIER
Can you not see what is happening? How one radiant form is taking shape, one power, from these elements?

YOUTH
Something like that — something like that!

ALIGIER
It's ever more clear. Do you not recognise that figure?

YOUTH
Against the background of that chaos, he alone, alone! So whole, so bright! With a living baldachin of golden eagles' wings outspread above his head! With a smile of benevolence upon his lips, while lightning, it seems, plays about his temples! An Emperor... It's Napoléon!

ALIGIER
It is the soul of Napoléon on the plains of human history. One soul, which yet contains whole ages — An idea formed of millions of thoughts, trembling, incarnate! And now the Lord says to him, "Onward!" And nothing, no one, can restrain him! That soul goes on, and finds his road among the darknesses!

CHOIR OF VOICES ALOFT
Who can equal him, of those who have passed away? Everything that ever existed scattered and divided, is given to him to unite in marvellous manner! Both the flesh of ancient demi-gods, unfatigued, sleepless, beautiful, and the Christian soul, of plumbless depth, tender and yearning, and the spirit creative, the magnetic master of time and space!

All the fates of humanity are gathered together in him: all trial and triumph, might and catastrophe, rejoicing and misfortune! Just as God created the world from nothing, so shall he appear among people, from nowhere, and arise! He shall be a hero like Alexander the Greek, an emperor like the Roman Caesar, and a martyr like a saint of the first springtimes of Christianity. He shall die, like Moses, alone, face to face with the Lord; he shall die prophesying the Lord's will to the future days of the tribe of man!

YOUTH
The eagles have gathered with loud, flaming wings and wheel about him in a fiery pillar. They burn and they wheel… He stretches up his hand from out of this whirl and, snatched up, flies. The sword in his hand is like a flame; it lights up the vacuum — the sky turns blue, again, down below, the human forms take shape, grow, gather — and the horizon before him spreads ever wider, endless!

ALIGIER
Not before him, for he must be dispersed, but before those crowds that he shepherds for a moment!

YOUTH
What voice of organs do I hear?

ALIGIER
You hear the thunders of his battles, transformed into harmony recalled!

YOUTH
And what are those black swarms, or layers, unmoving?

ALIGIER
Can you see — the closer the figure approaches them, the more they shine and begin to move!

YOUTH
True, like living shallows — and cries ascend from them, flashes of steel flare forth from them — thousands of arms; I see thousands of men arising!

ALIGIER
Had the nations not fallen asleep? Were they not covered over, like worms, those Divine thoughts in Europe?

YOUTH
From aloft, it is as if he magnetised them with his arms, in passing — some go along with him, others rise up against him!

ALIGIER
And of them all, both of these and of those, he is the Resurrection! From now on, neither kings nor peoples wield power, but Nationality and Humanity, and these in the name of the Lord!

YOUTH
Look, look — He pales now, though he flies on farther; he too pales, and now he stoops to descend! Let us run after him!

ALIGIER
We shall not catch up with that figure! Its time has run through. Eternity summons him!

YOUTH
The wheeling eagles stoop; he remains alone now, like a naked sun, setting lower, ever lower! The booms and murmurs grow silent. Again the horizon is dark. Night has fallen, and silence reigns — what now?

ALIGIER
Us! For now our hour strikes! Listen to but one more strophe as it runs its course…

CHORUS OF SUBTERRANEAN VOICES
Peek out from the bowels of the earth, you who took refuge among us, when the Titan thrashed you about like rubbish over the harvest fields of Europe! It is time for you to return to your old occupations. Hasten back, O hasten!

ALIGIER
Just watch — See what three forms are riding on those horses, all clad in phoney purple and tinsel!

YOUTH
They wear tall crowns, and have long sceptres wound about with olive branches. Their cloaks hang down past their stirrups — They drag upon the ground!

ALIGIER
They draw close — sink your eyes into them.

YOUTH
The same three, only swollen now, taller, longer — but still disgusting dwarves!

CHORUS OF SUBTERRANEAN VOICES
No longer through open violence, but rather, by hidden rapine, unending… Continue your labours! Announce a sacred peace! Unite in a Holy Alliance! And everything appertaining to you, call it sacred! Holy, holy, holy!

CHORUS OF VOICES ALOFT
Hearken to the truth, and perhaps you may still grow unto a man's stature! You go on to a grand council, be just, be righteous!

CHORUS OF SUBTERRANEAN VOICES
Varnish all injustice with the veneer of righteousness!

CHORUS OF VOICES ALOFT
If it was your desire to kill That, which is Immortal, confess your guilt. Raise not your arm to deliver a coup-de-grâce, but to return the stricken to life!

CHORUS OF SUBTERRANEAN VOICES
Go along with the pretense of raising the dead, pretend to regret murder!

CHORUS OF VOICES ALOFT
As Christ has commanded, be the first servants of the nations, and you will not fall into contempt!

CHORUS OF SUBTERRANEAN VOICES
Fatten people like cattle, and they shall shoulder your yokes of their own will!

CHORUS OF VOICES ALOFT
Become the architects of God's Will upon this earth; in all societal structures, make visible faith, hope, and love!

CHORUS OF SUBTERRANEAN VOICES
Diplomacy, police, and militias!

YOUTH
They've halted their horses; they take one another by the hand, and hearken!

ALIGIER
They make a vow to each other!

YOUTH
But in such whispers that their words cannot be heard.

ALIGIER
If their words were noble and reasonable and virtuous, they would pronounce those vows aloud!

CHORUS OF SUBTERRANEAN VOICES
O, yes! Good! And now go on — race like poisoned arrows! Onward, onward!

CHORUS OF VOICES ALOFT
In vain! No word of warning will untangle the knot of vipers that binds their hands together in that unbreakable vow — but as they are united in their vow, so shall they perish together!

YOUTH
Perish? When? For so long now archangelic blood has cried out against them, for vengeance! In vain you press me to your bosom, Aligier — I am oppressed with icy shivers. Ah! no further images present themselves — nothing — nothing more — nothing but this gigantic dungeon, so similar to an endless tomb. Heroes, prophets, saints have all passed by, and perished! Only dwarves endure — remain — live! O, Aligier! Such is the consummation of so many inspirations, so many

ages? And this is neither nightmare nor illusion. Just as it is here, in these depths, so it is there, on the plains of earth above — dead, dark, vile! Pettiness and ire fill the seventh day of Mankind! Such a rest has been given us!

ALIGIER
Do not blaspheme, child! The Sunday of mankind is transformation, the resurrection of the body, Angelic! But man still has far to go until then. You know not what you say — you know not where you are along the road, nor where that road is leading, but this you shall learn!

YOUTH
Is this not our age, now?

ALIGIER
It is — as it seems, not as it is!

YOUTH
What is it you show me?

ALIGIER
From this side, these two lit torches —

YOUTH
Like two sad moons… Ah! I see some huge doors below them, iron doors set in the wall!

ALIGIER
Let us approach them slowly. Read the inscription above them, in silver.

YOUTH
Gens aeterna, in qua nemo nascitur.[6]

---

[6] "An eternal clan, in which no one is born," Pliny.

ALIGIER
Here, finally, is the end of the Past! Beyond this threshold begins the Present, and the gathering of living spirits dreaming what *is to* happen, because it *should* happen!

CHORUS AFAR
Greetings to you, who approach the present time, you who have completed your journey along with the pilgrims, the angels of the Lord, the Ideas of Humanity!

YOUTH
I hear a swelling of voices, nearing, multiplying! It seems as if they were right at our side, those vibrating strings, those growing voices!

ALIGIER
Only this wall separates us from them.

CHORUS
In the name of the Lord I receive you at these doors! The Lord Triune, Three, though One, and the history of the world is threefold, though one!

YOUTH
I've never heard such tones as these. The whole air is vibrating with this music. This hymn enters my very core, like the Sound-Redeemer of all the groans of the heart!

CHORUS
At last the promised day approaches! The Age to be known as that of the Comforter! the Hour, to be known as that of the Fulfiller! Christ was not taken from us forever — not for always was the Light of the World darkened! At last the Son will be adored through the Spirit, and the Spirit is from both Father and Son, uniting Both in Love!

YOUTH
I was nearly finished, but now again I feel Eternity in my bosom! O blessed accord!

CHORUS
And on earth as it is in Heaven!

All that has passed, and was pained in its passing, shall return, come alive, rise, never to suffer again!

Thoughts, like separated brethren, contradictory acts, will love one another in reciprocity as the ages advance!

With a third inspiration, the Lord of All-Loving shall recall this planet of His; He shall remember the tribe of man!

ALIGIER
I shall knock — the door will open — and you must enter with me, at once!

YOUTH
I'm ready, as if these were the very gates of Heaven. Ah! How everything tends to life renewed, my Archangel as well!

CHORUS
We greet you with our peace. Enter!

VI

THE CATACOMBS OF VENICE

SCENE II

A gigantic hall. Lamps hang from walls and vault. In the depths, on an elevated throne, sits the President. To the right is a rostrum, affixed to the wall, with steps. The Choruses of the Nations are ranged along both walls; they are all dressed in their national colours. Pankracy leads the Polish chorus. Aligier, Youth.

UNSEEN CHORUS
Who dost thou lead unto the congregation? Is this not a body deprived of its soul?

ALIGIER
Such a body would merely be a slumbering stone. I do not drag stones behind me, my beloved!

UNSEEN CHORUS
Perhaps it is a soul then, without a body?

ALIGIER
Such a soul is like a stray, a nothing, a dream. I do not lead a dream to you, my beloved!

UNSEEN CHORUS
Who then might he be, who stands behind thee?

ALIGIER
A living spirit! A spirit without beginning, because he comes of the Lord; a spirit without end, because he tends toward the Lord again, and will not be confounded with Him! Soul and body have been given unto him for an eternal pilgrimage — He is ever the same, never to be lost; his elements but die and live again by turns. One day, someday, along with you he will cast aside his human shell, to clothe himself with another, higher, to be donned on the last day of remembrance and judgement! Yet first the fates of the planet common to you all must be unravelled, and he enters in amongst you to labour along with you and hasten on all the great preceding days, which are to come. I beg you, I say unto you: receive him!

UNSEEN CHORUS
Let him pronounce before us the merited name, the sacred name with which he was christened when born as a man.

YOUTH
Henryk.

UNSEEN CHORUS
Let him now confess the name common to the spirits, for whose sake the Lord determined that he should live and die, when he ordained his birth among them on the earth.

YOUTH
Poland.

UNSEEN CHORUS
The chorus aethereal receives thee, demanding no vow from thee. Because thou art, because thou knowest thyself to be spirit, thou hast already vowed fealty to the Lord and to mankind, and to the truth. Woe to thee, not to them, shouldst thou fall away, doubt, or betray. Now may the earthly choruses greet thee!

IRISH CHORUS
We, the first on earth to cast away the yoke with white hands; we, who come with the good news that already the merciful and meek are set

to conquer, greet thee! Trust in these harps, each string of which is a sword — 'tis they shall win Catholic freedom for Erin!

ITALIAN CHORUS
We, corpses who lie in graves covered twice over by glorious ash, the azure sky spread above us; we, desiring to live a third time, greet thee. Trust in these black cloaks of ours, although they signify a funeral, and our green caps, for they are premonitions of the spring!

GERMAN CHORUS
Torn asunder in body, but united in mind, we, the priests of Idea; we who were, without living; we, desiring to live, send thee our greeting! Behold our hair and the curls of our beards: the wisemen of Greece once looked similar to us. Trust these rapiers, handed down to us from our Gothic forefathers!

FRENCH CHORUS
The living greet thee!

SLAVIC CHORUS
O many, many are we, like the swelling ocean waves, like children who, from the cradle, yearn toward the rays of the sun — and all of our cradles are so similar to coffins! We know not ourselves, whether we are to be born, or resurrected, but we hear the voice that calls us. And so we rise, we look — to see before us a gigantic grave stretching from sea to sea. On our behalf, may those who are in that grave address thee — for they have not lain themselves down in it to sleep. For one hundred years now, darkness has been their light — death their life — despair their hope! May the Nation-King of us all, the Nation-Spirit of our tribe, greet thee!

POLISH CHORUS
Thou, our brother thrice over, thou spirit among spirits, thou man among mankind, thou Son of Poland among Her sons, we greet thee! And now as a spirit merely in the guise of a man, know that thou only art a man under the appearance of a Pole; shouldst thou take upon thee another guise, thou shouldst fall lower than cattle! Enclose thou within thy single bosom all of the might of both the quick and the

dead! Make do with nothing, like a corpse! Care not for any vanity or profit or pride, like a corpse! Show no pain on your face, though they drive nails through thy heart, like a perfect corpse! But be ever prepared to act, like a living man! Love thy brothers like a living man! Like a living man, trust in the God of the living! Now, approach the throne, and give ear!

PANKRACY
But first receive from my hands this white cloak and this crimson cap.

ALIGIER
Dress yourself in what you've been given. It is a sign that you belong to their number.

YOUTH
And you as well?

ALIGIER
As long as I am on the earth, I too am of their number!

YOUTH
And now?

ALIGIER
As they have ordered you, approach the throne!

PRESIDENT
Thou hast looked upon the shades of those bold ones, who throughout long ages in the depths of the earth have set themselves in opposition to those who govern its surface. Surrounded by them, through two worlds, what they have passed through, thou too hast experienced. Dost thou understand what the pre-Christian world was before, and what it has been since, following His Incarnation? What was desired by those in the truth of an eternal longing, and in the falsehood of instruments sometimes mistakenly chosen — those mysterious ones, straining toward an ever more distant future? Speak — what hast thou beheld this night?

YOUTH
In its first hours I beheld the fleshly pagan world, yearning toward the Christian soul, until the heavenly revelation was revealed!
PRESIDENT
And in its latter hours?

YOUTH
I saw a swarm of sacred thoughts hovering above the earth. But these did not descend to shower upon the earth; heavenly, they bloomed only in the heavens!

PRESIDENT
That is good, my son. And what next? Surely this was not the end of thy visions?

YOUTH
Then was I surrounded by the despair of all flesh. Long ago, they knew not the soul, though she was born unto them; they saw her above them, but were unable to draw her into their bosoms, and so they wept, and gnashed their teeth, and wallowed in blood.

PRESIDENT
Thou hast understood the plaints of the dead. The ancients anticipated the souls of the Church Universal, while the moderns, the universal society of the flesh. But can one exist without the other? And can no third arise from the mingling of these two? Only a divided Humanity was to be found beating in the hearts of these, and those; and halves are but illusions — sometimes they are crimes. The whole is a reality only when it is on earth as it is in Heaven. Thou knowest this?

YOUTH
I know it, Father.

PRESIDENT
Speak on! Dost thou believe in the Father, in the Word, in the Holy Ghost, in that Trinity existing from all times, in the image and likeness of Whom the universe and each portion thereof, and each of us, and every trifle, as well as each mighty power, the pebble and the Seraph,

were given a place in being, and bestowed with Thought, and with Life?

YOUTH
I so believe!

PRESIDENT
And dost thou believe that the Word became flesh, and dwelt among us?

YOUTH
I do believe.

PRESIDENT
If Christ became man, then He appeared in a certain place and at a certain time. If He is God, then He reigns over all places and all times. If He is God and man, He must have embraced all the fates of this planet. Dost thou remember how, on the eve of His torment, He prophesied the future of humanity, and promised the advent of the Comforter?

YOUTH
I remember His promise.

PRESIDENT
I shall repeat unto thee the words of Scripture. All who are present, kneel!

UNSEEN CHORUS
Father, all the choruses are now upon their knees. You may open the Gospel of John.

PRESIDENT
"I have yet many things to say to you, but you cannot bear them now —
 But when He, the Spirit of truth, is come, He will teach you all truth.
 He shall glorify me, because He shall receive of mine, and shall shew it to you."

This is what the Lord delivered unto all the future ages of the world, and many have since then passed away, and are passing now, without understanding it. This means that they were unable to bear it!

UNSEEN CHORUS
The Father has closed the book — You may rise!

PRESIDENT
There was no higher prophecy, nor is, nor shall there ever be! God, testifying to Himself! That He shall pour Himself upon the earth a third time! During the days of Jehovah, the prophets waited in anticipation upon the Son, nigh unto them! And when he was about to die, the Son beheld the Holy Ghost! It could not be otherwise. Man is a mirror of eternity. And so that Trinity, living in the eternal moment in Heaven, must be reflected too in the human history of this rapid globe — but has this fulfilment come? Which age of these eighteen Christian centuries has advanced Christ?

YOUTH
None, not a one, father!

PRESIDENT
To them all, to them all the Lord still says, "You cannot bear them," for only he adores Him, who makes visible and tangible His commandment in all its reality — only then shall the glory of such a world, being truly of God, bear testimony to itself. And so, my son? What now? The execution thereof will be the descent of the Spirit, the act itself, the Comforter! And where is that act? Dost thou see it?

YOUTH
No.

PRESIDENT
Look within thyself, for it is there!

YOUTH
How can that be, Father?

PRESIDENT
It is in thy breast, as it is in that of each human being!

YOUTH
How?

PRESIDENT
Eternal Grace can effect nothing at all for individual, or for nation, or for Humanity entire unless they lift their hands unto the heavens for it — for one half of creation is the will of the created! Although what was to pass away has passed away, and although the ages are drawing close to their fulfilment; although the wings of the promised Spirit already beat above this earthly vale, if we do not earn His coming, truly desire and indeed work earnestly toward it; if we do not become ourselves tabernacles[7] to house Him, he shall not shine forth to us, and we shall not be comforted!

YOUTH
What then is your command?

PRESIDENT
It is no longer for us to command anything. We can only reveal the truth, and he who comprehends it, will command himself! Give ear therefore to the truth! Until body and soul be poured into one spirit, until the universal act come to be, so long will the history of Humanity be war and chaos. Everywhere shattering and disintegration and disharmony — atomisation, with each tiny atom hating the other, greedily, seeking only its own selfish ends, exterminating others. In such a situation, nation and state, class and principle, edict and law have nothing to do with progress, but rather with regression — they strive ever backwards. That which endures the longer wins their praise, not because it is holy, but because it has cast down so many opponents. The expiration of legitimacy! Like a hangman approaching a skeleton on a throne, thus the future eternally approaches her

---

7   Another neologism: *Jeśli siebie samych nie przeołtarzym Jemu,* in which "przeołtarzyć się" would signify to "trans-altar ourselves," to "transform ourselves into altars/tabernacles for Him."

sister, the Past — and all the Present, befouled with the ashes of one and the blood of the other, is still nothing more than a puddle of misery! Do I not bear accurate testimony to the wretched fates of this planet?

YOUTH
Father, at times my tears have written this upon my face, as I read history — Every person, but especially every Pole, will testify to the truth of what you say!

PRESIDENT
To live thus is not to live at all; it is to be dying eternally! And the law of all life is quite otherwise — never to die that second death of damnation, but neither to die even in order to rise again from the grave — but rather to be constantly resurrecting from oneself without the swoon of death. Such is the development of spirits! Such is their life everlasting! The nations of the world ought to effect this already, before each individual attains it in the next world. For what is mankind if not a school — a testing ground for angels? Or are the altars of God only to be found beneath cathedral vaults? No, they are to be everywhere: in the house of representatives, on the tribunal, in the electoral circle, among the elected, upon the ruler's throne, and in the common market, the craftsman's workshop, the exchange, and in all the art and business of man. The Lord must be descried, recognised, adored and invoked everywhere — So must He be, and so shall He be! Each labour shall be transformed into a mission, each office into a priesthood, and praise will be given to Him who is, through our being, our living! Dost thou not feel in the depths of thy being that thou art anticipating just such a future, and that thou dost believe in it, love it?

YOUTH
Ever since I first drew breath, with each beat of my heart I have desired beauty, liberty, and happiness — and I live amidst monstrous catastrophes… I have never felt young, and you promise me a world grown youthful, Father! How can I not believe in your words, and thank you for them?

PRESIDENT
Speak on! Now, Christ was God, in one man?

YOUTH
Yes.

PRESIDENT
And who will be Christ in all people?

YOUTH
Humanity, I reckon!

PRESIDENT
But when? It was not yesterday. And not today? So, when?

YOUTH
At the final, greatest moment of Humanity's fulfilment!

PRESIDENT
And who shall bring about this fulfilment? Where are the members of that body in which one spirit resides? What sort of rites are celebrated in this Church universal, varied, and established by God? Where are the hues of that rainbow, from which the shining whiteness shall arise?

YOUTH
But I am not mistaken, Father, am I? It is of nationalities that you wish to speak?

PRESIDENT
Thou hast said it thyself. But look how in these our own days, everywhere the will of God providentially tempts their will! Some lack outer independence, others inner peace — all are longing for freedom, and, my son, dost thou know what freedom is?

YOUTH
Tell me, Father.

PRESIDENT
He alone achieves freedom, who has so masterpieced[8] his soul, that he no longer struggles with himself, nor with others, but possesses inner peace, and has love for others, and thus is self-extant, perfect, so that he can go out of his very self, can double himself, triple, become one hundred selves, in his works! Only the free create — and only free nations, like to various-sounding lutes, compose the score of Humanity, the most perfect harmony! So let them not forget about love, without which nothing can arise, nothing can be constructed! Without which God, although clothed in omnipotence, would have been unable to create anything! Their world — let them be that world themselves. Just like the sculpture from the block, so let them arise, from under the inner chisel of their will! Verily, verily, let them remember that that, which is immobile and compressed as a rock is not wisdom upon the earth, nor is it that which is frenzied, which blows the rock apart into the air by inspiration and act; rather, true holiness and exquisite beauty is that which is ever in motion, ascending ever higher — that which grows more broad by the moment, but is always the same, like an eternal sunrise.

PANKRACY
I beg leave to speak.

UNSEEN CHORUS
What does this mean?

PANKRACY
The choragos of the Polish chorus begs leave to speak.

UNSEEN CHORUS
Does the choragos of the Polish chorus not know that it is an offence to interrupt the president, whilst he is instructing an initiate?

PANKRACY
Once more, I demand leave to speak!

---

8   Coinage: *wyarcydzielował*.

PRESIDENT
My son, you are forgetful of the laws that govern the underworld, and with your stubbornness, you are risking much!

PANKRACY
And you, Father, are you not putting this young soul at risk of being lost, by thus speaking of love? And, instead of encouraging him to fortitude, you soften his heart to tenderness?

PRESIDENT
Silence!

PANKRACY
Listen to me, listen, your arch-reverence! Listen to me you all, however many nations and peoples are gathered here! If you be of the West, you yet have the luxury of dreaming that, through Christian mercy, you shall peacefully attain your goals! You've already guillotined your nobles, some of you, while others have cast them into mire and misery. Good! But what about the bankers, the financiers, and your bourgeoisie? Those monstrous parasites on the body of the people? But anyway, you are of little account, you Westerners. I am from the East, a Slav, a Pole! And therefore I shall say…

UNSEEN CHORUS
Disobedient soul! You are instructed to hold your tongue!

PANKRACY
As I've already made so bold… I shall not allow this scion of Sarmatian aristocrats, this descendant of ancient clans, to be mystified and misled by ideas which will some day be realised, perhaps, but before which realisation all of Slavdom, all of Poland, must become a sea of blood! Let the youngster see things as they really are. Let him renounce his noble identity, or let him go, leave, without looking back, and taking not our mysteries with him!

PRESIDENT
Perhaps your own, rebellious spirit! For ours contain no command to bloodshed. Our mystery is the sacred weapon of the sacred laws,

and defence of the oppressed. You will find no murderer among us!

PANKRACY
Listen, boy, you scion of fathers, you who know your fathers! I, who have none, I who walk the earth as if I had arisen directly from her womb, from the gravel and muck and the grass, as once the Titans, and as today the people of the peoples, I say unto you — there is to be an end to the Polish nobility, and that of all Slavdom! If you so desire, kneel down now and rattle off a rosary at their grave — you may do so if you wish. But I know you, I know, you shall not give an inch; you and all who are like you are ready to sacrifice all that you possess — half your lands and your clattering coins, but your real treasure, your relic, your pride — never! And thus you wriggle into power again by a new discipline, the allure of which power eternity itself is incapable of stifling in your soul. O, I am not one of you, but I know you, better than you know yourselves. So what is taking counsel with you worth, O Highborn one? There is only one counsel for our kind — We must force you to a different rebirth, forgiving none, allowing none to squirm free of the fatal net, so that once and for all your blood and marrow should be broken down, chemically, to disappear for all time into the thin air! Only then will there be Equality, and the People — and then, only then, will everything that that man in white there on the throne has said become a probability: Fraternity without force on this globe. But not before! Beware! Do you understand me, you son of so many fathers?

YOUTH
Aligier, where am I now? Where have you led me? I call him out…

ALIGIER
If you love me, hold your tongue! *To the president.* I kneel before you as a token of my respect, and my plea — for I do not wish to infringe upon the rules by speaking out of place. But please, most reverend Father, allow me to ascend the rostrum for a moment and to speak! Father, it is out of my concern for this bright and pure soul entrusted me — Behold, how pale his face is grown! Behold how his brow grows livid with the anger that flows through his veins! Behold how that hand, restrained from his blade, trembles with the anguish of a Laocoon! I

must arise and speak in order to calm him — For the first time ever such words meet his ears!

PRESIDENT
I cannot forbid what you demand, since that man has already trampled upon the laws.

ALIGIER
I thank you, Father.
Ascends the rostrum.

PANKRACY
I shall not take part in any debate, now! I am a choragos! I spoke from urgent imperative. And he who bears the word of necessity does not make answer to trifling human speech. Hey! Kiermasz, or you, Blauman — if they're about to indulge in sentimentalism and word-milling, stand before the rostrum there, look straight into the eyes of that melancholy friend of this youngster, and make answer on my behalf!

KIERMASZ
At once!

BLAUMAN
Sit down, Kiermasz — I can do it better.

OTHER
No! Let me speak! Blauman won't pull it off!

ANOTHER
No, Leader, choose me!

PANKRACY
Already you're quarrelling. Look how that half of the chorus, made up of the old nobility, who have drawn off to the side, keep a handsome dignity, although they are furious! Enough of this discordant screeching! Blauman, you speak!

BLAUMAN
To Aligier
You pale starveling of the aristocratic party! You, bending over the rostrum with your theatrically outstretched arms — I must admit, it's a beautiful pose, befitting the beauty of the nobles, just like your smooth features and clean white hands — Pah! Women, all of you! — Ha! So you take exception to what that great citizen has uttered, sincerely, yes, from his heart, bringing you notice of the logical and inexorable slaughter of the Polish magnates? Well, if you be a patriot, if anything Polish, anything of the fatherland yet remains in your heart…

PANKRACY
In a whisper.
Soft-pedal that fatherland stuff!

BLAUMAN
Too aristocratic?

PANKRACY
Yes, and no — Just do as I say!

BLAUMAN
Aha… I tell you, if there be at least a sliver of Humanity in your heart, how else would you bring salvation to the Polish land, in the iron grip of three tyrants, and trampled down ever lower by the noble caste? Only by a magnanimous massacre might…

ALIGIER
Pankracy! Pankracy! Choragos of the Polish chorus, yourself not a Pole at all! You who are constantly repeating "the People, the People," whereas "the Nation" is never found on your lips! You who wish to see great things come about through your own power, while you refuse to begin from God! You, who set massacre as the cornerstone of the edifice you would construct! You, possessed by a jealousy that you wish to transform into an eternal law of Progress, and who call the base itch in your own bosom by the name of Necessity! You, who know how to wound, and to infect wounds with venom whenever you come across a child, a woman, or a youth in the tenderness of

his springtime, but know not how to converse with God in prayer, or man in wisdom, or even with yourself in faith and conviction! You, greedy for power, you, a man powerful only in sensuality and passion, and some other horrid power secreted in yourself — Don't hide behind the back of the first best fellow you've seduced, but, in the name of God, the Judge of us all, the Lord of nations and spirits, my Lord and yours, answer! Do you believe in what you've just declared in our presence?

BLAUMAN
He? Does he believe? Who? Pankracy! Ah, this is too much already! Blaspheme not such a democrat, you, you… aristocrat, you!

ALIGIER
I conjure you with the power that has been given me, rooted in the depths of my being as a reward for all that my heart has suffered on behalf of all the sufferings of my brethren, from the very first time I opened my eyes and looked upon the world and found it beautiful; and the sun, beautiful; and God, all good, all merciful, and Humanity unfortunate, and among unfortunate Humanity, my Polish nation first in misfortune and pain! I command you, answer me! When I train my eyes on someone, usually he responds with truth. I have spent many hours in prayer upon mountain summits, upon the waves of the sea and among prisoners locked in citadels, in dungeons, in mines, at the foot of the gallows and in halls of justice — interceding with the Lord on behalf of the sentenced and praying for their judges as well, for a worse fate awaits them! I have erred long among the caverns of the earth, continually, as far as it lay in the power of a wretch such as I, by desire and thought and good work, to remain in Heaven — that, O, trust my words, man — in fain you try to slip past me! You must declare the truth in the presence of all these assembled brothers — and if you remain silent, that means you feel yourself incapable of speaking the truth; that means that you know yourself to be a hypocrite and a liar!

PANKRACY
Blauman, step aside! Ha, Aligier, you challenge me?

ALIGIER
As God is in Heaven and in each of us, as Christ once walked the earth and still spreads His Spirit throughout it, I do!

PANKRACY
So, speak less, and more plainly, practically. What is it you ask?

ALIGIER
I inquire after your conscience. Nothing more!

PANKRACY
Speak practically! I am a man of action — I have no grasp of metaphysics — Nor do I wish to have, nor have I any such need. So, again, what is it you ask of me, exactly?

ALIGIER
In the presence of Him Who is ever between us; Who, even were we two alone should be a Third among us, here! — O! — Who fills this space between us, wraps us round, is everywhere, however broadly stretches the horizon! In the presence of the Dearest Hidden One, as He is known amongst the people of Poland, I demand of you — Do you feel in your heart, and do you know, incontrovertibly in your mind, that the massacre of the Polish aristocracy is necessary for the salvation of Poland? That, in order to lift the stone lid that covers the grave of those who are to resurrect, it is hands stained with mire and blood that are necessary, and not the clean light of Heaven's lightning bolt? That for the third hour of the world — the hour of Christ — to begin, it is necessary to abjure that same Christ, even for a moment, setting His love aside for later, and to say to God Almighty, "Take a walk — You may return later, but at the moment, You are rather superfluous — You will be needed again only the day after tomorrow?"

PANKRACY
Julinicz, you bard of the people, you might be the one to make reply to him — For he is writing poems!

JULINICZ
Stepping out of the chorus.
I am a great Spirit, a Spirit prophetic! You all know me!

PANKRACY
So sing at this songster in reply!

JULINICZ
With nothing else, brothers, save riotous death, do the eras of this planet come to a close. And now is the time — twenty centuries are about to die, and before they do, they must be handed over to torture because of their great crimes, which is all they knew — continual crime, never knowing the Spirit! Today is different from all the days that went before! Back then there were prayers and tears and penitence — that was Christianity! Today there is might incarnate, motion, haste, whirl and tone, rule, command, the weaponising[9] of the Lord's inspiration! Today the Lord chooses even scoundrels as His instruments! Like thousands of hammers, sickles, flails, spears and swords — He trains them on all sides and wages a global war to destroy His enemies! The enemies of the people! What does the Polish aristocracy mean to the all-future? Some tens of thousands of people — would you prefer to multiply that number? Still, mere drops in the ocean! And this ocean is thirsty: toss them in! This is Christianity today, for the Lord has chosen to pass judgement upon the earth, and He shall judge it through us, His foresighted saints, His prophets! And, O! You shall remember, you infidel — storms and living tornados approach, gales of living people, myriads sweeping over the ruins and the ash pits, setting before God an offering of murder! And murder will be pleasing in God's eyes, as a continual holocaust ascending to Heaven from this spinning altar, this planet, upon which Humanity is the eternal priest and sacrificer, sending up the outmoded tribes and castes and thoughts as an offering!

ALIGIER
Pankracy! Pankracy! Do you not recall that voice calling down from the heavens to Adam in hiding, after he had committed the first

---

9   *Uorężnienie.*

sin? And to Cain escaping after his fratricide? You are hiding in just the same way — you would escape in the same fashion. Pankracy, Pankracy, answer me!

PANKRACY
You are unbearable. Hymn it out with Julinicz there.

ALIGIER
Pankracy! Pankracy! Where do you come from? And who was it poured the Polish language into your spirit? Who, Polish customs? Who set within you the desire for freedom? The strength of action? Were you born in the future? Of course not! So, what exactly are you, although you lack fathers that you can name, if you are not a son of the Polish Commonwealth? Tell me — what might you be able to say on the earth, with what might you form your lies, with what would you commit your treason, with what misappropriate the past, if not with all the gifts she has given you? You ungrateful thing! Who would give ear to your voice on behalf of the people, who among your own land, or among strangers, if not for the sword of Bolesław Chrobry,[10] the immaculate person of Jadwiga, the wise love of Zygmunt, the fortitude of Batory, the Roman virtue of the Zamoyskis, the heroic death of the Żółkiewskis, the heroic life of Czarniecki, the toils of Sobieski and his great European Deed? Without them there is nothing. And you choose to stand upon nothing? Why do you rise up against History and Immortal Deeds? Against that, which you yourself cannot do without, cannot make one step, or pronounce one single word? It is the very breath of your lungs! Lead further, man, if the Lord's blessing rests upon you; lead your own nation further! But lead your nation not

---

10   What follows is a catalogue of Polish nobility, chiefly kings and queens of Poland, who from the middle ages through the Baroque enlarged the Polish kingdom through wars in the east (Chrobry, Batory) or through diplomatic marriage (St. Jadwiga, who annexed Lithuania through her marriage with Władysław Jagiełło); who fought on behalf of Christian Europe (Jan Sobieski, who lifted the Turkish siege of Vienna in 1683), or against the Swedes (Stefan Czarniecki). In short, Krasiński paints a picture describing Poland defended on all sides by the sacrificial might of the Polish aristocracy. He also mentions the names of magnate families — such as the Zamoyskis, with whom his own family was affiliated.

out of its national identity, as the cruel tyrant would, those who have torn the motherland apart! Be not her fourth hangman, given by Hell in addition to the other three! Pankracy! Pankracy!

PANKRACY
Be damned with that past of yours, with that voice of the past that flies from your mouth like the exhalation of a grave, jabbering, jabbering!

ALIGIER
I warn you — because at this moment your future failure stands reflected before me! There is still time! You have free will! If you won't listen to me, perhaps you shall be powerful; perhaps you shall stand before people for a moment, a moment and a half. But you will fall away from the sight of God, and no trace of you will be found in His heart!

PANKRACY
O, how artful! Such superstitions — fallacies — divination! Such are the beginnings of all theocracy and all aristocracy! You think to bar me from my deeds, my power, my immortality… with your harp? So, know the truth — all of you, know this — You too, arch-reverend sir! He who believes in me, he who belongs to me, let him step away from the Polish chorus and take his place at my side!

KIERMASZ
Hail, our leader!

BLAUMAN
I am with you!

JULINICZ
I shall be a new Aaron in your camp!

SEVERAL OTHERS
We are democrats, at your command!

PANKRACY
The sermons they drone out here have bored me for some time now. Everything is so religious, so philosophical, so… languid…

Tortoises, not men! He who believes that he will soothe the world — has my congratulations. The world is rotten. The Polish nobility is rotten. There is no other thing for it. To be or not to be. And I want to be! Who aims at a goal grabs after the means that will get him there, even if they be poisoned arrows! Damned be those who sow confusion along the path of historical necessity! Damned be the lazy and the learned! The merciful and the pure! Mire is not dirty when it paves the pathway to Omni-humanity! Long live principles, though half of Europe perish thereby! I'm done with you all!

ALIGIER
Thus he answers in your presence, nations and peoples! Henryk, consider this, and learn! The man is a genius, a mighty spirit, but he has no power to reply to the simplest question — if that question be a noble one — for he has no nobility in him. Thus has the Lord determined that it should be. Blessed be the Lord!

UNSEEN CHORUS
Hold, hold, you errant soul! Do you not recall how deep the stain of shame is upon him who breaks his faith? Abandoned he is, on this and on the other side of the tomb; perverse, wretched, vile is he!

PANKRACY
I'll take that on the other side of your tomb, but not here. On this side, I am the son of my own deeds! I generate my own fathers. O my deeds, to my succour! Brothers, come!

PRESIDENT
All you choruses, block the path of this fatherless brother — let him not go!

ALIGIER
I beg you, Father, exempt from your order the faithful half of the Polish chorus! Order them not to stand against their own brethren — for though sinful, they are ever brethren!

PRESIDENT
You alone, faithful Poles, do we exempt from the execution of our order. Remain where you are!

PANKRACY
Do you think, most reverend sir, that by surrounding me with this crowd you shall force me to my knees before you? Do you think that — here in this cavern, at your nod, you, who know no bloody command — that your men will shed my blood? Unhand me, choruses of the nations!

PRESIDENT
Encircle the infidel in an unbreakable chain.

PANKRACY
Blauman, Kiermasz, Julinicz, your daggers!

PRESIDENT
Bring in coffins enough for every heretic.

PANKRACY
To arms, all! To arms! To me! If you wish to live and act, not to rot in indolence, to me! If you wish to behold with your own eyes what you conceive in your mind, and long for in your heart, to me! Whatever your clan or nation, to me!

PRESIDENT
Set the coffins up in a row, and set one infidel before each coffin.

PANKRACY
Depart these catacombs, these fantasies and poetries and visions! — To me, with me, out into the air where the sun is brilliant in the sky, and the essential enemies are upon the ground — Let us shed their blood to the delight of the sun, who will lap up the bright red liquor! Are you blind and deaf? Will no one from the Italians, Germans or French make answer beside me?

UNSEEN CHORUS
Several from each of the choruses pass over to the side of the rebel —
O, misfortunate ones!

PRESIDENT
More coffins, we need more coffins!

PANKRACY
What? You would nail us in those boxes? Can you not see the pistols in my hands? We will defend ourselves to the last man!

UNSEEN CHORUS
Man of misfortune! He thinks that this is about the death of the body! Misguided wretch!

PRESIDENT
You faithful choruses, move nearer to them — yes — in a half-circle. The coffins now suffice. There are no more traitors.

PANKRACY
Hey, to me! Trust me! You slumbering people! Choruses! Earthly majorities! Must it always be the minority that is brave and bold, and you — base? Is this the reason why the minority must always employ fear and violence to hammer you into the fetters of its will?

ALIGIER
Thus speaks the tyrant within you!

PRESIDENT
To the youth.
You came here, my son, in search of truth and salvation, and found but scandal. It would have been better for him, who scandalises the hearts of the innocent, had he never been born. Now hear the sentence pronounced upon him!

PANKRACY
If you don't allow us to leave, I will shoot!

PRESIDENT
I rend this pure, white garment on my bosom in the sight of you all, nations and peoples! For from this throne I must cast death upon one of the living; I must pronounce a curse upon a spirit whom I once blessed, as I blessed you all!

PANKRACY
I will shoot! I will shoot the most reverend gentleman himself!

YOUTH
Look here, you enemy of my fathers! Can you see the barrel of my pistol? Its black eye studies your brow. If your finger but twitch on that trigger, it shall not be he on the throne, but you, who dies! Beware!

PRESIDENT
Pankracy! Thou art branded with the mark of damnation! Such as thou have ever existed upon the earth, whose pride is temptation, and their deed, destruction! Each Heaven-born Idea, sent into the world by the Lord, they have thrust away from the world, deflecting it back into the heavens, serving it basely! For it is not the Idea they serve, but themselves, in its name. And God, received by them as if He were Satan, draws away, pale in anger, that He should have such servants! And thou art one of these. Thou betrayest the holy things revealed here! Thou betrayest Christ! Thou betrayest the Holy Ghost! To these thou art just such a Pharisee as a king's toady, as a hypocrite, an informer, a spy! Thou shalt either fall away utterly, or thou shalt impede the development of Humanity, shunting it from its proper track to the wayside wastes — forcing her to soil her white feet in puddles of mire! Thou dost terrorise the ages, which recoil hastily backward from thee! What the entire diapason of all monarchs has not effected in force and violence, thou dost grasp with one bold hand! And so in the name of Humanity, in the name of the Holy Ghost, I pronounce a curse upon thy head, thou lost spirit! For he who is against eternal Love, let him know — even though he may triumph, he shall perish!

PANKRACY
See you in eternity!

PRESIDENT
These coffins are your funeral. You have regressed many, many ages, you heretic! And you are dying at this moment, dying a death much worse than if I had you executed — for I could not command your spirit to be taken from you. You have flung her away with your own hands! Go then, with your bodies! In these coffins your nobility and virtues will remain — in these coffins are the thoughts God had of you, which were to become yourselves, but into which you were not able to mature — in these coffins lies whatever human there was of you upon the earth!

UNSEEN CHORUS
Counterfeiters of the Idea! Fiercest enemies of the Idea! You, who are to crucify it, and mockingly, for you will claim to be its offspring! You perishing ones, you — as soon as you pass over that threshold, you, the dead! Go! Begone!

PRESIDENT
Each earthly chorus, every nation and people, take candle in hand and intone the funeral dirge!

PANKRACY
Kiermasz, grow not so pale! Blauman, you too? Julinicz, are the nerves of poets like the strings of lutes, that they tremble so? What of it, that this circle glows with candles? Or that the sounds of a funeral dirge resound, echoing from the vault as if the granite itself were chanting, foretelling our death?

PRESIDENT
The choragos of the Polish chorus is dead — Aligier, assume governance of thy brethren and be their leader.

PANKRACY
Ah! The counsel of the aristocracy is my replacement! Kordecki, Rejtan, Ligenza, Rymszo, Kazanowski, will you not come with me?

POLISH CHORUS
We shall remain here. The sword and nobility! Not the dagger and shame — This is our device!

UNSEEN CHORUS
Intone, intone the funeral dirge unto them! They have trodden down the Past; they have not comprehended the Future — and the Present is become monstrous on their account! — And so they do not exist in Time, for they have offended, wounded, quartered Time! — Where are they? In the nothingness of the Spirit! Sing, sing unto them the funeral dirge!

PRESIDENT
Carry their coffins behind them — See them off to the very threshold of the mysteries. Open the wall of the underworld before them!

PANKRACY
My thanks to you, most reverend sir! We shall fight, you and I, for I — how well you spoke — I am the destroyer! But fear no treason — the surface of the earth will never hear of you, or your men!

PRESIDENT
Who has played Judas to the Idea, may yet turn Judas among men!

PANKRACY
No, no! You cannot think so of me!

PRESIDENT
The living hold no commerce with the dead. Enough already. Amen!

PANKRACY
The keys, the keys! Here is the threshold — How stuffy it is here! You ought not to strain your lungs so, singing in this atmosphere. Open it up, already!

UNSEEN CHORUS
Sing, sing them the funeral dirge to the end!

PRESIDENT
And now, let each say to them, "You are extinguished."
PANKRACY
Will this ritual ever end?

PRESIDENT
Now, let each snuff his candle, and fling spark and ash above their heads.

PANKRACY
Let us out!

UNSEEN CHORUS
The dead — the dead — the dead!

PRESIDENT
Ye nations and peoples, disperse now in silence and darkness! Scandalised and saddened, the judgement has followed hard upon the guilty, and the punishment soon after. Pray now and remember — and never give lodging to temptation in your hearts. For the spirit that sins against the Holy Ghost is never forgiven! Depart — the service is concluded for this night.

UNSEEN CHORUS
Nations and peoples, disperse in silence and darkness!

HERE ENDS THE MANUSCRIPT

Bibliography

PRIMARY SOURCES FOR THE TRANSLATION

KRASIŃSKI, Zygmunt. *Dzieła literackie*, ed. Paweł Hertz. Warsaw: PIW, 1973. Vol. I.

— *Irydion*. Paris: W drukarni i księgarni A. Jełowickiego i sp., 1836.

Nie-Boska komedyia. Paris: W typografji A. Pinard, 1835.

— *Niedokończony poemat (z pośmiertnych rękopismów)*. Paris: W księgarni polskiej, 1860.

SECONDARY SOURCES

LEDNICKI, Wacław, ed., *Zygmunt Krasiński: Romantic Universalist*. New York: PIASA, 1964.

MACIEJEWSKI, Jarosław, ed. *Archiwum Literackie: Miscellanea z okresu romantyzmu*. Wrocław: Ossolineum, 1972.

MIŁOSZ, Czesław. *The History of Polish Literature*. Berkeley and London: University of California Press, 1983.

SANDAUER, Artur. *Pisma Zebrane*. Warsaw: Czytelnik, 1985.

WITKOWSKA, Alina. *Literatura romantyzmu*. Warsaw: PIW, 1986).

About The Author

Zygmunt Krasiński (1812–1859) has been traditionally considered one of the "three national bards" of Poland, along with Adam Mickiewicz and Juliusz Słowacki. His fame mainly rests on his plays, especially the monumental drama *Nieboska komedia* (*The Undivine Comedy*, 1833-1835). *Irydion* (1835-1836) is the second closet drama which he completed during his lifetime. Set in the early Christian ages, in Rome, it is a broad allegory of Polish national aspirations in the face of the Russian occupation of his homeland. Two other dramatic works, unfinished and posthumously published, are included in this translation: *Rok 1846* (*1846*) and *Niedokończony poemat* (*The Unfinished Poem*), both of which were composed during the last decades of the author's life. The *Unfinished Poem* is of special interest, as it provides a look at the developmental years of the character of Count Henryk, the chief protagonist of the *Undivine Comedy*. Krasiński also wrote verse, chief among which is *Przedświt* (*Foredawn*, 1841-1843) and *Psalmy przyszłości* (*The Psalms of the Future*, 1844-1848), and fiction, such as the early novel *Agaj-Han* (1832-1833). Besides his plays, however, it is his copious epistolary output which is most highly valued by critics and historians of literature.

About The Translator

Charles S. Kraszewski (b. 1962) is a poet and translator. He is the author of three volumes of original verse (*Diet of Nails; Beast; Chanameed*). Several of his translations of Polish and Czech literature have been published by Glagoslav, among which may be found Adam Mickiewicz's *Forefathers' Eve* (2016) and Stanisław Wyspiański's *Acropolis: the Wawel Plays* (2017). His translations into Polish of the poetry of T.S. Eliot, Robinson Jeffers, and Lawrence Ferlinghetti have appeared in the Wrocław monthly *Odra*. He is a member of the Union of Polish Writers Abroad (London) and of the Association of Polish Writers (Kraków).

Acropolis – The Wawel Plays
by Stanisław Wyspiański

Stanisław Wyspiański (1869-1907) achieved worldwide fame, both as a painter, and Poland's greatest dramatist of the first half of the twentieth century. *Acropolis: the Wawel Plays*, brings together four of Wyspiański's most important dramatic works in a new English translation by Charles S. Kraszewski. All of the plays centre on Wawel Hill: the legendary seat of royal and ecclesiastical power in the poet's native city, the ancient capital of Poland. In these plays, Wyspiański explores the foundational myths of his nation: that of the self-sacrificial Wanda, and the struggle between King Bolesław the Bold and Bishop Stanisław Szczepanowski. In the eponymous play which brings the cycle to an end, Wyspiański carefully considers the value of myth to a nation without political autonomy, soaring in thought into an apocalyptic vision of the future. Richly illustrated with the poet's artwork, *Acropolis: the Wawel Plays* also contains Wyspiański's architectural proposal for the renovation of Wawel Hill, and a detailed critical introduction by the translator. In its plaited presentation of *Bolesław the Bold* and *Skałka*, the translation offers, for the first time, the two plays in the unified, composite format that the poet intended, but was prevented from carrying out by his untimely death.

Buy it > www.glagoslav.com

Forefathers' Eve
by Adam Mickiewicz

Forefathers' Eve [*Dziady*] is a four-part dramatic work begun circa 1820 and completed in 1832 – with Part I published only after the poet's death, in 1860. The drama's title refers to *Dziady*, an ancient Slavic and Lithuanian feast commemorating the dead. This is the grand work of Polish literature, and it is one that elevates Mickiewicz to a position among the "great Europeans" such as Dante and Goethe.

With its Christian background of the Communion of the Saints, revenant spirits, and the interpenetration of the worlds of time and eternity, *Forefathers' Eve* speaks to men and women of all times and places. While it is a truly Polish work – Polish actors covet the role of Gustaw/Konrad in the same way that Anglophone actors covet that of Hamlet – it is one of the most universal works of literature written during the nineteenth century. It has been compared to Goethe's Faust – and rightfully so...

Buy it > www.glagoslav.com

A Brown Man in Russia - Perambulations Through A Siberian Winter
by Vijay Menon

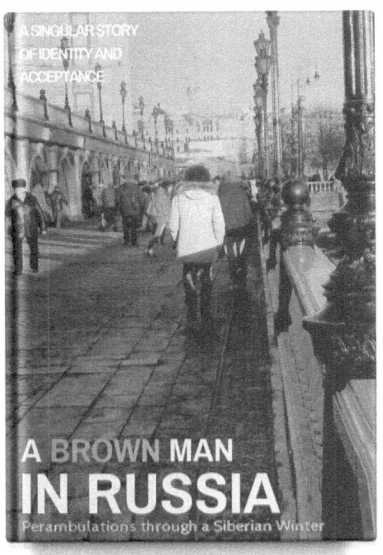

A Brown Man in Russia describes the fantastical travels of a young, colored American traveler as he backpacks across Russia in the middle of winter via the Trans-Siberian. The book is a hybrid between the curmudgeonly travelogues of Paul Theroux and the philosophical works of Robert Pirsig. Styled in the vein of Hofstadter, the author lays out a series of absurd, but true stories followed by a deeper rumination on what they mean and why they matter. Each chapter presents a vivid anecdote from the perspective of the fumbling traveler and concludes with a deeper lesson to be gleaned. For those who recognize the discordant nature of our world in a time ripe for demagoguery and for those who want to make it better, the book is an all too welcome antidote. It explores the current global climate of despair over differences and outputs a very different message – one of hope and shared understanding. At times surreal, at times inappropriate, at times hilarious, and at times deeply human, A Brown Man in Russia is a reminder to those who feel marginalized, hopeless, or endlessly divided that harmony is achievable even in the most unlikely of places.

Buy it > www.glagoslav.com

Dear Reader,

Thank you for purchasing this book.

We at Glagoslav Publications are glad to welcome you, and hope that you find our books to be a source of knowledge and inspiration.

We want to show the beauty and depth of the Slavic region to everyone looking to expand their horizon and learn something new about different cultures, different people, and we believe that with this book we have managed to do just that.

Now that you've got to know us, we want to get to know you. We value communication with our readers and want to hear from you! We offer several options:

– Join our Book Club on Goodreads, Library Thing and Shelfari, and receive special offers and information about our giveaways;

– Share your opinion about our books on Amazon, Barnes & Noble, Waterstones and other bookstores;

– Join us on Facebook and Twitter for updates on our publications and news about our authors;

– Visit our site www.glagoslav.com to check out our Catalogue and subscribe to our Newsletter.

Glagoslav Publications is getting ready to release a new collection and planning some interesting surprises — stay with us to find out!

Glagoslav Publications
Email: contact@glagoslav.com

Glagoslav Publications Catalogue

- *The Time of Women* by Elena Chizhova
- *Andrei Tarkovsky: The Collector of Dreams* by Layla Alexander-Garrett
- *Andrei Tarkovsky - A Life on the Cross* by Lyudmila Boyadzhieva
- *Sin* by Zakhar Prilepin
- *Hardly Ever Otherwise* by Maria Matios
- *Khatyn* by Ales Adamovich
- *The Lost Button* by Irene Rozdobudko
- *Christened with Crosses* by Eduard Kochergin
- *The Vital Needs of the Dead* by Igor Sakhnovsky
- *The Sarabande of Sara's Band* by Larysa Denysenko
- *A Poet and Bin Laden* by Hamid Ismailov
- *Watching The Russians (Dutch Edition)* by Maria Konyukova
- *Kobzar* by Taras Shevchenko
- *The Stone Bridge* by Alexander Terekhov
- *Moryak* by Lee Mandel
- *King Stakh's Wild Hunt* by Uladzimir Karatkevich
- *The Hawks of Peace* by Dmitry Rogozin
- *Harlequin's Costume* by Leonid Yuzefovich
- *Depeche Mode* by Serhii Zhadan
- *The Grand Slam and other stories (Dutch Edition)* by Leonid Andreev
- *METRO 2033 (Dutch Edition)* by Dmitry Glukhovsky
- *METRO 2034 (Dutch Edition)* by Dmitry Glukhovsky
- *A Russian Story* by Eugenia Kononenko
- *Herstories, An Anthology of New Ukrainian Women Prose Writers*
- *The Battle of the Sexes Russian Style* by Nadezhda Ptushkina
- *A Book Without Photographs* by Sergey Shargunov
- *Down Among The Fishes* by Natalka Babina
- *disUNITY* by Anatoly Kudryavitsky
- *Sankya* by Zakhar Prilepin
- *Wolf Messing* by Tatiana Lungin
- *Good Stalin* by Victor Erofeyev

- Solar Plexus by Rustam Ibragimbekov
- Don't Call me a Victim! by Dina Yafasova
- Poetin (Dutch Edition) by Chris Hutchins and Alexander Korobko
- A History of Belarus by Lubov Bazan
- Children's Fashion of the Russian Empire by Alexander Vasiliev
- Empire of Corruption - The Russian National Pastime by Vladimir Soloviev
- Heroes of the 90s - People and Money. The Modern History of Russian Capitalism
- Fifty Highlights from the Russian Literature (Dutch Edition) by Maarten Tengbergen
- Bajesvolk (Dutch Edition) by Mikhail Khodorkovsky
- Tsarina Alexandra's Diary (Dutch Edition)
- Myths about Russia by Vladimir Medinskiy
- Boris Yeltsin - The Decade that Shook the World by Boris Minaev
- A Man Of Change - A study of the political life of Boris Yeltsin
- Sberbank - The Rebirth of Russia's Financial Giant by Evgeny Karasyuk
- To Get Ukraine by Oleksandr Shyshko
- Asystole by Oleg Pavlov
- Gnedich by Maria Rybakova
- Marina Tsvetaeva - The Essential Poetry
- Multiple Personalities by Tatyana Shcherbina
- The Investigator by Margarita Khemlin
- The Exile by Zinaida Tulub
- Leo Tolstoy – Flight from paradise by Pavel Basinsky
- Moscow in the 1930 by Natalia Gromova
- Laurus (Dutch edition) by Evgenij Vodolazkin
- Prisoner by Anna Nemzer
- The Crime of Chernobyl - The Nuclear Goulag by Wladimir Tchertkoff
- Alpine Ballad by Vasil Bykau
- The Complete Correspondence of Hryhory Skovoroda

- *The Tale of Aypi by Ak Welsapar*
- *Selected Poems by Lydia Grigorieva*
- *The Fantastic Worlds of Yuri Vynnychuk*
- *The Garden of Divine Songs and Collected Poetry of Hryhory Skovoroda*
- *Adventures in the Slavic Kitchen: A Book of Essays with Recipes*
- *Seven Signs of the Lion by Michael M. Naydan*
- *Forefathers' Eve by Adam Mickiewicz*
- *One-Two by Igor Eliseev*
- *Girls, be Good by Bojan Babić*
- *Time of the Octopus by Anatoly Kucherena*
- *The Grand Harmony by Bohdan Ihor Antonych*
- *The Selected Lyric Poetry Of Maksym Rylsky*
- *The Shining Light by Galymkair Mutanov*
- *The Frontier: 28 Contemporary Ukrainian Poets - An Anthology*
- *Acropolis - The Wawel Plays by Stanisław Wyspiański*
- *Contours of the City by Attyla Mohylny*
- *Conversations Before Silence: The Selected Poetry of Oles Ilchenko*
- *The Secret History of my Sojourn in Russia by Jaroslav Hašek*
- *Mirror Sand - An Anthology of Russian Short Poems in English Translation (A Bilingual Edition)*
- *Maybe We're Leaving by Jan Balaban*
- *A Brown Man in Russia - Perambulations Through A Siberian Winter by Vijay Menon*
- *Death of the Snake Catcher by Ak Welsapar*
- *Hard Times by Ostap Vyshnia*
- *Nikolai Gumilev's Africa by Nikolai Gumilev*
- *Vladimir Lenin - How to Become a Leader by Vladlen Loginov*
- *Soghomon Tehlirian Memories - The Assassination of Talaat*
- *Duel by Borys Antonenko-Davydovych*
- *Zinnober's Poppets by Elena Chizhova*
- *The Hemingway Game by Evgeni Grishkovets*
- *The Nuremberg Trials by Alexander Zvyagintsev*
- *Mikhail Bulgakov - The Life and Times by Marietta Chudakova*

More coming soon…

www.ingramcontent.com/pod-product-compliance
Lightning Source LLC
Chambersburg PA
CBHW031052080526
44587CB00011B/658